BLUEBERRY HILL
MENU COOKBOOK

By the author

NOTHING WHATEVER TO DO
BLUEBERRY HILL COOKBOOK
OFF MY TOES!
BLUEBERRY HILL MENU COOKBOOK

BLUEBERRY HILL

MENU COOKBOOK

ELSIE MASTERTON

DECORATIONS BY THE AUTHOR

THOMAS Y. CROWELL COMPANY
ESTABLISHED 1834

NEW YORK

To Lucinda, who helped with the drawings—
To Heather,
To Laurey,
and, always, to John

CONTENTS

BLUEBERRY HILL
MENU COOKBOOK

INTRODUCTION

 When the *Blueberry Hill Cookbook* was conceived, well over five years ago, it was my feeling that there was a need for a truly conversational, yet functional, cookbook; that women, and men—for many of my readers have turned out to be men—like to know what to expect of food, how long a thing might logically take to be properly cooked. I was sure that, if I could take the time to point out the pitfalls, to warn, to admonish, to encourage, it would be the right way to do this book. I won't tell you how long it took me to find a publisher willing to go along with this premise. I was told that I was wrong; that a list of ingredients and a static set of instructions was all that was wanted in a cookbook. For a while it looked as if that book would never see the light of day, not to speak of a kitchen.

It turned out that my approach was a proper one. The *Blueberry Hill Cookbook* has the most loyal sort of friends, and my publisher, just the other day, said he was glad to see that in my *Blueberry Hill Menu Cookbook,* which this is, I have "kept in the conversation."

For a cookbook, I would say, is a most personal sort of book. People get to know the author of their favorite cookbook, or cookbooks, in a way that is perhaps true of no other sort. My mail has been filled with letters, week after week, to "Elsie," telling me, as one friend to another, of the cooking of my recipes in Mobile, Alabama, or St. Paul, Minnesota, or even

1

Aruba; often, in return for the favor of my recipes in my book, there is enclosed a "rule" from the writer, for me to try.

This, the *Blueberry Hill Menu Cookbook,* is a cookbook to cook by, yes. But it is also a cookbook to read in bed, to laugh with, to laugh *at,* if you will. As I write this book, I think that I am talking with someone; let's let it be you. You are a gal in my kitchen, at my elbow. I want you to know what I'm doing, every single thing I'm doing, and, as often as this is practical, why I'm doing it. This is true, as well, if you're a man. Some of the best cooks I know are men. Some of the finest recipes in this book have come to me from men who have been guests at Blueberry Hill and who have spent literally their entire holiday in my kitchen, perched on a stool, watching, giving suggestions, writing down things new to themselves.

Obviously I love to cook. But if I were to think back to the times when the food I have served forth has surpassed my best, it has been when someone has truly relished it, has chortled over the humor of it (and food can be humorous, just as talk can be), and given to me the greatest gift a cook can receive—sincere and utter culinary appreciation. Ah, to the cook a plate licked clean is as a diadem!

I hope, furthermore, that this book will not only sit by your stove, used and thumbed and familiar, but that you will like to read it even when you're not cooking. One of the nicest letters I have received told me that the writer had read my first cookbook "like a novel, right straight through." That's nice. I hope you'll want to do it again.

It is some four years now since the *Blueberry Hill Cookbook* was published. Those of you who may have seen it will know that it was a classified book: appetizers, soups, meats, leftovers, desserts, each in their own section. At the start of it, almost as an afterthought, I included a chapter of menus. These menus, which covered 29 days, included just about all the 275 recipes in the cookbook.

Since the publication of that book, I have been told time and again of the great help this menu chapter had provided in solving the one bugaboo facing most cooks—what to prepare *that very night*. I remember that my mother, who was a fine cook with a limited repertoire of dishes, would rock in her chair, look to heaven, and say: "What in the world can I have for dinner tonight?" Such a problem!

It's fairly simple to plan a party dinner. One has time for that, leisure between the decision to hold the party and the cooking of the dinner, time to mull the whole thing over. But on a hot summer day, who knows what to cook for dinner? How nice to be told.

And may I add, parenthetically, that there's just about nothing surer to irritate an otherwise loving husband than to ask him, just as he's leaving for his day's occupation, what *he* would like for dinner! How does *he* know? He's just had breakfast, for the Lord's sake! You'll get nowhere putting the onus on him.

So this time, in this *Blueberry Hill Menu Cookbook*, it is menus. Twenty-four of them. Two for each month: one party menu, one family menu. They are good, big menus with plenty in them so that, given a group with hearty appetites, you will have ample for them all; for people with more sensitive digestions, you might want to leave out one or two items, but you will still have a balanced, enticing meal. With each menu is an explicit section of directions on how to organize the meal, what can be done the day before, even the week before, and frozen, what needs to be done in the morning, the afternoon, just before dinner, and so on. Thus, through it all, you'll know that everything is going to come out at the same time, that the vegetables and the entree will emerge triumphant, hand in hand; that, in the end, you can relax and enjoy your own party.

Then, and this has been the most fun for me, I've tried to think of everything I might be apt to do with every part of each meal, were it to be left over. Obviously, you won't have some of each thing left, even in small quantities, but, in the event that you might, I've told you what I would do. To my surprise, in several chapters with ten or twelve main dishes, I've been able to give you thirty or thirty-one different ideas for leftovers. Some of these thoughts are just that; others, quite a few others, are complete recipes; once in a while, I'll just admit that there's absolutely nothing you can do with one item of food.

Some of these menus will be for lunches, some for dinners. Some outdoor barbecues. A garden club luncheon. A children's supper party. A meal for men alone—after bowling, perhaps. And so it will go.

But this I promise. Every meal will be the best I can give you, the most gracious—never less than that. I will back each recipe with my reputation as a cook. Don't worry about anything. If you trust me—and I hope you do—you will try everything in this book.

The meals are attuned to the seasons as well, though this is not as urgent a matter as it once was, what with the improvements in transportation of perishables and the invention of the freezer. Foods are used, however, when they are plentiful, as much as possible.

You will find the recipes colloquial affairs, the ingredients in bold type where they appear. I am aware, however, that the cook should have somewhere at his disposal a grouping so that he can, if he's systematic about these things, get everything out and have it before him before he starts. I like my own system better; I have everything that I'm apt to use in general cooking, such as flour, Worcestershire sauce, sugar, within my reach in my own kitchen. Thus I grab it when I want it. This may not be possible for you, and of course you do have to go to the refrigerator for milk and eggs.

All this being true, I'm presenting my recipes the way I like a recipe to be presented to me; conversationally, and in narrative form. At the end of each recipe, there is a list of ingredients.

At the beginning of each menu, I will tell you how many people the recipes in that meal are supposed to serve. If you wish to prepare a single recipe, check back to the start of the chapter to see how many it will serve.

Here, then, is my new cookbook, the *Blueberry Hill Menu Cookbook*. A timetable for each meal. A right meal for the right time. As those who know me from other writings will remember, I don't make a big thing about the right pots and pans. Immediately following, I shall make a few comments about the several items that I would not be without; other than these, I couldn't care less. Certainly I don't demand, when you use my cookbook, that you run right out and get a new supply of cooking dishes.

It's nice to be back with you again. Let's cook!

SOME IDEAS ON EQUIPMENT, ETC.

I WOULDN'T BE WITHOUT MY . . .

 WIRE WHISK. A simple device, French in origin, I believe, that is indispensable in making gravies, sauces, stirring up batters, combining eggs. Just a handle with some curved wires. As I said above, I wouldn't be without it.

BUNGALOW COOKER. You'll hear about this on and off throughout the book. There's a long description of its beginnings in the Masterton kitchen, which you will find in the early pages of my *Blueberry Hill Cookbook*. It's a steamer, made by Wearever. Just to confuse you, since my earlier cookbook came out, the Wearever people have changed its name to their dealers from Bungalow Cooker to Bungalow Steamer to, now, Rice Steamer, by which it seems now to be known in its listed state in their catalogue. All this information, in the event you go looking for one. Try your big department store housewares department first; if you're unsuccessful, as you well may be, write to Wearever, New Kensington, Pennsylvania; and, if that seems too much trouble, or doesn't produce results, write to me. I have them in self-defense and will be glad to ship one out if necessary. *Description:* It's an aluminum pot with a two-quart insert, large enough for three or four boxes of frozen vegetables, though one will do perfectly in it. It's the greatest for any sort of fresh vegetable, fish, in fact any steaming purpose. Steaming has supplanted boiling for me. I haven't boiled a potato in ten years. The juices in this Bungalow Cooker are retained; you can use them for soups, sauces, what have you! You should have one.

KITCHEN SHEARS. Buy a good, sharp pair and don't use them for paper. Fine for snipping parsley, chives, marshmallows (wet them first); use the shears to cut through chicken breasts when you want them in quarters and to snip the strings on a roast. If you have a pair, you'll be after them all the time. Makes a two-handed job a one-handed job.

DUTCH OVEN. A heavy pot, preferably iron, though club aluminum will do, with a tight-fitting lid. The perfect utensil for long-cooking sauces like spaghetti sauce, for stews, for pot roasts. The lid is a self-baster. Wouldn't be without it.

BLACK IRON FRYING PANS, ALL SIZES. These produce a fine crust, if you want one, but more than that they maintain an even heat without concern. Our grandmothers knew about these! Griswold and Wagner are two manufacturers of these.

ROAST THERMOMETER. This is the only way to keep track of what's happening in the oven. I speak of these frequently as you will see. Don't get a glass one—they frequently break in the roast. The Taylor Company makes a firm aluminum thermometer with a glass face that will not break, even in a dishwasher.

AND IT'S NICE TO HAVE A . . .

SALTON HOTRAY. These come in all sizes, and are a tremendous help in keeping food hot during buffets. They take a good bit of the frenzy out of timing everything to come out at the same time. They don't work indefinitely, because they're actually a very low heat, but for the duration of the average dinner party, they do their job. There's a rolling table with a Hotray top, too.

FOLEY FOOD MILL. For puréeing.

BLENDER. Any kind. I use these less often than other people because they don't hold the quantity of food I'm apt to be preparing, but for certain recipes, such as my caviar loaf, they're indispensable.

OVEN SHOVEL. I speak of these occasionally, and probably I ought to list this in the Wouldn't Be Without section. Saves so much in burned hands and lost tempers. These shovels will slide under the largest pie plate and smoothly lift it from the oven.

SHRIMP CLEANER. These are available in hardware stores of perspicacity and in many mail-order catalogues—and what a boon *they* are—the shrimp cleaners, not the catalogues. These pointed gadgets lift off the shrimp shell and remove the intestinal vein in one fell swoop. Get one.

AND A THOUGHT OR TWO ON

HOW I FEEL ABOUT . . .

GAS as against ELECTRIC RANGES. I like the gas ranges better. For me, they have worked more efficiently, particularly in the top-of-the-stove department. When the gas is turned on, it's on, and when it's off, it's off, and if something's ready to burn, you can do something about it without lifting large pots on and off the heating units of the electric ranges. Besides, living in the country, there's always the chance of a power shortage, and then where is dinner? However, all this being so, I do know that the electric ranges are improving all the time. I just wish they'd learn how to cool down as quickly as they've learned to heat up.

WINES FOR COOKING. I guess one of the questions I'm asked most often is, "What *sort* of wine?" when I call for a "light, sweet, red wine" or "light, sweet, white wine." The best way I can answer this is to say that practically every California winery now has a light red dinner wine on the market.

Since there's no actual name for this wine, they solve the problem by calling it, and I quote, "light, sweet, red [or white] wine." Sometimes they just call it a "light red wine." Sometimes they just call it a "red dinner wine" or "white dinner wine." It is much less sweet than a port, though it's not as dry as some of the Chiantis. There's a conspiracy among the liquor stores, however, who don't seem to want to sell these wines, or even acknowledge their existence, and many of my *Blueberry Hill Cookbook* readers have had problems getting the sort of wine I have asked for.

In Vermont, and in Florida, and in many other states, I presume, the liquor licensing laws are such that these wines are sold in every supermarket in every small town. In other states—most particularly to my knowledge, New York—you have to go to a liquor store for wines, even of this low alcoholic content. (Any wine under 14% alcohol can be sold in a supermarket in Vermont. Any wine of more than 14%, such as a sherry, must be purchased at the state liquor stores.) If you must do this, tell your liquor store salesman that you want *light, sweet, red [or white] wine,* and that Roma, Three Monks, Cella, Petri (and I'm sure the Eastern vineyards such as Taylor and Widmer) put this up by almost exactly this title. Make the man look it up in his catalogue; it will be there. Then make him order it. It's so inexpensive that you could buy a case of it and pass it around to the neighbors, if that's the only way you can make him get it for you.

JANUARY

PARTY MENU

Let's Begin the Year with an Eggnog Party

EGGNOG FOR GROWNUPS
CIDER ICE-CREAM FLOAT FOR CHILDREN
BAKED HAM WITH CRANBERRY SHERRY GLAZE
CHICKEN TETRAZZINI
MUSHROOMS A LA GREQUE
POTATOES IN CUSTARD
CARROTS IN COGNAC
CHEESE STRAWS
PEGGY'S MYSTERY SALAD
BING CHERRIES IN BRANDY
MIRACLE MERINGUE CAKE

It's many years since John and I have stayed up much later than midnight on a New Year's Eve. We prefer the fun of the New Year's Day eggnog party. For this one, we've provided for children as well as grownups. It's a buffet, the only sort of service possible for an elastic number of people. First, eggnogs for the adults and ice-cream floats for the youngsters, and then, very soon, a lovely, ample supper. I'm very much against eggnog parties which provide nothing but eggnog and beaten biscuits. Everybody always has too many eggnogs, which are much too rich to be taken in quantity without dire results. And, when the party is over, what do you do about supper?

9

The menu will serve 12 to 18. Multiply it if you'd like. There will be plenty of ham for any unexpected guests, anyway, so you're pretty safe to stick to the quantities set forth here. You can, of course, divide, given fewer numbers.

EGGNOG

A centuries-old recipe. I recommend it. Prepare this at least five days before you want it. Then hoard it in the refrigerator until New Year's Day—a difficult feat, I will admit. Mix **1 cup granulated sugar** with **1 quart light cream**. (Don't use that coffee cream mixture, but a cream rich in butterfat. Perhaps where you live it is called heavy cream; in Vermont, our light cream is, in fact, pretty heavy.) Beat **8 egg whites** and fold in. Don't overbeat these; they must not go past the glistening stage; they're supposed to stand in peaks, not fluff into cotton balls. When all the egg white is assimilated and unidentifiable—no white showing— add the **8 egg yolks**, beaten to a golden yellow first, and **1 tablespoon grated nutmeg.** If you can get whole nutmegs and a little nutmeg grater and grate these yourself, you'll have something very much worthwhile. Otherwise, a good grade of already-ground nutmeg will do. Stir it all around and then, slowly, add **1½ pints rum.** The best rum for this is Old Newburyport Rum, though you can suit yourself as to brand. That's all there is to that. Keep it till you want it. Serve in little eggnog cups, sprinkling as you go with **freshly ground nutmeg.** You will have about 2 quarts of eggnog. If you want to take my advice, you'll double the recipe. You can always use what's left over. It keeps in the refrigerator for weeks.

INGREDIENTS: 1 cup granulated sugar; 1 quart light cream; 8 eggs; 1 tablespoon grated nutmeg; 1½ pints rum; freshly ground nutmeg.

CIDER ICE-CREAM FLOAT

Well ahead of time, the day before or the morning of your party, heat **6 cups sweet cider** with **½ teaspoon ground all-**

spice, 1½ sticks cinnamon, 8 whole cloves, and ¼ cup packed
brown sugar. Heat this over low heat for about 10 minutes,
stirring just to dissolve the sugar. Strain the mixture and add
1 tablespoon grated lemon rind. Chill it in the refrigerator.
Serve in eggnog cups to the young with 1 tablespoon vanilla
ice cream in each, sprinkling the top with freshly ground
nutmeg.

INGREDIENTS: 6 cups sweet cider; ½ teaspoon ground allspice;
1½ sticks cinnamon; 8 whole cloves; ¼ cup packed
brown sugar; 1 tablespoon grated lemon rind; ½ pint
vanilla ice cream; freshly ground nutmeg.

NOTE: Some of the very young children might prefer
either a Coca-Cola or a Seven-Up float, a practically
universally acceptable small-fry drink. Keep them small,
however. There's a good supper coming along.

BAKED HAM
WITH CRANBERRY SHERRY GLAZE

For any buffet, there must be one main dish that is not only
strikingly beautiful to view, but that tastes marvelous and
unusual at the same time. This beautifully glazed ham an-
swers this description; it is a joy to view and is truly delicious.

Although there are many schools of thought about hams,
debating the various attributes of lightly and heavily smoked
animals, we have come, at Blueberry Hill, to the hams which
are ready-to-eat when we get them. These are lightly smoked
and tenderized, and require very little attention. When they
are properly heated through and glazed, they are juicy, pink,
and delicious. I buy them at the local supermarket.

Place a 12- to 14-pound ready-to-eat ham with bone in
(ask for it by this name) on a rack in a roaster which has a
tightly fitting cover. Bake it, covered, for 10 minutes for each
pound of weight, in a slow (325°F.) oven. (This will take
2 to 2½ hours.) Remove it from the oven at this point, lift the
lid (and step back, because the steam will burst forth), and
set the ham on a tray for a few minutes until it's cool enough
to handle. Pour out all the fat that has accumulated on the

bottom of the pan and wipe the pan out with a paper towel. Snip the skin of the ham right through the top with the kitchen shears (an indispensable object, kitchen shears) and, grabbing tight hold of one corner of the skin, a paper towel protecting your hands from the heat, pull it completely off the ham. It will come along easily. One or two places might be a little stubborn; help them along with a sharp little knife. Set the ham back on the rack in the roasting pan, fat side on top (trim off any of the fat that has become discolored, the part that did not have any skin on it), and score the fat with your little knife. "Scoring" just means cutting into the fat in fearless strokes, straight ones, so that you have symmetrical, diamond-shaped cuts. Stick a **whole clove** in each square, and then smooth over the top **1 can whole-berry cranberry sauce.** Dribble on, very carefully, so as not to disturb the cranberries, **½ cup light sherry.** If any of the cranberries do fall down into the pan, scoop them up with a spoon and pat them back where they came from. Return the ham, un-covered, to the oven, now set at 425°F., for 20 to 30 min-utes, until cranberries are well set and glazed. Ten minutes be-fore it's due out of the oven, add another **½ cup light sherry,** dribbling it directly on the ham. Watch the bottom of the pan; if any of the juices start to burn, add a little more sherry and turn the oven down. When the ham is ready to be served, lift it out of the pan onto a large platter or carving board and carefully pour onto it whatever wine is left in the bottom of the pan. Be sure there is served with each slice a few of the sherry-soaked cranberries with a little of the juice. This ham can be served hot or cold; hot's better, but don't be ashamed to serve it to late-comers after it's cooled down.

INGREDIENTS: 12- to 14-pound ready-to-eat ham; whole cloves; 1 can whole-berry cranberry sauce; 1 cup light sherry.

CHICKEN TETRAZZINI

A fine, classic casserole (named for Madame Tetrazzini, a famous opera singer), which the children will love as much as the grownups. Most of it can be prepared ahead, a comfort.

The best chicken for any sort of chicken pie or creamed chicken dish for which you're interested in having rich, fine broth, is a fowl. These are hens which have seen their day, but, given three or four hours of simmering, they, too, emerge tender as the hours of their youth. You may use a roasting chicken which will cook tender in about two hours, but the stock won't be so robust.

In either case, bring to a boil in a large kettle **6 quarts cold water; 6 peeled large carrots; 2 peeled large onions,** cut up a bit; **2 bay leaves; 2 or 3 celery stalks,** mostly tops; **8 peppercorns;** and **2 tablespoons salt.** Add **2 whole fowl** (or they can be cut up if you find this easier to fit into your pot— they're much more moist if they are cooked whole, however) or **3 roasting chickens.** You should have about 10 pounds of chicken, the weight of course being reckoned at the butcher shop, not after the chicken has been taken off the bones. Lower the heat and continue to simmer until the chickens are tender. And by this I mean really tender. The leg is the part to test. It must show no resistance to a firm poke with a fork.

Set the pot, still containing the chickens, uncovered, in a cool place such as your porch or fire escape. If you have neither, or if these are heated by the sun, place a stopper in your sink, fill the sink half full with cold water, add some ice cubes, and set the pot in that. It's of vital importance that the broth cool quickly and that it be uncovered. Warm chicken broth sours before you know it, if you let it sit around. As soon as it's at room temperature, you're safe. Remove the chickens and set about cutting them into fairly large bite-sized pieces.

As you remove the chickens from the bones, return the bones and the skin and carcass, with whatever meat is unremovable by normal means, to the broth and let it simmer again for another hour. The chicken itself should be refrigerated until it's needed; keep it in a bowl with enough strained broth to cover it. This keeps it from drying out.

After the broth has simmered its required hour, strain it. Taste; add salt and pepper if necessary. Cool, then refrigerate the broth until you need it. If you're not planning to use it within 24 hours, freeze it. I do this, using large-sized juice cans, labeled on the outside as to contents, and covered with aluminum foil or saran. You should have several quarts of broth.

The procedure this far is the basic process to be followed whenever you want chicken or broth. I won't repeat it in this book. Just read up to here, if any other recipe calls for **chicken broth** or chicken meat.

The morning of your party, cook **1 pound vermicelli** (the thinnest of the spaghettis, and if you purchase this in an Italian grocery, you'll really get the thinnest) in **4 quarts** rapidly boiling **salted water.** This will take no more than 2 minutes, so stay with it. You must add the vermicelli slowly to the water and keep stirring it with a fork so it won't cook in one glutinous mass. Taste it after 2 minutes, adding salt if needed, and, as soon as it has lost the raw taste of un-cooked spaghetti and is tender, but still somewhat *al dente* (means just as it sounds: your teeth—*dente*—must feel it), drain it in a colander and rinse it quickly with ice-cold water. If you use hot water, you will cook the vermicelli further. Get all of it wet and cool, letting it fall through your fingers, making sure all the starch has been removed. Set it in a bowl with **2 teaspoons salt, 4 tablespoons** (½ stick) **butter, 2 table-spoons grated Parmesan cheese.**

Get a 6-inch black iron frying pan hot. Sizzle in it, without burning, **1 tablespoon butter,** and, when the butter is hot, add **1 pound fresh mushrooms,** the stems trimmed and the mush-rooms sliced through vertically in thin umbrella-shaped slices. Sauté the mushrooms 3 minutes. They will be wilted, but far from cooked through. That's what you want. Sprinkle with ½ **teaspoon salt,** a few gratings of **pepper** from the pepper mill, and **1 small clove of garlic,** peeled and cut into slivers. Simmer another ½ minute. Stir them into the bowl with the vermicelli, scraping the pan for juices with a rubber spatula. Get everything in.

For the Sauce: Melt **6 tablespoons butter** or **chicken fat** in a heavy 2-quart saucepan; then stir in, with the back of a wooden spoon or a wire whisk, **¼ cup flour**, rubbing it until you have a smooth, thick paste. Add **1 quart** of the hot chicken broth, a little at a time, stirring constantly. If you're patient about this, and careful, you will have with each addition, a smooth, slightly less thick, *roux* or paste than the time before. Eventually, it will be quite thin and you can add more of the broth at once. When all the broth has been added, let the sauce simmer for five minutes over low heat. Then add, very gradually, **2 cups rich light** (not coffee) **cream, 1½ teaspoons salt**, and **¼ cup sauterne** or **sherry**. Simmer a minute more, until the wine and the cream are well mixed.

Add *half* the sauce to the vermicelli and the mushrooms waiting in the bowl. Remove the prepared chicken from the refrigerator, drain off the chicken broth (save it, of course; it's delicious), and stir the *other half* of the sauce into the chicken.

Place the vermicelli and mushrooms, already mixed with their sauce, in a very large, flat buttered earthenware casserole (or two smaller ones; in the event you have one casserole left over, it can be frozen as is). Make a hole in the middle of the vermicelli and pour into it the chicken and the sauce that comes with it. This much can be done ahead.

Refrigerate the casserole or casseroles, covered, until one hour before the party. Sprinkle the top of the Tetrazzini with **¼ cup grated Parmesan cheese.** Half an hour before serving, set the casserole in a moderate (375°F.) oven and, five minutes before serving, brown the cheese on top of the casserole under the broiler just slightly.

To serve, place casserole on one of those little electric hot trays, which will keep it warm for quite a while. If your party goes on past the keeping-warm stage, pour the mixture into a chafing dish, and keep it hot that way. Won't have the crust but it will be equally delicious.

INGREDIENTS:

For the broth: 6 quarts cold water; 6 large carrots; 2 large onions; 2 bay leaves; 2 or 3 celery stalks; 8 peppercorns; 2 tablespoons salt; 2 whole fowl or 3 roasting chickens (about 10 pounds in all).

For the vermicelli: 4 quarts water; salt; 1 pound vermicelli; salt; 4 tablespoons butter; 2 tablespoons grated Parmesan cheese.

For the mushrooms: 1 tablespoon butter; 1 pound fresh sliced mushrooms; ½ teaspoon salt; pepper; 1 small clove of garlic.

For the sauce: 6 tablespoons butter or chicken fat; ¼ cup flour; 1 quart hot chicken broth; 2 cups light cream; 1½ teaspoons salt; ¼ cup sauterne or sherry.

For the topping: ¼ cup grated Parmesan cheese.

MUSHROOMS A LA GREQUE

A day-before job. Simmer **caps of 2 pounds small fresh mushrooms,** wiped with damp paper towels if they have any dirt on them, in **1 cup dry white wine** with **¼ teaspoon salt** for 5 minutes. Add to the wine **½ cup pure olive oil; 2 tablespoons cider vinegar; ¼ cup chopped parsley; 1 bay leaf; ½ onion,** grated; and **2 cloves garlic,** minced. Simmer 5 minutes more. Cool in the marinade in the refrigerator. Serve chilled, draining just before serving.

INGREDIENTS: Caps of 2 pounds small fresh mushrooms; 1 cup dry white wine; ¼ teaspoon salt; ½ cup pure olive oil; 2 tablespoons cider vinegar; ¼ cup chopped parsley; 1 bay leaf; ½ onion; 2 cloves garlic.

POTATOES IN CUSTARD

You may not wish to have any potatoes, since you do have the chicken Tetrazzini with its spaghetti, but, for the benefit of those who select the ham, a dish of these might be appreciated. The recipe is intentionally given as a small quantity, as you surely will find many of your guests skipping this course.

Butter a 1-quart casserole lavishly, using **2 or 3 table-spoons butter.** Sprinkle over the butter **1 clove garlic,** minced. Slice, paper thin, **6 medium potatoes,** sprinkle them well with **salt** and **pepper,** and place them in the casserole. Be sure the potatoes are sliced paper thin, because if they are thicker they will take too long to bake and your custard will separate.

In a separate bowl, beat together with a fork **4 eggs, 1 cup milk,** and **¼ cup heavy cream.** Pour this over the potatoes, dot with **2 tablespoons butter,** and bake in a moderate (350°F.) oven until the potatoes are tender. This will take about 1 hour. Serve when done and still hot. Have a bowl of ice-cold **commercial sour cream** at hand for your guests to use as topping, if they wish.

INGREDIENTS: 4 or 5 tablespoons butter; 1 clove garlic; 6 medium potatoes; salt; pepper; 4 eggs; 1 cup milk; ¼ cup heavy cream; ½ pint commercial sour cream.

CARROTS IN COGNAC

Steam **4 dozen peeled small carrots** with **½ teaspoon salt,** until just tender. Those who know me know how I feel about steaming vegetables. It's the only way. I use what is called a Bungalow Cooker (see Some Ideas on Equipment, Etc., page 5) which retains the juices for future uses (a poem!), but there are now many other steamers on the market, probably of fairly equal value. If you can't see your way clear to getting one, use a colander over hot water with a lid on top of the colander. The carrots can be steamed well ahead of time. The rest is a last-hour job, but, even at that, once everything is prepared, the carrots can be kept hot in a chafing dish or an electric skillet with damage done to nothing.

Heat a 10-inch black iron frying pan, and, when it is hot

(test it with a drop of water—if the water sizzles, fine), add ½ cup (1 stick) **butter** or **margarine** (margarine's all right in this recipe), letting it sizzle. Then add the drained carrots, turning and moving them in the pan to cover the carrots thoroughly with the butter. Sprinkle with **4 teaspoons light brown sugar,** continuing to move the carrots back and forth to glaze them thoroughly. This part you can do as much as an hour before dinner. At the last minute, add ¼ **cup cognac.** Shake the pan and sprinkle the carrots with **2 teaspoons finely minced parsley.** Serve from the pan or transfer to something that will keep the carrots in shape through a long evening. You can flambé the cognac, lighting it with a match for remarkable effect, but this scares the devil out of me and I prefer to leave such goings-on to Le Pavillon. If you're one who prefers not to have things like cognac with your carrots, stop short of the last step. The carrots then will be plain glazed carrots.

INGREDIENTS: 4 dozen small carrots; ½ teaspoon salt; ½ cup butter or margarine; 4 teaspoons light brown sugar; ¼ cup cognac; 2 teaspoons finely minced parsley.

CHEESE STRAWS

These will serve as your "breadstuff"—horrid word!—as well as a nibble with the eggnogs. Blend together with a firmly held mixing spoon 1½ **cups flour;** ½ **cup** (1 stick) **soft butter or margarine; 4 ounces cheddar cheese,** grated; and ¼ **cup commercial sour cream.** When the ingredients are pretty well homogenized, work the dough with floured hands. Quickly it will merge into a rich, smooth dough, very malleable. Wrap in saran and leave in the refrigerator at least an hour—you can leave the dough there as much as a week without harm, actually. When ready to bake the straws, roll out the dough on a lightly floured board to ¼-inch thickness, trying to keep it in a rectangular shape. With a sharp knife cut strips ¼ inch wide and then cut them across so they are 2 inches long. Spread the top with **beaten egg yolk,** using a pastry brush.

Bake in slow (325°F.) oven for 15 minutes or until light brown. Makes about 100 two-inch straws.

INGREDIENTS: 1½ cups flour; ½ cup butter or margarine; 4 ounces cheddar cheese; ¼ cup commercial sour cream; 1 egg yolk.

PEGGY'S MYSTERY SALAD

The Peggy of the title is one of my cooking students who traveled to Vermont from St. Paul, Minnesota, last May. She attended all the classes and then, on parting, casually handed me this recipe. It's been a major part of my cuisine ever since. Always arouses admiring conversation. So you see, the pupil has taught the teacher.

Dissolve **3 regular-sized packages raspberry gelatin** in **1¼ cups hot water.** Stir in **3 cans** (1 pound each) **stewed tomatoes** (the kind that are already prepared with onion, celery, peppers), breaking the tomatoes up with a spoon. Add **6 drops Tabasco sauce.** Pour into a lightly oiled 12-cup ring mold. Chill until firm. Unmold on greens and fill center of ring with **1 pint commercial sour cream** to which has been added **1 tablespoon creamed horseradish,** ½ teaspoon salt, and ½ teaspoon sugar.

INGREDIENTS:
   For the salad: 3 regular-sized packages raspberry gelatin; 1¼ cups hot water; 3 cans (1 pound each) stewed tomatoes; 6 drops Tabasco sauce; mixed salad greens.
   For the dressing: 1 pint commercial sour cream; 1 tablespoon creamed horseradish; ½ teaspoon salt; ½ teaspoon sugar.

BING CHERRIES IN BRANDY

Add **3 tablespoons brandy** slowly to an **8-ounce glass currant jelly,** stirring jelly first. Be sure there are no lumps. Combine with **1 large can** (1 pound, 14 ounces) **Bing cherries,** pitted and drained. Chill.

INGREDIENTS: 3 tablespoons brandy; 8-ounce glass currant jelly; 1 large can Bing cherries.

MIRACLE MERINGUE CAKE

Since this is a party, let's have a definitely party cake. If you've never seen a cake like this before, as I hadn't before the recipe was sent to me, you will be amazed at its beauty and its individuality. It's like no other cake I've ever seen. Absolutely gorgeous, too. The cake is baked with the meringue, usually used only to top lemon pies, baked right along with the cake batter. It will keep in the refrigerator for a week, wrapped lightly in saran and, if anything, improves with age. One cake is more than enough for 10 or 12 people, and, since we are providing so much else to eat, including the fruit dessert, this recipe will be for just one cake. You can of course, bake two. As you know, if you know me, it has to taste as good as it looks for me to urge it on you. This one does!

Cream ½ cup butter or margarine with ½ cup sugar very thoroughly. Have your electric mixer at high speed. When they are thoroughly combined, ungranular in appearance and *creamy*, which is the definition of creaming, add 4 egg yolks, one at a time, beating after each addition until they are well combined with the butter and sugar mixture. Then add ¼ cup rich milk. If the milk you can get is not rich in butterfat, mix it half and half with cream. Add ½ teaspoon vanilla.

Sift onto a piece of waxed paper 1 cup sifted cake flour, 1¼ teaspoons baking powder, and ⅛ teaspoon salt. Add the wet to the dry mix, combining by beating thoroughly with an electric mixer, and beating for at least 2 minutes after they are combined.

Grease with any good vegetable shortening two 9-inch layer cake pans, then toss some flour around on top of the shortening and discard whatever flour does not stick to the shortening. Then spread the batter, which is very thick, in these pans. You'll probably do well to use a spatula to spread it around. It needs help.

For the Meringue: Just beat stiff the 4 egg whites (the distaff half of the eggs) with a pinch of salt and, gradually, in about four additions, add 1 cup granulated sugar, then 1 teaspoon vanilla. Beat at least another minute after all the sugar has been added, then spread the meringue right on top of the batter in the two pans. Do this lightly, as you would for a meringue pie, so that it is in uneven peaks, and make sure it touches the edges of the cake pans all around. On one of the layers, sprinkle ¼ cup broken walnut or pecan pieces.

Set the pans in a moderate (350°F.) oven and bake for 35 minutes, or until the cakes test done with a skewer or a broom straw. The meringue will be raised and light brown. Set the two pans on racks out of a draft and allow the cakes to cool in their own pans.

For the Filling: While the cakes are cooling, make the following apricot filling. Cook ½ pound dried apricots in 2 cups water, simmering until the fruit is tender, about 25 minutes. Add sugar to your own taste, usually about ¾ to 1 cup. Boil about 5 minutes then mash the fruit or put it through a food mill. I prefer to mash the apricots coarsely, as I like the solid bits of apricot more than a purée, but this is up to you. Cool the fruit and, when it is thoroughly cooled (remember the freezer as a quick-cooling agent if you're in a hurry), fold into it 1 cup heavy cream, whipped. Reserve ¼ cup of this filling for the top of the cake. For a less rich filling, omit the whipped cream and add, instead, 2 tablespoons lemon juice.

To put the cake together, remove the two layers from their pans. They come out beautifully; just don't worry about it. Don't be afraid to let them fall lightly on the meringue, nothing will happen to it. Of course I don't expect you to drop them on the meringue, but these cakes are marvelously malleable. Set one layer, meringue side *down*, yes, I said *down,* on a pretty cake plate. Save the layer with the nuts for the top. Spread the upside-down layer with apricot filling, set the other layer, right-side up (meringue-side up) on top of the apricot filling. Spread a small circle of the reserved filling on top.

This cake is truly delicious served very, very cold, but it is a gorgeous thing, no matter what you do with it. If you wish, you can substitute rhubarb crème (the recipe for this is in the *Blueberry Hill Cookbook*), folding the stewed rhubarb into the whipped cream just as you have here with the apricot. It is tart, yet sweet. Quite wonderful.

Think, if you will, of a lemon filling for this cake; or fresh strawberries in season. There is nothing more beautiful than this meringue cake, filled with fresh strawberries slightly crushed into whipped cream, and topped with perfect specimens of strawberries, dipped in sugar, their stems and a leaf or two still attached. Raspberries are perfect here, too. The variations are endless. I don't suggest freezing this cake, as the meringue doesn't take to freezing very well; however, with its long refrigerator life, you will never waste a bit of it.

INGREDIENTS:

For the cake: ½ cup butter or margarine; ½ cup sugar; 4 egg yolks; ¼ cup rich milk; ½ teaspoon vanilla; 1 cup sifted cake flour; 1¼ teaspoons baking powder; ⅛ teaspoon salt.

For the meringue: 4 egg whites; pinch of salt; 1 cup granulated sugar; 1 teaspoon vanilla; ¼ cup broken walnuts or pecans.

For the filling: ½ pound dried apricots; 2 cups water; sugar; 1 cup heavy cream or 2 tablespoons lemon juice.

TIMETABLE: I won't pretend that there isn't a lot to do in preparation for this party, but much of it can be taken care of beforehand, and there is little in the way of final, frantic activity.

The eggnog is prepared far ahead of time. Just stir it about a bit when you need it, keeping it refrigerated until the last moment. The day before your party, prepare the chicken and

the broth, getting the broth strained and setting the prepared
chicken pieces in a bowl in the refrigerator. The mushrooms
à la Greque, too, are marinated at least a day in advance.
It doesn't hurt them to be fixed two or three days ahead;
they improve, as a matter of fact. The cheese straws can be
prepared up to the point of cutting the dough into strips and
baking. These, too, may be left in the refrigerator for days,
baking them as you need them. Won't hurt the cider to be
prepared the day before either. Satisfying to have so much
ready, isn't it?

Bake your meringue cake, complete, the day before your
party. If you have this cake on some other, less complicated,
day, bake it the day you plan to serve it—but this time do
it ahead!

On the morning of your party, cook the vermicelli, make
the sauce for the Tetrazzini, prepare the mushrooms, and
get the casserole ready for the oven. It can remain in the refrigerator thereafter until an hour before you expect to serve
it. Let it relax at room temperature for a half hour, and
then bake it for a half hour as directed. Cook the carrots
for the carrots in cognac in the morning, steaming them as
directed. They don't need refrigerating; just leave them in
the steamer, uncovered. Prepare the mystery salad. Takes
all of five minutes and *that's* done. It will be set, in the
refrigerator, long before you need it. This can be done the
day before, if you prefer. Prepare the cherries in brandy.
Leave them in their cut-glass bowl in the refrigerator. Slice
the potatoes. Leave them in cold water until a little later.

Early in the afternoon of your party, place the ham in the
oven, as directed. An hour and a half before the guests are
due, put together the potato custard, and start it baking.
Glaze the carrots, leaving the cognac nearby in a cup, ready
for the last-minute addition. Roll and cut out the cheese
straws. Leave them on their baking tray, ready to bake; if
you have some time to wait, set the tray in the refrigerator.
Remove the ham from the oven, skin it, get the cranberries
and sherry in place, return it to the oven and, with it, the
chicken Tetrazzini.

About this time, probably, you'll want to get ready for your guests. Do that. They'll be arriving in a minute or two. Greet them. Get them started on their eggnogs. Leave them with somebody who will see to their comfort, and pop a tray of cheese straws into the oven. Let them nibble on these with their eggnogs or cider ice-cream floats.

You have nothing left to do, really, but to get your buffet table ready so: the ham on a welled-board so you can catch the luscious sherry gravy to serve with the slices; the chicken browned for a few minutes and then set on the table on a hot tray; the mushrooms drained and set out in a glass bowl; the potatoes in their own casserole; the carrots heated quickly, the cognac added and, if you're game, flambéed, or just set on a hot plate on the table in their own frying pan; the salad turned out on a bed of water cress or chicory, the center filled with the sour cream mix (this takes so little time to stir together, I haven't suggested doing it ahead of time, but if you'd feel more secure, by all means have it ready). The cheese straws were served once, and at this time you should have another hot tray of them ready.

In the center of the buffet table, for your guests to see and then return to, will be the cherries of which life is just a bowl, and the beautiful, beautiful meringue cake.

Nothing to it. Happy New Year!

LEFTOVERS

The eggnog, as I have said, goes on without damage until you've done away with it all. The mushrooms, too, improve, so don't fool with them, just eat them. If there is any of the Tetrazzini left, pile it into individual scallop shells, pour on each 1 teaspoon sherry, top with buttered soft bread crumbs and heat to bubbling. It'll be like new. The carrots in cognac, should you have some, can be combined with some freshly sautéed mushrooms, heating it all quickly in the sautéing butter.

Another nice thing to do with the carrots is to mix them

with a can of small white onions, drained, and heat in the oven with 1 egg yolk beaten into ¼ cup light cream.

Of course, the ham is going to be your biggest problem. There's always so much ham on a ham. You can do the usual things, such as serving it sautéed in sizzling butter with half a peach (sprinkle the peach with brown sugar), or having the most delicious ham sandwich in the world, which is achieved by slicing it thin, spreading it with a morsel of mustard, and then adding whatever of the glazed cranberries you can find. This makes a divine sandwich, particularly on old-fashioned homemade white bread. But after you've done these things, how about a beautiful ham mousse? You'll need 2 cups of minced ham—don't grind it, it's never the same, ground.

Leftover-Ham Mousse

Soak 1½ tablespoons unflavored gelatine in ¼ cup cold chicken stock (canned chicken broth will do, though home-made [page 13] is far superior. Keep some in your freezer, why don't you? An invaluable ingredient in so many things). After 5 minutes, dissolve the gelatine in ½ cup hot stock. Takes 5 or 10 minutes. Don't use bouillon cubes, by the way, for this. The pure chicken flavor is essential.

Beat the yolks of 3 eggs, add 1½ cups light cream, and, stirring madly in a heavy saucepan over direct heat, cook until smooth and thick. It takes no time, but you have to watch it. Use a double boiler, if you prefer—you won't have to watch it so carefully, but it will take longer. Remove it from the heat the moment it *starts* to thicken; it will con-tinue thickening away from the heat, so don't leave it where it will become pasty. Stir the gelatine mixture into this and fold in 2 cups minced, not ground, ham. Add salt to taste (you'll have to taste this, because there is variation in the sea-soning of the stock), a few gratings of pepper from your pep-per mill, 2 tablespoons chopped parsley, 2 tablespoons chopped walnuts, and refrigerate it. Keep your eye on it and, as soon as it is quite thick but not really set, fold in 1 cup heavy cream, whipped. Transfer to a moistened mold, continuing to chill. Unmold to serve. This will serve 8 and it's nice enough for another party.

INGREDIENTS: 1½ tablespoons unflavored gelatine; ¾ cup chicken stock; 3 egg yolks; 1½ cups light cream; 2 cups minced ham; salt; pepper; 2 tablespoons chopped parsley; 2 tablespoons chopped walnuts; 1 cup heavy cream.

Getting back to the Tetrazzini, if you have only a bit of this left, and only a little ham, put them together, heat a frying pan very hot, sizzle some butter, add the whole business, and let it fry slowly until the vermicelli is crisp and brown on the bottom. Serve with Peggy's salad, if there's any left. This salad keeps for days, and, if you want to build it up, chop it a bit and stir into it a cucumber, cut fine, and three or four sliced radishes.

There's always the good old ham hash, made by mixing about 2 cups each of chopped ham and chopped freshly boiled potatoes, adding 1 tablespoon parsley, and frying in a buttered hot frying pan with enough milk (1 to 2 cups) to cover both ham and potatoes. You should cook this slowly until the milk is absorbed and the mixture is very hot. At the end, add ½ cup of light cream. Taste; add salt and pepper, if you need it.

Another choice for the ham is ham croquettes. My *Blueberry Hill Cookbook* contains a quite superior recipe for these.

As for the Bing cherries in brandy, heat them and serve them with vanilla ice cream. Or add some raggy freestone peaches and a few whole peeled apricots for a lovely compote.

The meringue cake? Why would you want to do anything with that? You might, if you insist, make a custard at the very end, slice the cake thin, cover it with the custard, and bake it all. But I'd like to take bets you'll never have a chance to do this.

JANUARY

Why Don't You Ask the Boys In, Dear?

HOT TOMATO PUNCH
SMOKED SALMON, PUMPERNICKL, ETC.
SAUERBRATEN
KARTOFFELKLÖSSE
MAMA'S BAVARIAN CABBAGE
RHUBARB JELL
IRISH SODA BREAD WITH DILL
ROQUEFORT ROMAINE
APPLE-NUT THING

 In Vermont, the January days are the good days. Bright and cold and snow on the ground, though sometimes there's a January thaw. We're not deceived by it; "don't mean nahthin'," as our neighbors say, squinting at the sky. Lots of winter left. Bowling is a popular sport, not only in Vermont, but clear across the country—and this is a dinner planned for a cold night after your husband has spent an hour or two bowling with his friends. Or skiing, for that matter. Or sitting before the fire. Your husband's compatriots will approve of you, you can be sure, after an invitation to a meal such as this one. The recipes will feed 8; sufficient for leftovers, too.

HOT TOMATO PUNCH

Heat together 1 quart tomato juice and 1 quart beef broth (canned is all right, but homemade is better). Spike it with 1 teaspoon Worcestershire sauce and 1 tablespoon creamed horseradish. After it has reached a near-to-boiling point, serve in mugs with lemon segments studded with whole cloves.

INGREDIENTS: 1 quart tomato juice; 1 quart beef broth; 1 teaspoon Worcestershire sauce; 1 tablespoon creamed horseradish; 1 lemon; 1 teaspoon whole cloves.

SMOKED SALMON, PUMPERNICKL, ETC.

The "etc." stands for the other things, of course, an understatement. With the hot tomato punch, serve to the eager gentlemen (and arrange it neatly on a heavy white ironstone platter, if you have one) sliced smoked salmon (called "lox" in metropolitan areas). This is very salty and 8 to 10 slices will go a long way. Have it sliced to your order at a delicatessen, if you're near one, or use the smoked salmon now available in supermarkets in little plastic bags. The freshly sliced lox is far superior, being sliced, as you need it, from a large pink fish—but we can't always have everything. Surrounding, or sprinkled on top of the salmon, should be 1 tablespoon finely chopped chives. You can buy these in small pots, sometimes, or, if you're forehanded, you can grow your own in your kitchen window. The more you snip them, the more you will have. Nature's way, you know. Then, of course, you will want thin, thin slices of pumpernickl bread. The thinner, the better, and slice it yourself if you have to. A pepper mill is a necessary accompaniment here.

Along with this, on another plate, set 2 to 3 dozen radish roses (leave the stems on the radishes). To make these, simply cut thin slits down the sides of the radishes, not quite through, and leave them in water for an hour or so in a cold place. They will come out looking something like

roses—well, you'll know they're radishes, but they're pretty.
On the plate with the radishes, have little pats of **sweet
butter** (if this were a ladies' lunch, you'd make pretty butter
forms, but men are of a different mind) and a **salt** shaker.
The idea is for the men to salt the radishes and then spread
them with butter. They are an ideal accompaniment for the
smoked salmon and the hot tomato punch. The men will
want to use the butter to spread thickly on the pumpernickl
before they add the smoked salmon, too. These appetizers
are particularly good with beer, as well.

INGREDIENTS: 8 to 10 thin slices smoked salmon; 1 tablespoon
    finely chopped chives; pumpernickl bread; pepper; 2
    to 3 dozen radishes; ½ pound sweet butter; salt.

SAUERBRATEN

The best part about a sauerbraten, which is a classic German
marinated beef, is the fact that a good part of the preparation takes place days before you actually will be cooking,
and, during the marinating process, your home will be
redolent of the most gorgeous of aromas. By the time you
actually serve the sauerbraten, everyone concerned is so involved that they cannot, almost, wait for the time of the
eating. A good way to approach a dinner.

At least three, preferably five, days before you expect to
serve this, prepare the following marinade: Bring to a boil
and let simmer for 3 minutes **1½ cups red wine vinegar, ¾
cup light sweet red wine, 1 cup water, 12 whole cloves, 2
tablespoons sugar, 15 whole allspice, 10 whole peppercorns,
3 bay leaves, 3 large onions,** cut up any old way, **2 teaspoons
salt, 2 cloves garlic,** peeled and cut in half, **1 teaspoon
mustard seed, 2 or 3 strips lemon peel.** While this is simmering, wipe a **5- to 6-pound top round, rump round, or chuck
roast of beef** with a damp cloth and place it in a deep
crock. The crock should be made of glass or a ceramic sub-
stance, not metal, and ought to be not much larger than the
piece of beef so that the marinade will come up and over

the meat, or nearly. If you happen to be preparing this in hot weather (an unlikely possibility), it should be refrigerated during the marinating process. However, this being January, room temperature (65° to 70°F.) is all right. Let it remain in the marinade, turning it two or three times a day, particularly if the top of the sauerbraten is not completely covered with the marinade, for the already mentioned three to five days.

In the early afternoon of the day you want to serve it, remove the beef from the marinade (strain and save the liquid—you'll need it!), wipe the beef dry, and dredge the meat on all sides with **2 tablespoons flour.** You can do this by sprinkling the flour on it and pressing it in with your hands, by rolling the roast on a board covered with the flour, or by setting the roast in a heavy paper bag with the flour and shaking it. Gently is the word if you choose the last method, or the entire works will break through the bag and land on your kitchen floor.

Heat a heavy kettle, such as a Dutch oven, quite hot, on top of your range. Add **2 tablespoons vegetable shortening,** let it sizzle a little, and then slowly brown the sauerbraten in it on all sides. Very soon the fat in the meat will help to moisten the pan and you won't have a sticking problem. This browning takes a bit of time, but it is well worth it, even if you spend a half hour at it, as it gives you a lovely brown gravy later. After the roast is quite beautifully browned on all sides, drain away whatever excess fat there is in the bottom of the pan. Remove the meat from the heat and add to the kettle, with the meat, **2 small onions,** cut up; **8 large carrots,** peeled and left whole; **1 small white purple-top turnip;** and **1 cup strained marinade.** Cover tightly and roast in a slow oven, no more than 325°F., for 3½ to 4 hours, or until the meat is very tender. Start your testing in 3 hours with a long-tined fork.

If it's more convenient for you, you may cook this on top of your range, as you would a pot roast, covering it tightly and simmering over low heat until tender. This will take from 2½ to 3 hours. If you need more liquid, add some marinade. When you roast this in the oven, the liquid in the pan increases, if anything.

When the meat is tender, remove it to a hot platter and keep it warm while you cook the Kartoffelklösse (potato dumplings) right in the same marinade. (Recipe for these follows immediately after this one.) You should have at least 2 cups of the marinade in the pan when you cook the dumplings; if you haven't, add some from your reserve and simmer it a few minutes before you start with the dumplings.

When the dumplings are done, remove them from the marinade and crumble **6 gingersnaps** into the liquid. In a few minutes of boiling, the gravy will be thickened and mightily improved by the addition. Slice the meat against the grain and arrange on a large platter surrounded by the Kartoffelklösse and plenty of gravy, both on it and in a gravy boat.

INGREDIENTS:

For the marinade: 1½ cups red wine vinegar; ¾ cup light sweet red wine; 1 cup water; 12 whole cloves; 2 tablespoons sugar; 15 whole allspice; 10 whole peppercorns; 3 bay leaves; 3 large onions; 2 teaspoons salt; 2 cloves garlic; 1 teaspoon mustard seed; 2 or 3 strips lemon peel.

For the sauerbraten: 5- to 6-pound top round, rump round, or chuck roast of beef; 2 tablespoons flour; 2 tablespoons vegetable shortening; 2 small onions; 8 large carrots; 1 small white purple-top turnip; 6 gingersnaps.

KARTOFFELKLOSSE

Kartoffelklösse (potato dumplings) are the authentic and proper accompaniment to sauerbraten. These are not awfully light, and you may prefer to use the dumplings I tell you about in the recipe for chicken and dumplings in my *Blueberry Hill Cookbook*. However, for them that likes Kartoffelklösse (among which I am one), this is a fine, fine recipe.

Either the day before or the morning of the same day, boil
6 medium potatoes (not new; old!) in their skins. Cool them,
slip the peels off, and press through a ricer. They must
rest on a clean dish towel to dry out. Toss them around once
in a while over a period of an hour or two, until you can
make out no particularly moist areas. Then set the riced potatoes in a bowl and make a well in the center of them.
Drop into the well 2 large unbeaten eggs; 1½ teaspoons salt;
¾ cup flour; 4 or 5 gratings of black pepper, fresh, of course;
and ½ cup soft bread crumbs. Beat with a fork until fluffy
and manageable, and then, kneading first for a minute or
two with floured hands, roll them into one-inch balls. They
should not feel wet; if they do, add a few more bread
crumbs. If you don't do this, they will break apart when
you cook them later. Let them sit in the refrigerator on a
plate for about an hour after they're rolled into shape.

Bring the marinade (at least 2 cups of it) to a rapid boil
—remember, you've already removed the meat from it—
and, carefully, drop the balls into this, 4 or 5 at a time. You
should really let them slowly roll into the marinade, not
drop with a plop. Let them cook 3 to 5 minutes. Test one
after 3 minutes by removing it with a slotted spoon and
cutting through it with a sharp knife. If the center is cooked
through with no sogginess apparent, it's done. If not, let
it cook another minute or two. Let this be your guide with
your timing. Keep the Kartoffelklösse warm until they're
all cooked. When you're ready to serve them, heat a black
iron frying pan till it's really hot and add 4 tablespoons
(½ stick) butter letting it sizzle lightly and brown a bit.
Then throw in ½ cup soft bread crumbs. They will absorb
the browned butter and crisp up a little. Then quickly heat
the dumplings by rolling them about so the browned crumbs
will adhere to them. Serve with the sauerbraten.

Aren't you proud?

INGREDIENTS: 6 medium-sized old potatoes; 2 large eggs;
    1½ teaspoons salt; ¾ cup flour; pepper; 1 cup soft bread
    crumbs; 4 tablespoons butter.

MAMA'S BAVARIAN CABBAGE

The perfect, the correct, companion to sauerbraten. My mother's recipe.

Fry 1 **medium onion**, chopped small, in 1 **tablespoon butter** or **chicken fat**. Mama preferred the chicken fat. Look in the index for directions as to how to achieve proper chicken fat for cooking purposes. Wash a **medium-sized head of red cabbage** and shred it finely. Place it in a heavy saucepan with 1 **tart red apple**, unpeeled and cut into small pieces; ⅛ **teaspoon ground allspice**; and ½ **cup water**. Simmer over very low heat for 1 hour, stirring occasionally. When very little juice is left, add a **small piece of citric acid**, about the size of a diamond you'd be proud of (citric acid can be purchased in drugstores and in some supermarkets; it is used in many recipes instead of lemon or vinegar); ½ **cup sugar**; and **salt** to taste. If there is still a good bit of liquid in the pan, thicken it by stirring in ½ **teaspoon arrowroot** (which is also available at drugstores and is far superior to cornstarch or flour for thickening purposes) stirred into ½ **cup cold water**. In the absence of arrowroot, remove ½ cup of the juice, stir into it 1 **teaspoon flour**, making a paste. Be sure it's smooth, which it will be if you add the liquid to the flour a little at a time. Thin the paste down to the consistency of the liquid in the pan, adding liquid a little at a time, stirring as you go; then add the whole business to the cabbage, bring to a boil, and let it boil long enough to thicken. A few minutes at most. Serve it.

INGREDIENTS: 1 medium onion; 1 tablespoon butter or chicken fat; 1 medium-sized head of red cabbage; 1 tart red apple; ⅛ teaspoon ground allspice; ½ cup water; small piece citric acid; ½ cup sugar; salt; ½ teaspoon arrowroot with ½ cup cold water, or 1 teaspoon flour.

RHUBARB JELL

Rhubarb is generally available these days in the freezer sections of supermarkets, should you not have any frozen in your own freezer. This is a most unusual little fillip to any meal. Whenever I serve it at Blueberry Hill, it's a wow, both with men and women. As for my children, they whoop with joy at the news it's on the menu.

Place **5 cups cut-up frozen rhubarb** (uncooked and without sugar) in a very heavy pot with a lid. Add to it **3 cups granulated sugar.** Cook, covered, over low heat—it won't burn if you don't lose your head and turn the heat too high—until the sugar is liquefied and the rhubarb is tender throughout. A safer way, but much slower, is to do this in the top of a double boiler over rapidly boiling water. The first way takes about 5 minutes; the second, 15 to 30 minutes. Be careful, in either case, not to overcook it, as it will lose its rosy glow.

While the rhubarb is stewing, soak **2 tablespoons unflavored gelatine** (same as 2 envelopes) in **½ cup cold water** for 5 minutes. Then set the cup in a small pan of boiling water. The gelatine will dissolve and there will be no granular specks visible. Pour it into a bowl.

When the rhubarb is cooked, press it through a Foley food mill, if you have one (and you should have one—these little strainers press all the juice and pulp out of any sort of fruit, leaving only the dry skins that you don't want anyway), letting the rhubarb land right on top of the gelatine. As soon as it's all through the mill, combine it with the softened gelatine with a spoon. If you don't have a food mill, you can use a strainer, pressing the pulp through with the back of a large spoon. If the rhubarb has lost its color (sometimes it never had any, that's a possibility), add a few drops of **red food coloring.**

Grease sparingly a 1-quart mold with peanut oil or vegetable oil—not olive oil—using a pastry brush. Pour the rhubarb jell into the mold and chill 4 or 5 hours or until it's set. Unmold, when you need it, on a glass platter. All you'll need to do to accomplish this is to dip it quickly into hot water and, holding your platter tightly against the jell, watch it slide out. Serve with the sauerbraten. This is also an excellent accompaniment for any other meat or poultry or fish you can think of. Just tart enough. You may want to double the recipe to make a 2-quart mold—just in case. That's up to you. In summer, use fresh rhubarb.

INGREDIENTS: 5 cups cut-up uncooked rhubarb; 3 cups granulated sugar; 2 tablespoons (envelopes) unflavored gelatine; ½ cup cold water; red food coloring, if needed.

IRISH SODA BREAD WITH DILL

A superb, quickly produced bread. This recipe will make 2 loaves. Sift together **4 cups sifted all-purpose flour, 1 tablespoon baking powder, ½ tablespoon salt, 1 tablespoon sugar, and 1 teaspoon soda.** Mix in with a fork **1 cup seedless raisins or currants** (or 1 cup of raisins and currants mixed) and **1 tablespoon dill seeds.** Add **2 cups buttermilk** and blend with a fork until well mixed. Then flour your hands and, removing dough to a floured board, knead until smooth. Keep enough flour on your hands to prevent the dough from sticking. It won't take more than 2 minutes of kneading. Shape into 2 rounds and place in 2 greased heavy black iron frying pans, about 6 or 7 inches in size. Let rise in a warm spot for about 10 minutes. Then slash the top with a knife, shaping a cross, and bake in a preheated 350°F. oven for 45 minutes or until lightly browned and dry within, when tested with a sharp-bladed knife. The knife should be as dry and shiny when it comes out as it was when it was thrust into the breads. This bread should be baked at the very last minute, if possible. It's simply great when it is served immediately in thick slices dripping with butter. It will, however, reheat to its former state of glory if you simply can't manage to bake it at the last moment. In this case, place it in a heavy, slightly moistened paper bag and heat slowly for 10 minutes.

INGREDIENTS: 4 cups sifted all-purpose flour; 1 tablespoon
  baking powder; ½ tablespoon salt; 1 tablespoon sugar;
  1 teaspoon soda; 1 cup seedless raisins or currants (or 1
  cup of both, mixed); 1 tablespoon dill seeds; 2 cups
  buttermilk.

ROQUEFORT ROMAINE

A salad made to order for men. Wash **2 heads of crisp romaine** and separate the leaves. Dry them and keep them
cold and crisp in a linen towel, dampened, until you want
them. Serve them from a wooden platter, on one end of
which you have set a large wedge of **Roquefort cheese** (or
bleu, if you prefer), about ¾ pound, and a few butter
spreaders. Let the boys cut off a chunk of cheese, lay it on
a romaine leaf, roll it up, and eat it.

INGREDIENTS: 2 heads romaine; ¾ pound Roquefort or bleu
  cheese.

APPLE-NUT THING

This dessert is neither pie, cake, nor pudding. As my children
say, it's a *thing*. It's a delicious thing, however.

Sift together **1 cup sifted cake flour, 4 teaspoons baking
powder,** and **1 teaspoon salt.** Cream (which, of course, you
know means to combine—usually with an electric mixer—
until ungranular and creamy) **4 eggs** and **2 cups light brown
sugar.** Add the flour mixture to the creamed mixture and add
2 teaspoons vanilla, 2 cups chopped pecans or **walnuts, 2
cups tart apple cubes,** peeled. Mix it all up and bake it in
two greased 10-inch pie plates at 350°F. for 30 minutes. Use
butter for the lubrication here. Cool in the plates. When
cool, cut as you would a pie and serve with **1 cup heavy
cream,** whipped with **2 teaspoons sugar** added at the last
of the whipping, and **1 teaspoon sherry** or **Marsala wine.**

INGREDIENTS: 1 cup sifted cake flour; 4 teaspoons baking
  powder; 1 teaspoon salt; 4 eggs; 2 cups light brown

sugar; 2 teaspoons vanilla; 2 cups chopped pecans or walnuts; 2 cups tart apple cubes; 1 cup heavy cream; 2 teaspoons sugar, 1 teaspoon sherry or Marsala wine.

TIMETABLE: One hardly needs a timetable for this dinner. The sauerbraten rests, albeit fitfully, in its marinade for days ahead of time. The actual cooking of it can either be done the afternoon of the day you choose to serve it— starting it around 1:00 o'clock if in the oven or 2:00 o'clock if on top of the range—or you might cook the whole thing the day before, leaving only the reheating and the Kartoffelklösse to the last. The red cabbage can be cooked in the morning, too, or even the day before, reheating it just at the time of serving. The rhubarb jell should, by all means, be prepared in the morning or the day before. The romaine, also, should be washed and set in the refrigerator in its damp towel to crisp and chill in the morning. The boiling of the potatoes, too, is a morning job, as well as the ricing. Set them drying on their towel. Measure the ingredients for the hot tomato punch. Leave on range.

Since this is predominantly a dinner for your husband and *his* friends, there are few of the usual problems of finding time for preparation, inasmuch as it's fine for you to stay in the kitchen all the time. They'll have a better time without you, anyway. This is a boon.

Assuming service is to be about 6:00, start at 4:00 fixing radishes, chopping chives, and arranging the smoked salmon. Slice the pumpernickl and cut the butter into pats. Cover the platters involved with saran—the bread won't dry out under this. Refrigerate them. They're ready when you are.

This will have taken no more than 15 minutes. Now prepare the Kartoffelklösse, a 10-minute job at most, since the potatoes were ready and waiting. Set the dumplings in the refrigerator on their plate. Time to start the Irish soda bread. This, as I said before, is perfect if baked close to the time of eating, so I suggest that at this time you get all the dry ingredients together, measure out the buttermilk, and, it now being close to 5:00, put the breads together. If you're ahead of this schedule, leave the wet ingredients and the dry ingredients ready but not mixed until you think you ought to get at them.

While the bread is rising for the 10 minutes indicated in the recipe, prepare the apple-nut thing. Go ahead and bake it, setting your timer for 30 minutes. Go get your Irish soda bread and add it to the apple-nut thing in the oven. Remember when the apple-nut thing comes out of the oven in 30 minutes to reset the timer for the soda bread for another 15 minutes.

The meat should be tender now, so remove it from the marinade of which you make sure you have at least 2 cups in the pan. Cook the Kartoffelklösse as directed. Don't leave them for other matters; they need testing and should be removed as they are done. When all the dumplings are done, add the gingersnaps as directed to thicken the gravy.

Yipes, the men are here! Whisk out the platters of smoked salmon and radishes, meanwhile bringing the hot punch to a boil. Present the gentlemen with a mug of the spicy drink and let them get at the business at hand. Don't give them another thought. They'll be fine.

This, of course, is to be served as a buffet. Set on the table the rhubarb jell, unmolded. Now heat the Kartoffelklösse in the bread crumbs, slice the sauerbraten on a hot platter, surround it with the dumplings, slather it with gravy (having a side bowl of whatever gravy is available thereafter), and set this on the table. Pile the hot Bavarian cabbage in a bowl; set that on the table. The romaine next—no trick to this. Just arrange it with the cheese and the spreaders. Gather the men around the table and then go back to the kitchen and remove the first of the two breads from the oven. Slide it onto a bread board with a large pancake turner or one of those flat shovels you always see in mail-order catalogues, and just leave it on the table with a big bread knife. The first slice, cut by the first man to reach it, will be steaming and fragrant with dill and kitchens and *home!* Take the other bread out of the oven and just leave it around, casual like. When they've had what they will of the sauerbraten, the Kartoffelklösse, the bread, direct them to the apple-nut thing. You'll have had plenty of time to prepare the whipped cream with the sugar and the sherry.

That's it. I just won't talk about what this will mean to your husband. Husbands yearn for this sort of treatment from wives, and lots of them don't get it. Of course lots of them don't deserve it, either—but think about it a little.

LEFTOVERS

Sauerbraten, the second day, is better, if that's possible, than the first. The gravy might seem too thick, the meat might appear, as it comes from the refrigerator, rather dry. However, set the meat in a colander over hot water (or in a steamer, for that matter) and reheat it via the steam method. Then slice it thin, this time. Meanwhile thin the gravy with a bit of boiling water and bring it back to a boil, making sure that the resulting gravy is no thicker than heavy cream. Taste; correct seasoning if necessary. A little curry might go well at this time. Serve with chutney if you decide on this ploy.

The Kartoffelklösse that are left can be sliced and fried in a bit of butter, and, even when there isn't any more sauerbraten, the dumplings with some of the gravy are a fine idea for lunch.

Whatever sauerbraten you have around, later, cold, can be used to very good purpose in a sandwich on your leftover pumpernickl bread with leftover radishes and lots of butter.

Another good thing to do with it is to chop the meat rather coarsely, boil some fresh potatoes, sauté a few onions and a few slices of green pepper in butter or margarine in a black iron frying pan (get the pan hot before you do anything!), and then fry everything together just until the meat starts to get a little crusty and the potatoes are slightly brown. You'll have to add butter or margarine probably, to keep it from burning. As soon as it's all hot, add enough of the gravy to bind it together; say ½ cup of the gravy to 4 or 5 cups of the other things. Turn down the heat under the pan and let it cook slowly for about 5 minutes until you have a good brown crust on the bottom. Turn it once with a pancake turner, make a few holes in strategic places, exposing the bottom of the pan, and drop an egg in each hole. Sprinkle salt and freshly ground pepper on the egg. Cover the pan with a lid and continue to heat just until the egg is set. Takes about 10 minutes, usually, but keep your eye on it. This is called sauerbraten hash, I guess.

If you have just a half cupful of sauerbraten in the refrigerator, stir it into a small amount of onion soup. You'll like it.

The rhubarb jell will keep until it's "et," as they say in Vermont. However, it will not suffer from the addition of a few stewed apricots and a topping of whipped cream—making of itself a dessert. It can also become a salad all by itself, with some watercress and a dressing of sour cream thinned down with apricot juice.

The apple-nut thing, too, improves with age. Heat it, if you'd like, and cover it with fluffy hard sauce, instead of whipped cream. You make this by creaming ½ cup butter or margarine with 1 cup confectioners' sugar. When it's thoroughly combined and very creamy, fold in ½ cup heavy cream, whipped, with 1 teaspoon vanilla. This hard sauce won't keep the way real hard sauce will, but it's a nice variation.

As for the soda bread, this freezes perfectly. Slice it and butter it, in any case, and toast it for a divine afternoon tea bread. This has become one of our most favorite breads at Blueberry Hill. You'll see why when you bake it.

FEBRUARY

PARTY MENU
For the Ladies

CLEAR MUSHROOM BROTH WITH AVOCADO SLICES
GRILLED BREAD
RISOTTO WITH SHRIMP
BAKED PEAS
TOMATOES BROILED WITH DILL
SPICED PRUNES WITH CRANBERRY RELISH
CREAM CHEESE BISCUITS
GREEN BEAN SALAD
SWISS CHOCOLATE BRICK

 Sometimes it's nice just to have the ladies in. If you're a bridge player, this perhaps happens often—lunch and a few rubbers of bridge. Well, the menu above is fine for this purpose, or for a shower for one of the gals, or for a going-away party for one.

There is no honest reason for restricting it to women, however. This is not in any sense a tearoom-type meal, and, if you have anything around after the ladies have departed, just watch your husband devour it.

The recipes are for 8, the largest number of ladies, I think, anyone should cope with at one time.

41

CLEAR MUSHROOM BROTH
WITH AVOCADO SLICES

As in so many recipes in this book, this broth calls for a fine, robust chicken soup. Make it yourself as I've told you to do on page 13; you should have quarts of this in your freezer, if you have a freezer. In the event you are not situated comfortably for the making of things like chicken broth, you may use canned, but, even then, shop around for the best tasting variety of *this*. Some canned chicken broths are watery concoctions; one wonders how long, if at all, the chicken has spent in them.

Trim a thin slice off the bottoms of the **stems of 1 pound firm white fresh mushrooms;** then chop the mushrooms and stems fine. The best way to do this is in an old-fashioned wooden chopping bowl (a hardwood salad bowl kept for this and other chopping purposes would do), with an old-fashioned one-handed chopper. Taste **3 quarts rich chicken broth.** Make sure it is well flavored, properly salted and peppered. If it isn't, add a few chicken bouillon cubes, but I don't really recommend this. If you have a good broth, you won't need the bouillon. Simmer the chopped mushrooms in the broth for ½ hour. Cool, strain, and add **1 tablespoon fresh lemon juice, ½ teaspoon dried dill weed** (Spice Island, for one, puts this up), **½ teaspoon sugar,** and taste again for seasoning. Add **salt** and **pepper,** if you need it.

This soup can be served hot or cold. I suggest it be served hot, since it's February, but keep it in mind for summer.

If your frugal soul rebels at throwing away the mushrooms, don't strain the broth. You might consider mixing them into the green bean salad later, as a matter of fact.

Serve broth with thin slices of freshly cut ripe **avocado** floating about here and there.

INGREDIENTS: 1 pound firm white fresh mushrooms; 3 quarts rich chicken broth (homemade or canned); 1 tablespoon fresh lemon juice; ½ teaspoon dried dill weed; ½ teaspoon sugar; salt; pepper; 1 ripe avocado.

GRILLED BREAD

Trim thin-sliced firm **white bread,** cutting away the crusts.
Cut the slices into triangular halves. Heat a large iron or
electric skillet or grill, then sizzle in it a large lump, perhaps
2 tablespoons, of **butter.** When the butter is sputtering and
lightly brown, add as much of the bread as will fit in the
pan. Fry it to light brown, turn it, and fry the other side,
being sure not to let the butter burn. This can easily happen,
if you're not alert. You'll have to add lots of butter, as you
go—grilling bread uses enormous quantities—and, if you
worry about this from the point of view of cholesterol, just
use half butter, half margarine. Don't eliminate the butter
entirely, however; the flavor is important here. You will
probably need ½ **pound of butter** before you have done
enough to provide 4 to 6 triangles for each person—and
you may be sure this much will be eaten. Keep the already
grilled bread warm while you finish the others.

INGREDIENTS: 1 loaf thin-sliced firm white bread; ½ pound
   butter (or half butter, half margarine).

RISOTTO WITH SHRIMP

Divine is the word. In a heavy saucepan with a cover bring
to a boil **2 cups water, 4 or 5 peppercorns, a few celery
tops, 2 teaspoons salt.** Reduce heat and let stock simmer,
covered, for 5 minutes. Then add **2 pounds fresh shrimp,**
still in their shells. A good-sized shrimp is called 20–24,
which means that many shrimp to a pound; shrimp larger
than this are sometimes less flavorful, and always less manageable in this sort of dish; shrimp smaller than this take
too long to peel. Cover tightly. Allow the shrimp to boil
lightly from 3 to 5 minutes, or until all have turned pink.
Lift the lid and look, that's how you'll know. If you let
them boil past this point, they will toughen and shrink.
Get them off the range as soon as they are pink, not ten
minutes later.

In this case, you will want the shrimp to be peeled, so allow them to cool in their own broth, then peel them, one out of the broth at a time, using a shrimp cleaner. You'll find a description of these on page 7. As each shrimp is cleaned, return it to the broth which you should strain first. Keep the shrimp, in the broth, in the refrigerator, until you want to use them. The business of boiling and cleaning your shrimp can take place at any convenient time before your party. Just keep the shrimp in the broth and they will retain their tender succulence. If, for some other recipe, you just want boiled shrimp, you may boil them this way and keep them, *un*peeled, in the broth in the refrigerator for as much as three days without problems. Then peel them at the proper moment.

The aforesaid directions are the proper ones for boiling shrimp for any purpose. I'll refer to this recipe whenever boiled shrimp are needed. If you will always do your shrimp this way, you'll always have the sweetest, nicest shrimp you could ask for.

Early in the morning of your luncheon, heat a large, 11- or 12-inch black iron frying pan with a cover (or a Dutch oven) and, when a drop of water will sizzle on it, add ½ cup (1 stick) **butter** or **margarine** and **6 tablespoons olive oil.** Let the shortening sizzle a little and then add **2 cloves of garlic,** minced very fine, along with **3 cups uncooked long-grain white rice.** I prefer Uncle Ben's, but you do as you're a mind to. Now watch carefully! Sauté the rice and garlic over low heat until the rice turns golden yellow. It does this in a split second when it's ready to do it at all, and, if you're not right there to remove the rice from the heat, it will burn. If this happens to you (ah, woe!), don't try to salvage the rice. Throw it out and start over.

When the rice is golden, add **1½ cups dry white wine** of the sauterne type and simmer over moderate heat until the wine has been completely absorbed, about 10 minutes. Add **1 quart rich chicken broth** (page 13). Here it is again, that chicken broth. I hope you have some of your own ready in the freezer for just such recipes as this. If you haven't, use canned, the best you can find.

Cover the frying pan or Dutch oven tightly, turn the heat down and cook very, very slowly, for about 25 minutes. The broth should be absorbed and the rice nearly tender. Now drain the cleaned shrimp (don't discard the stock) and add them whole or, if they are unusually large, cut them in halves. Also add 1 tablespoon salt, ½ teaspoon freshly ground black pepper, ½ teaspoon marjoram, and 2 cups strained shrimp stock. Stir lightly with a fork, cover, and cook another 10 minutes over low heat, or until the rice is tender and dry. Stir in, at the last, ¼ cup (½ stick) butter, sprinkle with ½ cup chopped parsley, and serve with a bowl of grated Parmesan cheese.

If you want to have this all prepared ahead of time, do everything up to the addition of the butter and parsley, refrigerate, and reheat with these last two ingredients in the last ten minutes.

INGREDIENTS:

To prepare shrimp: 2 cups water; 4 or 5 peppercorns; a few celery tops; 2 teaspoons salt; 2 pounds fresh shrimp in shells.

For the risotto: ½ cup butter or margarine; 6 tablespoons olive oil; 2 cloves garlic; 3 cups long-grain white rice (Uncle Ben's); 1½ cups dry white wine; 1 quart chicken broth; 1 tablespoon salt; ½ teaspoon pepper; ½ teaspoon marjoram; 2 cups strained shrimp stock; ¼ cup butter; ½ cup chopped parsley; grated Parmesan cheese.

BAKED PEAS

Have you ever, I wonder, baked a pea? I did, one Sunday, and this is the way I shall care for frozen peas forevermore. Place 2 boxes (10 ounces each) frozen peas, chunk of ice that they be, into a casserole with a cover. Add 1 teaspoon salt, 2 teaspoons sugar, 2 grinds of fresh black pepper, and a large lump of butter (about 3 tablespoons). Cover this tightly. Set the oven at 350°F. Forget it for an hour. You'll be famous for these.

INGREDIENTS: 2 boxes frozen peas; 1 teaspoon salt; 2 teaspoons sugar; pepper; 3 tablespoons butter.

TOMATOES BROILED WITH DILL

Slice **4 large red tomatoes** crosswise in halves. Set them, 8 halves in all, in a greased Pyrex pie plate or cake pan. Try to select a dish that will hold them, just, so that they can bolster each other up. Sprinkle each half with ½ **teaspoon sugar,** a little **salt,** 2 or 3 grinds of **pepper** from a mill, ¼ **teaspoon minced onion** or **chives,** ¼ **teaspoon dried dill weed** (unless you have some chopped fresh dill in your freezer in a little package). Dribble over the top of each, carefully, **1 teaspoon heavy cream,** the heavier the better. At the last of your preparations, set these under the broiler and allow them to broil slowly at about 400°F. or moderate heat, for about 10 minutes or until the tomatoes are rather soft and the tops are light brown. A safer way is to set them in a slow oven (350°F.) for half an hour, then pop them under the broiler for the last minute for browning. Safer but slower. Suit yourself here.

INGREDIENTS: 4 large red tomatoes; 4 teaspoons sugar; salt; pepper; 2 teaspoons minced onions or chives; 2 teaspoons dried dill weed; 8 teaspoons heavy cream.

SPICED PRUNES
WITH CRANBERRY RELISH

A fussy matter, which fortunately may be prepared well ahead of time. Ladies love them. The prunes are fine without the cranberry, if you want to eliminate some of the bother; better with, however. These are good as accompaniments to a roast of any sort, pork particularly, and go quite naturally with duck, tame or wild. Remember them at such times.

The day before your party, simmer **1 pound dried prunes** very, very slowly in **1½ cups light sweet red wine** with **¼ teaspoon allspice**, **¼ teaspoon nutmeg**, **1 stick cinnamon**, and **4 whole cloves**. The prunes will cook tender in less than an hour, particularly if they are what is known as tenderized. If the wine boils down too much before the prunes are done, add a little more. While they're cooking, put through your food chopper **1 whole orange** and **2 cups fresh cranberries** (which can come out of your freezer, just as well as fresh). Stir in **½ cup sugar** and let it stand. When the prunes are tender, drain them (save the juice for a sauce on ice cream or custard), remove the pits and stuff the prunes with the cranberry-orange mix. Refrigerate, but take them out at least an hour before serving; they taste better at room temperature than ice cold.

INGREDIENTS: 1 pound dried prunes; 1½ cups light sweet red wine; ¼ teaspoon allspice; ¼ teaspoon nutmeg; 1 stick cinnamon; 4 whole cloves; 1 orange; 2 cups fresh or frozen cranberries; ½ cup sugar.

CREAM CHEESE BISCUITS

These are very rich, flaky biscuits, resembling, in a way, patty shells. They complement the shrimp dish as they should, and I can imagine them used as a base for a Newburg. For a tea party, make a dent in each biscuit, and drop into it a small bit of stiff **tart currant-type jelly.** Bake them as directed here.

Soften first, then mix well in your electric beater at high speed, **2 packages cream cheese** (the 3-ounce size) and **¼ pound** (1 stick) **butter or margarine.** I can't make out too much difference here, so choose your shortening. With the cheese and the shortening, mix in **⅛ teaspoon salt** and **1 cup all-purpose flour.** As soon as the beater blades rebel, remove the batter from them—you might have to scrape the blades as it's quite a stiff dough—and work it with floured hands for a few minutes. You'll find this a satisfactory dough to handle, practically right away. Refrigerate it, wrapped in saran, for at least one hour, or set it in the freezer for ten minutes. Chill it, is what I'm getting at. Then roll it on a floured board one-quarter inch thick. Yes, that is very thin, isn't it, for biscuits, but they will puff up. Cut them out with small biscuit cutters and lay them on a slightly greased cookie sheet. Use a vegetable shortening, always, for greasing tins. Bake at 400°F. for 15 minutes, or until light brown. You will have 2 dozen small or 4 dozen tiny biscuits.

INGREDIENTS: Tart jelly (optional); 2 packages (3-ounce size) cream cheese; ¼ pound butter or margarine; ⅛ teaspoon salt; 1 cup all-purpose flour.

GREEN BEAN SALAD

One of the large processors of frozen foods has been putting out whole green beans, very deluxe, in a gold wrapper. These are marvelously like the little whole green beans one can pick in one's own garden in the early, hot days of summer. Steam, in your Bungalow Cooker or in a colander over hot water, 2 boxes frozen whole small green beans until they are just done, not one moment longer. Marinate in Italian dressing for at least 2 hours. You can buy quite satisfactory Italian dressings these days but, if you're like me, you will prefer to have some of your own making.

To prepare your own Italian dressing, combine, in a screw-top jar, ¾ cup pure olive oil; ¼ cup wine vinegar; 2 cloves garlic, peeled and halved; ½ teaspoon oregano; ½ teaspoon dried sweet basil; ½ teaspoon salt; 4 or 5 grindings of fresh black pepper. Shake well and keep in a cool place. Shake when needed. This makes 1 cup of dressing.

Don't use too much of this in marinating the green beans; just add it, a teaspoon at a time, turning the beans carefully until all the beans are gleaming. Add no more dressing;

turn the beans four or five times during the marinating process.

An hour before serving, arrange the beans in neat bundles of 6 or 8 beans each. They can be left, covered with saran, on a platter in the refrigerator until just before serving time. Turn them once more to moisten and set them, each bundle on a leaf of fresh Boston lettuce and arrange across each bundle of beans a thin strip of **pimiento**. Pour the Italian dressing left on the platter over the beans and the lettuce. Serve.

INGREDIENTS: 2 boxes frozen whole green beans; Italian dressing (¾ cup pure olive oil, ¼ cup wine vinegar, 2 cloves garlic, ½ teaspoon oregano, ½ teaspoon sweet basil, ½ teaspoon salt, pepper); 1 head Boston lettuce; pimiento strips.

SWISS CHOCOLATE BRICK

The ladies won't be able to resist this. Melt **3 squares unsweetened chocolate** in **6 tablespoons black coffee** in the top of a double boiler over boiling water. You can do this in a heavy saucepan directly over the heat if you'll not take your eyes off it. As soon as the chocolate is melted in the coffee, stir it smooth, remove it from the heat and allow it to cool while you beat together (*cream* is another term for this process) **1 cup** (2 sticks) **margarine** or **butter** and **6 tablespoons superfine sugar**. In this case, margarine is fine unless you're a purist on the matter of butter. Add **2 egg yolks** when the creamed mixture is smooth and ungranular and beat them in. Use your electric beater at a moderate rate and continue beating until it's very smooth, and then gradually add the now-cooled chocolate. Beat just until the chocolate is blended.

The result will be a bitter chocolate flavor, which I prefer. However, if you would rather have it sweet, substitute **3 ounces Baker's German's sweet chocolate** and add **2 more tablespoons sugar**.

Cover the bottom of a regular bread pan (Pyrex, if you'd like) with **2 dozen ladyfingers,** split. If you happen to have some leftover sponge cake like my mama's sponge cake (see my *Blueberry Hill Cookbook*) this is perfect. Slice it thin and line the pan with fingers of cake instead of ladyfingers.

Spread one-third of the chocolate mixture thinly over the cake.

Whip **1 cup heavy cream** until very stiff, short of the butter stage. Blend into the cream **1 teaspoon granulated sugar,** ½ **teaspoon vanilla** and spread one-third of it over the chocolate.

Arrange another layer of the cake, this time crosswise. Spread with the chocolate, then the whipped cream. Repeat a third time, ending with the whipped cream.

This must chill in the refrigerator three or four hours. If you're in a hurry, you may set it in the freezer for 15 or 20 minutes. Slice and serve.

This dessert can be frozen very satisfactorily and, should you have any left, I suggest that you do freeze it. Whipped cream desserts don't survive very long in the refrigerator. You're lucky if you get 24 hours out of a whipped cream dessert before it starts changing. However, if you wish to omit the top layer of whipped cream, you can prepare this the day before, leave it in the refrigerator, and finish it off at the time of serving.

INGREDIENTS: 3 squares unsweetened chocolate; 6 tablespoons black coffee; 1 cup margarine or butter; 2 egg yolks; 6 tablespoons superfine sugar (for sweeter brick, use 3 ounces Baker's German's sweet chocolate and add 2 tablespoons sugar); 2 dozen ladyfingers; 1 cup heavy cream; 1 teaspoon sugar; ½ teaspoon vanilla.

TIMETABLE: Since this is a luncheon, with not so much time for same day preparations, you'll be glad to know that a good part of this meal can be done well ahead of time.

The mushroom broth can be made the day before, or the week before, or the month before. Freeze it; when you're ready to serve it, reheat it. While you're at the preparation of the chicken broth, by the way, set aside an extra quart for use in the risotto with shrimp.

Also the day before, prepare the prunes and their filling; don't put them together until the morning of your luncheon. They may be kept, refrigerated, until an hour before you need them; then let them come to room temperature. Uncover when ready to set them on the table.

The shrimp, too, may be cooked, cleaned, the stock strained, and the shrimp kept in the stock in the refrigerator a day, even two days, before the party. If two days before, don't peel them until the morning of the party.

The morning of the party prepare, first thing, the chocolate brick. It'll take about half an hour. Wash the lettuce for the salad, chill it, cook the beans and set them to marinating. Slice the pimientos; prepare the biscuit dough and refrigerate it.

Around 11:00 o'clock, prepare the risotto. If you have to clean the shrimp, you'll need to allow another 15 minutes for that job. The risotto should be ready by 12:00 at the latest. Leave it on your range, ready to be reheated at the last minute.

An hour before lunch, which I am assuming will be at 1:00, put together the casserole of peas and set it in the oven. Now roll and cut out the biscuits; leave them on their tray. Slice the tomatoes, season them, and set them in the oven half an hour before lunch.

At ten or fifteen minutes before 1:00, arrange the salads and set them on the tables. Grill the bread, which you should have all cut, and heat the soup. Shortly after your guests have arrived, serve the soup and the grilled bread in the living room, the soup in cups.

At the moment of ladling out the soup, pop the biscuits in the oven; they'll come out just about the right time. Also, start the risotto heating, stirring it lightly with a fork. Set the tomatoes under the broiler for a moment just before serving them.

Your ladies may be seated now. Their salads are waiting; the biscuits, flaky and delicious, are being passed. The prunes are on a pale green cut-glass plate.

Arrange, on a rolling table if you have one, the risotto, the casserole of perfect peas, and the tomatoes, which have emerged from the broiler a bubbling light brown. Let the ladies help themselves from the cart or you may help them and ask one of them to pass the plates for you. That's all there is to that.

Time for dessert. While coffee is being passed, slip into the kitchen, take the Swiss chocolate brick from the refrigerator, slice it, and set the slices on dessert plates.

LEFTOVERS

The mushroom broth should be frozen, if any is left, and used next summer. It's so good, cold, with chopped chives. If you're too impatient for that, sauté a cup of fresh mushrooms in butter, sprinkle them with a little flour and gradually add some of the broth—enough to make a rather thin gravy. Season with salt, pepper, and a bit of soy sauce and serve over a small steak or a cubed steak or any sort of leftover, heated meat. A very acceptable sauce.

The broth itself can be combined with any number of canned soups. It's particularly good with black bean soup. Serve this with chopped hard-cooked eggs and chives. Try the mushroom broth to thin down canned cream of mushroom or cream of chicken or cream of celery soup, using the resultant sauce as the cohesive agent of baked macaroni or lima beans.

The grilled bread revives in the oven. Revive it. There will be less than a perceptible change. Or freeze it and re-heat it when it seems appropriate.

The risotto? This tastes even better the second day. If you wish to doll it up, add whatever peas are left and enough sauterne (or whatever wine you used in the first place) to moisten, top with whatever broiled tomatoes there are about, sprinkle with Parmesan cheese, bake in the oven until bubbly. Might as well invite the neighbors in, don't you think?

The prunes and cranberry relish are fine, as is. They can, however, be chopped and stirred into a fine quality creamed cottage cheese (large curd is more flavorful than small curd, if you can get it), a bit of commercial sour cream added, and there you have a beautiful centerpiece for a fresh fruit salad. Serve with a dressing made by adding 1 6-ounce can frozen lemonade concentrate to 1 pint commercial sour cream. A bit of sugar, if you think so.

As for the cream cheese biscuits, as I hinted earlier, these are the equivalent of the flakiest of patty shells. Use them as a base for a lobster or crab Newburg, or for chicken à la king (which I despise but mention in deference to those who do not).

If you have any green beans left, all marinated, try heating them for your next evening's meal. Turn them again and again in a heated frying pan with a bit of olive oil, and the moment they are thoroughly warm, serve them. Sprinkle a few pignolia nuts on top.

The Swiss chocolate brick, if not eaten within 24 hours, should be frozen. I can't believe this will be so, however. If there is just a bit, too little to do much with, slice it paper thin and top with vanilla ice cream.

FEBRUARY

FAMILY MENU

Your Family Deserves the Best!

CLAMS AND OYSTERS, HALF SHELL
POPOVERED CHICKEN
CHOPPED KALE WITH BACON
BUTTERED HULLED CORN
BAKED BEETS
HEARTS OF LETTUCE WITH CAPER DRESSING
OLD-FASHIONED APPLE PIE WITH CHEESE CRUST

 This is one of my most favorite dinners. Each part of it is beloved in our family, and, when company does drop in, we're proud to serve it to them. There is no bread provided in this menu, as the popovered chicken supplies ample starch. If your husband is one who insists on bread with each meal, a plain French or Italian bread will do nicely. For 8.

CLAMS AND OYSTERS, HALF SHELL

This is an R month. Some of us like clams; some like oysters. I say, have some of each. There's really nothing to this recipe except the method of opening the stubborn beasts. Here's how to do it without anguish.

54

Place 1 **dozen clams** and 1 **dozen oysters** in a shallow pan (or two pans) in a 400°F. oven for 6 or 7 minutes. As soon as you see the shells start to open, remove them, one at a time, and plunge each mollusk into a bowl of ice water. Insert a knife (not sharp!) at the rounded edge. It will respond. That's all. Continue, setting each clam or oyster on a bed of shaved ice.

Serve with **lemon juice** or, if you must, 1 **cup chili sauce** with 2 **teaspoons horseradish.** A delicious accompaniment, fine enough for the most posh dinner party, would be a dab of **commercial sour cream** topped with ½ **teaspoon black** or **red caviar** for each oyster or clam.

INGREDIENTS: 1 dozen clams; 1 dozen oysters on half shell; lemon juice, or 1 cup chili sauce with 2 teaspoons horseradish, or 1 cup commercial sour cream; 4 teaspoons black or red caviar.

POPOVERED CHICKEN

As you perhaps know, there is no recipe in this book that I do not recommend; in fact, vouch for heartily. It wouldn't be here if I didn't think it deserved to be. There are, nonetheless, several recipes that I not only set forth for you to try, but *urge* you to try. This popovered chicken recipe is one of them. It is a dramatic-looking casserole of unsurpassed flavor and texture. Try it, not only for your family but for your most honored guests.

Have 2 **3-pound chickens,** broiler or fryer type, cut into ten pieces each. The breast should be cut in fourths; there should be two second joints; two legs; two wings. Have the backbone cut out right down the line. Simmer the wings, the backbone (which has the neck connected to it) and the giblets in 4 **cups water** with 1 **small onion,** 2 **teaspoons salt,** and 6 **to 8 peppercorns.** After an hour of slow simmering, strain and reserve the broth. Of course, if you have some good, strong chicken broth in your freezer, you may eliminate the preparation of this broth and simply set out 2 cups from your cache.

Sprinkle the other pieces of chicken with salt, pepper, and a light dusting of flour. Turn them over and repeat on the other side. Go easy on the flour; a little is enough here. Get a heavy black iron frying pan hot—about 9- or 10-inch size would be fine. When the pan is hot enough to sizzle a drop of water, add ¼ cup peanut oil (you can use other cooking oils, if you wish—I prefer peanut oil) or chicken fat, and, when that is hot—it will look wavy—lightly brown the seasoned chicken on all sides, removing each piece to drain on paper towels or brown paper bags as it is browned. Don't try to cook the chicken—just brown it. Save the frying pan, as you'll want the brown drippings later for gravy.

Sift 4 cups flour with 2 teaspoons salt into a medium-sized bowl. Make a well in the middle, into which drop 10 large eggs. Beat the eggs lightly in the well, without touching the flour any more than necessary. When the eggs are combined and have a light yellow appearance, add 4 cups milk and 3 tablespoons melted butter or margarine. Either is fine, here. Blend all together now with an electric beater. Do not continue to beat after the mixture is well blended.

Coat a heavy, shallow baking dish (earthenware or stainless steel, about 4-quart size—or two smaller ones) with a rich coating of Crisco or other vegetable shortening. Spare it not. Place the casserole in a hot oven (425°F.) for about 5 minutes, or until the fat in it is smoking hot. Quickly remove the dish and pour the batter into it. Then, on top of the batter, arrange the chicken pieces and return the whole thing to the hot oven. Set your timer for 25 minutes and, at that time, reduce the heat to 325°F. Continue baking for 15 more minutes, without opening the door. At the end of this time, turn off the heat, open the oven door (the batter will be a great puff all over the chicken) and let it all rest in the oven for 5 minutes. If you have an oven with a glass door, it is marvelous fun to observe this popovered chicken bake and see the batter rise before your very eyes.

For your gravy, reheat the fat in the frying pan, and, if there is less than ¼ cup of drippings in the frying pan, add enough chicken fat or butter to make up this amount. When the fat is melted, add ¼ cup flour, blending in with a wire whisk or the back of a wooden spoon, until all the little brown bits are distributed. Then pour in 2 cups light cream and 2 cups chicken broth made earlier from the wings or defrosted from your freezer stock. Stir while letting it boil until it thickens; don't expect it to be very thick—just the consistency of a light cream is correct. Season with salt and pepper to taste, add 2 teaspoons chopped chives or dill, according to your preference.

Serve the chicken with some of the crusty popover business, pouring the cream gravy over each portion as you set it on the plates. The pudding will be brown on the outside, soft on the inside and of incomparable flavor. The chicken will be thoroughly cooked and still brown and crusty. Bon appetit!

INGREDIENTS: 2 3-pound chickens (fryers or broilers); salt; pepper; flour; ¼ cup peanut oil or chicken fat; 4 cups flour; 2 teaspoons salt; 10 large eggs; 4 cups milk; 3 tablespoons butter or margarine.

For the broth: 4 cups water; 1 small onion; 2 teaspoons salt; 6 to 8 peppercorns. (Or 2 cups homemade or canned chicken broth.)

For the gravy: ¼ cup drippings with butter or chicken fat to make up this amount; ¼ cup flour; 2 cups light cream; 2 cups chicken broth; salt; pepper; 2 teaspoons chives or dill.

CHOPPED KALE WITH BACON

The frozen chopped kale is very nice here. If you can get it fresh, it's twice as good. Use 3 boxes frozen kale or 4 pounds of fresh kale, since it subsides in cooking. In either case, steaming is the way to cook it. If frozen, steam directly from the box; it will be ready after about 3 minutes from the time it defrosts. If fresh, wash it in several waters, trim off the tough stems and steam it, preferably in a Bungalow Cooker, over boiling water. Or you can use a colander over boiling water, or cook it in a covered heavy saucepan with a few tablespoons of water. It will take perhaps 10 minutes after the water in the lower section of your steamer comes to a boil; check it to be sure it's tender. Remove, drain, and chop coarsely.

Sauté **8 slices bacon** slowly, drain the bacon on a paper towel, and crumble it. Place the chopped, drained kale in the frying pan with the bacon drippings, stir it around, add **1 tablespoon cider vinegar, 1 tablespoon lemon juice, ½ teaspoon sugar, ½ teaspoon salt,** and a few grinds of fresh black **pepper.** Stir it around. Taste for seasoning; correct it if it needs it. Bring to a boil, add drained bacon bits, and serve.

INGREDIENTS: 3 boxes frozen chopped kale or 4 pounds fresh kale; 8 slices bacon; 1 tablespoon cider vinegar; 1 tablespoon lemon juice; ½ teaspoon sugar; ½ teaspoon salt; pepper.

BUTTERED HULLED CORN

Hulled corn, which comes in cans, has a rather bland flavor which makes it a proper companion to the chicken gravy. Some people like to dress hulled corn a bit with maple syrup and cream, which is very nice with cold meat some Sunday supper time. However, this time, **2 cans** (1 pound, 3 ounces each) **Collins hulled corn** or **whole hominy,** if you can't get the hulled corn, should be heated in its own liquid. Boil it until the liquid is reduced by half, a 5- or 10-minute job. Then add **1 teaspoon salt, ¼ cup** (½ stick) **butter, ¼ cup sugar,** and 4 or 5 gratings of fresh black **pepper.** Stir around thoroughly. Continue cooking until the liquid is quite thick, perhaps 5 minutes more. Serve in sauce dishes. If you wish to serve this on another occasion without the chicken and its gravy, add **½ cup heavy cream** at the end.

INGREDIENTS: 2 cans (1 pound, 3 ounces each) Collins hulled corn or whole hominy; 1 teaspoon salt; ¼ cup butter; ¼ cup sugar; pepper; ½ cup heavy cream (optional).

BAKED BEETS

What could be easier? Have stems and leaves removed from **2 dozen medium beets,** leaving about 2 inches of stem attached to each. Place them in a pie plate or tray in a 325°F. oven and bake them for an hour or so. As soon as they can be pierced easily with a fork, they can be removed. Plunge them in cold water and you will see that their skins will slide off with just a little prodding. Trim off the stems and place the beets in a saucepan with **3 tablespoons butter, 2 tablespoons sugar, ½ teaspoon salt,** and **½ cup concentrated orange juice.** Heat to boiling, turning beets in the sauce several times. Serve.

INGREDIENTS: 2 dozen medium beets; 3 tablespoons butter; 2 tablespoons sugar; ½ teaspoon salt; ½ cup concentrated orange juice.

HEARTS OF LETTUCE WITH CAPER DRESSING

Clean **2 heads iceberg lettuce** by cutting out the cores with an apple corer and pouring ice-cold water into the openings. Let the water rest there a minute or two, turn the lettuce over and drain. When all the water has come forth, wrap the lettuce in a damp tea towel and chill. When ready to serve, cut each head into serving-sized segments (you probably will not need both heads—1½ will doubtless do) and pour over the lettuce sections the following dressing, which you can mix in a jar beforehand. Combine **¼ cup cider vinegar, 1 cup pure olive oil, ½ teaspoon salt, ¼ teaspoon freshly ground pepper, 4 tablespoons capers,** with the vinegar that comes with it, and **½ clove garlic,** chopped or pressed through a garlic press.

INGREDIENTS: 2 heads iceberg lettuce; ¼ cup cider vinegar; 1 cup olive oil; ½ teaspoon salt; ¼ teaspoon pepper; 4 tablespoons capers with vinegar; ½ clove garlic.

OLD-FASHIONED APPLE PIE
WITH CHEESE CRUST

This is a plain old apple pie, dressed up. The basic piecrust is my favorite one, given in my *Blueberry Hill Cookbook* and again with the recipe for Mama's lemon pie on page 287. This is a well-known piecrust to any of the readers of my first cookbook and I won't again go into its attributes except to say that it has spoiled me for other piecrusts.

Prepare one recipe of piecrust, using 3 cups flour, and divide the dough in halves. Roll one half out to fit a 10-inch pie plate and set it into place. You'll use a pastry cloth, if you're wise. As for setting the crust in place, you know it's easy to carry piecrust around from place to place if you will roll it on your rolling pin, around and around, lightly, and then, holding it over the empty pie plate at the far end, unroll it toward yourself. The pastry will fall right down into its place, right where you want it. If you've not been accurate about it, it doesn't matter. You can lift it and move it slightly to its proper spot. Trim it a bit so there's a little overhang, no more.

Now prepare the top crust. Use the other half of the piecrust and roll it out to approximately the right size. Sprinkle it with ½ **cup grated cheddar cheese,** distributing the cheese evenly. Dot the surface of the crust with **1 tablespoon soft butter,** spreading it lightly with a butter spreader, what else? Now roll the crust as you would a jelly roll. Fold it so the two ends meet in the middle and then fold it again. Work it with your fingers, just for a minute or so, until it has formed a nice round shape with the cheese well distributed. If it seems the cheese is spottily located, roll it out and refold it. Wrap it in saran and chill it in your freezer for 5 minutes or for 30 minutes in your refrigerator.

For the Filling: Peel enough green apples—or the tartest apples you can come by—to fill a 10-inch pie plate. I should say this would come to about **10 medium apples,** but apples vary, as do men, and you'd better be prepared for one or two more or less. Core and slice the apples, rather thin, letting them fall into a bowl.

Combine in a bowl and sift over the apples 1½ teaspoons flour, ¾ cup sugar, and ¼ teaspoon salt. Add 1 tablespoon lemon juice (or more if the apples are bland) and ½ teaspoon nutmeg. Stir the apples around a few times and let them sit there until you have rolled out the top crust.

Remove the top crust from wherever it has been chilling and roll it to fit the 10-inch pan. Place the apples in the bottom shell, scraping all juices and spices along with them. Dot with 1 tablespoon butter and set the prepared top crust over them. Press top and bottom crusts together, fluting edges. Be sure you have enough apples to fill the bottom crust very, very full; they will sink as they cook. Nothing worse than a convex pie. Protect the outer edges of the fluted crust with a 2-inch strip of aluminum foil, tucking it over and under. This will keep the crust from browning excessively. Slit the top crust symmetrically here and there. Bake at 425°F. for 10 minutes; then lower the heat to 325°F. and continue baking for about 30 minutes, or until the apples bubble out of the slits in the crust. The cheese crust will be an interesting brown and will be a perfect complement to the apples.

If you want a plain apple pie, omit the top crust directions and bake with a plain crust on top. In this case, why don't you spread the plain crust with egg white, then sprinkle it with granulated sugar. Nothing wrong with that kind of pie either.

You will have some piecrust left, probably enough for a few tarts or a chicken pie.

INGREDIENTS: 1 recipe piecrust (page 287); ½ cup grated cheddar cheese; 1 tablespoon butter.

For the filling: 10 medium-sized green or tart apples; 1½ teaspoons flour; ¾ cup sugar; ¼ teaspoon salt; 1 tablespoon lemon juice; ½ teaspoon nutmeg; 1 tablespoon butter.

TIMETABLE: This dinner should be managed, all of it, within 2½ hours.

First prepare pastry for the pie. Roll out the bottom crust; prepare the top crust as directed. Refrigerate both until later. Should take about half an hour.

Then prepare the beets and bake them at 325°F. While they're baking, brown the chicken, meanwhile simmering the broth. If you have broth on hand, just brown the chicken. Set it aside. If you have just one oven, you can't bake it until the beets come out, anyway. Measure out the wet and the dry ingredients for the popover mix; don't combine them now.

Steam the kale, either fresh or frozen. Chop it, if you need to, and prepare the bacon and the sauce. Combine everything except the bacon bits. Set this aside, to be reheated at the last moment.

The hulled corn can be prepared now, too. Reheat it later.

Prepare the sauce for the beets. Wash the lettuce, prepare the dressing for the salad, if you're going to use homemade dressing.

All these matters should take you no more than an hour.

An hour before dinner, remove the beets from the oven. They should be done; raise the oven temperature to 400°F. for the clams and oysters. While the oven heat is rising, peel the beets and drop them into their sauce, ready to be reheated at dinner time.

The oven should now be at 400°F. Take care of opening the clams and oysters, a 10-minute problem, and refrigerate them, preferably in a pan of shaved ice. Drape a light covering of saran over them. Turn oven heat to 425°F. and set into it the heavily greased pan in which you are going to bake the popovered chicken. Now combine the wet and dry ingredients for the popover, beat them together as directed, and get the chicken in the oven according to the directions in the recipe. Set the timer for 15 minutes.

If you're an experienced hand with pastry, you can now roll out the top crust for the pie, and peel and prepare the apples. If you're not, hold off setting the chicken in the oven until you have the pie pretty much in shape.

When the bell rings, quickly open the oven door and set the pie in with the chicken. Be swift about it, for the popovers will fall if a draft hits them before they're set. Reset the timer for 10 minutes and let both pie and chicken bake for 10 more minutes at the 425°F. setting. Then reduce the heat of the oven to 325°F., the correct setting for both, and set the timer for 15 more minutes.

As soon as the pie and the chicken are in the oven, prepare the gravy. Keep it warm. Serve the clams and oysters; set the salads on the table; call your family. The kale, the hulled corn, and the beets can be heating while you're having your first course. When the bell rings, turn off the oven, open the door and let the popovered chicken dish rest. This will, of course, stop the pie from baking, but just let it sit there and, once you have taken the chicken out, continue baking the pie, still at 325°F., for another 10 or 15 minutes, or until done as directed.

These directions assume you have just one oven. If you have two, use one for the chicken and one for the pie and you won't have to worry about the oven temperatures. The pie can be baked in the morning, of course, and reheated without losing much of its flavor.

In any case, as you can see, everything's ready at one time. Set the three vegetables on the table with the casserole of popovered chicken and a bowl of the creamy chicken gravy. Let Daddy serve. Don't forget the pie in the oven—be sure to get it out when the bell tolls. It's a great pie to be eaten hot, hot as can be.

LEFTOVERS

You won't be likely to have clams or oysters left; however, if this should happen, dump them, with whatever liquor there is in each shell, in a jar and refrigerate overnight. The next day make for yourself a clam or oyster hash—a quite delectable dish, not necessarily fashioned of leftovers.

Clam or Oyster Hash

You should have at least **1 cup of chopped clams** or **oysters** or a combination of both. Sauté **1 small, finely chopped sweet onion** in **¼ cup butter** or **margarine** in a heavy iron frying pan. Do this slowly so that the onion does not get brown—just golden, no more. Add 1 to 1½ cups drained clams or oysters or both and an equal quantity (**1 to 1½ cups**) **freshly cooked, diced, peeled potatoes.** Season with **salt** and freshly ground **pepper,** tasting a bit of the potato to decide when you've had enough, and sauté slowly in the butter. Press the hash down with a pancake turner, letting it form a little crust. Stir some of the crust in, and let sauté 5 minutes longer. Beat **2 egg yolks** very well, combine with whatever **clam or oyster liquor** you may have salvaged, adding ¼ **cup heavy cream** and **2 tablespoons grated parmesan cheese.** Pour the egg-yolk mixture over the hash, cover, and let it continue cooking until the eggs are set. Run it under the broiler for a minute to brown the top. Surround edges with **2 tablespoons chopped parsley** and **2 tablespoons chopped chives,** mixed, and serve. There will be a good crust on the bottom. Some people like catsup with this. You should have enough for 4 or 5 very fortunate people.

INGREDIENTS: 1 to 1½ cups leftover clams and/or oysters; 1 small sweet onion; ¼ cup butter or margarine; 1 to 1½ cups cooked, diced, peeled potatoes; salt; freshly ground pepper; 2 egg yolks; leftover clam or oyster liquor; ¼ cup heavy cream; 2 tablespoons grated Parmesan cheese; 2 tablespoons chopped parsley; 2 tablespoons chopped chives.

Of course, there are always chowders (there's a nice New England one in the *Blueberry Hill Cookbook*), or, given sufficient clams or oysters, you can sauté them, salted, peppered, and floured, in butter, to good advantage. And, unless you're planning to use the leftover chicken gravy for a repeat of your popovered chicken, you might heat the clams and oysters in their liquor until the edges curl, then add them to the chicken gravy, reseasoning it, if necessary, and serving it on toast. Or add a sufficient quantity of milk, stirring to avoid lumps, and you have a stew; lace this with a bit of sherry.

The popovered chicken reheats perfectly. The popovers, of course, become somewhat nondescript, but if you will chop them up a bit and heat them with the leftover chicken and whatever gravy there is, you would have to be pretty fussy not to admit the whole thing is heartily satisfactory.

The hulled corn should be reheated in enough cream and maple syrup just to be visible in the pan. This is fine for breakfast, particularly with fried little country sausages. The beets can be chopped fine, mixed with hard-cooked eggs and sweet onion, held together with either mayonnaise or commercial sour cream (add a bit of sugar if it's the sour cream you decide on) and served as a salad on a bed of crisp greens. Very good, too. The beets, as well, can be chopped and heated in sour cream with a bit of butter, a little sugar, some salt and pepper. Don't boil these, just heat them, and serve with ham or sliced tongue. A good enough reason to serve tongue, beets fixed this way.

The kale with the bacon can be added, as is, to a tossed salad. Helps.

I'll wager you won't have any apple pie left, but, if you should, heat it till it's hot, divide it into dessert dishes, top with heavy cream. Shake a little nutmeg over the cream.

MARCH

PARTY MENU

Fish Through the Ice

MELON AND PROSCIUTTO
BAKED SMELT IN WINE
HERBED ZUCCHINI AND CARROTS
NOODLE CAKES
BELGIAN ENDIVE SALAD WITH WATERCRESS DRESSING
PEPPER BREAD
OLD-FASHIONED LEMON RICE PUDDING

 A truly great delicacy in Vermont are smelt that are caught through the ice of our lakes. As soon as the lakes are frozen over, little shacks appear. They are set up here and there on the surface of the lakes—many of them right out in the middle. Of course the ice has been tested and is strong enough to hold a well-filled automobile, so it is probably sufficiently safe for the shacks. The fishermen just have to be sure to fold their tents before the spring thaw comes. Some of the shacks are truly luxurious—and all are warm enough to comfort a fisherman who is willing to sit and wait for the smelt to run. When they do, the haul is mighty and well appreciated.

The smelt are usually served quite simply, sautéed, after flouring and seasoning, and are delectable in flavor and in texture. We eat them by the dozen and never grow weary of them. However, given the quantity of smelt that are available to us, we do like to serve them in other ways. This method is our solution to the problem of inviting guests in for our local smelt, and still pampering them with a truly Lucullan method of preparation. The main recipe in this company dinner, should you not have access to smelt, is acceptable for any small whole fish, or even brook trout.

Dinner is to be prepared for 8. I had a buffet in mind.

MELON AND PROSCIUTTO

A cocktail version of an old favorite. Use a melon that is fully ripe, but not overripe. You'll have problems, if it's too soft. Several hours before dinner, slice **1 large honeydew melon** in 1-inch-thick rings. Trim off the peel and discard the seeds. Cut the melon into bite-size cubes—about 1 inch each. The melon can then be refrigerated in a bowl until shortly before serving time. You will find that you have about 60 or 70 cubes, which will be just about right.

The **prosciutto**, which is Italian smoked ham, must be purchased in an Italian grocery store or a gourmet shop. I sometimes can find it in the delicacy department of our supermarket, shaved thin, in plastic packages. If you can't find prosciutto, use any thin-sliced boiled ham. You should have **½ pound prosciutto** or **boiled ham**, sliced thin. Just before your guests are due, wrap each square of melon in a piece of the ham, fastening with a toothpick. An easier way of serving, however, is to set the melon and the ham out on plates, side by side, with toothpicks close at hand. Direct the first guest in the combining of the two, and you're set. They will enjoy doing it for themselves.

INGREDIENTS: 1 large honeydew melon; ½ pound prosciutto or boiled ham.

BAKED SMELT IN WINE

Preheat oven to 450°F. Butter thoroughly a flat baking dish, which can go directly over the heat, with **2 tablespoons but-**

ter. Sprinkle over the top of the butter **1 large or 2 medium onions,** peeled and chopped into small pieces. On top of the onions, arrange **3 dozen smelt,** which have been cleaned and beheaded. I do this with a pair of shears, snipping off the head and the fins; then the insides will wash out under rapidly running cold water from the tap. Fit the smelt close together, preferably in one layer. Season with ½ **teaspoon salt,** freshly ground black **pepper,** and ½ **teaspoon crushed rosemary,** sprinkled evenly over the top. Dot with **2 tablespoons butter.** Add enough **dry white wine** (1 to 1½ cups should do it) to the bottom of the dish to cover the entire surface of it to a depth of about a quarter inch.

Bake quickly in a hot oven; you'll find the smelt will cook through in less than 10 minutes. Check with a fork to be sure that they will flake. Now set the pan on the range over high heat, bring the wine to a boil, baste the fish, and pour over the top ½ **cup heavy cream,** distributing it very carefully. Run the smelt under the broiler just until the cream is a little brown. Serve from baking dish.

If you prefer, you can omit the cream and sprinkle the top of the smelt with **2 cups buttered soft bread crumbs** and broil till brown.

INGREDIENTS: 4 tablespoons butter; 1 large or 2 medium
    onions; 3 dozen smelt; ½ teaspoon salt; pepper; ½ tea-
    spoon crushed rosemary; 1 to 1½ cups dry white wine;
    ½ cup heavy cream or 2 cups buttered bread crumbs.

HERBED ZUCCHINI AND CARROTS

I never think of zucchini that I don't recall that wonderful Helen Hokinson cartoon in which one of her typical ladies is haranguing the little vegetable store man for some imagined oversight. She is saying: "And to think that I introduced zucchini to Darien!" or it might have been Westport.

In the top of a Bungalow Cooker (which has no holes on the bottom and thus preserves the juices that come forth from fresh vegetables—juices which are usually thrown out when the vegetables are drained), steam **1 pound small carrots,** peeled and left whole (or larger ones, sliced diagonally) with ½ teaspoon salt, 1 teaspoon thyme, and ½ teaspoon sugar. If you have no steamer of this type, you can boil the carrots in ½ cup boiling water in a heavy saucepan with a tight-fitting cover, adding the seasoning as above. Let the carrots steam about 25 minutes; they should not be completely done when you add **2 pounds small zucchini,** unpeeled, washed, and sliced thickly on the diagonal. If you can get the truly tiny zucchini, halve them. Cover and steam them for an additional 5 minutes. Both zucchini and carrots should be tender by this time. Remove the top of the steamer from the lower section and set it on direct heat. Simmer the carrots and the zucchini in their own liquid until it is reduced to a very small quantity, 3 or 4 minutes at most. Add **2 tablespoons butter,** heat again; taste for seasoning, adding **pepper** and more salt if needed, and serve.

This can be prepared early in the afternoon up to the addition of the zucchini. Do that just before dinner.

INGREDIENTS: 1 pound carrots; ½ teaspoon salt; 1 teaspoon thyme; ½ teaspoon sugar; 2 pounds small zucchini; 2 tablespoons butter; pepper.

NOODLE CAKES

Early in the day, or the day before, boil **1 pound fine noodles** in accordance with the directions on the box. However, don't let them boil more than two or three minutes. Test them with your teeth. If you can just sense their texture, they're done. If they're soft, they're overdone. Add **salt** as directed, too.

Drain the noodles and rinse them in cold water, washing them thoroughly to remove any unwanted starch. (This is really redundant. All starch is unwanted.)

Beat lightly **2 large eggs,** add to them **1 teaspoon salt, 1 teaspoon sugar,** and ⅛ **teaspoon freshly ground black pepper.** Add the mixture to the noodles and stir around until they are thoroughly homogenized. Just before serving, heat a griddle very hot, grease it with a fine flavored **sausage fat** or **fresh butter,** lavishly, and let the fat come to a sizzle. Then drop the noodle mixture on the griddle in large spoonfuls, and bake slowly until both sides are brown. They can be kept warm in a slow oven, but not for too long.

Besides serving these cakes for dinner, try them for breakfast with syrup and sausages.

INGREDIENTS: 1 pound fine noodles; 2 large eggs; 1 teaspoon salt; 1 teaspoon sugar; ⅛ teaspoon pepper; ¼ pound sausage fat or fresh butter.

BELGIAN ENDIVE SALAD
WITH WATERCRESS DRESSING

Belgian endive, I admit, is very expensive when you compare its price to that of ordinary greens. But it goes far and means much. In the end it's cheap.

Arrange **5 or 6 leaves of Belgian endive** on each individual salad plate. One head usually serves two or three people. Sprinkle with **salt** and **pepper.**

In a pint jar, mix together the following: **½ cup chopped watercress** (if you can't find watercress in your market, substitute **1 tablespoon capers;** you will then have, instead of watercress dressing, caper dressing), **1 cup pure olive oil, ⅓ cup wine vinegar, 1 teaspoon Worcestershire sauce, 1 teaspoon sugar, ½ teaspoon salt,** and **⅛ teaspoon pepper.** Shake the mixture in the jar. Chill it in the refrigerator. Just before serving, shake it again and spoon a little over each salad.

INGREDIENTS: 4 heads Belgian endive (about 4 dozen leaves); salt; pepper.

For the dressing: ½ cup chopped watercress (if unavailable, 1 tablespoon capers); 1 cup olive oil; ⅓ cup wine vinegar; 1 teaspoon Worcestershire sauce; 1 teaspoon sugar; ½ teaspoon salt; ⅛ teaspoon pepper.

PEPPER BREAD

A veritable breeze. Cut **2 loaves fresh French or Italian bread**
nearly through, on the diagonal. Mix coarsely ground black
pepper with **melted butter.** You'll have to be the judge as to
how much black pepper you're safe with here, but I can
tell you that you'll need anywhere from ¼ to ½ pound butter.
Dribble the butter in the cut places. Heat in a slow (325°F.)
oven for 10 minutes, or a hot one (450°F.) for 5, on a
cookie tin. Serve hot.

INGREDIENTS: 2 loaves French or Italian bread; pepper; ¼
to ½ pound butter.

OLD-FASHIONED LEMON RICE PUDDING

I don't know why it is that so few hostesses think of rice pudding for a company dessert. Most men will order it in a
restaurant whenever they see it on a menu. Thus, to satisfy
the men who yearn for it and the hostess who insists on serving to her guests something unusual and quite superior, here
is a really deluxe rice pudding: creamy; lemony; a creation.

Rinse a heavy 2-quart saucepan with cold water. Without
drying it, place in it **½ cup uncooked long-grain white rice**
with **1 quart milk** and allow it to soak for half an hour. Then
add **2 teaspoons salt** and simmer, uncovered, stirring occasionally with a fork, until the rice is very tender and the
milk is almost absorbed. This will take about an hour.

At the same time, place in a bowl **1½ cups golden seedless
raisins** and **¼ cup cocktail sherry.** Let this stand, so that the
sherry will soak into the raisins and plump them.

When the rice is tender, remove it from the heat. Separate
4 eggs. Beat the yolks lightly, add a little of the hot rice
mixture to the eggs (not the eggs to the hot mix or they will
hard-cook before you know it). Then pour the eggs into the
hot rice and cook, stirring, for 2 minutes. Let it cool while
you cream together with your electric mixer **¼ cup** (½
stick) **butter or margarine** and **1 cup granulated sugar.**
Blend in **2 tablespoons grated lemon peel, 2 tablespoons fresh**

lemon juice (same lemon), and **1 teaspoon mace**. Now stir in the puffed raisins and add this mixture to the rice. Whip **1 cup heavy cream**, being careful to avoid the butter bit, and fold it into the rice. Then beat the whites of the 4 eggs until they form soft peaks. Fold these in.

Butter lightly a 2-quart casserole, turn the mixture into this, and set the casserole in a shallow pan or tray of hot water in a 325°F. oven. Bake 30 minutes or until the pudding is set. Serve warm with additional cream or whipped cream, if you're ready to live dangerously.

INGREDIENTS: ½ cup long-grain white rice; 1 quart milk; 2 teaspoons salt; 1½ cups golden seedless raisins; ¼ cup cocktail sherry; 4 eggs; ¼ cup butter or margarine; 1 cup granulated sugar; 2 tablespoons grated lemon peel; 2 tablespoons fresh lemon juice; 1 teaspoon mace; 1 cup heavy cream.

TIMETABLE: Practically everything here is a morning job. The smelt can be completely prepared and the baking dish, covered with saran, can spend the day in the refrigerator until time for baking. The carrots can be steamed in the morning, ready for the addition of the zucchini later in the day. The noodles, of course, can be cooked as far ahead as the day before—indeed, two days before. Mix them with the egg mixture any time during the afternoon of the party; the frying should be done close to consumption time.

The salad dressing can be made in the morning. There's no preparation necessary for the endive itself except to chill it; then simply arrange on salad plates just before meal time. The pepper bread can be prepared any time during the day, just needing the oven to complete it. The rice pudding can be prepared, except for the baking, early in the day. You should, however, bake it while dinner is being eaten, so that it can be served hot—or, at the very least, warm. The melon can be cut up in the afternoon.

What does this leave to be done? Very, very little. This is a dinner that allows you plenty of time with your guests. After things are well under way, get the melon and prosciutto started and slip into the kitchen. Somebody will take over for you for a bit. Don't worry about it, just go!

Have the oven ready at 450°F. You can have done this easily when you went in to get the melon. At that time, too, it would have been wise to take the smelt out of the refrigerator so they're not too cold when you set them in the oven, though this is not an urgent point.

Start the fish baking. Finish the carrots and zucchini, a mere matter of cooking down the liquid and adding the butter and seasonings. Heat a griddle or iron frying pan and start frying the noodle cakes—of course, it would be better if you had someone else around to do them for you—but, once they're under way, turn down the heat and, keeping an eye on them just for safety, arrange the Belgian endive salad. After 5 minutes, place the pepper bread in the oven and turn the noodle cakes.

Pour dressing over salads and set them on your buffet table. Turn the carrots and zucchini into a heated casserole. Remove the fish from the oven; add the cream or bread crumbs and set them under the broiler. Arrange the noodle cakes on a platter, remove the fish from under the broiler, place everything on the table, including the pepper bread. Serve the bread from a bread board with a knife nearby to finish slicing through the cuts.

Call your guests in. You've been away from them no more than half an hour, if that long. Place the pudding in the oven now set at 325°F., and let it bake during dinner. It will be just done (½ hour) when you want it to be. If it isn't, pass the time with the coffee and clearing away dinner plates. You won't have long to wait.

LEFTOVERS

There won't be any melon with prosciutto left, so let's drop that subject. The smelt are fine served cold with a hot German potato salad (a fine such salad appears in *Blueberry Hill Cookbook*); or, for breakfast, try them drained and heated in sizzling butter with some capers, vinegar and all.

The zucchini and carrots can be tossed with any leftover cut-up endive, provided you do this within 24 hours, adding 1 small can of pineapple chunks and binding it all with mayonnaise, Durkee's dressing (if you can get it), and pineapple juice to thin it down to salad dressing consistency. I frequently do this with leftover fruits and vegetables, folding in a small quantity of tart cranberry sauce, preferably of my own making. Well, if you did happen to have some melon, add it to the salad. And you might remember that, basically, zucchini has an affinity for pineapple.

The dressing you have left, you have left, that's all. Use it when you need it.

The pepper bread reheats in a moistened brown paper bag, like new. The lemon rice pudding is as good cold as hot; you can heat it in a pretty glass baking dish, thinning it down a bit with rich milk, and topping with a meringue. Grate some lemon peel on the meringue before baking it.

MARCH

FAMILY MENU
Blow the March Winds!

ORANGE CONSOMME
PUFFED MONTPELIER CRACKERS
FAMILY PORK CHOPS WITH CREAM GRAVY
RHODE ISLAND POTATOES
PEAS AND CORN, OREGANO
PICKLED HORSERADISH BEETS
GOLDEN APPLESAUCE
HOT- OR COLD-PAN POPOVERS
FRESH FRUIT BOWL WITH VERMONT CHEESE

March, at Blueberry Hill, means sugaring. Not that we do this ourselves; we never do have the number of hours needed to spend cooking down the sap. One must reduce it forty times, if you can believe it. But, all around us, the trees are being tapped, the sap collected. One of our neighbors has a sugar bush (which is the term for a grove of sugar maples) which consists of maples that are, it seems, over a hundred feet tall, each. We feel as if we were in a cathedral when we go there to visit. It is hushed, the sun dappled through the leaves. The trees are majestic.

So, after our regular menu here, I have given two rules for our first-run Vermont maple syrup. One is for lemon maple dumplings, the other for sugar on snow. This is fun to do and is possible whether or not you tap your own trees. When we have such a party here in Vermont, it is a great occasion. The syrup is cooked down to a thick liquid which, on contact with a plate of freshly piled snow, will become soft, chewy, taffy-like. It is served with unsweetened raised doughnuts, sour pickles, deviled eggs.

The recipes for this family dinner will serve 6.

ORANGE CONSOMME

Mix together **1½ cups fine quality tomato juice** and **1½ cups chicken or beef consommé,** undiluted. Add **¼ cup frozen concentrated orange juice** and **1 cup boiling water** and stir together. Bring to boil, simmer 5 minutes. Sprinkle top of soup with **1 tablespoon orange rind,** grated.

INGREDIENTS: 1½ cups tomato juice; 1½ cups chicken or beef consommé; ¼ cup frozen concentrated orange juice; 1 cup boiling water; 1 tablespoon grated orange rind.

PUFFED MONTPELIER CRACKERS

Hard as rocks, almost, when you buy them, easily split, easily toasted, these are the perfect crackers for cheese. Try one heated, buttered, cheesed, and accompanied by a large, red gillyflower apple—also a Vermont favorite. You won't forget it soon.

You may know these Montpelier crackers as "common" crackers. There are several names for them. One firm calls them, simply, Vermont crackers, but it is the Montpelier cracker, made in Montpelier by the Cross Bakery, which is the name best known to the old Vermonter. They can be purchased in some gourmet shops in other parts of the country, I suppose; the best place to buy them, however, is in Vermont. Several of the Vermont country stores will ship them to you.

Puffing them is the right method of approach, sometimes called souffléing. Pick a rainy day when you haven't much else on your mind—there's not much work involved here, just time. These crackers, when properly puffed, have a quite extraordinary flavor, rich and crusty. Try them with guava jelly or beach plum jam for tea.

Split **12 Montpelier crackers.** This will give you 4 halves for each person. After you've tried them once, you may want to serve more than this, but this is a fairly average portion. Place them in a large bowl of ice water with 4 or 5 ice cubes floating around; be sure it's really cold. Watch them and, in 6 or 7 minutes, or as soon as they seem to be uniformly soft, remove them, using a slotted spoon that will drain the water away quickly. The centers will be very soft, the outside crusts less so. They must be removed from the water before they disintegrate. Let them rest on a clean linen tea towel, draining as much of the excess water away as is possible. Turn them once, so both sides get the benefit of the dry cloth. Press lightly to get rid of the last bit of excess moisture. Place them on a rack over a roasting pan, cut side up, and dot each cracker with ½ **teaspoon soft butter,** or as much as it will take when thickly spread. Bake them in a 450°F. oven for about 15 minutes, or until they are lightly puffed. Lower oven temperature to 375°F. and continue baking until they're somewhat brown, about 30 minutes. They will be crisp, with no sign of dampness about them; the insides, when you bite into them, will be soft as velvet. If they are still a little wet, add a bit more butter and continue baking until they're thoroughly free of water.

These are the natural accompaniment to New England clam chowder, as well.

INGREDIENTS: 12 Montpelier crackers (common, or Vermont crackers); ¼ cup butter, or more if needed.

FAMILY PORK CHOPS
WITH CREAM GRAVY

Have **12 center-cut pork chops** cut 1 inch thick each. That's thicker than they come in packages; you'll probably have to have them cut especially for you. They do this cheerfully, even in supermarkets. Score the fat, making two or three cuts in each chop. Sprinkle them liberally with **salt** and **pepper.** You'll need a large, heavy iron skillet with a tight-fitting lid for this. Get it very hot, and start the chops by standing a few of them on their fatty edges. The fat will immediately start melting. Move the chops around, still on their edges, so that the pan is quickly covered with a thin coating of the fat. Then let the chops fall down on their sides and brown each side quickly, till golden. You won't be able to do all 12 chops at once, so remove those that are done while you brown the others. When all are brown, get them back in the pan and cover it tightly. Let them cook slowly, turning once, until they are done. Test them with a knife; they must show no sign of pink. On the other hand, it's nearly as bad to overdo them. It should take about 20 to 30 minutes; start testing at 20.

Remove the chops from the pan and set them on a warm platter in a just-turned-off oven. Drain off all the fat. Add **2 tablespoons butter** to the drippings in the pan, stirring in the brown tidbits with a wire whisk or a pancake turner. Sprinkle over the whole **2 tablespoons flour,** continuing to stir until well blended. Wait a minute or two, letting the flour brown a bit, and then start adding, gradually, **2½ cups rich milk.** Stir all the time you're adding the milk, combining the browned butter-and-flour mix as you go. Let it bubble and thicken. It should be the consistency of heavy cream; if it's thicker than that, add a little milk. Season to taste with **salt** and **pepper.** Lay the pork chops on top of the gravy and serve, directly from the pan. If you prefer your gravy on top, not under, let the chops stay on the platter where they are, and pour the gravy over them.

NOTE: You will see that I have allowed 2 chops for each person; they shrink a good bit and this is not too much. However, you may reduce the number for children or maiden aunts.

INGREDIENTS: 12 center-cut pork chops, 1 inch thick; salt; pepper; 2 tablespoons butter; 2 tablespoons flour; 2½ cups rich milk.

RHODE ISLAND POTATOES

Cut **5 peeled medium potatoes** into slices ¼ inch thick. Add them to **2 cups boiling water,** or enough to just cover them, and **½ teaspoon salt** and cook them for 5 minutes, no longer. Drain and spread in an 8-inch-square cake pan, first buttering it lavishly with about **2 tablespoons butter.** Combine, in the saucepan in which you've just finished simmering the potatoes, **½ cup** (1 stick) **butter, 1½ teaspoons Worcestershire sauce, ¾ teaspoon salt,** and **¼ teaspoon paprika.** Heat this sufficiently to melt the butter and pour the whole thing over the potatoes. Bake at 450°F. until tender, which should take about 25 minutes, basting three or four times. Serve at once, if possible.

INGREDIENTS: 5 medium potatoes; 2 cups boiling water; 1¼ teaspoons salt; 2 tablespoons and ½ cup butter; 1½ teaspoons Worcestershire sauce; ¼ teaspoon paprika.

PEAS AND CORN, OREGANO

My family is more partial to peas and/or corn than most other vegetables. They're a nice combination, not only in color contrast, but they take approximately the same time to cook and so can be concluded "to onct," as they say in Vermont.

Steam, both at the same time, **1 box frozen tiny peas** (or regular ones; the tiny ones are sweeter, if you can get them) and **1 box frozen corn,** off the cob. After the water in your steamer has come to a boil, break up the peas and corn with a fork and continue to cook them for 2 or 3 minutes. As soon as they are tender—taste one to see— remove them from the steamer, using a slotted spoon if you're using the Bungalow Cooker with the bottom that catches the juices. Set the top section of the steamer, with the juices, on top of your range and simmer them until the liquid is reduced to about 2 tablespoons. Add **1 table-spoon butter** and **½ teaspoon dried oregano** (or thyme, or rosemary, if you prefer). Heat until butter is melted and sauce is hot. Pour the herbed butter over the vegetables. Toss gently and taste; you may want **salt** and **pepper,** but usually the oregano is sufficient.

If you have no steamer and have boiled the vegetables, do as instructed on the box, using the smallest possible quantity of water in a heavy saucepan; if you have steamed the vegetables in a steamer with holes on the bottom or in a colander over hot water, you will not have the vegetable juices; just melt the butter, add the oregano, and toss the vegetables in this before serving.

INGREDIENTS: 1 box frozen tiny peas; 1 box frozen corn; 1 tablespoon butter; ½ teaspoon dried oregano (or thyme or rosemary); salt; pepper.

PICKLED HORSERADISH BEETS

To **2 cups canned sliced or small whole beets,** drained, add **1½ teaspoons sugar, ¾ teaspoon salt, ¾ teaspoon horse-radish, ¼ cup cider vinegar.** Allow these to chill for at least 2 hours before serving. At the last slice into them **8 to 10 sweet onion rings.** Taste. If you'd like a bit more horseradish, don't hesitate to add it. These keep nicely in the refrigerator.

INGREDIENTS: 2 cups canned sliced or small whole beets; 1½ teaspoons sugar; ¾ teaspoon salt; ¾ teaspoon horse-radish; ¼ cup cider vinegar; 8 to 10 sweet onion rings.

GOLDEN APPLESAUCE

A new way, and a most superior sauce. Core, pare, and quarter **8 large apples,** Winesaps, Cortlands, or any good tart apple. If they're small, use 10 or 11. Place them in a good-sized kettle, add **1 small can** (6 ounces) **frozen concentrated orange juice, ½ cup water,** cover the kettle tightly, and simmer slowly until the apples are tender. This depends on the apple, so take a look inside the kettle occasionally. Don't let the sauce burn. When the apples are soft, add **¾ to 1 cup granulated sugar,** according to their tartness—taste and see—and **⅛ teaspoon nutmeg.** You can press the sauce through a sieve if you'd like. I never do. A few **raisins** tossed in in the last five minutes, just long enough to plump them up, gild the lily.

INGREDIENTS: 8 large apples, or 10 or 11 smaller ones; 1 small can frozen concentrated orange juice; ½ cup water; ¾ to 1 cup sugar; ⅛ teaspoon nutmeg; a handful of raisins (optional).

HOT- OR COLD-PAN POPOVERS

Though I have always been an advocate of popovers baked in smoking hot shortening in smoking hot popover pans, I must admit that this recipe, which contradicts that rule, produces very lovely popovers. If you want my other popover rule, look in my *Blueberry Hill Cookbook,* please.

Grease thoroughly with any good vegetable shortening 2 popover tins. These are not tin, at all; they're iron, and right for popovers. They also are deceiving in that, instead of a dozen popovers, they have cups for only 11. But there's nothing like them for popovers; never wash them—just wipe them with paper towels after each baking. If you do use muffin tins, try to get heavy ones. You'll need 2 to 3 tablespoons vegetable shortening for the greasing process.

Break **4 eggs** into a bowl, add **2 cups milk, 2 cups flour,** and **1 teaspoon salt.** Stir these together with a spoon, disregarding lumps. Don't beat them. Pour them into the greased popover tins and set them in the oven. If oven is cold, just set it at 450°F. when popovers go in. If oven is already heated, fine. Bake them for 25 minutes without looking, then lower heat to 300°F. for 10 minutes. They'll need 5 minutes less baking if oven was preheated.

Of course, if your oven happens to be on for something else, I don't suggest that you turn it off and wait for it to chill. In this event, I would cut 5 minutes from the time, that's all.

INGREDIENTS: 4 eggs; 2 cups milk; 2 cups flour; 1 teaspoon salt.

FRESH FRUIT BOWL
WITH VERMONT CHEESE

This has been a rich, filling dinner. The right dessert is a bowl of fruit in season; pears, if they are ripe and juicy, are best; grapes, too. And, with the fruit, a wedge of Vermont cheese, called sometimes "rat cheese," which is a true, sharp cheddar that has not been duplicated elsewhere.

INGREDIENTS: Fruit; Vermont cheese.

Lemon Maple Dumplings

One of the nicest things to do with first-run maple syrup. Set this recipe aside for some Sunday breakfast or supper.

In a heavy iron skillet, about 6 inches in diameter, bring to a boil **2 cups pure Vermont maple syrup, 2 lemons,** sliced thinly, rinds and all, and **1 tablespoon butter.** As soon as the mixture comes to a boil, lower the heat and simmer gently 20 minutes. The lemon slices will become transparent. Set aside.

With your electric mixer, cream thoroughly **1 tablespoon butter** or **margarine** and **3 tablespoons granulated sugar.** When they are completely homogenized and ungranular, blend in **1 beaten egg.** You can set the creamed butter and sugar to one side of the bowl and beat the egg in the same bowl before you work them together; saves another bowl from the dishwasher.

In another bowl, sift together 1 cup flour, 2 teaspoons baking powder, and ¼ teaspoon salt. Add the dry mix to the egg mixture alternately with ⅓ cup milk, combined with ½ teaspoon vanilla.

Bring the syrup to a simmer, drop spoonfuls of the batter on the hot syrup and cover tightly. Steam over low heat for 15 to 20 minutes. Take a look after 15; break one of the dumplings open to be sure it's done right through the middle. If it is, fine; if not, use the other 5 minutes.

Serve the hot dumplings with **melted butter** and a bit of the syrup spooned over the top.

INGREDIENTS:

For the syrup: 2 cups pure maple syrup; 2 lemons; 1 table-spoon butter.

For the dumplings: 1 tablespoon butter or margarine; 3 tablespoons granulated sugar; 1 egg; 1 cup flour; 2 teaspoons baking powder; ¼ teaspoon salt; ⅓ cup milk; ½ teaspoon vanilla; melted butter.

Sugar on Snow

The traditional sugar-on-snow party is held when the syrup has finished its run, and the pressure of work can be relaxed. There is nothing more backbreaking than "sugarin' it," as any Vermonter will tell you. Nowadays there are modern methods of piping the syrup through an intricate system of pipes or gathering it in plastic bags instead of the heavy cans. However, nothing can relieve the farmer of the hours and hours of slow, painstaking cooking that is necessary to produce the golden nectar. Usually it goes on through the night, the hungry fire gobbling the enormous quantity of wood that has been stacked up through the winter—a major undertaking in itself—against this cooking time.

When it is all over, when the syrup has been canned, the evaporator emptied, there is the sugar-on-snow party. If you can't find snow in March where you live, when the first-run syrup is available, buy some shaved ice. Keep it in the freezer until you're ready for it. You'd need a bushel of either snow or ice for a gallon of syrup, which would be enough for a party of between 25 and 30 people.

In any case, whether preparing this for a crowd or for three excited little girls such as ours, it is all the same: Fill a deep kettle with only a few inches of **pure maple syrup.** Grease the top of the kettle to keep the syrup from boiling over. Let the syrup boil rapidly, but watch the pot so that it does not burn. Turn the heat down when the syrup has reached a symmetrical pace of boiling all over, and simmer, keeping the syrup at a low boil. Set a candy thermometer in the pan and, after about 15 minutes, when the thermometer has reached a reading of 230°F., begin testing the syrup. Don't ever let the syrup get down below one inch in depth; it will burn.

Drop a teaspoonful of the syrup into a glass of water and stir with a fork. If the sugar dissolves, it's not ready. Keep boiling it. Test again, every minute or so, until the sugar clings to the fork when you stir it in the water. It will be soft, like waxy taffy. As soon as this stage has been reached, remove the kettle from the heat. Leave the thermometer in it and let the sugar cool down to 150°F., stirring occasionally. Don't let it go below 125°F. as it will then harden.

While the sugar is cooling, get out the snow or shaved ice, fill a soup plate with the snow, firming it down, and lay some sugar over the snow in several little pools. If it's been cooked to the proper stage, it will be waxy. If it dissolves in the snow, it needs another minute or so of cooking. If it's too hard, too chewy, add a little water to it and reheat slightly.

If there's anything left, just place the kettle on the snow and stir the pan rapidly, keeping it on the snow, and soon it will form Maple Cream, an experience in itself.

With the sugar on snow, it is imperative to serve, always, unsweetened raised doughnuts and sour pickles. They will be needed to counteract the sweetness.

INGREDIENTS: Maple syrup; snow.

TIMETABLE: Prepare the soup in the morning or early afternoon. Reheat it when you're ready for it. Also in the morning, you can prepare the beets—or the day before or the week before.

The rest of the dinner should be fixed at dinner time, a proper function for a mother and a homemaker surely at that time of day. Two hours before dinner, peel and parboil the potatoes. Arrange them in the baking dish with the seasonings. Set them aside.

An hour before dinner, start the pork chops; they'll take about 10 minutes of your time for the browning; after that, until time to fix the gravy, they're on their own.

Peel the apples, mix them with the orange juice and water, and let them wait their turn. They won't darken; the orange juice takes care of that.

Now set the Montpelier crackers in the oven. While they're puffing, reheat the soup, steam the peas and corn, and prepare the herbs and butter for them. Mix up the popover ingredients, grease the popover tins and fill them.

Remove the Montpelier crackers from the oven and keep them warm a few minutes. Set the popovers in the same oven, as well as the potatoes. Set the applesauce on; look at it occasionally, while you finish the peas and corn, adding the butter sauce, and leave them in the top of the steamer over hot water.

Serve the soup and crackers; have yours with the family. When you're through, excuse yourself, go to the range and prepare the gravy for the pork chops. If you don't think you can do this speedily, take care of it before you have your soup —just keep the family waiting a few more minutes. However, the preparation of the gravy is neither difficult nor time-consuming, and, if it's the way it is at our house, your youngsters will be glad to use the time reporting on their day's activities. Remove the potatoes from the oven. Let the popovers continue baking. Set the timer, if you're apt to forget them.

Now the rest of the dinner can come to the table. The pork chops resting in the frying pan atop the rich, hot gravy;

the potatoes in their own pan; the peas and corn, oregano in the nice casserole; and, of course, the applesauce and the beets in their own serving dishes.

By the time you have everything in front of the master of the house or whoever is going to serve, the popovers should be finished. Let service begin while you pass them, right from the iron pan.

This has been a filling meal, and fearful for the fate of a fancy dessert, I'm sure you will agree that the fruit and cheese are the right ending to it.

LEFTOVERS

The orange consommé makes a fine bedtime hot drink. Reheat some Montpelier puffed crackers to go with them. The unpuffed crackers can be served with hot milk; you've heard of crackers and milk, haven't you? Heat milk, or half milk-half cream, and pour it over a bowlful of heated Montpelier crackers. Drop a lump of butter in the bowl, add a pinch of salt, a dash of pepper, and let the butter melt. This is nourishing, as well as heart-warming, at bedtime.

As for the main part of this dinner, it all goes so well with itself that it's only a matter of combining the components of it. Cut up whatever pork is remaining into bite-size squares, and layer them with the remaining potatoes in a buttered casserole, including the leftover peas and corn and the leftover gravy. If there is not enough gravy to moisten it well, add some milk, although, if you're down to only a tablespoonful or two of the gravy, it would be well, probably, to add a can of one of the cream soups, undiluted. Sprinkle with a bit of poultry seasoning or some thyme, dot the top with butter, heat to bubbling, sprinkle with Parmesan or cheddar cheese, and brown under the broiler.

If you have no potatoes left, just meat and gravy and vegetables, boil some broad noodles, drain them, and proceed as directed.

The applesauce is delicious, hot or cold. My youngsters

like it on hot oatmeal, sprinkled with brown sugar, eaten with cream. Try that, one cold morning.

Popovers, too, are fine for breakfast. Heat them smoking hot in a dampened heavy brown paper bag, place them in a cereal bowl, and open them. Spread them with melted butter and hot maple syrup; or butter and heated jam—such as blueberry.

Freeze the dumplings you don't eat and, when you want them again, heat them to their original temperature in the top of your steamer. Reheat the syrup and pour a bit of it over the dumplings. If you're against serving them the same way twice, slice them, set them in a buttered baking dish, heat and serve with chocolate sauce or whipped cream.

APRIL

PARTY MENU

Shall We Go into the Dining Room?

MELON BALLS IN WHITE WINE
ROAST SPRING LAMB, CAFE
KASHA IN BROTH
MUSHROOMS LUCULLUS
BRUSSELS SPROUTS WITH ORANGES
TOSSED SPINACH SALAD
FRY-PAN BREAD
CHOCOLATE MOUSSE

This menu, our party meal for April, fancy though it appears, is simple beyond words. It's a perfect company meal; still it's not too much if you are in the mood to pamper your family.

It's the meal I love to plan. Use everything for everything. And, whether it's your family that's eating this, or guests, it's definitely a dining-room meal. This meal is planned for 6, with allowances for leftovers.

MELON BALLS IN WHITE WINE

Any time during the day, but at least 4 hours before dinner, cut a little cap out of the top of a **large ripe melon** (honeydew, Persian, casaba, whatever you can get in the market). Make the opening large enough to scoop out the seeds with a spoon. Drain the melon upside down for a few moments. Then set it right-side up and pour into it enough **white wine** (sauterne, Chablis, or just a simple domestic light sweet white wine) to fill the melon, about 1 to 1½ cups. Return the little cap. Set the melon in the refrigerator; it might be wise to put it in a bowl of its own size to keep it from tilting. Ten minutes before dinner, remove the cap, pour off the wine. You should save the wine; you'll want ½ cup for your mushrooms and ½ cup for your gravy later on.

Now cut the melon in half, scoop out neat little balls with a melon cutter and arrange the balls in a pretty glass dish with perhaps a grape leaf on the side. Serve with a little of the wine poured over them. **Lemon** only for those who insist.

INGREDIENTS: 1 large ripe melon; 1 to 1½ cups wine (sauterne, Chablis, light sweet white wine); lemon (optional).

ROAST SPRING LAMB, CAFE

The gentle young lamb one gets in the markets these April days takes to this treatment beautifully. The lamb is basted with coffee and, even if you think this is not sane, I ask you to try it before you pass judgment. The coffee, as a matter of fact, becomes anonymous somewhere in the cooking; you have then a beautiful brown crust on the lamb and a sauce which is a natural for the kasha you'll be serving with this roast.

Have the butcher cut off the lamb shank of a **small leg of spring lamb**, weighing 6 or 7 pounds. You'll use the shank later for broth for the kasha. Set the lamb on a rack in a shallow roasting pan. Season it well with **salt, pepper,** and a few dashes here and there of **garlic powder.** Smear it all over, topside and underneath, with **prepared mustard.** You'll use perhaps a cup of this. Then pat on top of the mustard about ½ **cup light brown sugar**—enough to cover it well, the sugar on top of the lamb only. It'll stick right onto the mustard. Try to keep the sugar from falling into the bottom of the pan, if you can. Add to the bottom of the pan **1 cup strong coffee,** hot or cold, new or leftover. The coffee should not be poured over the mustard–brown sugar coating on the lamb at this time. You want that to get set before basting it.

Place the lamb in a 300°F. oven with a meat thermometer in the meaty part of the leg (be sure the thermometer doesn't touch any part of the bone or come out the bottom of the roast—it won't read accurately). Let the lamb roast slowly, starting to baste it not earlier than 45 minutes after it has gone into the oven. This gives the mustard-sugar coating a chance to get brown and crusty. You should watch the roast and see that the bottom of the pan is constantly covered with the coffee; should the coffee cook away and sugar fall into the pan, it will burn very quickly. Baste every 15 minutes or so (after the first 45 minutes without basting) until the thermometer reads 150°F., not a degree more. This will give you a rare, juicy roast of lamb. If you insist on having it well done (and I urge you to try it rare if you never have) let the thermometer go up to 160°F. or, heaven forbid, 170°F. When the lamb has reached the required reading on the thermometer, which ought not to take more than 2 hours, remove it and the rack from the roasting pan, setting the lamb on a warm platter. Keep it in a warm spot, or in a warm, turned-off oven. Then set the pan itself over the direct heat on the top of the range and let the juices bubble up hard. Add ½ cup of the **wine** poured out of the melon (or use wine directly from a fresh bottle if you're not fixing the melon), ⅛ **teaspoon garlic powder,** and let it boil and bubble, using a wire whisk to get all the juices and brownness mixed together. A wooden spoon will do nearly as well as the whisk if you haven't one. The gravy will thicken, almost glaze, but, if you've added a bit too much coffee, you might need to thicken it with a little **cornstarch** mixed with a little **cold water** (½ teaspoon cornstarch to 2 tablespoons cold water should do it), letting it boil up heartily afterward. Serve the gravy separately, to be eaten with the lamb itself or poured over the kasha.

INGREDIENTS: 6- to 7-pound leg of spring lamb; salt; pepper; garlic powder; 1 cup prepared mustard; ½ cup light brown sugar; 1 to 3 cups strong coffee; ½ cup white wine; ½ teaspoon cornstarch and 2 tablespoons cold water (optional).

KASHA IN BROTH

When you start roasting the leg of lamb, cover the **lamb shank** with **cold water**, about 1½ **quarts.** Add 1 carrot, peeled and left whole; 1 onion, peeled and quartered; 4 **peppercorns;** and 1½ **teaspoons salt.** Bring to a boil and simmer all the time the lamb is roasting. About ½ hour before the lamb roast is done, strain the broth in which the shank has been cooked. You should have 4½ cups. If you haven't, add boiling water to make up that amount. Mash the carrot and return it to the broth. Refrigerate the meat of the lamb shank—it makes wonderful sandwiches with hot mustard.

Bring broth with carrot back to a boil and add, gradually, stirring all the while, ¾ cup kasha (called, in grocery stores, brown buckwheat groats). It comes in sizes: fine, medium, and large, or coarse grain. One's as good as the other, though I'm a shade prejudiced toward the large grain. As soon as it's all boiling in fine fashion, lower the heat and let it simmer. It'll take about 10 to 15 minutes to cook. It should be chewy, not overly soft. You'll be amazed at the way this swells up—instead of the broth cooking away, the kasha expands to fill the whole pan. Add 3 table-

spoons butter, 1 teaspoon sugar. Taste for salt and pepper.
Add them if needed and then a dash of garlic powder. As
soon as the kasha is done with no water left in the pan, set
it over low heat or in a very slow oven and keep it warm.
If you want to fix this kasha some time when you've no
lamb broth, use homemade or canned rich chicken broth.
When you serve this, scoop out a well in the middle and fill
it with gravy from the lamb.

INGREDIENTS: 1 lamb shank; cold water; 1 carrot; 1 onion;
    4 peppercorns; 1½ teaspoons salt; ¾ cup kasha (buck-
    wheat groats); 3 tablespoons butter; 1 teaspoon sugar;
    salt; pepper; dash of garlic powder.

MUSHROOMS LUCULLUS

These are mushrooms worthy of their name. Trim bottoms
from stems from 1½ to 2 pounds (depends how much you
like mushrooms!) firm, fresh white mushrooms. Slice them,
cutting straight down through the stems. They will look
like silhouettes of small umbrellas. Heat (until it's truly
hot) a black iron frying pan, about 8-inch size. Then drop
into it 3 tablespoons butter. When the butter is bubbly,
and a little brown, add the mushrooms, all at once. (They'll
fill the pan at first, but they'll shrink very soon.) Stir
them around quickly while they heat through. As soon as
they are limp, sprinkle them with 1 teaspoon parsley,
chopped, and ¼ teaspoon dill weed (Spice Island puts this
up, among others) or 1 sprig fresh dill, chopped. Then pour
over them ½ cup white wine (left from the melon or fresh
from a bottle). Let this simmer 3 or 4 minutes. As soon as
the gravy thickens, it can be served. Taste first, of course,
and add salt and pepper as it is needed. A dash of garlic
powder, carefully controlled, does nothing but good here.

INGREDIENTS: 1½ to 2 pounds fresh mushrooms; 3 table-
    spoons butter; 1 teaspoon parsley; ¼ teaspoon dill weed
    or 1 sprig fresh dill; ½ cup white wine; salt; pepper;
    dash of garlic powder.

BRUSSELS SPROUTS WITH ORANGES

The simplest sort of vegetable and guaranteed sensational. At this time of year, the sprouts will be frozen. But don't forget this recipe, come September. Steam **2 boxes frozen Brussels sprouts**—or boil them in a small amount of salted water; steaming's by far the better method. (See pages 5–8 for talk about steamers and such.) This needs to be done the very last minute; it takes actually something like 2 minutes after the sprouts have defrosted for them to be done enough. They must still be green and crunchy or you've spoiled the whole thing. When they are ready, add **1 can** (11-ounce size) **mandarin oranges, drained** (if you're not dieting, drink the juice that comes off—it's delicious). These need just to heat through. If you do more than that, they will fall apart. Remove the sprouts and oranges to a lovely serving dish, meanwhile sizzling **3 tablespoons butter** in a frying pan until brown, watching it so it won't burn. Arrange over the sprouts **2 thin slices red onion**, separated into rounds. Sprinkle with ½ **teaspoon salt**, add **pepper to** taste, and pour over the whole, at the last, the brown butter. If you do this with fresh sprouts later, they must be trimmed and cleaned, then steamed 10 minutes.

INGREDIENTS: 2 boxes frozen Brussels sprouts; 1 can (11 ounces) mandarin oranges; 3 tablespoons butter; 2 thin slices red onion; ½ teaspoon salt; pepper.

TOSSED SPINACH SALAD

Look over **1 pound spinach;** it should be fresh, unwilted, crisp. Remove the heavy stems, wash it if it needs it, and set it in a salad bowl, drying it first with a paper towel. Set the bowl of spinach, covered with waxed paper or saran, in the refrigerator, ready to be tossed. Any time in the afternoon, prepare the dressing. This is done in a heavy black iron frying pan, preferably. A small one will do. Fry in it **4 slices bacon** until it is crisp. Remove the bacon with a slotted spoon, setting it on a paper towel to drain. Crumble it. Set it aside. In the bacon drippings, sauté **1 small onion,** chopped, until it is limp, not brown. Then add all at once **¼ cup water, 3 tablespoons cider vinegar, 3 tablespoons lemon juice** (fresh or bottled, doesn't matter), **1 teaspoon salt, 1 teaspoon sugar,** and **½ teaspoon dry mustard.** Bring all this to a boil. Turn off the heat and forget about it. When you're ready to toss the salad, reheat the dressing to boiling. Pour it over the ice-cold spinach, toss again and again, at the end adding the crumbled bacon. Serve as soon as each leaf is gleaming with dressing.

INGREDIENTS: 1 pound spinach; 4 slices bacon; 1 onion; ¼ cup water; 3 tablespoons cider vinegar; 3 tablespoons lemon juice; 1 teaspoon salt; 1 teaspoon sugar; ½ teaspoon dry mustard.

FRY-PAN BREAD

A crazy bread. Some Sunday supper, try it with gobs of butter and blueberry jam! You will notice, if you notice that sort of thing, that there is a goodly amount of salt *and* pepper, of all things, right in the batter. Don't worry about it. This gives it character. You need a heavy skillet, an 8-inch one. My black iron jobs do yeoman service, as you see. Nothing like them.

NOTE: This bread can be baked directly in an electric skillet or on top of the range. In this case, you would need a tight-fitting lid and would set your skillet at 375°F., your heat on the range top at medium. You would get a bread without a brown crust, but it's marvelous anyway. The recipe I give here, done in the oven, I like better.

Preheat oven to 375°F. Beat **yolks of 4 eggs** until thick and lemon-colored. I use a wire whisk for this and keep using it right through the preparation of this bread except to beat the egg whites. Add **½ cup flour** which has been sifted with **1 teaspoon baking powder, ¼ teaspoon salt,** and

¼ teaspoon pepper. Keep whipping with the whisk. At the last, add **2 tablespoons melted butter.** (Note: If you add melted butter right on top of the eggs, you cook the eggs and have lumps that won't come out. So add the hot butter *after* the eggs have been mixed with the dry ingredients.) Now add, gradually ¼ **cup milk.** The batter should be quite thick and, since eggs are variable, you may not need all of the ¼ cup milk. So go easy and stop when the batter is like a waffle batter. Beat the **whites of 4 eggs** until stiff but not dry. They should glisten. For this you'll need an egg beater in the interest of time. If you've loads of that, the whisk will accomplish it eventually. Fold the whites into the batter carefully, until no white is perceptible. Heat the skillet on top of your stove. When it is hot enough to make a drop of water dance, add **1 tablespoon butter.** Let the butter sizzle up, covering the entire surface of the pan and, when it is hot, pour the batter into the pan. Place in the 375°F. oven for 20 to 25 minutes. It will puff up like an omelette and brown lightly on top. Poke at it with your finger. If it is completely dry on top, test it with a cake tester. If it comes out clean and dry, you're in business. Serve right out of the frying pan at the table. It cuts into nice wedges, easy as pie.

INGREDIENTS: 4 eggs; ½ cup flour; 1 teaspoon baking powder; ¼ teaspoon salt; ¼ teaspoon pepper; 3 tablespoons butter; ¼ cup milk, or less.

CHOCOLATE MOUSSE

A classic recipe; a classic dessert. This has not as much whipped cream as some mousses; in fact only 6 tablespoons cream for 6 people. This to salve your conscience. Do the mousse in the morning, for convenience sake. It can be served, however, within an hour of its preparation, a good point in its favor.

Over low heat, melt **6 ounces Baker's German's sweet chocolate** (if you can't get that, get some kind of semisweet chocolate—not unsweetened chocolate here) with **3 tablespoons leftover strong coffee** and **3 tablespoons sugar.** When it is thoroughly melted, remove from heat and let it cool a few minutes. Then separate **4 eggs,** setting the whites aside. Add to the chocolate the yolks of the eggs (again, this is why you cool the chocolate, to keep from hard-cooking the eggs), and **1½ tablespoons softened butter.** Stir it all thoroughly. Whip **6 tablespoons heavy cream with 1½ tablespoons sugar.** You know you whip the cream first, until it's almost as stiff as you want it, then add the sugar and finish the process. Fold the whipped cream into the chocolate mix, carefully, until it is completely blended. Then beat the 4 egg whites until stiff but not dry. Fold them into the chocolate. Pour into a lovely glass bowl or into individual sherbet glasses. Chill in the refrigerator for several hours or overnight. If you're in a rush, set it in the freezer for about 20 or 30 minutes, until it's chilled, not frozen. Serve out of the same bowl. This will freeze marvelously, by the way. Fill parfait glasses with it, freeze it, and serve from same.

INGREDIENTS: 6 ounces Baker's German's sweet chocolate; 3 tablespoons leftover strong coffee; 4½ tablespoons sugar; 4 eggs; 1½ tablespoons butter; 6 tablespoons heavy cream.

TIMETABLE: In the morning, prepare the melon and the mousse, and wash the spinach. Get these three things in the refrigerator. You can prepare the lamb broth in the morning, too, but it's just as easy, as directed in the recipe, to do it while the lamb is roasting. At 5:00 o'clock, prepare the lamb (takes 5 minutes), get it in the oven, start broth simmering. Prepare salad dressing in frying pan, leave it on stove until needed. You can leave the kitchen then, having used about 30 or 40 minutes. Come back at 6:15 (dinner is planned for 7:00), having just come in occasionally to check the roast for basting purposes. Now prepare the melon balls, refrigerate them. Prepare fry-pan bread batter, getting it in the oven a little after 6:30. Take lamb *out* of oven same time, setting it in warm place. Strain lamb broth, bring it to a boil, add kasha, cook that. Cut mushrooms directly into pan as directed and, while they're simmering, prepare the gravy for the meat. At the last minute, combine and toss the salad.

If this seems too much for you to do in the time allotted, come back at 6:00 instead of 6:15. Several of the items in this timetable could be done in the morning, or early in the afternoon, such as preparing the lamb for the oven, preparing the salad dressing, etc., but I do think that's asking them to sit around a long time without attention.

Contrary to the advice in women's magazines about the hostess always joining her guests while the dinner magically gets itself done, all I will say is that this is possible only when you have a casserole that has gone into the oven hours before, has been finished hours before, and is quietly drying out in a warm oven. What I'm trying to do here is to show you how to prepare and serve a magnificent dinner, and it can't get done all by itself. If you have a husband, let him greet the guests (you can do so, too, then duck) and give them drinks. *You're* busy!

Once I had decided on this course, my food benefited. I don't often join my guests for appetizers. I honestly don't think they miss me; I feel it's preferable not to be there at all rather than to sit down for five minutes and then jump up and run frantically into the kitchen. While my guests are having the melon balls, and while John is serving them the hot spinach salad and slicing them large wedges of steaming fry-pan bread, I have had loads of time to prepare the Brussels sprouts, to arrange on our rolling table the lamb on a carving board, the lamb gravy in a gravy boat, the mushrooms in their own frying pan, the kasha in *its* frying pan, the sprouts, last of all, on a nice little platter, all green and orange. The table then comes into the dining room with me; I sit down; John carves the lamb, serves the plates; they are passed. My part in all this is over, it has been successful, my guests are delighted. The mousse is ready and waiting, a creamy chocolate dream. Such a dinner! Try it. It's easy.

LEFTOVERS

This lamb is simply delicious as a leftover, if you will add to it whatever mushrooms were left, slice the lamb you will want, and heat it in a combination of the lamb gravy and the remains of the mushroom gravy. Sprinkle it with snips of chives, serve on toasted rolls.

If there is no gravy around, the thing to do is to slice the lamb or cut it up into small bits. Heat a black iron frying pan hot, add peanut oil to cover the bottom of the pan (about 2 tablespoons for an 8-inch pan) and, when the oil is wavy, which means it is hot, add the lamb, searing it quickly until it starts to brown—takes a few minutes only. Then pour over it soy sauce in sufficient quantity to moisten the whole (again about 2 tablespoons for a small panful), sprinkle with ½ teaspoon sugar, a sprinkling of garlic powder. Stir this all around, adding a little more soy sauce if it looks dry. Serve this with rice and shredded Chinese cabbage.

Then again, there's a curry. Always possible with leftover lamb. If you have gravy left, use that, adding milk to thin it down and curry powder (1 teaspoon of this to each 3 cups of gravy is a good starting point), 1 small sautéed onion. Actually you should sauté the onion in butter in a frying pan and pour the gravy over the browned onion. If there's no gravy, use some chicken broth (canned will do). You'd have to thicken the broth with a little flour, of course, stirring the flour into the sautéed onion, then pouring over the whole the chicken broth. Same proportion for curry powder. Taste it, and, if you like curry to taste the way I like it to taste, you'll add some sugar, about a tablespoon. If you don't care for the sweetness of this, omit the sugar. You may need to add some salt and pepper, but that's the fun of cooking. Rice with this.

Any of these three leftover lamb things can be served on the leftover kasha, if you'd like. This should be fried. To do this, heat a black iron frying pan sizzling hot, add butter, let the butter sizzle, then lightly sauté a small chopped onion in the butter. Add the cold kasha, mashing it around with the back of a tablespoon until it's well distributed. Then fry it slowly over medium heat until it's brown and crusty on the bottom. Turn it with a pancake turner, adding more butter if the pan is dry, and brown on the other side.

If, by chance, there is any fry-pan bread, heat it in a heavy brown paper bag, slightly moistened, in a 300°F. oven. Serve the lamb in its gravy over a wedge of the bread.

One final suggestion for lamb leftovers. If, when you make your spinach salad, you will save some spinach out without dressing, you will find a delicious dish can be contrived by mixing some chopped raw spinach with the cubed leftover lamb, adding 2 or 3 small cooked potatoes, cubed, and frying it as you would a hash in a hot buttered frying pan until the meat is brown and the spinach has wilted. This will need a goodly amount of salt and pepper.

If you have melon balls left, stir them into a box of frozen raspberries, just defrosted, for dessert the next day. Or frozen sour cherries.

The chocolate mousse can be used as is for four or five days; perhaps with a bit of whipped cream and some shaved chocolate on top. Or fill a pie shell with it, why don't you? Freeze what you can't use, as advised before.

APRIL

Mommy, May I Ask Some Friends of My Own for Supper?

PINEAPPLE CUBES DIPPED IN GRENADINE
DORIS EDDY'S HAMBURGER PIE
BUTTERED CHERRY TOMATOES
RELISHES, POTATO CHIPS
HOT CHOCOLATE, VIENNA STYLE
HOMEMADE GINGER-COOKIE ICE-CREAM SANDWICHES

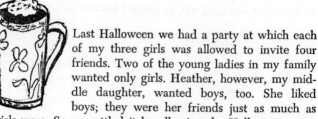 Last Halloween we had a party at which each of my three girls was allowed to invite four friends. Two of the young ladies in my family wanted only girls. Heather, however, my middle daughter, wanted boys, too. She liked boys; they were her friends just as much as girls were. So we settled it by allowing the Halloween party to be for the friends of the other two Masterton girls and, some weeks later, we had a supper party which could include boys. As it turned out, it was all boys, or nearly; only one other girl could come, though every boy who was invited was able to make it. The two ladies had a charming evening; they graciously allowed Heather's sister, Laurey, who had just turned eight, to join, since they were short on the female angle. Laurey had a great time.

100

This is the supper, which was eaten, every bit. An efficient measure of the success of any children's meal. Planned for 10.

PINEAPPLE CUBES
DIPPED IN GRENADINE

Youngsters, like their elders, love things they can pick up on toothpicks. Arrange 1 large **can pineapple chunks**, drained, on a platter. It will need draining several times; there's a great deal of liquid lurking in each chunk of canned pineapple. (Note: Children seem to like canned pineapple better than fresh, unless the fresh is unusually sweet and juicy.) If you have a fancy toothpick holder such as one uses at cocktail parties, pierce each cube with a toothpick and set it in the holder. Otherwise, leave them on the platter, the toothpicks in place. Pour ¼ **cup grenadine** into a shallow container, aluminum, pyrex, what-have-you, and, as each youngster takes a toothpick-impaled pineapple square, allow him to dip it in the grenadine. The pink syrup will be quickly absorbed, the color of the pineapple cubes will be rosy, and consumption will be rapid. Add grenadine to the dipping dish, if needed.

INGREDIENTS: 1 large can pineapple chunks (or 1 large fresh, sweet pineapple); ¼ cup grenadine syrup.

DORIS EDDY'S HAMBURGER PIE

Doris Eddy is a quite inspired lady who has a horse farm near us, just outside of Middlebury, Vermont. She teaches riding to many of the Middlebury College students and to uncounted young people in the environs of her marvelous, peaceful farm. There are thirty or forty horses there, and usually thirty or forty young people. She is completely "with it," both in the horse and the young people department. Come summer, twelve or thirteen teen-aged girls live in her farmhouse, caring for their own or her horses, learning not only how to live with horses but how to live with each other—

and consequently the world. My Lucinda has been one of these girls for several summers.

Doris does the cooking, the resident girls do the cleaning up—a fair division of the indoor chores. Doris tells me the most popular dish she serves these ravenous maidens is her hamburger pie. She "made it up, I guess," she says, laughing, so that, in giving it to you, I cannot in fairness dub it other than hers. I've tried it on many young people with enormous success and on enough grownups to know it's not to be kept away from them, either.

Line a 10-inch pie plate with **piecrust.** Use mine, please, page 287, the outer rim protected with aluminum foil. Bake it 4 or 5 minutes in a 425°F. oven; this will keep it from getting soggy when you add the filling. Set it aside.

Sauté **1 medium onion** in **1 tablespoon butter** until the onion is golden. Do this slowly, and you won't burn it. Add **2 pounds ground chuck steak** and stir it around until it is well crumbled and cooked through. If meat is fatty, drain away excess fat. Season with **1 teaspoon salt** and **¼ teaspoon freshly ground black pepper.** Place the onion and meat mixture in the partially baked crust. If you wish, you may add **¼ teaspoon dill weed,** sprinkling it around.

In a bowl, mix together **3 beaten eggs** and **1 pound creamed cottage cheese** until it is homogenized. Season with **⅛ teaspoon salt, ⅛ teaspoon imported Hungarian paprika** or, again, if you're more favored toward dill, the same quantity of **dill weed.** Spread the egg-cheese mix evenly over the hamburger.

Bake in a 375°F. oven until the crust is brown and the top is set, about 30 minutes. The topping becomes a lovely, truly enticing brown, too. Serve in pie-shaped wedges. If you serve this to grownups a dab of sour cream goes nicely on top.

INGREDIENTS: Piecrust to fit a 10-inch pie plate; 1 medium onion; 1 tablespoon butter; 2 pounds ground chuck steak; 1 teaspoon salt; ¼ teaspoon pepper; ¼ teaspoon dill weed.

For the topping: 3 eggs; 1 pound cottage cheese; ⅛ teaspoon salt; ⅛ teaspoon imported Hungarian paprika or dill weed.

BUTTERED CHERRY TOMATOES

If you can get some of the little cherry tomatoes, which are sometimes available at this time of year in the better markets, you will find that young people are fascinated with them. Either serve them, as is, with your dish of relishes, or heat a black iron frying pan, sizzle **2 tablespoons butter** until it bubbles lightly, add **2 pounds cherry tomatoes** and toss them around. Move the pan constantly for just a few minutes until the skins pop here and there. If you need more butter, add it. Sprinkle with **salt** and **pepper.**

INGREDIENTS: 2 pounds cherry tomatoes; 2 to 4 tablespoons butter; salt; pepper.

RELISHES, POTATO CHIPS

Just that. As to relishes, the most beloved in my home are **black olives.** My children will eat as many as they can get away with—and I mean a dozen or more each at a time. Second is **kosher dill pickles.** Lucinda asked for them for Christmas and meant it. Then, though not quite as popular, come **celery sticks** and **carrot sticks.** These they seem to like *before* dinner, more than with it, but I would say they are fine for the young. Arrange all these in sections of a large platter, preferably a divided one; if you've heated the tomatoes, set them on a separate plate. Have a large wooden bowl of **potato chips,** just plain ones, not barbecued! I haven't met a child yet who liked the flavor of a barbecued potato chip. Save them for grown-up parties.

INGREDIENTS: 1 large jar black olives; 1 large jar kosher dill pickles; celery and carrot sticks; potato chips.

HOT CHOCOLATE, VIENNA STYLE

You can do this in a double boiler, if you want to be cautious about it, but it will take a long time. I prefer to use a heavy pot, perhaps a Dutch oven, stay with it, and keep stirring. It'll be done in no time.

Combine **1 cup sugar, ½ cup water,** and **8 ounces** (8 squares) **unsweetened chocolate.** Stir this constantly, but *constantly,* until the chocolate is melted and combined with the water and sugar. Keep the heat below the pan very low while you're about this. Now add, slowly, stirring all the time, **2 quarts rich milk.** As the chocolate blends with the milk, the rate of addition can increase. When everything is combined, continue to heat, beating all the while with a rotary or electric hand beater. The chocolate will become frothy as it heats. As soon as it is very hot, but not boiling, remove from the heat and serve. There's a definite point, you know, where this is true. The best way to tell is to taste; you can't really know how hot something is by looking. You might drop a drop on your wrist, but sometimes that is a little risky; might be boiling. Add **1 teaspoon vanilla.** Serve with large gobs of **whipped cream,** topped with **shaved sweet chocolate.**

INGREDIENTS: 1 cup sugar; ½ cup water; 8 ounces (8 squares) unsweetened chocolate; 2 quarts rich milk; 1 teaspoon vanilla; ½ pint heavy cream; 1 sweet chocolate bar.

HOMEMADE
GINGER-COOKIE ICE-CREAM SANDWICHES

Make your own ginger cookies for these. This is a very, very old recipe, given me by one of my good friends. A quite special cookie for grown-up occasions too.

With your electric beater, cream together until very light **½ cup margarine** and **1 cup maple sugar** or **light brown sugar.** The maple sugar is better, but it's not so easily obtained. Add **1 egg,** well beaten, and combine thoroughly. With a fork stir ½ teaspoon soda and 2 teaspoons ground ginger to ½ cup commercial sour cream and add to the first mixture. Add 2 cups flour or enough to make a stiff dough, stiff enough to roll; you might need as much as 2¼ cups. When you think it's reached this point, flour your hands and take up a cupful of the dough. Toss it around from hand to hand and place it on a well-floured board. It will be a smooth, rich, easily rolled out dough. If it sticks at all, scrape it up with a knife, toss it in flour a minute more, and try again. As soon as you can roll it with a floured rolling pin, without any sticking, you're in business. Roll very thin, about ¼ inch, and cut into cookies 3 inches around. Bake on lightly greased cookie sheet about 8 minutes in a 450°F. oven. Don't overbake them. They should be somewhat chewy when they come out of the oven.

Invert one cookie, spread with **vanilla ice cream,** top with another cookie.

INGREDIENTS: ½ cup margarine; 1 cup maple sugar or light brown sugar; 1 egg; ½ teaspoon soda; 2 teaspoons ginger; ½ cup commercial sour cream; 2 to 2¼ cups flour; 1 pint vanilla ice cream.

TIMETABLE: The component parts of the hamburger pie can be prepared ahead: the piecrust baked 4 or 5 minutes; the filling ready; the topping ready. Bake it when you need it, that's all. As a matter of fact, Doris Eddy often bakes hers in the morning, goes out and teaches riding all day, comes in and, while she's fixing a salad, reheats the hamburger pie. Says it mellows somewhat and, if anything, is better. So you can do that.

Nothing else in this meal requires advance thought. Bake the ginger cookies any old time, morning or afternoon, or far ahead to be frozen, and fix up the relishes, if you'd like. But, without any of these preparations, you can have this meal ready in about an hour all told, unless you don't have any piecrust on hand in your freezer and need to fix that.

This is certain to be successful with young people, the whole meal. See if it isn't.

LEFTOVERS

The pie is great the next day, hot or cold. Something like Cornish pasties, except for the topping. So just reheat it, if you wish, or go after it late at night. Eat a slab of it with a tart apple, settle back with a good book. Luxury!

The pineapple can be used in a fruit salad or fruit cup, or can be mixed with cut-up softened marshmallows (soften them with pineapple juice) and ½ cup of commercial sour cream. Add some chopped walnuts.

The rest is academic. Who doesn't know what to do with leftover ginger cookies? If, by some fluke, you have them and nobody honestly wants to eat them, thicken a pot-roast gravy with them or crumble them on a lemon pudding. But how silly can you get? Who ever heard of leftover ginger cookies?

MAY

Dinner for a VIP

PIROSHKIS
HOT CLARET CONSOMME
FISH FILLETS IN SOUR CREAM WITH DILL
GLAZED ORANGE DUCKLINGS
WILD RICE
SWEET AND PUNGENT CARROTS
ASPARAGUS WITH WHIPPED CREAM
CHICORY AND WATERCRESS SALAD
ELSIE'S ROSEMARY BISCUITS
COFFEE CREAM TORTE

The dining room is coming back. A setting formal; a meal to match. At Blueberry Hill, the dining room is pine; the beams are gnarled and curly; the fireplace is enormous. The dinner I have planned for this month is a truly VIP dinner, more courses than usual, more fussing than usual. You may cook the entire menu as it is, thereby impressing without a doubt the most important people possible—ambassadors, your husband's boss. Or, if you'd like, you may omit either the soup or the fish course—keep the recipes for another time—and still make your mark as a fine cook and hostess.

This is a beautiful dinner, prepared with care, with love, for 10 or 12.

PIROSHKIS

These are flaky meat turnovers, traditionally served hot with Russian borscht. For this rather elaborate dinner, however, borscht would be too much. A clear, light soup is more in order. Think of the piroshkis with the borscht, however, on another occasion; with a salad and a dessert you will have an excellent, quite complete lunch.

You can prepare these ahead and freeze them.

For the Pastry: Combine in a bowl **2 cups flour** and **1½ teaspoons salt.** Blend into the flour and salt **¼ pound** (1 stick) **butter** until there are lumps the size of peas. Think ahead and have the butter at room temperature for at least an hour ahead of time, so it will work more easily. With a fork, work in **1 cup commercial sour cream** until the dough starts to hold together. Then use your floured hands, pressing the dough until it is combined. It will take only a few minutes. Don't keep handling it after this point is reached; the dough will stay flaky and tender if you don't misuse it. Toss the ball of dough in a little flour and roll out on a floured pastry cloth to a rectangle about 12 x 16 inches in size. Dot with **2 tablespoons rather soft butter,** little dots here and there covering a good bit of the surface of the dough. Fold into three layers, press together, and roll again. Repeat, folding the dough into threes, pressing together and then rolling it out. The folding and refolding creates flaky leaves of pastry. Do it three times in all. Then wrap the pastry in saran and set it in the coldest part of your refrigerator while you prepare the filling.

For the Filling: Heat a small, about 6 inches in diameter, black iron frying pan very hot. Then sizzle **1 tablespoon butter** or **margarine** (either will do) in it. Let the butter lightly brown and sauté **1 chopped small onion** in this, slowly, until golden. Add **½ pound ground chuck steak,** breaking it up with a fork, until the meat has just lost its red color. Remove pan from heat, add to it 1 **chopped hard-cooked egg, ¼ cup commercial sour cream, 1 tablespoon chopped parsley, ½ teaspoon sugar, ⅛ teaspoon garlic powder, ⅛ teaspoon freshly ground black pepper, and ¼ teaspoon dill weed.** Mix this together thoroughly with a fork.

Remove pastry from refrigerator and divide the dough in two. Roll each half into a rectangle about 8 x 12 inches, then cut each rectangle of dough into six thin squares 4 x 4 inches. Add 1 tablespoon of the meat mixture to each square, folding over to make triangular shapes. Press the edges together with the fingers, fluting or pressing with the tines of a fork around the edges to make them look fancy. Prick the turnovers with a fork and set them on ungreased trays in a moderate oven, 375°F., baking until golden brown, about 15 or 20 minutes. These can be prepared and kept in the refrigerator for about an hour before baking without harm, but they shouldn't wait longer than that. It's better to bake them and reheat them, which they do beautifully; as I said before, you can freeze them and defrost them for your party. Do the defrosting in a slow oven; should take about 20 minutes or so from freezer to hot turnovers. Makes 12 large piroshkis. You can make 24 if you prefer smaller ones. Serve with hot consommé.

INGREDIENTS:

For the pastry: 2 cups flour; 1½ teaspoons salt; ¼ pound and 2 tablespoons butter; 1 cup commercial sour cream.

For the filling: 1 tablespoon butter or margarine; 1 small onion; ½ pound ground chuck steak; 1 egg; ¼ cup commercial sour cream; 1 tablespoon chopped parsley; ½ teaspoon sugar; ⅛ teaspoon garlic powder; ⅛ teaspoon pepper; ¼ teaspoon dill weed.

HOT CLARET CONSOMME

Combine 3 **cans undiluted chicken** or **beef consommé** (preferably chicken) with 1½ **cans cold water.** Bring to a boil, add **1 cup claret** and allow to simmer a few minutes. Float a few **thin slivers lemon peel** on the top. Serve from cups with the piroshkis.

INGREDIENTS: 3 cans undiluted chicken or beef consommé; 1½ cans cold water; 1 cup claret; lemon peel.

FISH FILLETS
IN SOUR CREAM WITH DILL

The quantity given here is sufficient for a small serving of this fish for each of 10 or 12 people. The same quantity is correct for 4 or 6, should you prepare this as a main dish for a smaller group, a matter you should consider doing, as this is a quite superb and very unusual fish entree. The sauce, as well, can be made in quantity and used with plain boiled shrimp or as a topping in the baking of any fish at all. Use it to bake a whole haddock, mackerel, or whitefish. A jar of this sauce in your freezer and some frozen fillets, and you'll be ready to take on any unexpected guests with equanimity.

Prepare the sauce first. In a heavy saucepan, melt ¼ **pound** (1 stick) **butter.** When it is melted, add to the saucepan, *away from the heat,* ¼ teaspoon thyme, 1 bay leaf, 1 tablespoon minced onion, 1 tablespoon chopped fresh dill or ¾ teaspoon dill weed, ¼ teaspoon salt, ⅛ teaspoon freshly ground black pepper, 1 teaspoon sugar, and 1 cup commercial sour cream.

Season 6 fillets of sole (or flounder or haddock) on both sides with salt and pepper. Lightly. Cut the fillets in half, butter a flat baking dish, and arrange the 12 small pieces of fish symmetrically on the buttered surface. Spread the sauce over the fillets. Reserve a little of the sauce, if possible, perhaps ½ cup, keeping it in the saucepan.

Bake at 375°F. until the fish can be flaked with a fork. This varies with the thickness of the fillets. It should not take sole longer than 5 minutes after the sauce starts to bubble a bit. A larger piece of fish might take 15 minutes, and last night I baked a whole haddock under this sauce in 25; it was perfectly done.

When ready to serve, see that each portion has some of the sauce from the baking pan. Heat the small quantity of reserved sauce and pass that, as well, while your guests are eating; they'll want a bit more. Remember this sauce. It's worth making in large amounts and freezing.

INGREDIENTS: ¼ pound butter; ¼ teaspoon thyme; 1 bay leaf; 1 tablespoon minced onion; 1 tablespoon chopped fresh dill or ¾ teaspoon dill weed; ¼ teaspoon salt; ⅛ teaspoon pepper; 1 teaspoon sugar; 1 cup commercial sour cream; 6 fillets of sole, flounder, or haddock; salt; pepper.

GLAZED ORANGE DUCKLINGS

Very beautiful, very delicious, and very easy. Place 4 ducklings (4 to 4½ pounds each) on a rack in a large roasting pan. This may seem like a great many ducklings, but most ducklings will serve no more than three hungry people. Sprinkle them with salt and pepper, inside and out, and roast them, uncovered, at 325°F. Place a roasting thermometer between the leg and breast of one of the ducklings and roast them until the thermometer reads 160°F., or nearly done. In the absence of a thermometer, you can tell if a duckling is done if the drumstick wiggles very easily or if, when you poke it with a fork, the liquid which emerges is not pink. Pierce the skin occasionally so the fat will run out during the roasting. You'll find that about 20 minutes to the pound is approximately correct.

When the thermometer reads 160°F., or the ducklings are very nearly done, pour off the fat and smear the tops of the ducklings with a mixture of ¼ cup maple syrup and ¼ cup frozen orange juice, undiluted. Use a large can of the orange juice; you'll want the rest of it for your sauce. Return the ducklings to the oven, raise temperature to 375°F., and glaze them for about ½ hour.

While the ducklings are roasting, simmer the giblets and necks (save the livers for broiling with a bit of butter; they're marvelous) in salted water to cover. By the time the tops of the birds are crisp and brown, the broth will be rich. If the tops of the ducklings don't glaze by the time the thermometer reads 180°F. or the ducklings are done, set them under the broiler for a few minutes. They'll brown all right; as a matter of fact, if you don't watch them carefully, they'll burn.

For the Sauce: Add the balance of the **orange juice** in the can, **1 cup crabapple or currant jelly** (try guava sometime, too), and **1 cup strained giblet broth**. Bring to a boil, stirring, and heat until the jelly is diluted into the gravy. Add ½ **teaspoon powdered ginger** and ½ **teaspoon dry mustard**, if you want a bit of spice added.

Cut the ducklings into serving-size pieces with poultry shears; most of the fat will be out of them and can be used, if you haven't burned it, for pastries and frying other things. There is no such thing as a thoroughly defatted duck, unless you discard the skin, but this method of preparation is pretty close to it. There will be a little fat under the skin, but, with a sharp knife, this can be cut away and the skin may still be savored. The ducklings are delectable with the glaze and covered with the sauce.

INGREDIENTS: 4 ducklings (4 to 4½ pounds each); salt; pepper; ¼ cup maple syrup; ¼ cup frozen orange juice.
    For the sauce: Balance of large can orange juice; 1 cup crabapple, currant, or guava jelly; 1 cup strained giblet broth; ½ teaspoon powdered ginger; ½ teaspoon dry mustard.

WILD RICE

Plain wild rice is the perfect accompaniment to the glazed ducklings. Don't try to fancy it up. A substitute would be brown rice, also served plain, but if you can afford it, *riz sauvage*, as they say in Quebec, is right, here.

Wash **2 cups wild rice** well. Set it in a colander and run cold water through it for several minutes. Lift it and turn it as the water flows through. If you see any bits of foreign particles in it, remove them. Bring **2 quarts water** to a wild boil; add **2 teaspoons salt.** Slowly add rice to water, stirring as you do, and, when all the rice is added, reduce heat to a modest boil and continue to cook for about 45 minutes. The rice will be tender and the water should be completely absorbed. Look at it after about 35 minutes and be sure the water doesn't cook away when you're not around. Place the rice in a chafing dish; it will keep warm and stay dry. Serve with the ducklings, ladling a bit of sauce on it.

INGREDIENTS: 2 cups wild rice; 2 quarts water; 2 teaspoons salt.

SWEET AND PUNGENT CARROTS

Steam, in the top of your Bungalow Cooker or other steamer, **12 large carrots,** peeled and sliced in thin slices on the diagonal. They will take no more than 10 minutes to steam tender. At the end of about 8 minutes, add **¾ cup seedless white raisins** and **1 tablespoon slivered green pepper** (peeled and membraned). Let them steam with the carrots for 2 minutes.

Lift out the carrots, raisins, and peppers (save those good juices; add them to a glass of tomato juice tomorrow) and place them in a black iron frying pan with **4 tablespoons** (½ stick) **butter, 2 tablespoons light brown sugar, ¾ teaspoon salt, 1 tablespoon lemon juice.** When ready to serve, heat, stirring around; make sure the carrots are thoroughly hot and shiny before serving.

INGREDIENTS: 12 large carrots; ¾ cup seedless white raisins; 1 tablespoon slivered green pepper; 4 tablespoons butter; 2 tablespoons light brown sugar; ¾ teaspoon salt; 1 tablespoon lemon juice.

ASPARAGUS WITH WHIPPED CREAM

For this recipe, if you cannot get the early fresh asparagus, you can use the frozen asparagus cuts and tips. I'm not advocating this particularly, but you might wish to serve asparagus fixed this luscious way during the winter months or later in the summer after the fresh asparagus season is past.

Clean **4 pounds fresh asparagus,** snapping the stalks off at the point where they become tough—a very easy trick; try it. Cut away the little points along the sides of each stalk. Don't peel the asparagus unless you have had the misfortune to have purchased some which is nearing retirement age. If you have fresh, crisp, newly cut asparagus, use it as it comes.

Steam the asparagus in your Bungalow Cooker or other steamer, crisscrossing it. Your steamer will be available because the carrots have long since been prepared. When the asparagus is just tender, in 3 or 4 minutes, stop the steaming process. You should watch it carefully, using a paring knife to poke the stalks and see what state they're in. You may prepare the asparagus and arrange it in the steamer a few hours before dinner, but don't steam it until you want it.

Have ready in a large black iron frying pan ¼ cup (½ stick) **melted butter** and ½ **cup heavy cream.** As soon as the asparagus is ready, add it to the cream and butter and shake it around so that it is well coated. Sprinkle it with **salt** and **freshly ground black pepper** while you're doing this. When every stalk of asparagus is pretty much covered with the butter and cream, transfer it to a deep platter, leaving an opening in the middle of the platter. Whip **1 cup heavy cream** till it's stiff. Add, the last thing, ¼ **teaspoon salt,** combining it by a few turns of the beater. Pile the cream in a small bowl which may be set in the middle of the platter, surrounded by asparagus. Sprinkle the cream with **1 teaspoon chopped chives.**

INGREDIENTS: 4 pounds fresh asparagus; ¼ cup butter; 1½ cups heavy cream; salt; pepper; 1 teaspoon chopped chives.

CHICORY AND WATERCRESS SALAD

For this salad, the emphasis is on the watercress. Chicory can be rather bitter and is better understated.

Wash and dry 2 bunches watercress, unwilted and fresh at the start. Tear off and discard most of the stems, using only those to which there are leaves attached. Wash ¼ medium head chicory. If the stalks themselves are young and crisp, they can be used; if not, trim and discard the spiny sections, using only the chicory leaves. Dry the chicory, tear it and the watercress into bite-size pieces and wrap them both in a slightly dampened linen dish towel. Leave the greens in the refrigerator in this towel to crisp.

When ready to prepare the salads, arrange a mixture of the chicory and watercress on small, flat glass salad plates, covering the bottom of each plate with the greens. Wash and slice in thin rings 12 to 15 radishes. Slice 1 kosher dill pickle in thin rounds. Press through a sieve 2 hard-cooked eggs. These ingredients can be prepared ahead, combined in a bowl and refrigerated. When ready to serve the salad, divide the radish-pickle-egg mixture among the salads.

In a small bowl, mix together with a fork ¾ cup imported pure olive oil, ¼ cup wine vinegar, ¼ teaspoon salt, a few grinds of fresh pepper, ¼ teaspoon garlic powder, ½ teaspoon sugar, 1 tablespoon crumbled Roquefort or bleu cheese. When well mixed, distribute this dressing over the salad greens, using about 1½ tablespoons for each salad.

INGREDIENTS: 2 bunches watercress; ¼ medium head chicory; 12 to 15 radishes; 1 kosher dill pickle; 2 eggs.

For the dressing: ¾ cup olive oil; ¼ cup wine vinegar; ¼ teaspoon salt; pepper; ¼ teaspoon garlic powder; ½ teaspoon sugar; 1 tablespoon crumbled Roquefort or bleu cheese.

ELSIE'S ROSEMARY BISCUITS

These are a variation of Elsie's biscuits, a well-known recipe to readers of the *Blueberry Hill Cookbook*, with the addition of a well-chosen herb.

Sift 4½ cups flour with 3 tablespoons baking powder, ½ teaspoon crushed dried rosemary, and 1½ teaspoons salt. Cut in ¾ cup (1½ sticks) margarine or butter, using, preferably, a pastry blender. Two knives will do, but they're harder to manage. When there are only small lumps left, rub the flour mixture between your hands until you have something approximating a fine cornmeal. Now add, one after the other, ¾ cup sweet milk, ¾ cup buttermilk, and ½ cup commercial sour cream. Stir with a spoon until all the dry ingredients are moistened. As soon as this has been achieved, stop! The dough should be rather on the wet side and, if you see this is not true, add, grudgingly, a little more buttermilk.

Flour a bread board or pastry cloth thoroughly, turn the dough out on this and, with floured hands, toss it around until it is possible to handle it without your hands getting sticky. Pat, don't roll, the dough into a flat, round shape, ½ inch thick, always keeping flour under it and on your hands. Cut the biscuits with a small cutter, anywhere from 1 inch in diameter to 2 inches, not larger. Arrange them on two lightly greased trays or cookie tins. Bake in a hot (475°F.) oven for 8 to 12 minutes, depending on their size. You will have plenty of biscuits to serve 10 to 12 people, with leftovers. Serve them hot, the minute they emerge from the oven, if possible.

It's quite all right to get the wet ingredients combined and the dry ingredients put together in the early afternoon. The biscuits shouldn't be put together and cut out until as late in the afternoon as you think it is safe, and then, once cut, they should be refrigerated on their tray until time to bake them.

INGREDIENTS: 4½ cups flour; 3 tablespoons baking powder; ½ teaspoon crushed dried rosemary; 1½ teaspoons

salt; ¾ cup margarine or butter; ¾ cup milk; ¾ cup
buttermilk; ½ cup commercial sour cream.

COFFEE CREAM TORTE

An outstanding dessert. When I tested it, some years back,
I wrote across the card "great, great." This torte will serve
10 or 12, but with just one serving each. You'll bake two of
them, if you're wise.

Grease, with any good vegetable shortening, the bottoms
of three 8-inch layer cake pans. Sprinkle with flour, tossing
the flour around to cover the entire bottom surface. Set
oven at 350°F.

Beat 2 **very large eggs** with your electric beater until they
are light and lemon-colored. Add **1 cup sugar, ¼ teaspoon
salt,** and **1 teaspoon vanilla** and beat until the sugar is ungranular in appearance. Heat **½ cup milk** and **1 tablespoon
butter** just to boiling and pour it over the egg mixture. Beat
it in at medium speed, beating for about 1 minute after it
is assimilated.

Mix and sift together **1 cup sifted flour** and **1 teaspoon
baking powder.** Beat this into the batter and continue beating
at moderate speed until very well blended, about 2 more
minutes.

Divide the batter equally among the three prepared pans.
The batter will just about cover the bottoms of the pans.
Don't worry about the very small amount of batter; that's
the way it's supposed to be. Bake in preheated oven for 20
to 25 minutes, or until lightly browned and done when tested
with a skewer.

You will now have three very thin cakes, about ½ inch
high, each. They will turn out of the cake tins easily with
the aid of a spatula and should then be cooled thoroughly on
cake racks. When cool enough to handle (about room temperature), which should be in something like 10 minutes,
slice them horizontally so you have six very, very thin layers.
They will slice surprisingly easily with a sharp bread knife;
there's plenty of body to them and, if you do happen to slip

and break through one, don't worry about it. It will patch together easily.

While the cakes are cooling, prepare coffee syrup by boiling together for 10 minutes ½ **cup sugar** and ¼ **cup double-strength coffee.** At the end of this time, add 1 **tablespoon rum** or **rum flavoring** (optional, dependent on your affinity for this flavor; the torte will be a success without the rum). Also whip 1 **pint heavy cream** quite stiff, to the consistency of cake frosting, not runny at all.

Spread all cut sides of each layer *except one* with the syrup. This one layer, only, reverse and spread the syrup on the top, not on the cut side. Spread each layer, except the reversed layer, with the whipped cream, setting it atop the one before, so that you have five layers, each covered with coffee syrup and whipped cream. Set the top layer with the uncut side up, on the very top. Spread a bit more syrup on this. Spread the sides with the remaining whipped cream.

The torte should chill for three or four hours so that the cream and the coffee will be somewhat assimilated by the cake. The next day it will be better, if that's possible. And, should there be any left for a third day, it will be just divine, that's all. This freezes perfectly.

INGREDIENTS:

For the cake: 2 very large eggs; 1 cup sugar; ¼ teaspoon salt; 1 teaspoon vanilla; ½ cup milk; 1 tablespoon butter; 1 cup sifted flour; 1 teaspoon baking powder.

For the glaze and filling: ½ cup sugar; ¼ cup double-strength coffee; 1 tablespoon rum or rum flavoring (optional); 1 pint heavy cream.

NOTE: This recipe will make one torte, only.

TIMETABLE: This is a fussy party. You really ought to have some help. However, if you will stay calm and progress quietly toward your appointed goal, this is not absolutely essential.

The piroshkis can be made weeks ahead of time, or days, anyway, and frozen at no disadvantage to themselves. If you have no freezer, bake the piroshkis the day before your party, refrigerate them, and stop worrying.

Also the day before your party, bake the three layers for the torte. When they're thoroughly cool, wrap them in saran and refrigerate them. You can also make up the coffee syrup and put that in the refrigerator. The sauce for the fish is fine combined and refrigerated the day before. If you want to do it much further ahead of time, you can freeze the sauce; it's so easy to put together, however, you oughtn't to be worried about it.

First thing, morning of your party, whip the cream and complete the torte. Refrigerate it. Nice to know your dessert is ready and out of the way. Then prepare the soup. Leave it in its saucepan. Nothing will happen to it.

Still morning, wash the salad greens, prepare the other salad ingredients and the dressing. Refrigerate as directed, all except the dressing. Set that aside. Measure the wet and the dry ingredients for the biscuits.

This is enough for the morning. Have your lunch. Lie down for an hour, why don't you? In the early afternoon, get the ducklings ready for the oven, steam the carrots and leave them to be reheated in their frying pan. As soon as the steamer is free, arrange the cleaned and prepared asparagus in it. Wash the fish fillets, prepare them, covered with sauce, as directed, then refrigerate, covered with saran until time to bake.

Late in the afternoon, combine and cut out the biscuits. Set them in the refrigerator, to be baked a little later. A more ideal preparation is to have someone do this for you while you're arranging the salads so that the biscuits may be baked while your guests are having their fish. However, unless you have a gal in the kitchen, you'll come out nearly as well if you get the biscuits ready an hour or two ahead of time.

Two hours before dinner, set the ducklings in the oven. Get the glaze ready, prepare the duck broth, and mix the ingredients for the sauce ready for the addition of the broth. Prepare the wild rice.

Half an hour before dinner, raise the oven to 375°F., add glaze to ducklings and let them glaze and brown. Ten minutes later, set the piroshkis in the oven, either frozen or unbaked. They will either bake or reheat in about 20 minutes. Arrange the salad plates, adding the dressing, and set the salads on the table. For this dinner your best silver, crystal, china, is not too good. Look the table over; be sure it's perfect, not less.

Whip the cream for the asparagus; refrigerate it.

Bring the consommé to a boil, turn down to a simmer and pour the water. Set the hot consommé on the table in soup cups, thin slivers of lemon floating on top, and call your guests. Make sure they're primed for this before you set the soup on the table. They should come when they're called, of course, but not everyone is of like mind on the importance of this matter. As soon as they are seated, remove the piroshkis from the oven, have them passed (or pass them) and slide the fish into the oven. Place the wild rice in its chafing dish, light it.

Unless you have a gem in your kitchen, I'm afraid I shall suggest that you do not, in fact, cannot, join your guests until the main course. Somebody has to see that the fish isn't overcooked and, if you have a reliable soul whom you can trust to do that and to get the rest of the dinner properly ready to be served, sit right down with your guests and enjoy yourself. If you haven't, let your husband do his best to keep things moving without you for a while.

If you would prefer, skip the fish course, serve the piroshkis and consommé in the living room (in fact, if you're in the skipping mood, skip the consommé and serve the piroshkis with drinks), arrange everything else on a rolling table, and, at that point, get your guests, your dinner, and yourself into the dining room at the same time.

However, given the dinner as presented, either you, or someone equally concerned, must now watch the fish. While it's baking, reheat the extra sauce, set it in a bowl, and, the minute the fish can be flaked, send it into the dining room to be served. It can be served from its casserole, while everybody drools, and the extra sauce can be handed around as it is needed.

As soon as the fish is on its way, remove the ducklings from the oven and cut them into serving portions; turn up the oven and set the biscuits on a center rack in it. At the same time, turn on the heat under the steamer of asparagus, start heating the carrots, and, as soon as the asparagus is ready, arrange it on its platter, adding the bowl of whipped cream as directed. Add the duck broth to the sauce, heat that, and set it in a gravy boat on a rolling table with the duck, arranged on a platter. Ladle a little sauce over the pieces of duck; keep the rest in the gravy boat.

This sounds like a lot to do at once, but it really isn't. It's one, two, three: one, heat the carrots; two, heat the asparagus; three, finish the sauce. Arrange them all, according to color contrast, on a rolling table with the duck and the chafing dish of wild rice.

Send it in. The fish will have been cleared, conversation will be on its own, and the appearance of this beautiful table of food will be inspiring. If you haven't a rolling table, have the platters carried in and set down; almost equally inspired. They may be placed on the dining-room table, or you can use a sideboard, if you own one. The point is that your guests should view your creation in its undisturbed state.

By this time, the biscuits will be done. Send them in in a basket or two, steaming hot. If they are ready before you are, fine. Let your guests have them right out of the oven, in any case, no matter what!

If you haven't been sitting with your guests right along, join them now. You'll need a chair, I know, but what a dinner you have prepared!

Nothing more for you to do but eat and glow. Wine is right with this meal, but I've decided against suggesting wines in this book. I know, if you're a lover of fine food, you'll agree that a dinner such as we have served here does deserve a lovingly selected wine or series of wines. There are many good books for you to consult on this point. Do so.

When the dishes are cleared for the main course, bring forth (or have it brought forth) your beautiful torte. Serve it in rather small slices; it's very rich; and anyway you have only enough for 12 people. If you want to be safe, and have leftovers, you will have prepared two tortes.

LEFTOVERS

The piroshkis are amenable, as I've said before, to freezing. When they reappear, heated to their original just-out-of-the-oven temperature, they're like new. Serve them for lunch with hot Russian borscht.

Assuming you'd like a recipe for borscht, here's an old-fashioned one, which is the beet borscht, not the cabbage borscht. My mother always had some of this around, our family was so fond of it. Serve it hot or cold. It will be ample for 6.

Beet Borscht

Boil 1 **bunch beets,** unpeeled, with their tops, both beets and tops well washed, in **2 quarts water** for 1 hour. Remove the beets, slip off their skins, trim off the tops, and grate the beets. Throw away the peels and tops and return the grated beets to the water. Add 1 **small piece citric acid** (obtainable from any drugstore, and some supermarkets), 1 **tablespoon salt, 1 cup sugar.** Boil 5 minutes longer. Taste. If you think it is not sweet enough to your taste, you may add a little more sugar. Serve hot with 1 **tablespoon commercial sour cream, 1 freshly boiled peeled small potato** in each bowl. If you wish to serve this cold, the hot potatoes are wonderful in the cold soup. You can refrigerate the borscht, so it is ready for use at any time; it'll keep at least a week in the refrigerator. Its freezer life is indefinite. If you're serving it cold, 1 **tablespoon cut-up peeled cucumber** is very nice in it.

INGREDIENTS: 1 bunch beets; 2 quarts water; 1 small piece citric acid; 1 tablespoon salt; 1 cup sugar; 6 tablespoons commercial sour cream; 6 small potatoes; 6 tablespoons cut-up cucumber.

As to the other leftovers, the consommé will reheat to its former state; chilled, it is an excellent madrilene. Try heating it with a can of fine quality green turtle soup; a spoon of sour cream or whipped salted heavy cream floats nicely on top.

The fish fillets, whatever is left of them, should be refrigerated. The next day break up the fish, add enough half-milk half-cream to the fish and sauce to make it a chowder; heat and taste for seasoning. It will need salt and pepper and a little dill weed, probably. Drop a large lump of butter on top of the chowder, let it melt, and pour the very hot soup over two or three Montpelier (common) crackers in each soup bowl.

Or you can break up the fish, mix it with some sautéed mushrooms, stir it into some leftover whipped cream, season with salt, pepper, a bit of imported paprika, all to taste, pile into coquille or clam shells, sprinkle the top with fine bread crumbs, dot with butter or with little squares of bacon. Brown under the broiler at high heat until it bubbles and the bacon is crisp.

It will also make a fine fish salad; follow the rule for chicken salad, marinating the fish, cleansed of its sauce, in a tart oil and vinegar dressing. Then mix with mayonnaise and sour cream. A bit of parsley.

The duckling and wild rice are just elegant reheated in the sauce you served them with the first time. Add a few pignolia nuts or pecans, and chopped parsley to the rice. I've never gone any farther than this with it, but, with just a small amount on hand, this would take to Chinese treatment very easily. Add some pineapple chunks, some of the leftover carrots, slivered, a bit of green pepper (seeded and membraned), cut in squares, and perhaps a can of mixed Chinese vegetables, drained well. Use the sauce you have on hand, adding soy sauce and bead molasses, a little at a time, to your taste—not too salty, not too sweet. Pour it all over the duck pieces, heat, and serve with hot Chinese mustard. In the absence of enough sauce, add a bit more of the pineapple juice that came in the can of pineapple, thicken it with arrowroot or cornstarch, season as directed, and serve.

If you have any asparagus left, it's fine combined with leftover carrots and heated. Or it will make an excellent filling for an omelette. Prepare a light omelette (see my recipe in the *Blueberry Hill Cookbook* or use your own—just be sure it's a proper omelette), heat the asparagus quickly, cream and all, sprinkle with a bit of nutmeg and fill your omelette with it. You'll like it. As for the carrots, mash them, add whatever sauce there is, and heat in a buttered pie plate, topped with brown sugar. Broil at the end, for a crust.

The rosemary biscuits, if any are left, can be frozen and remembered another time as a topping for a chicken pie. Or a beef or kidney pie. They also go particularly well with a chicken salad; which reminds me of a marvelous recipe you ought to know about.

Chicken Salad

Cut up your **chicken**; marinate it in **French dressing** (not the gummy orange kind) or **Italian dressing** ("boughten" will do) and mix it up with enough **commercial sour cream** to moisten it. Add a **pinch of dry mustard,** a little **salt,** a little **sugar,** a bit of **paprika,** a few drops of **lemon juice,** and some **chopped celery.** A rather vague recipe, but it's a guess and by golly one, indeed, that tests your taste buds. It's truly delicious with, to bring you full circle, the leftover rosemary biscuits, split, buttered, and toasted.

INGREDIENTS: Cut-up chicken; French or Italian dressing; commercial sour cream; pinch of dry mustard; salt; sugar; paprika; lemon juice; celery.

The torte? Unless you've made two, there'll be none left. If you've been wise and done as I hoped you would, keep on eating it until its lovely end. I've kept mine for as long as four days and it gets better each day; doesn't look so good as it did when it was new, wouldn't want it for company, that's for sure, and it is, as a matter of truth, a little too moist to brag about, but flavorwise, it does nothing but improve with age. At the very end, if it's a matter of a few scraps, lay them out in a buttered dish, dribble sherry over them, lots of butter, and bake in a slow oven. Serve with whipped cream. Of course, if you've frozen it, defrost it slowly when you want it. Room temperature does this.

MAY

FAMILY MENU
The Crocus and the Daffodil

FENNEL AND BLACK OLIVES
MRS. JOHN DE POMPEO'S LASAGNA
ASPARAGUS OR FIDDLEHEADS WITH BUTTERED CRUMBS
DANDELION SALAD
GARLIC BREAD
BROILED FRESH PEACHES
RHUBARB MERINGUE PIE

It takes quite a while for spring to arrive in Vermont, finally. Even in May, it sometimes snows. But the days are longer, they are gentler. The crocus and the daffodil are budding, sometimes blooming, in carpets on the lawn. By the end of the month, there are the apple blossoms, the lilacs, the asparagus. Best of all, the rhubarb—called pie plant by lots of Vermont folk. Large pink stalks, tart and colorful.

This is a very favorite spring supper at Blueberry Hill. Mrs. John de Pompeo's lasagna, which is given here, is a beautiful Italian recipe given me by her husband, John, who cuts my hair at the New York Best's when I'm in that city. He's called Frank at Best's because there was another John there when he came to work. Frank-John and I talk about food a lot and he gave me his wife's recipe one day while

he was snipping my locks. I haven't changed it, not a word;
I think the directions are beautifully given and clear, and I
wouldn't do a thing to them to spoil them.

This is a meal with generous servings for 6 or even 8.

FENNEL AND BLACK OLIVES

In Vermont we can find fennel these days in supermarkets.
Called *finocchio,* in its true authenticity, it's a licorice-tasting
celery-like stalk; it looks rather like celery, too. Slice **1 large
stalk fennel** in thin slices on the diagonal. Trim off the leaves,
discarding the top, which is tough. Chill for several hours.
Drain **1 large can** very large **black olives** (about 2 cups) reserving ¼ cup of the liquid. Add to the liquid **½ cup imported olive oil** and **1 large clove garlic,** peeled and chopped.
Return olives and liquid to the can, cover with saran and
refrigerate for 2 hours. Shake olives around on occasion.
When ready to serve, arrange fennel on a flat, rather deep
platter, sprinkle with **salt** and **freshly ground pepper,** lift
olives out of can with spoon and arrange them here and there
on the fennel, dribbling a little of the liquid on the fennel in
the process. This is finger food. Whatever is left of the olives
can be kept in a glass jar in the marinade.

INGREDIENTS: 1 large stalk fennel; 1 large can large black
     olives (2 cups); ½ cup olive oil; 1 large clove garlic;
     salt; pepper.

MRS. JOHN DE POMPEO'S LASAGNA

A verbatim recipe. Several remarks by Elsie within the recipe
are in brackets.

"The most important single item for a good tasty pasta is
the sauce. Any pasta. So let's concentrate on *it.*

"Use a pot in which you can boil comfortably 3 pounds of
meat and 3 quarts of liquid.

"In bottom of pot, in **3 to 4 tablespoons olive oil,** brown 1
sliced medium onion, 1 clove garlic, chopped fine, **1 pound**

meaty **pork spareribs,** salted and peppered, **1 pound lamb neck or shank,** all fat possible removed, salted and peppered. [I have made this with 2 pounds of spareribs and eliminated the lamb; the sauce was wonderful that way, too.]

"When well browned, remove meat from pot temporarily. Now brown in fat that is left **1 pound chopped round steak,** broken in small bits. When this is well browned, put back in the pot the lamb and the spareribs and add **6 cans tomato sauce** [8 ounces each] and **equal parts of water.** Season with **2 teaspoons salt,** ½ **teaspoon pepper, 1 teaspoon chopped parsley, 1 teaspoon chopped basil.** Let simmer, uncovered, about 2 hours. Add boiling water if sauce gets too thick. Stir occasionally. [It should be a rather thin sauce, thinner than spaghetti sauce, for instance.]

"When sauce is done and before adding to the lasagna, skim some fat from the top if it appears to be too much. Remove spareribs and lamb. This may be or may not be served with the lasagna, as you please. [Succulent are these tidbits of meat and ribs.]

"While sauce is simmering, slice **1 pound Mozzarella cheese** in thin strips; mix **1 pound Ricotta** with **4 beaten eggs** in adequate dish; grate **1 cup Parmesan cheese** [or buy it grated, not as good]. Get everything ready for the preparation of the lasagna.

"Bring to boil **6 quarts water** in a large pot. Add to it **2 tablespoons salt** and **1 tablespoon olive oil.** [This will prevent lasagna from sticking.] Add **1 pound lasagna,** piece by piece, crisscrossing it, and let boil for 12 minutes. Stir with wooden ladle a few times. Blanch [rinse] with cold water. Drain.

"Now for baking. We use a 15 x 10 x 2½-inch casserole. Start by putting some sauce in bottom of casserole. Then arrange a layer of lasagna piece by piece, sprinkle some grated cheese, add Ricotta, Mozzarella strips, sauce. Continue until all lasagna is used. Arrange layers of lasagna crisscross, top with Ricotta, grated Parmesan cheese, and sauce.

"Cover casserole with heavy-strength aluminum foil. Bake for 30 minutes or so in moderate (325°F.) oven, until Mozzarella is melted. Serve hot. Makes 8 generous servings."

This really is a generous amount, but the lasagna reheats gorgeously, freezes without a murmur, and my suggestion is, if you don't think you want all this for one meal, arrange it in two smaller baking dishes, bake one and freeze one.

Also, please notice, after the lasagna has cooked for the 12 minutes directed, it will be very chewy. I'm sure you'll think it's underdone and will want to cook it longer, but it will soften in the baking process and the time is perfect as given in this recipe. This is, I assure you, a lasagna to end lasagnas.

INGREDIENTS: 3 to 4 tablespoons olive oil; 1 medium onion; 1 clove garlic; 1 pound meaty spareribs; 1 pound neck or shank of lamb; salt; pepper; 1 pound round steak; 6 cans (8 ounces each) tomato sauce; 6 cans water; 2 teaspoons salt; ½ teaspoon pepper; 1 teaspoon chopped parsley; 1 teaspoon chopped basil; 1 pound Mozzarella; 1 pound ricotta; 4 eggs; 1 cup grated Parmesan cheese; 6 quarts water; 2 tablespoons salt; 1 tablespoon olive oil; 1 pound lasagna.

ASPARAGUS OR FIDDLEHEADS
WITH BUTTERED CRUMBS

Asparagus, fresh picked this month, should have little if anything done to it. Crisscross **3 pounds asparagus** in your steamer but don't cook it until 5 minutes before you expect to serve dinner. Then, and only then, bring the water in the lower part of the steamer to a boil and proceed to steam them for 3 or 4 minutes or until they are just pierceable with a sharp-tined fork. Don't let them lose their bright green color. The nice thing about a steamer, rather than a pressure cooker, is that you can quite easily lift the lid and see what's going on.

Lift the asparagus from the steamer with a pair of tongs—an invaluable item of kitchen equipment—and set the spears on a hot platter, symmetrically lined up. Squeeze a few drops **lemon juice** on the asparagus, season with **salt** and **pepper** and pour over them buttered crumbs, fixed so: Heat a small

heavy skillet, preferably iron, and drop into it ¼ **cup butter.**
Let the butter sizzle and lightly brown; then drop into it ½
cup soft bread crumbs, no crusts. Let the bread crumbs
brown a bit.

If you are fortunate enough to be near a wooded area, as
we are, you will find, quite easily, the little **fiddleheads.** These
are ferns, all curled up, and, if picked before they mature,
they are delicious morsels, approximating asparagus in a way.
They are picked when they are between 6 and 8 inches tall;
you'd better get the countryfolk to show you which are the
right ferns to select, however. Serve them prepared exactly
as you would asparagus. They're delicious raw, too, in salad.
I have been able to buy them frozen in gourmet shops and
they're rather good that way too, but, to be honest, I don't
think they're worth hunting for in this form.

INGREDIENTS: 3 pounds fresh asparagus or fiddleheads; lemon
    juice; salt; pepper; ¼ cup butter; ½ cup bread crumbs.

DANDELION SALAD

The only dandelion greens you should eat are the first tiny,
tender shoots that sprout up around your lawn. Mature dandelion greens are bitter. If you are fortunate enough (or un-
fortunate enough, depending on whether you're a gardener
or a cook) to have a "mess" of these, which should be about
6 cups, dress them simply with an oil and vinegar dressing, as
follows: Dribble over the washed **tiny dandelion leaves, 3
tablespoons pure olive oil.** Toss lightly to distribute the oil
evenly, then add **1 tablespoon wine vinegar** and toss again.
Season with **salt,** freshly ground **pepper,** and ¼ **teaspoon
sugar.** Sprinkle with **1 chopped hard-cooked egg.**

Dandelion greens are very nice wilted, as in my recipe for
wilted lettuce in my *Blueberry Hill Cookbook.* In the absence
of dandelion greens, use new leaf lettuce or bibb lettuce.

INGREDIENTS: 6 cups dandelion greens (if unavailable, use
    lettuce); 3 tablespoons olive oil; 1 tablespoon wine vine-
    gar; salt; pepper; ¼ teaspoon sugar; 1 egg.

GARLIC BREAD

The only really proper accompaniment to an Italian main dish, we think. Slice a long loaf of **Italian or French bread** diagonally, not quite through, keeping the slices about 1½ inches apart. Soften **¼ pound** (1 stick) **butter**, squeeze **1 clove garlic** through a garlic press and work together with a butter knife. Spread both sides of the cut bread lavishly with the prepared butter. Place on open tray or cookie sheet and heat bread through, in a slow (325°F.) oven along with the lasagna. Serve in loaf, letting the family break off hunks as they wish.

INGREDIENTS: 1 long or 2 short loaves Italian or French bread; ¼ pound butter; 1 clove garlic.

BROILED FRESH PEACHES

The new peaches are in the market, up from Georgia. Peel and slice into halves and remove pits from **6 very ripe large freestone peaches.** Lay them on a buttered Pyrex or other pie plate, the right size just to hold them; sprinkle each half with **¼ teaspoon lemon juice** and **1 teaspoon light brown sugar.** Dot with **½ teaspoon butter** for each half. Bake in a slow (325°F.) oven 10 minutes or until rather soft, then broil under high heat for a few minutes to brown.

INGREDIENTS: 6 ripe large freestone peaches; 1 tablespoon lemon juice; ¼ cup light brown sugar; 2 tablespoons butter.

RHUBARB MERINGUE PIE

This is a well-known pie to my Vermont neighbors. We too love it dearly, particularly when it is made of freshly pulled pink "pieplant" rhubarb.

You will need an unbaked 10-inch pie shell. Use my recipe for this on page 287, unless you have some pastry on hand. Roll out the piecrust, fitting it on your 10-inch pie plate. Flute the edges and tuck a 2-inch-wide strip of aluminum foil over and under to keep the pastry from browning too much. There's no piecrust needed for a topping here, so if you have even a small amount of piecrust on hand, you can fix this pie without too much effort.

For the Filling: Place in a bowl 1½ to 2 cups granulated sugar, ¼ cup flour, 3 cups cubed unpeeled rhubarb (trim away the tough root end), ½ teaspoon grated orange peel, and 4 unbeaten egg yolks. The amount of sugar will depend on the tartness of the rhubarb. Start with the smaller amount, taste when partly baked and add more, if needed, then.

When the fruit is well coated with the other ingredients, place it in the prepared pie shell. Bake in a 425°F. oven for 10 minutes, then turn heat down to 325°F. Bake until the fruit bubbles all over, from 30 to 40 minutes. Remove the pie from the oven, allowing it to cool a little, while you prepare the meringue.

For the Meringue: Beat 4 egg whites until they will hold a peak without effort and, adding very little at a time, stir in gradually ½ cup sugar. Don't beat the sugar in; it will melt and the meringue will lose its body. Just stir the sugar in slowly; as soon as it's combined with the egg whites, stop. Pile meringue on the pie, very unevenly, being sure that it touches the edges of the pie shell. If it doesn't, it will shrink. Place in oven for 10 to 15 minutes at 350°F., or until the peaks are light brown.

INGREDIENTS: Unbaked 10-inch pie shell; 1½ to 2 cups granulated sugar; ¼ cup flour; 3 cups cubed unpeeled rhubarb; ½ teaspoon grated orange peel; 4 egg yolks. *For the meringue:* 4 egg whites; ½ cup sugar.

TIMETABLE: Fix the sauce for the lasagna in the morning, or, if you prefer, the day before. If you wish, prepare it at your leisure and freeze it. Defrost over direct heat. In any case, the lasagna itself can be boiled in the morning, or, again, even the day before. It can be kept wrapped in saran in the refrigerator; a sheet of saran between layers of it will make it easy to handle whenever you need it. I have frequently used lasagna that has been refrigerated for 4 or 5 days before adding the sauce and the component parts. It shows no deterioration in this period of time. Also in the morning, grate the Parmesan cheese and get together all the other lasagna ingredients, ready to put it together. The fennel and olives, too, are either a morning or an early afternoon job. Wash the dandelion leaves at the same time.

Late in the afternoon, make up the lasagna. Cover with foil. Clean the asparagus; leave it in the steamer. Prepare the bread crumbs; leave them in a plate nearby. Fix the garlic butter; prepare the pie shell, or, if you have some piecrust on hand, roll it out. Combine the rhubarb and sugar mix.

Forty minutes before dinner, fill the pie shell with the rhubarb and set this in the oven at 425°F. After 10 minutes, reduce the heat to 325°F. and place the lasagna in the oven with the pie. Peel the peaches, prepare them, and, within 15 minutes, place them in the oven with the lasagna and the pie. Set the garlic bread in the oven, too. Get out the ingredients for the salad dressing. Beat the egg whites and prepare the meringue.

Now remove the peaches; they should go under the broiler for a minute. Toss your salad. Let the family, meanwhile, munch on the fennel and the olives. Take the lasagna and the bread out of the oven. Pile the meringue on the pie. Return pie to oven, now raised to 350°F. Start the asparagus steaming. Sauté the bread crumbs.

Everything ought to be just fine, now. The lasagna, the bread, the asparagus with its bread-crumb topping, all ready. The salad should be passed. The peaches are ready to be served, alongside the lasagna. Serve more fennel and olives, if you'd like. Remove the pie from the oven, all fluffy and lightly browned.

Join the family for dinner. The pie will be just right, still warm, when you're ready for it.

LEFTOVERS

The fennel will stay crisp and delicious for several days, kept in a plastic bag or wrapped in saran. It can be used in a chicken or crabmeat salad, much as celery is used; its elusive anise-like taste makes a conversation piece. If you have any of the feathery leaves, they can be added to omelettes or tomato juice for some more of the same attractive flavor. You'll find many uses for fennel, once you're accustomed to having it in your vicinity. As a last resort, use it in a flower arrangement; might win a prize at the next meeting of your garden club.

The lasagna reheats perfectly. Rearrange it in a fresh baking dish, lay a few strips of Mozzarella cheese across the top, recover with foil, and reheat till it's bubbly. For the second serving, serve the spareribs and/or lamb which were used in the original sauce. A fine way of handling these is to heat them in the oven with the leftover lasagna, the meat in a dish of its own, well covered with sauce. The ribs, particularly, are great; they deserve a meal of their own. If you have just a little lasagna left, tuck the lasagna in the sauce around the meat.

If you are out of sauce, place the spareribs and the lamb on a broiling rack and quickly heat them under the broiler; there will be enough of the sauce adhering to them to keep them moist.

If you have a bit of asparagus around, after the lasagna is fully reheated, set the leftover asparagus on top of it, cover with the foil again, allow to heat another 5 minutes, remove the foil, sprinkle the asparagus with Parmesan cheese and run it under the broiler just to melt and brown the cheese. Serve.

If you've prepared the dandelion greens with the oil and vinegar and have quite a bit of it left, sauté a few slices of lean bacon, drain off most of the fat when the bacon is crisp, remove the bacon too, and add the greens to the frying pan. Shake the pan over a moderate heat, turn the leaves over, and reseason, if necessary—you'll probably like a little more pepper. Serve as a hot vegetable, the crisp bacon crumbled over the top.

Garlic bread, in our house, is placed in a plastic bag, frozen, and, when called for, reheated in a hot oven, each slice of bread out flat on a pan. More toast than bread, this way, but as delicious as on the day it was prepared.

Whatever leftover peaches might be about should be poached in a small quantity of whatever wine you have on hand; just long enough to heat through. Drop in a clove or two, whole, that is, and serve with a large spoonful of commercial sour cream.

The pie is simply marvelous right out of the refrigerator until its very end. The meringue part doesn't freeze, but, given more than you can handle in the way of leftover pie, I will suggest that you scoop off the meringue and freeze the rest of the pie. Then, when you're after the pie again, there's nothing to prevent you from whipping a bit of heavy cream, adding a little sugar and some cognac, perhaps, or some sauterne, defrosting the pie, adding the whipped cream and enjoying same.

JUNE

CAVIAR MOUSSE
CHINESE STEAMED LOBSTERS
BAKED STEAK
MUSHROOM AND BARLEY CASSEROLE
GREEN BEANS, GREEN ONIONS
ARTICHOKE HEARTS IN WINE
TINY BEETS A L'ORANGE
CHINESE CABBAGE SALAD
APRICOT LOAF
OLD-FASHIONED STRAWBERRY SHORTCAKE

 June's the time for outdoor din-
ing and for taking care of your
winter's dinner obligations, both
at a swoop. I refuse to say a fell
swoop. I would not recommend this meal for a barbecue or
a picnic; still it's a perfect rather formal, yet casual, meal
alfresco. If you have a patio or an outdoor porch, closely
aligned to your kitchen area, this is the meal to serve there.
If not, keep it indoors. It is a meal to be eaten at table, not
on a lap, so, should you decide on a buffet, have small tables
for your guests to settle around with laden plates.

Everything in the dinner is worth your doing, if not all

136

on the same night as I have done here, certainly some time. I will recommend, far beyond the usual, both the caviar mousse and the strawberry shortcake. Dinner here for 12.

CAVIAR MOUSSE

This is one of the most successful and attractive appetizers we've ever served at Blueberry Hill. It's simple beyond words to prepare; it's stunning to view. You will have your reputation made for you if you will serve this mousse (which is actually a loaf and a spread) at your next party. Whatever is not eaten will keep, covered with saran, for several days in your refrigerator. It will also keep well in the freezer; give it several hours to defrost at room temperature before serving.

You will need a blender to do this; I don't think you can manage without one, here. Melt ¼ **pound** (1 stick) **fresh, preferably unsalted, butter** and pour it into a blender. Add, in about three stages, **2 7-ounce cans water-packed white tuna fish,** the best quality you can find, drained, and blend with the butter until it is the consistency of a paste. Turn off the blender, now and then, to scrape down the sides.

Add, all at once, **1 teaspoon chopped green-onion tops** (these can be the tops of any onions that have sprouted, or can be scallion tops); **1 jar** (6 ounces) **herring tidbits in wine,** drained; **1 heaping teaspoon black caviar** (which can be imported caviar, but this dish is nearly as good with the much less expensive lumpfish caviar; you'll want 4 ounces in all); ¼ **teaspoon garlic powder** (not salt); ½ **teaspoon sugar.** Continue to blend until there are no perceptible lumps. It should now be of the consistency and texture of whipped cream.

Pack the paste into a buttered 1-pint mold (a small bread pan is perfect for this) and refrigerate. It will quickly resume the consistency of the butter it began life as, which is what you want.

When ready to serve, or anyway within an hour of serving time, turn out the mold by running a knife dipped in hot water around the edges, letting it settle on a wood bread board.

NOTE: A few strips of waxed paper laid across the mold in both directions before you pack in the paste will make it a little easier for you to get the mousse out in good shape. However, even if it breaks a little, coming out, don't be concerned; just shape it back with a butter knife.

Spread the *sides* only (of the mold, of course) with the remains of the jar of black caviar. It will just make it. Spread the *top* of the loaf with the contents of a **4-ounce jar of red caviar,** drained for 5 minutes to remove excess liquid (salmon or whitefish caviar is fine). It will be a thing of singular beauty. Shiny black all around. Glistening red on top. Surround with small pumpernickl bread or rye bread rounds. Let your guests spread their own canapés.

INGREDIENTS: ¼ pound butter, unsalted preferably; 2 cans (7 ounces each) water-packed white tuna; 1 teaspoon chopped green onion tops; 1 jar (6 ounces) herring tidbits in wine; 1 jar (4 ounces) black caviar; ¼ teaspoon garlic powder; ½ teaspoon sugar; 1 jar (4 ounces) red caviar.

CHINESE STEAMED LOBSTERS

Lobsters, you know, should be cooked alive. You can tell if a lobster is alive when you get it home, if its tail is tucked under. If you pull it out straight, the tail of a live lobster will pop back under. No matter how many times you pull it out, it will spring back.

For this recipe you should have a steamer large enough to hold 6 small lobsters. This will provide a half lobster for each person and, in light of the size of the meal, this will be enough. If you wish to make the lobster the main deal here, increase all proportions.

I have a steamer, a large vessel, which is actually made to steam clams. The lower part of it which contains the water which steams the clams or lobsters just above (the upper section has holes) will catch the clam or lobster juices as the crustaceans steam; there's a faucet so that you can draw off this rich liquid to drink as broth or to use in a chowder later.

If you haven't something of this sort, use a large vessel such as a roasting pan and set a rack in the bottom. Raise the rack about two inches, resting it on wood sticks, and fill the bottom of the pot with about an inch of water.

Have 6 small lobsters (1 to 1½ pounds each) split, alive, at the market. This is a feat I have never wanted to try at home, myself, but you may know some intrepid soul of adventurous spirit who is willing to do it. I won't bother to tell you how— I'm just going to assume you will have it done at the market. Have the claws cracked too. Keep the lobsters refrigerated, preferably wrapped in seaweed, until you're ready for them.

Place the halved lobsters in the upper part of your steamer or on the rack in your homemade device, cut side up. Mix together in a bowl ½ cup soy sauce, ¼ cup sherry, 1 tablespoon sugar, a few grinds of black pepper, ¼ cup chopped green onion tops, 1 clove garlic, peeled and finely chopped. Pour this carefully over the lobsters, dividing it evenly among them.

Cover the steamer tightly, bring the water in the bottom to boil (you'll hear it) and steam 5 to 10 minutes only. Open the steamer after five minutes, cut into one of the meatier parts of the lobster meat and, if it is white and thoroughly cooked, remove them all and serve them. If it isn't, let the steaming continue, but in no event should it take more than 10 minutes in all. One of the great troubles with lobster is that it is often overcooked and dry. If you will watch carefully, these lobsters will be *just* done—no more than that— and at their perfection point. They will need no further sauce. You can, if you wish, melt some butter, squeeze a little lemon into it and have it handy for those who insist on it.

INGREDIENTS: 6 small lobsters (1 to 1½ pounds each); ½ cup soy sauce; ¼ cup sherry; 1 tablespoon sugar; pepper; ¼ cup chopped green-onion tops; 1 clove garlic.

BAKED STEAK

For this very lush main dish, you should order a **sirloin steak** of the best quality. Have it cut three inches thick from the top section of the sirloin. It will weigh about 8 pounds. Early in the day, sprinkle both sides of the steak with **salt** and freshly ground **pepper**, and spread both sides with 1½ teaspoons **dry mustard**, combined with 1½ teaspoons **Worcestershire sauce** (a tablespoon in all). Set the steak on a rack in a roasting pan with the fat side up, and now spread the top thickly with **chili sauce**, using about ½ **cup**, or more if you need it. Slice **1 lemon** in thin slices and arrange on the chili sauce. Then in the spaces you have left, set thin slices of **1 small onion**, peeled. Dust lightly with **imported Hungarian paprika**. Marinate in the refrigerator for at least 2 hours; won't hurt it to marinate longer than that.

Bake at 375°F. for 2 hours for a rare steak. Check with your oven thermometer; it should read a little below 140°F. in the center of the steak. Just before serving, dot with butter, letting the butter melt and join the other juices. Slice with the grain, ¼ inch thick, ladling some of the juice over the meat on each plate.

INGREDIENTS: 8-pound top sirloin steak, 3 inches thick; salt; pepper; 1½ teaspoons dry mustard; 1½ teaspoons Worcestershire sauce; ½ cup chili sauce (or more, if needed); 1 lemon; 1 small onion; Hungarian paprika.

MUSHROOM AND BARLEY CASSEROLE

Heat a heavy kettle, such as a Dutch oven, and, when a drop of water will sizzle, add **1 tablespoon butter** or margarine. Let that melt, start to brown, and add **2 cups washed pearl barley**. For this recipe, the regular barley, not the quick-cooking, gives you a better result. The quick-cooking barley, however, may be used, thus cutting down the cooking time. As soon as the barley is a little brown, pour over it **2 quarts chicken, lamb, or turkey broth**. This should be, preferably, homemade and consequently rich in flavor (see page 13) but canned broth will do. In the absence of any broth, this can be made with water, **boiling** when you add it, with the addition of 1 teaspoon salt.

Boil until the barley is cooked through but still crunchy to the teeth; something like the *al dente* spaghetti. This will take 30 to 40 minutes unless you've used the quick-cooking type. The broth or water should be cooked away. If it evaporates before the barley is done, add a little more liquid and continue cooking. Taste for seasoning. You will need **salt** and **pepper** in quantities depending on the flavor of the original broth. Might not need any. Taste and you'll find out what to do.

Turn the barley into a 2-quart casserole and stir it around with 1 tablespoon sugar, 1 tablespoon butter, ¼ teaspoon **garlic powder**, 2 **teaspoons chopped parsley**, 1 **teaspoon chopped chives** (or tops of green onions), and 1 **cup fresh mushrooms**, sliced and sautéed for one minute only in 1 **teaspoon butter**.

This much may be prepared in the morning or the day before. Keep it refrigerated in the casserole and, 45 minutes before serving time, place it, uncovered, in the oven. It will heat through in this time in a 325°F. to 350°F. oven; it will take only 10 minutes in a hot oven.

INGREDIENTS: 1 tablespoon butter or margarine; 2 cups pearl barley; 2 quarts chicken, lamb, or turkey broth (or water with 1 teaspoon salt); salt; pepper; 1 tablespoon sugar; 1 tablespoon butter; ¼ teaspoon garlic powder; 2 teaspoons parsley; 1 teaspoon chopped chives; 1 cup fresh mushrooms; 1 teaspoon butter.

GREEN BEANS, GREEN ONIONS

Another quick and easy recipe. Snip off the ends of **4 pounds tiny whole new green beans,** the more recently removed from your garden the better. (Warning: don't pick them on a rainy day or while they're still wet with dew.) Steam them over boiling water in your Bungalow Cooker or boil them (if you must!) in very little water in a heavy pot with a cover. Season with ½ teaspoon salt, or more to taste. They must be steamed only until they are tender, and, if they're new to the world, this will take a very short time. So watch your pot, poke a fork in the beans after 7 or 8 minutes, and, the moment they are tender, remove them with a slotted spoon to a serving casserole. Note that they are still bright green. If you overcook them, they lose the vibrant green which lends so much to your color scheme in the serving, not to speak of their flavor. Snip over them the tops of 4 or 5 green onions, also freshly pulled from the ground, washed and trimmed. Brown lightly ¼ cup (½ stick) butter. Take it easy, just heat the butter slowly and watch it melt, bubble, sizzle, and then brown. Remove it from the heat before the next step, which would be burned butter, a doleful sight. Pour butter over the beans and onion tops, toss, taste, and serve.

If you have no garden, or if you're out of the bean season when you do this recipe, use 5 boxes of frozen green beans; handle them the same way. No green onions? Use the tops of a grown-out onion (these we have with us always!)

INGREDIENTS: 4 pounds tiny whole green beans (or 5 boxes frozen whole green beans or Frenched green beans); 1 cup water (if boiling beans); ½ teaspoon salt; 4 or 5 green-onion tops; ¼ cup butter.

ARTICHOKE HEARTS IN WINE

An extra. In a heavy saucepan, combine and bring to a boil 1 small white onion, minced very fine; 1 clove garlic, peeled and split; 2 cups dry sauterne or other white wine; 1 tablespoon salt. Allow this to simmer until it is reduced to one-half. Remove garlic, add 4 packages artichoke hearts, frozen and still unthawed, and ¼ cup butter (½ stick). Simmer another 5 minutes or until the artichokes are completely thawed and heated through. Squeeze the juice of ½ lemon over all. Baste with butter-wine sauce. Serve.

INGREDIENTS: 1 small white onion; 1 clove garlic; 2 cups dry
    sauterne or other dry white wine; 1 tablespoon salt; 4
    packages frozen artichoke hearts; ¼ cup butter; ½
    lemon.

TINY BEETS A L'ORANGE

Try to purchase the smallest size canned beets you can find.
It's a bit early for your own beets, but if you have those, cook
them in their skins, slip the skins off, and proceed as directed
here. To return to the canned variety, the tiny beets are a
little more expensive than the regular beets, but they are
worth the extra cost. Drain **4 cans** (1 pound each) **tiny whole
beets**. Place in a heavy saucepan with **¼ pound** (1 stick)
butter. Heat, shaking pan so that the beets are covered on
all sides by the butter. With a sharp knife, peel **1 California
navel orange**, discarding as much of the white as possible.
Sliver the peel, cover it with boiling water, allow it to boil for
2 minutes, drain it, and add it to the beets with **1 tablespoon
light brown sugar**. Cut the orange segments inside the membrane, drop them in at the last minute and heat just hot so
that they don't lose their shape. Serve.

INGREDIENTS: 4 cans (1 pound each) tiny whole beets; ¼
    pound butter; 1 California navel orange; 1 tablespoon
    light brown sugar.

CHINESE CABBAGE SALAD

Wash **1 large head or 2 small heads Chinese cabbage** by
holding it under cold water, spreading apart its leaves, and
rinsing out any dirt that you can see. Usually it's fairly clean
and needs little of this sort of attention.

Arrange thin (1½ inch thick) rounds of **Chinese cabbage**
on a large platter, allowing one or two small rounds for each
person. Mix together in a bowl **1 cup fine quality mayonnaise,
½ cup commercial sour cream, 1 tablespoon chili sauce, 1
teaspoon finely minced onion** or **chives, 1 teaspoon creamed**

horseradish. Just before serving, place 1 large spoonful of the dressing on each round of Chinese cabbage. Serve.

INGREDIENTS: 1 large head or 2 small heads Chinese cabbage; 1 cup fine quality mayonnaise; ½ cup commercial sour cream; 1 tablespoon chili sauce; 1 teaspoon finely minced onions or chives; 1 teaspoon creamed horseradish.

APRICOT LOAF

A nice, rather tart bread, quickly made. Add 1½ **cups cold water** to 1½ **cups dried apricots,** finely cut. Kitchen shears do this. Heat just to boiling, remove from heat, add **2 tablespoons lemon juice** and cool to room temperature.

Sift together **6 cups flour, 1½ teaspoons baking soda, 1 teaspoon salt.** With your electric beater, cream at high speed until very smooth ½ cup (1 stick) **margarine** and **1 cup sugar.** Add **2 eggs,** slightly beaten, and the apricots with their juice. Mix all together well.

Fill 4 small or 2 regular-sized greased and floured bread pans. Bake in 350°F. oven for 1 hour, or until the breads test done with a skewer; in dry, out dry. Done. This bread slices better the second day; rather convenient of it. It also freezes well. Defrost it from the frozen state in slow oven for 10 or 15 minutes until it is good and hot. Like new.

INGREDIENTS: 1½ cups cold water; 1½ cups dried apricots; 2 tablespoons lemon juice; 6 cups flour; 1½ teaspoons baking soda; 1 teaspoon salt; ½ cup margarine; 1 cup sugar; 2 eggs.

OLD-FASHIONED STRAWBERRY SHORTCAKE

A dramatic sight, perfectly flavored. Wash and hull **3 quarts berries.** Leave some whole (the nicest ones), cut some in halves, crush the rest. There are always some berries in each basket that are cut out for crushing (just like some people, unfortunately). Add sugar to your taste. The best way to do this is to sprinkle the crushed ones with a few tablespoons of sugar, let it settle awhile, taste them, and add more sugar if you think you need it. Berries vary so, it's difficult to give you a precise amount of sugar. The whole berries need only a thorough sprinkling. Do all this an hour or more before dinner.

The shortcake itself should not go into the oven until your guests have started their appetizers. It takes about 25 minutes to bake and is at its perfect best if it is brought directly from the oven to the table, steaming hot.

However, you can have all the ingredients ready to combine well ahead of time so that all you need to do, the last thing before your guests arrive, is to roll it out, pat it into shape, and then, the right moment having arrived, get it in the oven.

For the Shortcake: Sift **4 cups flour, 2 tablespoons baking powder, 2 teaspoons salt, ¼ cup sugar.** Cut in **¼ pound (1 stick) butter and 2 tablespoons margarine.** Stir in **1½ cups light cream** to make a soft dough. You may not need quite this much, so don't add it all at once. As soon as it can be managed with floured hands and seems pliable and smooth, stop adding the cream. You may need no more than 1¼ cups. Turn the dough out on a floured board, slice it in half with a floured knife, and roll out each half to fit your pan.

The best size and shape for this is a 13 x 9 x 2-inch baking pan, well buttered. Set the first half of the dough into this, pat it into place in the corners, and, using a pastry brush, spread the top of it lavishly with **melted butter;** about **1 tablespoon** or more will probably do it. Then roll the second piece and set it directly on top of the first. This arrangement will make it possible for you to lift the top of the shortcake off the bottom when you want to fill it, as you will later.

Bake the shortcake in a hot (450°F.) oven for 25 to 30 minutes, or until it is nicely browned and done through. Test this by lifting a small corner of it and looking; the center should be thoroughly baked. If it isn't, set it back in the oven for 5 or 10 minutes. Remove the shortcake to a large serving platter that will accommodate it—a bread board is fine. You'll have to do this with two pancake turners. If you have one of those large oven shovels, it's great for this job, because this is very short shortcake, particularly delicate when it's still warm. Now lift off the top layer of biscuit— you'll have to poke at it and pry it up with your shovel or two pancake turners. Set it down carefully nearby, and fill the lower part of the shortcake with the crushed berries, which by this time are very juicy. Replace the top, putting it back the way you got it off. Don't worry if it breaks, just piece it together. No one will tell in the end. Now, using the halved berries, arrange the fruit on top of the shortcake. Top with 1 **pint heavy cream, whipped,** to which you have added **1 teaspoon superfine sugar** and **½ teaspoon pure vanilla or almond extract.** Arrange the whole berries symmetrically over the whipped cream.

This should definitely be served under the eyes of the guests. Set the bread board with the shortcake on another larger tray, so that it won't dribble on your tablecloth, and cut large squares of the shortcake. The best dish for this is a rather deep one.

INGREDIENTS: 3 quarts fresh strawberries; 1 pint heavy cream; 1 teaspoon superfine sugar; ½ teaspoon vanilla or almond.

For the shortcake: 4 cups flour; 2 tablespoons baking powder; 2 teaspoons salt; ¼ cup sugar; ¼ pound and 1 tablespoon butter; 2 tablespoons margarine; 1¼ to 1½ cups light cream.

TIMETABLE: Prepare the caviar mousse the day before you need it, all except the trimming of it. Be sure to butter your mold, add the waxed paper for insurance and, if the mold is nicely hardened, it will fall out as you want it.

The rest of the meal should probably be done the day of your party. Nothing complicated needs preparation, so, if you know what you're about, and get at it with dispatch, you'll have time and to spare.

The morning of the party, combine the sauce for the lobsters. The lobsters themselves should be prepared at the market and delivered early in the day; keep them in seaweed; they'll be content in your refrigerator. You might as well fill the bottom of the steamer with water as directed, when the lobsters arrive. Keep the soy sauce mix in a bowl nearby.

Also the morning of the party, bake the apricot loaves. Nothing nicer than to have the baking out of the way early. As mentioned before, they can be done the day before, if you'd prefer. They will reheat beautifully later, in the pans in which they were baked. Wash the Chinese cabbage. Slice it, set it on its platter, cover it with saran, and refrigerate. Prepare the dressing now; refrigerate it, too.

In the early afternoon marinate the steak and prepare the mushroom and barley casserole for the oven. As I mentioned before, you can do this as early as the day before your party. Now prepare the beans. No preparation needed, if they're frozen. Snip the green onions; leave them, wrapped in a bit of waxed paper or saran, near the beans. Set the butter to be browned in a small saucepan, nearby. *That's* ready.

Prepare the tiny beets up to the final heating.

Two hours before dinner set the steak in the oven. You'll have to check the temperature of the beef later, but that's all the trouble it will cause you.

Take the mousse from its mold now, set the red caviar in a sieve to drain, then decorate the loaf. Set it on a board, surround it with rye-bread rounds, lightly cover it with saran— hold the saran away from the caviar with toothpicks, strategically placed. Refrigerate it. The saran will keep the bread from getting stale.

Prepare the fruit for the shortcake. Combine the dry ingredients with the shortening; measure out the cream; grease the baking pan.

You should have plenty of time now to set the table, arrange the flowers, have a cup of tea. Maybe you won't, but you should have.

Half an hour before your guests are due, place the mushroom and barley casserole in the oven with the steak. Combine the artichoke recipe as given. You could do this earlier, but it's better not to have the artichokes defrost too long before they are cooked and the recipe is a snap; if you worry about things like this, however, combine everything but the artichokes, ahead of time. Add them now.

Combine the shortcake ingredients, already prepared, with the light cream. Roll out the dough, place it in the prepared baking pan. Whip the cream for the shortcake, add the vanilla, the sugar, and refrigerate.

Look at the steak. If it has reached a temperature of a little under 140°F., remove it from the oven and set it in a warm spot until ready to serve. If it hasn't, let it continue baking.

Your guests, I assume, have assembled. Remove the saran from the mousse, stick a few little butter spreaders around the edges and set this before them. Wait for the hosannahs; they'll come. Then, while your friends are settling down to the delectable mousse, you must return to the kitchen.

Set the lobsters in the steamer. Pour the sauce over them. Steam them. Steam the beans. Brown the butter. Heat the beets. Heat the artichokes. As you can see, it's a mere matter of heating one thing after the other. Not so hard. If you run out of space on top of your range, leave the butter for the last and do that quickly. If you still have not enough top burners, either the beets or the artichokes can be heated first, removed to a casserole, and kept warm in the oven while you're getting the other things ready. Take the mushroom and barley casserole from the oven and keep it warm.

Reheat the apricot loaves in the oven with, or without, the steak—depending on whether or not it's been removed. Set out the salad, add the dressing. Set out the lobsters, the steak, sliced, the mushrooms and barley, the beans, the beets, the artichokes, and call your guests.

Last of all, while your guests are being served, place the shortcake in the oven. Set the timer for 25 minutes, join your friends and have your own dinner. When the timer rings, which should be just when you want it to, excuse yourself, get the cake out of the oven, do as you've been told with the strawberries and the whipped cream, and by the time everyone has been served with coffee, you'll be able to show them the most beautiful strawberry shortcake they've perhaps ever seen.

LEFTOVERS

The caviar mousse retains its perfection of flavor, if not of appearance, until you've eaten the last of it; within limits, of course; I wouldn't push it too far. Several days is about right in the refrigerator. After that, freeze it. A good way is to slice it first and freeze the separate slices. Then when you want just a little, you have no need to defrost more than that. The mousse makes quite a wonderful sandwich late at night between two slices of black, black pumpernickl bread. Lots of butter on this, and a sweet onion.

As to the lobster, should you have any of the meat left, pick it out and refrigerate it. It is a great thing to have about for an omelette.

Lobster Filling for Omelette

A particularly excellent filling is made by heating a black iron frying pan, then sizzling in it **2 tablespoons butter**. Add the **lobster pieces**—you ought to have about ¾ cup at least; probably if you have any lobster left at all, it will be claw meat which will not have absorbed the soy sauce and sherry. This being so, season the lobster with a little **salt**, perhaps ¼ **teaspoon**, a few grinds of fresh black **pepper** from a mill, ½ **teaspoon flour**, and stir it all around. If you have lobster that does have the soy sauce mix on it, omit the salt. When the lobster is hot (don't cook it, just heat it), stir into it **3 tablespoons light cream** and **1 tablespoon cocktail sherry**. Allow this to combine and heat for just a moment or two. Use this as a filling for a 4-egg omelette. There's a good one given in my *Blueberry Hill Cookbook*.

INGREDIENTS: 2 tablespoons butter; leftover lobster pieces; ¼ teaspoon salt; pepper; ½ teaspoon flour; 3 tablespoons light cream; 1 tablespoon cocktail sherry.

Chafing Dish Lobster

Melt ¼ cup (½ stick) **butter;** add **½ pound sharp cheddar cheese,** grated or cut up into little bits, and **a few dashes Worcestershire sauce.** When the butter and the cheese are well combined, add **3 tablespoons fine light rum.** Heat thoroughly, stir in the **lobster meat** you have left (1½ cups is about right for this recipe), heat for another minute. Serve over heated leftover green beans on grilled bread (see page 43).

INGREDIENTS: ¼ cup butter; ½ pound sharp cheddar cheese; Worcestershire sauce; 3 tablespoons fine light rum; 1½ cups leftover lobster meat.

For either of the recipes just given, should you not have enough lobster, don't hesitate to add the contents of a can of crabmeat, deboned first.

Chinese Lobster

Should you chance to have **1 cup or more of the lobster meat** which *was* inundated with soy sauce, make this recipe. Add to the lobster **½ cup of the broth** left in the bottom of the steamer; **1 can Chinese mixed vegetables,** drained thoroughly; and **1 can bean sprouts,** drained equally well. Simmer the mixture for 2 minutes, add **1 tablespoon Chinese bead molasses** (called "brown sauce" in some supermarkets), **½ tablespoon soy sauce, ½ teaspoon dry mustard, 1 teaspoon sugar.** Thicken with **1 teaspoon arrowroot** or **cornstarch** stirred into **½ cup cold water.** Taste for seasoning and add if needed. Shred some Chinese cabbage, ladle hot Chinese lobster over it, and sprinkle a few canned Chinese noodles over the top. This will serve 3 or 4 nicely. Rice, plain rice, would be nice, too.

INGREDIENTS: 1 cup or more leftover lobster meat; ½ cup leftover broth; 1 can Chinese mixed vegetables; 1 can bean sprouts; 1 tablespoon Chinese bead molasses; ½

tablespoon soy sauce; ½ teaspoon dry mustard; 1 teaspoon sugar; 1 teaspoon arrowroot or cornstarch; ½ cup
cold water.

Chill the leftover artichoke hearts, adding 1 tablespoon olive
oil to them and the sauce. Serve with sliced sweet Bermuda
onions and fresh tomatoes on a bed of whatever Chinese
cabbage is about. This time, shred the cabbage very fine.
Makes a nice salad. If you haven't any of the sauterne sauce,
simply marinate the artichoke hearts in a good quality Italian
dressing; proceed from there.

Chop the leftover beets, add a little frozen concentrated
orange juice, a little chopped onion, a bit of sugar, and
reheat. Press a hard-cooked egg, yolk and white, over the
top. Makes another vegetable of it.

There are many leftover possibilities for the baked steak,
but one of the best is the following.

Beef Bordelaise

Heat a black iron frying pan, sizzle in it **1 tablespoon butter,**
and lightly brown **1 medium onion,** chopped. Add **¼ teaspoon salt,** a dash of freshly ground **pepper;** push onions to
one side and quickly sauté **thin beef slices** until they are
lightly browned on both sides. Remove beef from the pan,
keep it warm on a platter, and, to the pan juices add **¼ cup
beef broth** (homemade, if you can manage it; just use the
bony part of the sirloin, boiled an hour or so with an onion
and salt and pepper); **⅓ cup dry white wine; 1 clove garlic,**
mashed through a garlic press; **1 tablespoon chopped parsley;**
and **1 chopped shallot** (optional, mostly because they're
hard to find). Simmer all together until the sauce has cooked
down about one third and has slightly thickened, a matter of
less than 10 minutes. Add **1 tablespoon butter,** let this melt
into the sauce, and pour it over the beef slices. This sauce
should not be more than just a little thickened. If you like
a thick sauce, stir **2 teaspoons potato starch** or **arrowroot** in a
little water, and add. Let it boil up; it will thicken. Try **this**

without the thickening the first time; I'm sure you'll find it suits you.

INGREDIENTS: 2 tablespoons butter; 1 medium onion; ¼ teaspoon salt; pepper; thin slices leftover beef; ¼ cup beef broth; ⅓ cup dry white wine; 1 clove garlic; 1 tablespoon chopped parsley; 1 chopped shallot (optional); 2 teaspoons potato starch or arrowroot (optional).

Here is another very popular leftover dish, particularly with my youngsters:

Yesterday's Chinese Beef

For 4 people, heat **2 cups beef squares** in whatever **juices** you have around. In the absence of juice, heat them in **butter.** When the beef is hot, stir in **1 cup cooked fine noodles** (obviously this is a good thing to have when you're trying to get rid of some cooked fine noodles, too; cook some fresh if you have to, however; that's a 2-minute job); **¼ cup pecans,** chopped or whole; **2 tablespoons soy sauce;** and **2 tablespoons sugar.** You can always add mixed Chinese vegetables and/or bean sprouts to any of these Chinese recipes, but be sure to drain them dry as the liquid in them will dilute your sauce. Heat quickly, stirring around until everything is hot. Serve, accompanied by a small amount of Chinese mustard— which is dry mustard, thinned down with cold water. It's very hot, so be careful.

INGREDIENTS: 2 cups leftover beef squares; beef juices or butter; 1 cup cooked fine noodles; ¼ cup pecans; 2 tablespoons soy sauce; 2 tablespoons sugar.

If it happens that you have a sizable chunk of the steak left over, you will have a quite superlative pot roast type meal of it, if you will follow this advice.

Pot Roast

Use a heavy pot with a lid, of the proper size for the piece of steak you have on hand. Sauté in this pot **2 or 3 onions,** thinly sliced, in **1 tablespoon butter** until they are golden. Lift out the onion with a slotted spoon, sprinkle your **left-over steak** with **salt, pepper,** and enough **flour** to show and lightly brown the unbrowned cut edge or edges of the steak in the sizzling butter. Then lay the steak out flat, spread the onions over the top of it, add **½ cup red wine**—I use Burgundy, but any dry red wine would do the same. Cover tightly and let it simmer for 15 minutes. Turn once. The flour will thicken the gravy. Add, to your taste, a bit of **sugar, a** bit of **garlic powder.** Serve, sliced, with the gravy and onions, accompanied by buttered wide noodles.

INGREDIENTS: 2 or 3 onions; 1 tablespoon butter; leftover baked steak (at least 1½ pounds); salt; pepper; flour; ½ cup red wine; sugar; garlic powder.

Left Bank Soup

The scraps of steak combined with the barley and mushrooms casserole makes a most excellent beginning for a soup that you will relish, I'm sure. Use the scraps of beef that you have around and prepare from them a strong broth. This is done by adding the **beef** and the **bones** to enough **cold water** to cover, about a quart, and simmering it with **1 large onion,** peeled and quartered; **4 medium carrots,** peeled—they may be cut up or not, doesn't matter; **1 small purple-top turnip,** also peeled and cut up (a white turnip with a purple top supplies an incredible sweetness to soups and stews of any sort); **1 cup celery tops; 1 bay leaf; salt** (start with 1 teaspoon, and taste); **3 or 4 peppercorns.** Let this all bubble away merrily at a moderate pace for at least 2 hours—3 is better—and, if you can think of anything else to add, do so. It should be rich and full of flavor before you add the barley; if it isn't, add a little consommé, but I don't think you'll need to. Taste and decide. Now strain the broth if you prefer—I like all those things in there—and add whatever **mushrooms** and **barley** you have left from the casserole; you can add the leftover **asparagus** and the leftover **carrots;** they'll all go fine. The more the merrier.

Now that everything's in, simmer the soup for 10 minutes, then turn off the heat under it and let it rest in the rear of your stove overnight; if it's a hot night, refrigerate it, but if your kitchen's cool, it will keep and improve. The next day, set your table with a red checkered cloth, purchase and heat a long loaf of Italian or French bread, open a tall, romantic-looking bottle of red wine, reheat your soup, and serve it from a large earthenware casserole. Just like the Left Bank. This soup, with a simple bibb lettuce anointed with oil and vinegar, and life will be complete.

INGREDIENTS: Leftover bits of beef and bones; cold water to cover; 1 large onion; 4 medium carrots; 1 small purple-top turnip; 1 cup celery tops; 1 bay leaf; salt; peppercorns; leftover mushroom and barley casserole.

The apricot loaf freezes, if you don't eat it first, very nicely, as do all such breads. Spread with softened cream cheese, this is a fine tea sandwich; sliced thin and buttered, it's the right thing for a fruit salad accompaniment. If you have any perceptible quantity of the bread on the premises after it has passed its peak, break it up, dot it with butter, pour sherry on it, and bake it to very hot. Serve it with whipped cream, that's the way. Apricot purée, warm (apricots, water, and sugar cooked together a little while, then mashed—and tasted to see if you have enough sugar to your taste), is nice in modest amounts under the whipped cream.

As for the shortcake, the next day it will be soaked together, the cake, the strawberries, and the whipped cream; a delicious mixture. Serve it in a deep dish, a pitcher of heavy, creamy cream nearby to be poured over it. Don't eat too much else, this time.

JUNE

June Is Busting Out All Over

ARTICHOKES, SOUR CREAM RADISH DIP
SWORDFISH KEBABS
RICE OR BULGUR WITH RAISINS
FRESH PEAS IN BUTTER
ZUCCHINI-PINEAPPLE SALAD BOWL
FRENCH MUFFINS
SWISS PIE

 There's something very important about June, particularly in the northeastern states. It's a month of promise—the winter is over; summer is here, or nearly. This is a happy meal for a happy family; consequently it is one not to hesitate to serve to guests. The swordfish kebabs are fabulous cooked over charcoal, similar to shish kebab made with lamb. Here is a method of handling swordfish that negates the old straw about this being a very dry fish. By marinating it and then cooking it quickly, the swordfish remains moist and very delicious. The peas are the first June peas, tiny and sweet, and handled simply; the pie a very dream.

This dinner is arranged for 6. Multiply or divide as you wish.

155

ARTICHOKES, SOUR CREAM RADISH DIP

To some people, artichokes are exclusively a company item. Not to the Mastertons. The children adore them, particularly with the mousseline sauce which is told about in my *Blueberry Hill Cookbook*. My girls, young as they are, can actually spell *mousseline*. The sour cream radish dip given here is another equally delicious way, and I will tell you, as well, how to prepare the artichokes so that the fuss and fear of the prickly choke is eliminated.

If your family relishes artichokes, serve a whole one to each. If they're so-so about the matter, half an artichoke will be sufficient per person. Since we Mastertons revel in them, my directions are for six artichokes for six people.

With scissors snip the pointed ends of the outer leaves of **6 large artichokes**, which must be fresh and green and without black spots. With a large, sharp knife, trim the stem so it is level with the artichoke itself. With the same knife, slice across the center leaves, cutting them off about an inch from the top. The artichokes should have flat tops, now. Cover the 6 artichokes with cold water, adding about **1 tablespoon salt**, and let them soak for an hour. Drain the water away, cover again with cold water (and it's wise to use a pot that will hold just the 6 artichokes, thus keeping them from bobbing around too much in the boiling; you will want the bottoms to stay under water). Add **2 tablespoons salt** to the fresh water and bring the artichokes to a boil. Reduce heat and simmer for 30 to 40 minutes, or until a long-tined fork will easily enter the bottom of the choke. Start testing at 30 minutes. Don't overcook them; as soon as the bottoms are tender, they've cooked long enough. Drain the artichokes, set them upside down on a tray and let them cool, at the same time getting rid of the excess water.

When they are cool enough to handle, turn the artichokes right side up, pull apart the outer leaves, and there you will see a circular, prickly area with a purplish tinge, deep down in the center of the artichoke. This is the part called the "choke," presumably because it will indeed choke you if, by accident, you get one down your throat. It consists of many little needle-like points with which you don't want any truck. Grab hold of the entire section, getting a good grip on the center, and pull. The choke will come right out in your hand. There will be perhaps some soft little fronds left, and, using the back of a teaspoon, you can scrape the exposed heart of the artichoke easily to get rid of these remaining bristles. Thus you will have left an outside ring of leaves, attached to the heart. The choke is gone, without regret.

For the Sauce: Combine in a bowl, any time in the afternoon, **1 cup mayonnaise** (and I don't mean salad dressing; use the best quality mayonnaise you can get); **½ cup commercial sour cream; 2 or 3 radishes,** sliced in thin rounds; **½ teaspoon sugar;** and **½ teaspoon garlic powder.** When ready to serve the artichokes, fill the exposed center with the sour cream mixture. I like to serve the artichokes at room temperature rather than chilled. They're better still, hot, but, in this event you would do better to serve the sauce in a side dish so the heat of the artichoke doesn't thin it down too much too soon.

You know how to eat artichokes, I assume. The leaf is pulled from the heart, the center of it is dipped in whatever sauce you have provided (and just plain Italian dressing is fine, too), and, holding the leaf as you have pulled it, you must scrape from the center the soft part, the meat of the artichoke. Use your teeth for this job. A mere morsel per bite, but a delicious one. At the end, there is the heart, which may be cut into bite-size pieces and dunked. It is a delicacy much appreciated.

INGREDIENTS: 6 large artichokes; 3 tablespoons salt; water to cover.

For the sauce: 1 cup mayonnaise; ½ cup commercial sour cream; 2 or 3 radishes; ½ teaspoon sugar; ½ teaspoon garlic powder.

SWORDFISH KABOBS

First prepare your marinade. To do this, squeeze into an enamel, pottery, or glass bowl (not aluminum, that's the point), the juice of 1 lemon. After squeezing the lemon juice into the bowl, toss in the rind of the lemon. Add 1 clove garlic, peeled and crushed; ¼ cup pure olive oil; 2 tablespoons white wine; 1 teaspoon salt; 4 or 5 peppercorns; 1 bay leaf; ½ teaspoon rosemary; 12 tiny white onions or 2 large sweet onions, cut in quarters. Mix this all together lightly, then add to it 2 large swordfish steaks, cut at least 1 to 1½ inches thick, and then cut up into squares of approximately 1½ inches square. Trim away the bones and the skin. (I'd cover these with cold water, if I were you, add an onion, some salt, a few peppercorns, a bit of bay leaf, and simmer it for 15 or 20 minutes. You would then have what is called a "court bouillon." Freeze it and use it for the liquid in a sauce for a Newburg or any baked fish. Not to leave you hanging, you do this by following any recipe for a medium cream sauce or a Newburg, using the fish liquid instead of the milk called for in the recipe, or at least for half the amount of milk. You'll have a very flavorful sauce, needing little or no extra seasoning.)

Allow the swordfish to marinate for at least 3 or 4 hours, turning it gently two or three times. When ready to serve, cut 2 firm large red tomatoes in sections about the size of the fish pieces, do likewise with 1 firm large green pepper, the seeds and membranes of which have been trimmed off, and wipe dry caps of 2 dozen medium mushrooms, removing any grit with a damp cloth or paper towel. Remove the mushroom stems and drop the mushroom caps into the marinade for a few minutes before grilling. Chop the stems, drop them in a plastic bag, and freeze them.

Have a charcoal grill ready; the coals should be still quite hot and red, not flaming. Thread the fish on long skewers, starting and ending with a mushroom cap, alternating the fish, the tomato, the green pepper, and the tiny white onions or a section of the larger onion on the skewer. They will require just a few minutes of grilling. You can baste once or twice with the marinade that is left. I prefer to let the skewers rest right on the coals, which grills the lower section of the food on the skewers first; as this half is ready, the fish cooked through and crusty on the outside (test a piece to see), push the tasty fish and vegetable morsels off the skewer onto a heated platter. A kitchen fork serves as a good pusher. Move the top part of the fish and vegetables down to the lower section of the skewers and continue grilling that section. In any case, grill the kabobs close to the coals and quickly. Eat them quickly, too.

INGREDIENTS:

For the marinade: juice and rind of 1 lemon; 1 clove garlic; ¼ cup olive oil; 2 tablespoons white wine (sauterne or any dry white wine); 1 teaspoon salt; 4 or 5 pepper-corns; 1 bay leaf; ½ teaspoon rosemary.

For the kebabs: 12 tiny white onions or 2 large onions; 2 large swordfish steaks; 1 firm large green pepper; caps of 2 dozen medium mushrooms.

RICE OR BULGUR WITH RAISINS

Since bulgur is rather difficult to obtain in some cities, I am giving you, as well, an excellent rice recipe. Bulgur is an Armenian wheat product which is chewy and nutty and a superior accompaniment to any sort of shish kabob or, in this case, to the swordfish kabob. You can buy it in delicacy departments of supermarkets or gourmet shops, where it will cost you a fabulous sum. If you have an Armenian grocery store, however, in your city or town (in New York, there are, I believe, a raft of them on Third Avenue), the bulgur can be purchased in bulk for pennies.

The bulgur, just as rice, expands greatly. One cup will go a long way; it will be ample for 6 servings.

Bring to a boil **2 cups well-seasoned chicken broth, bouil-lon, or lamb broth.** Either the chicken broth or the lamb broth might very well be in your freezer against a use such as this; boil up the bones from your most recent leg of lamb, season them well, add a carrot and an onion or two, simmer for a few hours, strain, freeze. What have you? Lamb broth.

Taste the broth for salt and pepper. It must be robust before you add the bulgur. When the broth is boiling rapidly, add **1 cup bulgur**, a little at a time, so as not to stop the boiling of the broth. In about 10 or 15 minutes, the broth will be absorbed and the bulgur should be tender, though still crunchy, almost nutty in texture. If it isn't, add a little more broth and continue boiling. At the last three or four minutes, add **1 tablespoon butter** and ½ **cup raisins**, any old kind. Heat long enough to plump up the raisins. You will have 3 cups cooked bulgur.

INGREDIENTS: 2 cups chicken or lamb broth or bouillon, or more if needed; salt; pepper; 1 cup bulgur; 1 tablespoon butter; ½ cup raisins.

For the rice, brown **1 cup raw long-grain white rice** in a heavy pan *without fat*. Keep it moving around, watching it to keep it from burning, and you will see, very shortly, that the kernels are starting to brown lightly. When this happens, don't delay: put it in a 1-quart casserole. Add **2½ cups boiling water, 1 teaspoon salt**, cover tightly and bake in a 350°F. oven for ½ hour. It will come out with each grain separate and fluffy; the browning of the rice without fat of any sort will give it a very different and interesting flavor. Stir in in the last five minutes **1 tablespoon butter** and ½ **cup raisins**, as for the bulgur. Re-cover and continue baking. The raisins will plump up in the steam of the dish.

INGREDIENTS: 1 cup raw long-grain white rice; 2½ cups water; 1 teaspoon salt; 1 tablespoon butter; ½ cup raisins.

◆ FRESH PEAS IN BUTTER

Melt, in a heavy saucepan with a tightly fitting lid, **4 table-spoons** (½ stick) **butter**; fresh and sweet it must be. Add **4 cups peas**, freshly picked, freshly podded, the smaller the better. Turn the heat down very, very low and heat the peas for 30 minutes. Lift the lid, taste a pea, and, if done, fine. If not, re-cover and give them 5 or 6 more minutes. Season with salt, pepper, and, if you wish, a few snips of chives or green-onion tops. These last are optional.

If you're lucky enough to have grown or know where to get edible podded peas, which are the Chinese snow peas, pull the strings on them as you would on old-fashioned string beans, and treat them in the same manner as you have been told to do the peas themselves. You then eat the pods in which are the still undeveloped peas, and a more delicious morsel you will never know.

INGREDIENTS: 4 tablespoons butter; 4 cups peas; salt; pepper; chives or green-onion tops (optional).

ZUCCHINI-PINEAPPLE SALAD BOWL

Wash, dry with a towel, and set in the refrigerator to chill and crisp 1 head Boston or romaine lettuce. Wash, dry, and slice very thin 4 small zucchini, none of them more than 4 or 5 inches long and an inch around. Drain 1 medium-sized can pineapple chunks. Peel 1 red sweet onion and slice into rings. Wrap the onion in saran, if you prepare them much ahead of time; they'll stay moist that way.

When ready to serve, line a wooden salad bowl with the crisp lettuce leaves. Mix together in a separate bowl the sliced zucchini, the pineapple chunks, and the red onion rings with 2 tablespoons sugar, 2 tablespoons white vinegar, 1 tablespoon mashed Roquefort or bleu cheese, and ½ cup light cream. Toss several times, making sure the zucchini and pineapple are well saturated with dressing. Pile into lettuce bed in bowl. Serve.

INGREDIENTS: 1 head Boston or romaine lettuce; 4 small zucchini; 1 medium-sized can pineapple chunks; 1 sweet red onion.

For the dressing: 2 tablespoons sugar; 2 tablespoons white vinegar; 1 tablespoon mashed Roquefort or bleu cheese; ½ cup light cream.

FRENCH MUFFINS

Excellent, rich, all-purpose muffins. Try them sometime with blueberries or currants.

Grease 2 dozen muffin-pan sections. The best lubricant for greasing tins is a vegetable shortening; it doesn't burn as butter or margarine has a tendency to do. Toss a bit of flour into each section. Heat oven to 350°F.

Separate 2 eggs. Mix together 1 cup light cream and 2 egg yolks. Stir the yolks in, don't beat them. Add 2 tablespoons melted butter. You have now provided for the wet ingredients.

Now sift 2 cups sifted cake flour, 1 tablespoon baking powder, ¼ cup sugar, and ½ teaspoon salt. Dry ingredients ready.

Combine, quickly, the wet and the dry, in whichever bowl is larger, stopping when they are together, as it were, in one mass. Don't try to get the batter smooth; just be sure there are no lumps which, on investigation, turn out to be bits of dry flour. Beat 2 egg whites (the two you were wondering about) until they are glistening and make a peak, but not, no never, dry. Gently fold these into the batter.

Fill the prepared muffin pans half-full. Sprinkle each muffin with ¼ teaspoon sugar. Bake at 425°F. for 15 minutes or until lightly browned and test done when poked with a straw. The straw must come forth dry.

INGREDIENTS: 2 eggs; 1 cup light cream; 2 tablespoons butter; 2 cups sifted cake flour; 1 tablespoon baking powder; ¼ cup sugar; ½ teaspoon salt; 2 tablespoons sugar for topping.

SWISS PIE

This luxurious pie calls for a custard which is just about the best custard in the world, I think. Some night fix it by its lone self and serve it in sherbet glasses, topped with a bit of whipped cream. You'll thank me for this.

As you perhaps know, most custard recipes are full of warnings. Be careful of this. Be careful of that. Stir. Add. Fold. One feels the blessing of the Lord is necessary for true success.

This custard can be performed by my Laurey with ease. She's nine.

You need a baked **9-inch pie shell**. Use my recipe on page 287 unless you have thought ahead and have an extra pie shell in the freezer. If you did as you were told, here's your chance to cash your ticket. If you didn't, when you prepare crust this time, fix an extra one for the freezer. Use it when you need it.

The whole pie can, in fact should, be fixed in the morning. It needs sitting in the refrigerator to blend the velvet flavors.

Mix **½ cup sugar** with **2 tablespoons flour**. Do this in a 1-quart heavy saucepan (or double boiler) away from the range. Slowly, stirring all the time, add **2 cups milk**. Then, still stirring, add **2 egg yolks**. You won't use the egg whites for this pie, so put them in a jar, mark the lid "2 egg whts," and freeze them.

Set the pan over moderate heat and, stirring constantly, in fact like crazy, keep the custard cooking until it starts to boil and you have a thick custard. Takes very little time, once the milk is hot, so watch it. If you're the kind who burns things of this sort, cook your custard in the top section of a double boiler over boiling water. Doesn't need so much watching but takes at least twice as long. When you have a thick custard, remove the pan immediately from the heat and allow it to cool thoroughly, stirring it once in a bit. Add **1 teaspoon pure vanilla**, blend it in, and pour the custard into your baked 9-inch pie shell; sprinkle with **2 tablespoons finely chopped walnuts**. Whip until stiff **1 cup heavy cream**. Stir in **½ teaspoon pure vanilla**. Spread this smoothly over the custard.

This pie is finished! Do not bake it. Just leave it in the refrigerator at least 4 or 5 hours. If you're in a hurry, place it in the freezer until it's thoroughly chilled, not frozen, then refrigerate for another hour.

INGREDIENTS: Baked 9-inch pie shell; ½ cup sugar; 2 table-spoons flour; 2 cups milk; 2 egg yolks; 1½ teaspoons vanilla; 2 tablespoons finely chopped walnuts; 1 cup heavy cream.

TIMETABLE: Little to worry you, here. Fix the pie in the morning. That's done. Prepare the artichokes in the morning, too. Leave them, chokeless, in the refrigerator on a plate, covered with saran. Mix up the sour cream radish dip in the morning, as well. It improves with a few hours' neglect. The salad greens can be washed and set to chilling.

Early afternoon, prepare the marinade, cut up the fish, start marinating it. That's ready. Very late in the afternoon, mix up the zucchini-pineapple salad bowl ingredients; leave them in their bowl. Shell the peas.

Thread the kabobs. If you're having rice, get that in the oven. Start the peas cooking. Start the grill (your husband can take care of that, of course, if you have one). If you have no grill, preheat your oven. The kabobs are fairly good, done under the broiler of your range, if you must.

Prepare the bulgur, if that's what you're having; start it boiling. Mix up the muffins. If you have the ingredients ready, the wet in their bowl, the dry in their bowl, this takes no time. To get them quickly in the muffin tins, use a small ice-cream scoop. Scoop up just enough, press the handle, neat as you please, a muffin with each scoop. Easy, that way. Place the muffins in the oven; finish putting the salad together; arrange the artichokes and their sauce on their dishes, and everybody sit down.

Just about when you have finished eating the artichokes, the muffins will be ready. Since the kabobs take such a short time to do, it's best to have the artichokes over and done with before you start the kabobs. They can now be grilled; they'll cook in a matter of minutes. Don't let the keeper of the grill overdo them. As soon as they flake, take 'em off! While the broiling is going on, remove the muffins from the oven, pass them, hot, to be reveled in. The peas should be done; turn them into a serving dish. The bulgur will be ready for the raisins; add them, set the lid back on. Pass the salad.

Ready is the platter of swordfish with its tomatoes and onions and green peppers, the bulgur, the peas. The muffins are hot, the salad is cool and refreshing. Nothing more to do, unless it is to check on seconds of swordfish.

When you're ready for dessert, it's ready for you. The Swiss pie, cool and inviting, awaits your attention and that of your family.

NOTE: *Practically* everything in this meal can be done ahead, if necessary, except the broiling of the kabobs. The bulgur, the rice, the peas, the muffins, all could be made in the morning or early afternoon and reheated. This, in case you want to make this an outdoor meal and want to be there through it all. I've presented to you what I consider an ideal, because there is truly no substitute for muffins right out of the oven, and so forth. If it isn't practical for you, your dinner will be, still, an exceptional one. Perhaps not perfect, but exceptional.

LEFTOVERS

Thinking of leftovers, you should save about a half cup of the marinade. The swordfish with its tomatoes and vegetables, the bulgur or rice, and the peas can be combined in a casserole, if you have very much left. Scrape into the casserole whatever marinade you can find settled onto the platter from which you've served the kabobs. Dot with butter, moisten, if it's dry, with a little more of the marinade, cover the casserole with aluminum foil, and bake in a 325°F. oven only until it is hot. This will take about 15 minutes, probably; when you lift the foil, if the steam pours forth, it's ready. The foil will keep this delicious casserole from drying out. Sprinkle with a little cheddar or Parmesan cheese, if you'd like, and slide it under the broiler—just to fancy it up a little.

The bulgur itself can be reheated with a little broth. It'll taste as good as it did yesterday. If you haven't any fish left, combine the peas with the bulgur and a few pignolia nuts, heat in butter, and serve with lamb chops.

Any time there is fish left after a meal, I remember the story of the lady in my cooking school and the fish hash. She was a lovely, elderly New Englander who had been a high school Latin teacher until her retirement a few years before. Now that she had some time to herself, she proposed to learn to cook, and so she came to my spring cooking session. The first evening she was there, she told me, quietly, that if I could teach her how to prepare a fine "fish hash," so that it would be brown and crusty and still didn't stick to the pan, her faith in me would be complete and the course consequently worthwhile. I couldn't admit to her, didn't dare, that up to that moment, I had never made a fish hash myself, no less heard of it, and we started the course.

She was very happy about everything she learned but, each day, she gently reminded me that she wanted, above all else, to learn to fix that fish hash. Finally, the last day, I obviously had to come through, and, in the absence of left-over fish, I asked her if a can of corned beef hash would do. After all, it was the method, not the ingredients, that worried her.

"Fine!" she declared. She knew the recipe for the hash, all she needed was to see how to make the brown crust. By this time, my other students were fascinated too at the challenge, and we gathered round my range while I heated a black iron frying pan.

"Get the pan hot first," I said.

"Oh!" she exclaimed, admiringly. "I never heard of *that!*"

"Yes," I continued, "things stick to cold pans."

"Now," she said, turning to the others, "you see! I've learned something already!"

I took heart. "Of course," I went on, "there's nothing like an old-fashioned black iron frying pan to make a fine crust —on a hash."

She folded her hands across her apron. "Well, my stars! And I've been using a thin aluminum pan."

One of the other students said: "There you are! You've been using the wrong frying pan."

I dropped a lump of butter on the surface of the pan. It sizzled. "Let the butter sizzle a bit," I went on. We all watched while the butter slid around as I tilted the pan until the whole surface was well covered with the melted butter. "Drop a little of the hash on the hot butter. If it sizzles, it's the right temperature. Add the rest then." And with that, I added, first a speck, then the contents of one poor can of corned-beef hash. It settled into place with a hiss. I patted it with a pancake turner, turned it. It hissed again.

"Now," I went on, courageously, "turn down the heat so it will cook slowly."

There was silence as this was done, and silence as I patted the hash once in a while. "It *should,*" I promised, "be browning nicely."

My New England lady watched, fascinated. "My!" she said.

I looked at it. It would not let me down, surely. It would brown. We watched, we waited. Finally, the top of the hash was moist and steam was curling through from the bottom. "Let's turn it over," I said, bravely, and I slid my pancake turner under it. The implement slid under, smoothly. I leveled the hash on the turner and, with one quick turn, had it over on its back.

"Ah!" The sigh of relief came from us all. There it was, crisp and brown and crusty. A perfect crust. A perfect "bottom."

"I've learned what I came to learn," my lady said. "Now I'll go home and practice." I leaned back, exhausted. "My," she said, "that looks good!"

The other ladies thought so too. They all had some of the canned hash.

Since then, I've learned how to make a fine New England fish hash. Won't catch me twice.

This can be made of any sort of leftover fish. If you have

swordfish from this meal that will do fine. It's simple: equal parts of flaked cooked fish and chopped cold cooked potatoes. Boil the potatoes fresh for the hash and let them cool. Day-old potatoes aren't as good as just made. Add whatever green pepper you have on hand from the kabobs. Season with salt, pepper, and Worcestershire sauce (about 1 teaspoon Worcestershire for each cup of fish and cup of potatoes). Heat a black iron frying pan very hot; sizzle in it sausage fat or butter, and add the hash. As soon as all the hash is spread around, turn it over, once, so all is moistened with the fat. Turn down the heat, continue frying slowly until you have a brown crust, turn again, brown the other side, and serve.

The Swiss pie keeps beautifully in the refrigerator for about two days. It will also freeze nicely. Arrange to consume it, if frozen, at the moment of its complete defrosting. It will break down if allowed to wait around. Serve it with any sort of fruit sauce—blueberry, crushed strawberry, raspberry. It's fabulous with a bitter orange sauce, such as I tell you about in my *Blueberry Hill Cookbook*.

JULY

CURRIED VICHYSSOISE
SMOKED BEEF TONGUE A L'ORANGE
NEW POTATOES AND PEAS WITH CAPERS
ROSEMARY ZUCCHINI
JULY TOMATOES
TINY CARROTS AND ONIONS IN WINE
HOT BUTTERMILK BISCUITS
OLD-FASHIONED LEAF-LETTUCE BOWL
OMELETTE-RUM SOUFFLE

This will not be a garden party in the sense of large-brimmed ladies' hats and chiffon dresses, but one in which the bounty of a summer of good gardening comes to its ultimate use. A cold soup first, then a delicious sliced tongue with orange sauce, and, proudly displayed, zucchini, tomatoes, leaf lettuce, new potatoes and peas, carrots, onions, all home grown. If you haven't a garden, make friends with someone who has. A menu for 8, this time.

CURRIED VICHYSSOISE

Wash **6 large leeks,** stripping off the outer coatings and trimming off the roots. If you can't get leeks, which are the traditional green for this soup, you may use **2 bunches scallions,** instead. Slice the leeks, or scallions, into thin rounds, tops and bottoms, and sauté them in ½ cup (1 stick) **butter** with **1 medium-sized white onion,** peeled and cut into small pieces. When the onions are wilted and golden—don't let them burn, or even turn brown—add **1½ quarts rich chicken broth** (homemade preferred, see page 13; reserve about ¼ cup); **3½ cups cut-up raw potatoes,** peeled (about 6 medium); and let it come to a boil. Turn down to a simmer, and allow the soup to cook slowly until the potatoes are cooked through, about 25 minutes. Pour the soup through a coarse sieve, pressing the potatoes through, as well. Add **salt** to taste, the amount depending on the saltiness of the broth you are using. Taste, and add 4 or 5 grinds of **pepper** from your pepper mill, **1 cup milk,** and **2 cups light cream.** Mix **1 teaspoon curry powder** to a smooth paste with a little of the cold reserved chicken broth, add it to the vichyssoise, mix well, and bring to a boil. Don't let it actually boil. Chill. Just before serving add ½ **cup watercress,** broken into small pieces, and ¾ **cup heavy cream.** Taste for seasoning, adding salt if it's needed. Serve from bouillon cups, sprinkling each cup of vichyssoise with **1 teaspoon chopped chives.**

If you wish a smoother texture, you can press this through a fine sieve just before adding the watercress and cream, or buzz it in a blender. I prefer the coarseness of my way.

For a traditional vichyssoise, omit the curry.

INGREDIENTS: 6 large leeks or 2 bunches scallions; ½ cup butter; 1 medium-sized white onion; 1½ quarts chicken broth; 3½ cups cut-up raw potatoes; salt; pepper; 1 cup milk; 2 cups light cream; 1 teaspoon curry powder; ½ cup watercress; ¾ cup heavy cream; chopped chives.

SMOKED BEEF TONGUE A L'ORANGE

I know there are people who do not wish to contemplate a beef tongue on a plate. All I can say is they are missing one of the truly marvelous foods devised by man, particularly as prepared according to this recipe.

Use a ready-to-cook smoked beef tongue, if possible. These are not as salty as those which are not so treated. If it is not this sort, you must soak the tongue overnight, drain it, and continue as follows.

Cover a **4- to 5-pound ready-to-cook smoked beef tongue** with **cold water**. Add **1 bay leaf; 1 onion,** cut in quarters; **3 or 4 peppercorns; 2 carrots,** peeled and cut up. Salt is not necessary. Bring to a boil, let it boil a few minutes, skim off whatever scum appears, if any, then reduce the liquid to a simmer. Simmer until the tongue is tender, about 3½ hours. You'll know when it is tender, as a fork will enter it easily at any point. Lift the tongue out of the broth now, let it cool until you can handle it. You will notice that, if the tongue is really done, the little bones in it will fall out at a touch.

Remove the skin. This is very easy to do at this time, as the skin will be quite loose. You will need only to start it with a sharp knife for it to slip off. If it is at all recalcitrant, help it along with a knife or kitchen shears. Then cut away all the odd-looking gristle and funny little bones and fat at the back end of the tongue. If you have a cat or a dog, it will love the discards. Heavens, you yourself could make a meal of the lovely morsels of tongue that come along with the unusables. When the tongue is trimmed, if you're not going to use it right away, return it to the stock until you do need it, refrigerating it if this will not be for some time. It will stay in good shape, in the broth, for several days, covered.

You can prepare the sauce immediately after the tongue is cooked; it, too, will keep perfectly in a jar in the refrigerator. What I'm trying to say is that literally this entire dish can be prepared a day or even two in advance of your party.

For the Sauce: Trim the orange part only from the **rind of 2 California oranges.** This will give you thin bits of peel; keep away from the white. Place these peelings on a wooden board and, with a sharp knife, cut them into the thinnest slivers you can manage, paper-thin if possible. Set them aside for a few minutes.

Now peel away the white membrane, and, again using a very sharp knife, cut neat segments of the oranges, keeping within the membranes which divide the oranges into sections. Set these neat pieces of orange pulp on a saucer. Squeeze out the juice which will remain. Measure, and if you do not have **½ cup orange juice,** add some juice, either from another orange or whatever frozen juice you may have in your refrigerator.

Now you're ready to put the sauce together. Use a heavy 1-quart saucepan.

Melt **¼ cup** (½ stick) **margarine** or **butter** (margarine is very good, here) and, over low heat, stirring constantly with a wire whisk or a wooden spoon, add **2 tablespoons flour.** Keep rubbing until you have a smooth paste, light brown in color, in other words a *roux*. (I don't approve of words like *roux*, but, since you see them in other cookbooks and may wonder what the devil *that* means, I repeat: in other words, a *roux*.) Add slowly, stirring constantly, the ½ cup orange juice you have ready, and **1 cup strained tongue stock.** When it starts to thicken, add **½ cup light brown sugar, ¼ cup wine vinegar, ¼ cup light sweet red wine,** and continue cooking until it is of the consistency of a light cream. Remove from the heat and add **½ cup seedless white grapes** or **½ cup seedless raisins** and the prepared orange rind. Taste for seasoning. You shouldn't need anything; just see that you don't consume too much of this luscious sauce, tasting it. If it is too thick, add a bit more orange juice or wine. If you're a teetotaler, omit the wine and substitute orange juice. Add the orange sections, (Note: Do not heat again until just ready to serve.) The orange sections will disintegrate if boiled.

When ready to serve this, reheat the tongue in the stock, reheat the sauce, without boiling it, slice the tongue in neat, thin slices, on the diagonal, ladle some sauce over the meat, and serve. Nothing will be harmed if you slice the meat a bit ahead of time, cover it with some of the sauce and keep the whole thing warm in a low, low or just-turned-off oven, ready to set on the table when wanted. The additional sauce, containing the orange slices, can be passed.

Despite these directions, I much prefer to slice the tongue just when my guests are ready to eat it, ladling the sauce with the oranges as I go. The juices and tenderness are enhanced by this, though I cannot, again, deny that many people withdraw from the visualization of a tongue in process of being sliced.

INGREDIENTS: 4- to 5-pound smoked beef tongue; cold water; 1 bay leaf; 1 onion; 3 or 4 peppercorns; 2 carrots.

For the sauce: 2 California oranges; ½ cup orange juice; ¼ cup margarine or butter; 2 tablespoons flour; 1 cup strained tongue stock; ½ cup light brown sugar; ¼ cup wine vinegar; ¼ cup light sweet red wine; ½ cup seedless white grapes or seedless raisins.

NEW POTATOES AND PEAS WITH CAPERS

The potatoes should be tiny and new. These will be available in some parts of the country right now in your own gardens; in any case, they are on the market, imported from Florida and California, so make these do until your own come along.

Use your steamer. You have one, haven't you? Leave the skins on **4 dozen new potatoes,** scrub them, peel one strip around the middle of each, and steam them until they're tender. Fork tender, I mean. While they're steaming, shell **4 pounds fresh peas,** the smaller and the more recently picked, the better. When the potatoes are done, add the peas. Steam them for no more than 2 minutes after the water in the bottom of the steamer resumes a boil. If the peas are truly small, they will probably be done too. Keep watch over them, looking at them every minute or two. As soon as they are tender to the bite, remove the potatoes and the peas from the steamer. If it's a Bungalow Cooker, you'll want to drain them, reserving the liquid for soup or sauce; if you've steamed them in a steamer with holes in the bottom or in a colander over hot water, draining is not necessary.

In either case, turn them into a heated serving dish. Don't let all the peas sink to the bottom; arrange them nicely on top of and around the potatoes. Brown ¼ cup (½ stick) **butter,** letting it sizzle and brown quickly. Stop it there; next step is burnt butter. Remove butter from heat and add **2 tablespoons capers** with their own liquid. Pour butter-caper mixture over the potatoes and peas. **Pepper,** freshly ground, is the only spice you'll need.

INGREDIENTS: 4 dozen new potatoes; 4 pounds fresh peas; ¼ cup butter; 2 tablespoons capers; pepper.

ROSEMARY ZUCCHINI

A perfect marriage: rosemary with zucchini. If you can get the tiny zucchini, no more than 3 inches long, wash 8 of them. Trim the blossom ends of the **8 tiny zucchini,** slice lengthwise and continue as directed. Otherwise, trim off the blossom ends, wash and slice into paper-thin slices, unpeeled zucchini to measure 10 cups, when sliced. Arrange it in layers in a 2-quart casserole or baking dish, lavished with **butter, 2 or 3 tablespoons** at the least. Don't worry if the zucchini piles high; it will sink when it's baked. If you start with a level dish, you'll have a half-filled one later. Sprinkle each layer lightly with **salt,** liberally with freshly ground **pepper,** sparingly with sugar (you'll want no more than ½ **teaspoon sugar** in all), and toss over each layer about **4 or 5 bits of rosemary,** crushed in your fingers, no more than that. This is an herb with a fine, strong way of its own; you don't want to overwhelm the zucchini, just complement it.

Again, about ½ teaspoon rosemary is more than enough for the entire casserole. Dot each layer with ½ teaspoon butter. Continue until you've used all the zucchini.

Bake in 375°F. oven for 15 or 20 minutes or until the zucchini is cooked, yet crisp—a subtle point, that. The casserole can be stirred in about 10 minutes, so that the top, which is not as moist as the bottom, may have a chance at some of the juices. This casserole can be prepared for baking several hours in advance. The juices that are left are divine; don't throw them away. Use them in a soup stock or a gravy; they can be frozen until they're needed.

INGREDIENTS: 8 tiny zucchini or 10 cups sliced zucchini; ½ cup butter; salt; pepper; ½ teaspoon sugar; ½ teaspoon rosemary.

JULY TOMATOES

This can be done either with bright red tomatoes or green tomatoes; either is delicious. In the case of green tomatoes, they will need to be sautéed quite a bit longer—perhaps 5 minutes longer, perhaps 10—to get them tender throughout. Assuming, however, that you have loads of tomatoes in your garden or that you have access to them in quantity, cut 8 medium-sized firm bright red tomatoes in thick slices, crosswise. Trim off the blossom end and cut a thin slice from the other end, making of it, too, a slice. Poke out the seeds and the runny pulp with a knife and let the tomato slices drain for about 1 hour to get rid of the rest of the seeds.

Now make a smooth garlic butter (and this is the way you prepare a garlic butter for other recipes, too) by combining ½ pound soft butter with 2 mashed cloves of garlic. Mash the garlic after it's peeled, using a mortar and pestle, if you have one (the only proper way of crushing a bud of garlic) or with a garlic press (next best way). Combine the butter and the garlic thoroughly in a blender, an electric mixer, or with a fork. Season the cut tomatoes with a good sprinkling of **salt,** a grind or two of **pepper,** and a bit of **sugar** (½ teaspoon in all should be plenty).

Get a heavy 9- or 10-inch black iron frying pan very hot. Add the garlic butter, enough of it to cover the bottom of the pan rather lavishly. When the butter is sizzling, add the slices of tomato and sauté them at moderate heat until one side is brown. Turn and brown the other side. Remove the tomatoes to a warm platter as they are finished and continue until you have fried all of them. You'll need the rest of the garlic butter as you go along. When all the tomatoes are lightly browned and done, pour into the pan **1 cup heavy cream.** Stir it around so that the brown juices are combined with it. Heat, but do not boil, the sauce. Taste it for seasoning; you might need salt, pepper, or sugar. Decide which. Pour the sauce over the tomatoes on the platter, or, if you prefer, you can return the tomatoes to the sauce in the pan and spoon some of the sauce of them in the frying pan. In that case, serve from the pan; otherwise from the platter. If you prefer to serve these tomatoes without the sauce, they will be delicious by their own selves—a Masterton daughter's colloquialism.

INGREDIENTS: 8 medium-sized firm red (or green) tomatoes; ½ pound butter; 2 cloves of garlic; salt; pepper; ½ teaspoon sugar; 1 cup heavy cream (optional).

TINY CARROTS AND ONIONS IN WINE

Try these! If you cannot get the thinnings from a carrot row, tiny carrots 1 or 2 inches long, use larger ones cut into shoestrings. The little ones need a thorough washing, but don't try to peel them; it'll drive you mad. Trim off the tops and the little tail on the bottom. Most of the carrot skin will come off in the wash job, and what's left won't hurt anyone.

In a heavy saucepan with a tight-fitting cover, sauté **4 medium onions,** preferably pulled from a July garden, in **¼ pound** (1 stick) **butter.** Let them simmer for about 10 minutes, until they are golden and tender—don't brown them. You know, I'm sure, that browned onions have a completely different taste from golden ones—and, particularly in combination with other foods, a rather unpleasant one.

Now add **2 pounds carrots**, either tiny new ones or cut into shoestrings. Cover with **1 cup chicken broth**, homemade or canned, and **1 cup light sweet white wine.** If you should happen to use a dry, unsweet, white wine, add a pinch of **sugar** here. There should be sufficient broth to just about cover the carrots and onions; if there isn't, add a little of the combination of the broth and the wine; if there's more than you need, hold off a bit of it. Simmer now, slowly, slowly, until the carrots are cooked through but not overly tender, and most of the liquid has cooked away. These can be cooked ahead, transferred to an earthenware or Pyrex casserole, and reheated in their broth when needed. Taste for seasoning. If the broth was well seasoned, you probably won't need any. Add **salt** and **pepper** if you need it.

INGREDIENTS: 4 medium onions; ¼ pound butter; 2 pounds carrots; 1 cup chicken broth; 1 cup light sweet white wine (sugar, salt, pepper, if needed).

HOT BUTTERMILK BISCUITS

Sift **4 cups flour** with **1 teaspoon salt** and **1 tablespoon plus 1 teaspoon baking powder.** Cut in **½ cup margarine** (that's 1 stick) to a texture similar to corn meal. A pastry blender is excellent for this; 2 knives will do. Add **1½ cup buttermilk.** Combine.

This will give you a soft dough. Turn it out on a floured board and knead it lightly. Do this only until it is a homogenous mixture; flour your hands and toss the dough, pressing it lightly, to this point. Pat, don't roll, it out to ½-inch thickness. Flour your biscuit cutter, whatever size you fancy, and cut out the biscuits. You should get about 3 dozen regulation-size biscuits, many more if they're smaller. Bake on a greased tray (use a vegetable shortening for this job) or a cookie sheet at 475°F., which is a rather hot oven, for 10 to 12 minutes. Split them, slip a lump of butter in each biscuit, put them back together right away, and serve them.

INGREDIENTS: 4 cups flour; 1 teaspoon salt; 1 tablespoon plus 1 teaspoon baking powder; ½ cup margarine; 1½ cups buttermilk.

OLD-FASHIONED LEAF-LETTUCE BOWL

For this salad you should, if possible, have the tender leaf lettuce freshly pulled from your own garden. Otherwise, Boston or bibb lettuce will be acceptable. Wash the lettuce several hours before you expect to use it; dry by patting with a linen towel, with paper towels, or, best of all, if you have a French wire salad basket, dry the greens by swinging this in the open air, letting the moisture fly away. An amusing gambit, and effective. Chill the greens in a plastic bag or wrapped in a linen towel in the refrigerator.

You'll need a lot of this lettuce, probably three times more than you think. Fill a salad bowl which will hold enough salad for 8 so that it is piled high with the lettuce—about 4 quarts of leaf lettuce, I would say. If you're using heads of lettuce, you'd need 3 or 4 heads of Boston or bibb lettuce. Break the greens lightly; never cut them, but never. When ready to serve, slice over the top 2 **cups chopped green onions** (scallions) and 4 **hard-cooked eggs,** chopped coarsely.

In a small frying pan, fry until crisp 6 **slices lean bacon.** Lift the bacon from the fat with a slotted spoon and allow it to drain. Crumble it and set it aside. In the pan, with the fat, add ½ **cup cider vinegar, 1 teaspoon salt,** several grinds of fresh black **pepper** from the mill, 2 **tablespoons light brown sugar.** Heat to boiling, simmer 2 minutes, remove from heat. At serving time, reheat to boiling and pour over the lettuce, eggs, and onions. Toss until lettuce is wilted. Add broken bacon bits. Taste for seasoning. Adjust, particularly as to pepper. Serve at once.

INGREDIENTS: 4 quarts leaf lettuce or 3 or 4 heads Boston
    or bibb lettuce; 2 cups chopped green onions; 4 eggs.
    For the dressing: 6 slices lean bacon; ½ cup cider vinegar;
    1 teaspoon salt; pepper; 2 tablespoons light brown
    sugar.

OMELETTE-RUM SOUFFLE

This is a quick way of doing a soufflé. It requires attention,
of course, but not as much as a regular soufflé. If it's impossible for you to manage this recipe and still run your party
as you would like, save the soufflé for a less harried time
and serve instead fresh, ripe freestone peaches, peeled and
soaked all day in a fine red wine or champagne.

The soufflé, however, is a beautiful thing. This recipe will
serve 8 modestly; if your guests have large appetites, I'm
afraid it will do for only 4.

Heat your oven to 375°F. Separate **8 large eggs.** Beat
the yolks until they are lemon-colored and very light. Then,
gradually, beating all the time, add **½ cup superfine sugar**
and **⅓ cup good-quality light rum.** Now beat the egg whites
until they hold a peak, glistening. Don't overbeat these. Fold
into the yolk mixture, one-third at a time.

Now heat a 10-inch iron frying pan. Add **1 tablespoon
butter.** It should sizzle as it hits the pan. Distribute the butter
so that the entire pan is greased and pour in, carefully, the
soufflé mixture. Cook it over a very low heat for 3 minutes
without stirring; then transfer the soufflé to the preheated
oven and bake for 15 minutes. Remove it from the oven
at once, let it slip out of the pan onto a heated platter, waiting nearby to receive it. Sprinkle the top of the soufflé immediately with **granulated sugar** and dribble **¼ cup light
rum** over the top of that. You're supposed, at this point, to
flambé it. To do this, hold a match about an inch above the
top; the fumes from the rum will ignite, flare up, and praise
be, die down. Keep it away from paper, nylon gowns, and
frightened people. It will be very effective, of course, before

your guests and will enhance the flavor of the soufflé. If you're against this sort of shenanigans, forget the flambéing and serve the omelette with the rum un-flambéed, if there is such a word. It's divine, anyway.

INGREDIENTS: 8 eggs; ½ cup superfine sugar; ⅓ cup light rum; 1 tablespoon butter; granulated sugar; ¼ cup light rum (optional).

TIMETABLE: The vichyssoise is a do-ahead job. It can be prepared except for the watercress and heavy cream, as much as three days ahead for the refrigerator. Its freezer life is practically indefinite; of course leftover vichyssoise will freeze perfectly, too.

The beef tongue, as I've told you, is nothing to worry about. Do it a day or two ahead of time, the tongue and the sauce, remembering not to boil the orange sections until ready to serve.

The lettuce should be washed and left to crisp in the refrigerator the morning of your party. The dressing can be prepared any time of the day, needing to be reheated when you're ready to serve. Hard-cook the eggs at the same time, chop the scallions, and leave them nearby, the whole to be combined at the proper time.

These things done, you can save the latter part of the afternoon for the preparation of the vegetables. The potatoes, washed and peeled as directed, can be steamed and ready for the addition of the peas. The zucchini can be prepared and in its casserole, while the potatoes are steaming. The garlic butter next, ready for the tomatoes. The tomatoes sliced and draining. The carrots can be cooked, seasoned, and allowed to wait for reheating. Shell the peas now and last thing, not more than 1 hour before dinner, prepare and cut out the buttermilk biscuits. Leave them in a cool place on their tray; refrigerate them if there's no other cool place available.

Half an hour before dinner, reheat the tongue in the stock in which it's been resting; less than 10 minutes at low heat should do this job. Heat the sauce separately and, if you don't want to slice the tongue at table, slice it now, lay it out on a platter, cover it with a minimum of sauce and keep it warm until you wish to serve it. A slow oven or a warm spot on the back of the stove will do. I prefer, as I've told you, to slice it at the last moment, which would require your serving the tongue on a welled board, with the gravy on the side, and slicing it at the table.

While the tongue is heating, you can now set the casserole of zucchini in the oven to be baked. Add the garlic butter to a sizzling frying pan, proceed with the frying of the garlic tomatoes, arranging them on a preferably white platter as they are finished, each slice in its turn. Reheat the carrots and onions. Bring the potatoes back to hot, add the peas. Prepare the butter for browning; set the capers near them.

Set the oven at 475°F. and, when it hits that heat, slide in the biscuits. Heat the salad dressing, combine the salad ingredients, and toss the salad.

Add the heavy cream to the vichyssoise, ladle it into soup cups, place the cups on the table, and call your guests. As soon as they are seated, have a look at the biscuits. They should be done, or nearly—they take 10 or 12 minutes, re-member—and as soon as they are lightly browned and done through (break one open before you serve any, to tell), they can be passed. I like to loosen them with a pancake turner and serve them to my guests right from the baking tray; but, more formal and, of course, more proper, they can be served from a bread basket, nestling in a linen napkin. Turn down the oven now to 375°F. for the omelette soufflé. Give the zucchini casserole a turn, now, and a poke.

Next comes the salad, and while your guests are eating that, you can be setting the resplendent dinner on your serv-ing table—a table on wheels is an invaluable aid here—the platter of sliced tongue with its sauce (or the whole tongue with the sauce on the side) first of all. Keep whatever sauce is left to be passed again later. Sizzle the butter, which will take just a minute, browning and all; add the capers and dress the potatoes and peas as directed, placing them next to the tongue. Next the carrots, hot and steaming in their own casserole; then, a contrast of color, the zucchini. The tomatoes last, in their white platter. A beautiful table of beautiful food. How fortunate we are to have, at our touch, bounty such as this.

Sit down, why don't you? Join your guests. Have dinner.

The soufflé omelette, which will be your dessert if you're game, takes just 15 minutes. I suggest that you do not attempt to prepare it until the main course is over. Have the egg yolks beaten with the sugar and rum ahead of time. While the table is being cleared, beat the egg whites, fold them in, and do the initial business with the frying pan—a matter of 3 minutes and you can let your guests observe this, if you'd like. This is dependent on the state of your kitchen, and the quality of your guests. In any case, slip the soufflé into the oven as directed and the 15 minutes needed for baking it is easily passed in conversation and coffee. At the proper time, sprinkle the omelette with the sugar and rum. The flambé procedure, if you decide on it, will compensate for the wait—which wasn't very long, really. Serve the soufflé immediately.

LEFTOVERS

The vichyssoise can be served hot the second time, accompanied by hot buttermilk-cheese biscuits. Sprinkle the split halves of leftover buttermilk biscuits with grated cheddar cheese. Bake until hot and see that the cheese is lightly browned. A bit of grated onion is nice, mixed into the cheese.

The tongue, heated in a little of its stock, makes a marvelous sandwich. Serve it, sliced, on Jewish rye bread with mustard. It can be used this way, cold, too, but heating it multiplies its joys. Slices of it, moistened with tongue stock, can be laid out in a buttered casserole, and covered with some chopped parsley, chives, capers, topped with the leftover tomatoes, sauce and all. Sprinkle soft buttered bread crumbs atop, heat in a moderate oven, then brown quickly under the broiler.

A German potato salad, using the leftover potatoes, the peas, and morsels of tongue is achieved by combining these ingredients with whatever leftover leaf lettuce salad you have about. You will need enough dressing to moisten everything moderately. Heat quickly, stirring, and serve.

Slices of the tongue, laid out on piecrust with Swiss Gruyère cheese, make a change of base (ooh!) for a Quiche Lorraine. Follow the recipe for the custard in the Quiche recipe in my *Blueberry Hill Cookbook,* or see the recipe for asparagus tart here on page 218. Either recipe will do nicely.

Bits of tongue bound together with the orange sauce make an excellent filling for an omelette. And chopped tongue, held together with a very extra thick cream sauce, makes a delicious tongue croquette—save enough sauce to serve on top of the croquettes, too.

I think that's quite enough about tongue.

The rosemary zucchini, unbelievably, is at its best in a leftover state in a salad. Add it, at the end, to a tossed green salad. Toss it with the rest of the greens. An interesting texture and flavor, even cold.

The juices from the zucchini casserole, as I mentioned earlier, will make a lovely creamed soup. Add them to some chicken broth, bring it to a boil, add heavy or light cream, taste for seasoning, sprinkle with chopped chives. You can add a few slices of leftover zucchini at the end, too, if you'd like. Speaking of soups, make one of the leftover tomatoes.

Creamed Tomato Soup

Sauté a **medium onion** in a heavy saucepan in melted **butter** until golden. Then chop whatever tomatoes you have, coarsely is the way, and add them to the onion with your leftover cream sauce. Stir it around a minute or two until all is one. Add, slowly, **1 pint milk** for each **1 cup tomatoes.** Heat thoroughly, season with a little **basil, salt,** and freshly ground **pepper** to taste, adding a hint of **sugar.** Sprinkle **chopped chives** on top, and serve with Montpelier crackers, toasted and buttered or puffed as on page 76.

INGREDIENTS: 1 medium onion; butter; 1 pint milk; 1 cup tomatoes; basil; salt; pepper; sugar; chopped chives.

You will find the carrots and onions benefit from mashing just as you do potatoes. They are an exquisite combination. Whip them in your electric mixer or blender. If you have 3 cups in all, you should use about 1 tablespoon of the juice that came with them and 1 tablespoon light cream and 2 tablespoons butter. Whip them to a froth, adding more cream if you need it. Taste for salt and pepper.

Most of the vegetables from this one meal can be combined into one fine casserole. Put together whatever you have left of the potatoes, the peas, including the capers and butter, the zucchini, the carrots, and the onions. Toss them around lightly, sprinkle with garlic powder—just a pinch—dot with butter, cover tightly, and heat to steaming. Uncover, set the leftover tomatoes on top, sprinkle with Parmesan cheese, slide under the broiler long enough to heat and brown the tomatoes. Serve.

The buttermilk biscuits are nice dessert biscuits. They should be hot, split, buttered, and covered with crushed fruit. Pass the heavy cream and brown sugar.

I'm afraid the omelette soufflé should not be served in any leftover capacity. It needs to be eaten right away and, since I'm sure it will be, all of it, I'm not going to worry about giving you a recipe for a second time use.

JULY

FAMILY MENU
A Blueberry Festival

BLUEBERRY SHRUB
BLUEBERRY SCONES
OLD-FASHIONED BLUEBERRY MUFFINS
BLUEBERRY PECAN BREAD
BROWN SUGAR BLUEBERRY MUFFINS
BLUEBERRY SPICE CAKE (OR BREAD)
BLUEBERRY KUCHEN
MAINE BLUEBERRY CAKE
BLUEBERRY GRUNT
BLUEBERRY-PEACH COBBLER
BLUEBERRY SHORTCAKE
LITHUANIAN PANCAKES WITH SPICED BLUEBERRY SAUCE
BLUEBERRY DESSERT PANCAKES
QUICK BLUEBERRY PIE

In this chapter I have departed from the format of the rest of this menu cookbook. Because of my affinity for and association with blueberries, I have had given to me, and I have worked out by myself, an almost infinite number of blueberry recipes. Were I to give you each of these recipes, which I call the best of them all, as a dessert for an individual dinner, there would be nothing in this book but blueberry desserts. Instead, I have decided to call this chapter, as you see, A Blueberry Festival.

And why not? There are strawberry festivals, many of them. Why shouldn't there be, in blueberry country, a blueberry festival? If you are in an area where the blueberries flourish, think of this for your next church or PTA function.

None of these recipes has appeared in my other cookbook. I hope you'll try them all and perhaps some of my blueberry recipes in the *Blueberry Hill Cookbook*. I recommend them, each of them, as the best of the hundreds of blueberry recipes I have come upon in the last few years.

BLUEBERRY SHRUB

A handy drink to have about on summer evenings. Crush **5 quarts ripe blueberries**, fresh or frozen dry, and cover them with **1 quart cider vinegar**. Let them stand 24 hours. Then crush again and squeeze through a cloth. To 1 quart of the juice, add **2 pounds granulated sugar**. Bring to a boil, let simmer 15 minutes. Cool, bottle, refrigerate, and use as a base for drinks, adding ginger ale or soda water, ice, and further sweetening if you wish. Makes about 3 pints.

INGREDIENTS: 5 quarts ripe blueberries; 1 quart cider vinegar; 2 pounds granulated sugar.

BLUEBERRY SCONES

Mix and sift together **2 cups sifted flour, 1 tablespoon baking powder, 1 teaspoon salt,** and **2 tablespoons sugar**. Cut in ⅓ cup margarine or butter until mealy. Combine in a bowl ⅓ cup buttermilk with **1 egg**. Reserve a little of the unbeaten egg white; then beat the rest of the egg and combine it with the buttermilk. Combine, quickly, the wet and the dry ingredients. Toss **1 cup blueberries**, fresh or frozen dry, in **1 teaspoon flour**. Fold them into the dough which should be a wet, rather heavy consistency. Toss the dough around with lightly floured hands, long enough to remove the stickiness. Pat it out, about ½ inch thick, and cut into uneven triangular shapes. Lay them out on an ungreased cookie sheet or a tray, brush the tops of the scones with the reserved egg white, sprinkle each scone with **½ teaspoon granulated sugar** and bake in a hot (425°F.) oven for 10 to 15 minutes, or until done. This makes 1½ dozen scones. Serve them hot with butter.

INGREDIENTS: 2 cups sifted flour; 1 tablespoon baking powder; 1 teaspoon salt; 2 tablespoons sugar; ⅓ cup margarine or butter; ⅓ cup buttermilk; 1 egg; 1 cup blueberries in 1 teaspoon flour; sugar for topping.

OLD-FASHIONED BLUEBERRY MUFFINS

Set oven heat at 425°F. Grease thoroughly 2 dozen muffin-pan sections. Cream **¼ cup softened butter** with **½ cup granulated sugar,** until smooth and ungranular. Break **1 egg** into a measuring cup and add **milk** to make a full cup. Beat the liquid into the butter mixture; use the electric mixer and see that it's smooth before you leave it for other things. Sift together **1¾ cups sifted flour, 2½ teaspoons baking powder, ½ teaspoon salt.** Combine the wet ingredients with the dry, quickly, just moistening the flour. The batter will be lumpy. Toss **1 cup blueberries,** fresh or frozen dry, with **1 tablespoon flour.** Fold into the batter. Fill muffin pans two-thirds full. The recipe given to me suggests greasing the pans with butter, but this has a tendency to burn; I suggest that you use a vegetable shortening, instead.

Bake the muffins 15 to 20 minutes in a 425°F. oven. Test for doneness at the end of 15 minutes.

INGREDIENTS: ¼ cup butter; ½ cup granulated sugar; 1 egg and milk to make a cup; 1¾ cups sifted flour; 2½ teaspoons baking powder; ½ teaspoon salt; 1 cup blueberries; 1 tablespoon flour.

BLUEBERRY PECAN BREAD

An excellent bread, not too sweet, which freezes perfectly. Preheat your oven to 350°F. Grease thoroughly, with vegetable shortening, 2 small loaf pans (7½ x 3½ x 2¼ inches) or one regulation-size bread pan; then toss 2 tablespoons flour in them.

In a mixing bowl, sift together 1¾ cups sifted flour, ⅔ cup sugar, ½ teaspoon salt, 1½ teaspoons baking powder, and ½ teaspoon baking soda. Make a well in the flour mix and drop into it 1 large egg. Beat it thoroughly within its own well, not mixing it with the dry ingredients. Grate the orange part of the rind of 1 orange—keep away from the white part—and brush that into the bowl on top of the egg, using a pastry brush for the purpose. Squeeze the juice of the orange into a cup, add to it 2 tablespoons margarine or butter (margarine does well here). Fill to the ¾ cup mark with boiling water. Mix the juice, water, and butter to melt the butter, then add it to the bowl. Quickly combine the dry ingredients with the wet ingredients. As soon as they are combined, stop. Toss 1 cup blueberries, fresh or frozen dry, and ¾ cup chopped pecans with 1 tablespoon flour. The flour will keep the fruit from sinking to the bottom of the batter. Add the blueberries and pecans to the batter, blending gently, distributing evenly. Pour the batter into the loaf pans, or pan, and bake for 35 to 45 minutes, or until the bread tests done. With frozen blueberries, it will take at least 10 minutes longer than it will with fresh to bake this bread. Makes 2 small loaves or 1 large loaf.

INGREDIENTS: 1¾ cups sifted flour; ⅔ cup sugar; ½ teaspoon salt; 1½ teaspoons baking powder; ½ teaspoon baking soda; 1 large egg; rind and juice of 1 orange; 2 tablespoons margarine or butter; boiling water; 1 cup blueberries; ¾ cup chopped pecans; 1 tablespoon flour.

BROWN SUGAR BLUEBERRY MUFFINS

An excellent blueberry muffin. For 1 dozen muffins, proceed as follows; multiply for more. I like to bake about 4 dozen at a time; the leftover muffins will freeze and reheat as new.

Preheat oven to 425°F. Mix **1 beaten egg** with **¾ cup light brown sugar** and **½ cup milk**. Add and mix in **1 tablespoon melted butter or margarine**. Sift together **1½ cups flour**, **¼ teaspoon salt**, and **1 tablespoon baking powder**. Combine wet and dry ingredients, quickly, just to the point of assimilation. Fold in **1½ cups blueberries**, fresh or frozen dry, tossed with **2 tablespoons flour**. Fill 1 dozen well-greased and floured muffin-pan sections two-thirds full. (Vegetable shortening for greasing is best.) Bake 12 minutes in a hot (425°F.) oven, or until they test done with a skewer in and out. Loosen muffins and serve hot.

INGREDIENTS: 1 beaten egg; ¾ cup light brown sugar; ½ cup milk; 1 tablespoon butter; 1½ cups flour; ¼ teaspoon salt; 1 tablespoon baking powder; 1½ cups blueberries tossed in 2 tablespoons flour.

NOTE: The best way to reheat any muffin is to place it in the muffin pan in which it was baked in the first place. Heat quickly until very hot. The muffin pan keeps the edges tender and fresh.

BLUEBERRY SPICE CAKE (or BREAD)

This recipe came to me from South Newbury, Vermont. The note with it said: "This is my mother-in-law's blueberry cake which her three boys always looked for each year, come blueberry season, and which I still try to have when they visit." The lady, whose recipe it was, died in 1941. I shall give it to you as the Lady from South Newbury had it in her file. Notes from Elsie within the recipe are in brackets. We at Blueberry Hill have it often and love it dearly.

"Cream **⅓ cup butter** and **1 cup sugar**. Add **1 egg**, well beaten. Beat very light, all together. Add **1 cup milk**, alternately with the following dry ingredients: 2½ cups sifted flour (measured after sifting), ½ teaspoon salt, 4 teaspoons baking powder, ⅛ teaspoon cinnamon, ⅛ teaspoon allspice, and ⅛ teaspoon cloves. Beat after each addition thoroughly, so that it is very, very light.

"Add 1 pint blueberries [fresh or frozen dry] well floured with ¼ cup flour. Bake at 375°F. in a greased and floured angel food mold for about 45 minutes. [This amount will not fill a 10-inch angel food pan more than half-full; maybe in the old days they had smaller-sized angel food cakes.] Test for doneness, using judgment.

"You can eat it cold or hot. The boys liked it fresh, with or without butter. You can even serve it hot, with lemon sauce."

I would like to add that the pan needs to be cooled right side up. Don't invert it. The weight of the blueberries will be too much for it, as I discovered to my sorrow, and it will fall out. It must cool thoroughly before you remove it from the pan. Better still, cut it right in the pan. A delicious bread—or cake—call it what you will.

INGREDIENTS: ⅓ cup butter; 1 cup sugar; 1 egg; 1 cup milk; 2½ cups sifted flour; ½ teaspoon salt; 4 teaspoons baking powder; ⅛ teaspoon cinnamon; ⅛ teaspoon allspice; ⅛ teaspoon cloves; 1 pint blueberries; ¼ cup flour.

BLUEBERRY KUCHEN

Here is an authentic kuchen, the dough rich. You should be proud to serve it. The recipe for the pastry will be sufficient for two kuchens. You may either prepare two of them at one time or make just one and refrigerate the balance of the dough. It will keep in the refrigerator, wrapped in saran or aluminum foil, for a week. In the plum season, you will find that this recipe will be equally fine for a plum kuchen; in this case, dot the plums with butter and omit the lemon.

Blend together with a fork 1½ cups unsifted flour, ⅓ cup sugar, and ½ teaspoon salt. Cut in ¼ pound (1 stick) butter—and this time butter is essential for the flavor—using a pastry blender. It should reach the texture of fine gravel. Add **1 beaten egg.** Work with floured fingers until the egg is thoroughly blended into the dough, and forms a ball. Cut it in half.

For one kuchen, use one half of the dough, rolled to line an ungreased 8-inch Pyrex round cake pan. Fit the dough up the sides of the dish; flute the edges casually.

For Filling for One Kuchen: Mix together **1 quart blueberries,** fresh or frozen dry; **¼ cup sugar; 1 teaspoon flour;** and **1 teaspoon lemon juice** and fill the kuchen shell with this mixture. Sprinkle the top with **1 teaspoon cinnamon-sugar.** Bake at 450°F. for 15 minutes; turn heat down to 325°F. and continue baking for 20 minutes. When the blueberries are cooked through and bubbling all over, the kuchen is finished. Serve warm with, or without, **whipped cream.**

INGREDIENTS:
For pastry for two kuchens: 1½ cups unsifted flour; ⅓ cup sugar; ½ teaspoon salt; ¼ pound butter; 1 egg.
For filling for one kuchen: 1 quart blueberries; ¼ cup sugar; 1 teaspoon flour; 1 teaspoon lemon juice; 1 teaspoon cinnamon-sugar.

MAINE BLUEBERRY CAKE

We have lots of friends in Maine. They have good blueberries, too.

Preheat oven to 350°F. and lightly grease a 13 x 9 x 2-inch cake pan, Pyrex or other. Toss **1¼ cups blueberries,** fresh or frozen dry, with **2 tablespoons flour.** Set them aside.

Cream together in your electric beater at high speed **1 cup sugar** and **½ cup (1 stick) margarine** or **butter.** Add **2 eggs;** continue beating until very light. Slowly add **½ cup light cream** until thoroughly combined. Then add **2 cups sifted flour** and **2 teaspoons baking powder,** beating slowly and only until the mixture is combined. Fold in the floured blueberries. **Pour** the batter into the pan. Sprinkle the top of the batter with a combination of **¼ cup sugar** and **¼**

teaspoon nutmeg. Bake 35 minutes or until your cake tester comes out clean and dry. Serve directly from the pan while the cake is warm, with butter, if you wish to serve this as a hot bread; if you consider it a dessert, serve it warm with whipped cream or heavy cream from a pitcher. This makes enough cake for 12.

INGREDIENTS: 1¼ cups blueberries; 2 tablespoons flour; 1 cup sugar; ½ cup margarine or butter; 2 eggs; ½ cup light cream; 2 cups sifted flour; 2 teaspoons baking powder; ¼ cup sugar; ¼ teaspoon nutmeg.

BLUEBERRY GRUNT

An old-time Vermont favorite. Simmer in a large iron skillet, covered, **1 quart** (4 cups) **blueberries,** fresh or frozen dry; **1 cup sugar; 1 teaspoon lemon juice;** and **¼ cup boiling water,** until the berries are soft and the liquid in the pan increases. This will take between 5 and 10 minutes.

Prepare a rich baking powder biscuit dough (see recipe for strawberry shortcake dough, page 145) using 2 cups of flour (half the recipe given for the shortcake) and roll or pat it out ¼ inch thick. Cut the dough into 1½-inch squares with a floured sharp knife and drop it onto the berries. Cover the pan and cook for 20 minutes. Serve hot from the skillet, with chilled heavy cream. Makes 6 servings.

INGREDIENTS: 1 quart blueberries; 1 cup sugar; 1 teaspoon lemon juice; ¼ cup boiling water; 2-cup recipe shortcake dough; heavy cream.

BLUEBERRY-PEACH COBBLER

Peaches and blueberries have a natural affinity, one for the other. Bring to a boil over moderate heat **1 cup blueberries,** fresh or frozen dry; **1½ cups sugared, sliced, very ripe peaches; ⅓ cup light brown sugar; ⅓ cup water;** and **1 teaspoon arrowroot** or **2 teaspoons cornstarch.** When the fruit has thickened somewhat, stir in **2 tablespoons butter** and 1½ teaspoons fresh lemon juice. The butter will melt quickly. Stir it in. If the blueberries are at all overripe, increase the lemon juice to 2 teaspoons; if they are not ripe, still on the red side, decrease the lemon juice to 1 teaspoon. Place the fruit in an earthenware or Pyrex baking dish, 1-quart size.

For the Crust: Sift together 1 cup flour, 1½ teaspoons baking powder, ½ cup granulated sugar, and ¼ teaspoon salt. Add ¼ cup (½ stick) soft margarine or butter, beat until combined, then add ½ cup rich milk, beating until just smooth, no more. Drop the topping in large spoonfuls over the fruit, sprinkle with 1 tablespoon cinnamon-sugar, and bake in 350°F. oven for 20 to 25 minutes, or until the top crust is done all the way through. Be sure it is; lift up a section of it with a fork and see. Serve warm with cream, thick and heavy. Serves 6.

INGREDIENTS: 1 cup blueberries; 1½ cups sugared, sliced, very ripe peaches; ⅓ cup light brown sugar; ⅓ cup water; 1 teaspoon arrowroot or 2 teaspoons cornstarch; 2 tablespoons butter; 1½ teaspoons fresh lemon juice.
For the crust: 1 cup flour; 1½ teaspoons baking powder; ½ cup granulated sugar; ¼ teaspoon salt; ¼ cup margarine or butter; ½ cup rich milk; 1 tablespoon cinnamon-sugar; heavy cream.

BLUEBERRY SHORTCAKE

Prepare shortcake as in recipe for strawberry shortcake (page 145) using one-half the recipe (2 cups flour) or follow the biscuit recipe in my *Blueberry Hill Cookbook*, using light cream instead of milk. Roll into one large rectangle, about ½ inch thick, fitting it into a baking dish, 13 x 9 x 2 inches. Over the top of the unbaked dough, spread 2 cups ripe blueberries, fresh or frozen dry, sweetened with ¼ to ½ cup light brown sugar (sweetening must depend on the ripeness of the blueberries), ¼ teaspoon nutmeg and ½ teaspoon lemon juice added. Bake at 375°F. until the dough is baked through and the berries have formed a blueberry sauce on top. Serve hot with **heavy cream** or whipped cream. Makes 6 servings.

INGREDIENTS: ½ recipe shortcake dough (page 145); 2 cups ripe blueberries; ¼ to ½ cup light brown sugar; ¼ teaspoon nutmeg; ½ teaspoon lemon juice; heavy cream.

LITHUANIAN PANCAKES
WITH SPICED BLUEBERRY SAUCE

These are a very light dessert pancake. They can be served at breakfast as well, and are particularly good for a company brunch menu. An authentic Lithuanian recipe.

Separate **4 eggs.** Beat the yolks until they are very light. At low speed, stir into the yolks **1 cup sifted flour, 1 tablespoon commercial sour cream, 1 cup milk, ¼ teaspoon salt.** Fold in the stiffly beaten whites of the 4 eggs.

To fry, get a large iron frying pan hot, sizzle a large lump of **butter** in it, add 1 large tablespoon batter for each pancake. Brown lightly, then turn and brown on the other side. Be sure the cakes are cooked through before serving; test one for an approximation of cooking time. Add more butter to the pan as you need it. If you prefer, for breakfast, these may be fried in **sausage fat.** Serve with a spoonful of hot spiced blueberry sauce. Makes 4 to 6 servings.

Spiced Blueberry Sauce: In a saucepan, heat **2 cups blueberries,** fresh or frozen dry; **½ cup sugar; 1 tablespoon water; 1 tablespoon lemon juice; 1 stick cinnamon** tied in a bag with **4 whole cloves;** and **2 tablespoons sherry.** Bring to a boil, let it boil for 3 or 4 minutes, remove the spice in the bag. Thicken, only if necessary, with **½ teaspoon cornstarch** dissolved in a little **cold water.** This should not be necessary but depends on the variety of blueberry. Yields 2 cups.

INGREDIENTS:

For the pancakes: 4 eggs; 1 cup sifted flour; 1 tablespoon commercial sour cream; 1 cup milk; ¼ teaspoon salt; butter or sausage fat to fry.

For the sauce: 2 cups blueberries; ½ cup sugar; 1 tablespoon water; 1 tablespoon lemon juice; 1 stick cinnamon; 4 whole cloves; 2 tablespoons sherry; ½ teaspoon
cornstarch; cold water.

BLUEBERRY DESSERT PANCAKES

A delightful affair to be served as an after-theatre supper
with lots and lots of hot coffee.

Soften **2 packages** (3 ounces each) **cream cheese,** a matter
taken care of simply by leaving them around at room temperature for a few hours. Combine the cheese with **¼ cup
milk,** using a fork to mix them together until the mixture is
smooth and very creamy. I'd suggest doing it in a blender or
an electric mixer, but then you have all the trouble of getting the cheese off the blades. A fork's best. Set this aside.

Add **¼ cup sugar** to **3 cups blueberries,** fresh or frozen
dry. Toss lightly. Set aside.

Sift **1½ cups flour** with **2½ teaspoons baking powder, ¾
teaspoon salt,** and **3 tablespoons sugar.** Combine, in a bowl,
1 cup milk; 1 egg, beaten; and **¼ cup** (½ stick) **butter,**
melted. Add the egg-milk mixture to the dry ingredients. Stir
only to mix; don't overmix. The batter should be very thin;
if it isn't, add a little extra milk, again stirring just to mix.

Bake pancakes, about 4 inches in diameter, on a hot griddle or in a small frying pan. If you have a properly seasoned
griddle, you'll need no shortening. Turn once, and as soon
as each side is brown, remove to a clean linen towel. Spread
each pancake with some of the cream cheese mixture, add
a spoonful of the blueberries, roll quickly and sprinkle with
confectioners' sugar. Serve at once. You will have enough
for 6.

INGREDIENTS:

For the filling: 2 packages (3 ounces each) cream cheese;
¼ cup milk; ¼ cup sugar; 3 cups blueberries.

For the pancakes: 1½ cups flour; 2½ teaspoons baking
powder; ¾ teaspoon salt; 3 tablespoons sugar; 1 cup
milk; 1 egg; ¼ cup butter; confectioners' sugar.

QUICK BLUEBERRY PIE

Mix together in a heavy saucepan 1 quart blueberries, fresh
or frozen dry; ¼ cup flour; 2 tablespoons butter; ½ teaspoon
salt; 2 tablespoons lemon juice; 1 cup granulated sugar; 1
cup light brown sugar. Cook at low heat, stirring, until the
mixture thickens, about 5 minutes after it comes to a boil.
Cool. Add 1 quart blueberries, uncooked. Stir to combine
the cooked and the uncooked berries.

Have ready a baked **pie shell**, 10-inch size. Perhaps you
have one in your freezer. If not, bake one, following the
recipe on page 287; better still, bake two, so you *will* have
one in the freezer.

Fill the baked pie shell with the blueberries, cooked and
uncooked. Whip ½ pint heavy cream to a good, stiffened
state, add 1 teaspoon superfine sugar, ½ teaspoon vanilla,
and spread the cream over the berries. Chill. A most superior blueberry pie.

INGREDIENTS: 2 quarts blueberries; ¼ cup flour; 2 tablespoons butter; ½ teaspoon salt; 2 tablespoons lemon
juice; 1 cup granulated sugar; 1 cup light brown sugar;
10-inch baked pie shell; ½ pint heavy cream; 1 teaspoon
superfine sugar; ½ teaspoon vanilla.

AUGUST

PARTY MENU

Wasn't It a Lovely Wedding?

MELON CHAMPAGNE CUP
COLD BEET SOUP
WHOLE POACHED SALMON WITH DILL SAUCE
FINE-NOODLE BAKE
GRATED ZUCCHINI
SAUTEED FRUIT COMPOTE
GREEK SALAD
PUMPERNICKL WATERCRESS ROLLS
CREME AU CARAMEL
TAKE-HOME CANADIAN WEDDING CAKES

Given a balmy day, a puff of cloud in a blue sky, a garden wedding in mid-August is a perfection. Your luncheon could be platitudinous: tiny sandwiches, punch, the usual thing, or, as it is here, it might very well emerge as an exquisite affair, the food delicious, unusual, and perfectly prepared and served. I don't suggest this meal if you expect hundreds, even fifty people to attend. This is a luncheon for the close friends and relatives of the bride and groom—no more, I should say, than 25 people. It's a meal to be served to sitting-down guests, each part of it to be savored slowly, appreciated fully.

The recipes for the soup and the salmon are for either hot

or cold; if one is served hot, let the other be cold. Vice-versa, too.

This menu is for 25.

MELON CHAMPAGNE CUP

Be sure the melons are completely ripe. Slice in half, remove seeds and scoop out balls from **1 large honeydew melon, 1 casaba melon, 2 canteloupes, 1 Persian melon.** Leave the balls in a large bowl, covered with a liberal sprinkling of **superfine sugar.** The amount of sugar depends on the sweetness of the melon, so taste them as you go. Just before serving, place the melon balls, some of each, in champagne glasses, filling each glass with the balls. Sprinkle each glass of fruit with a few dashes of **angostura bitters.** When the guests are seated, pour enough **champagne** into each glass to fill it.

INGREDIENTS: 1 large honeydew melon; 1 casaba melon; 2 cantaloupes; 1 Persian melon; superfine sugar; angostura bitters; champagne.

COLD BEET SOUP

You will need **4 quarts rich chicken broth** or **chicken consommé.** Homemade chicken broth is best (see recipe on page 13); prepared weeks in advance, it freezes perfectly, packed in fruit juice cans, the large ones. Reheat the broth in the same cans, right from the frozen state, and, as soon as the broth is melted on the edges sufficiently to remove it, transfer it to your soup kettle and finish the defrosting process there. Wash thoroughly **1 dozen large beets,** peel them with a potato peeler, and grate them. Cover them with the broth and allow the beets to simmer until they are soft, about 15 minutes. If you prefer, you can use, instead of the fresh beets, **4 cans** (12-ounce size) **julienne beets,** juice and all. The canned beets should be brought just to a boil with the chicken broth. Continue now, as with fresh beets.

Chop very fine, preferably with a hand-chopper in a

wooden bowl, **8 scallions**, tops and all; **8 blossoms fresh dill**
or **2 teaspoons dried dill weed.** Pour the hot broth over the
vegetables and allow them to sit for about an hour.

You can now strain the soup so as to have it clear. I like
the taste and texture of the vegetables and do not always
strain them out. In either case, add **1 cup light dry sherry**
and **1 teaspoon sugar.** Refrigerate if you're not planning to
serve the soup within a few hours. Reheat at serving time.
Pass a bowl of **commercial sour cream** with it.

This soup can be served chilled. A delicious contrast to the
cold soup is achieved if you will place in each soup bowl one
tiny freshly boiled, still hot, new potato. Pour the cold soup
over this, pass the sour cream and serve with pumpernickl
watercress rolls.

INGREDIENTS: 4 quarts rich chicken broth or consommé; 1
dozen large beets or 4 cans julienne beets; 8 scallions;
8 blossoms fresh dill or 2 teaspoons dill weed; 1 cup
light dry sherry; 1 teaspoon sugar; 1 quart commercial
sour cream.

WHOLE POACHED SALMON
WITH DILL SAUCE

Find a pot big enough to hold a whole salmon. It can be
a washtub or something like that. You'll want a fish weighing about 15 pounds. Wash the **whole salmon,** with head and
tail removed, and wrap it in a triple or quadruple thickness
of cheesecloth, sewing it up so that it fits the fish snugly, and
leaving a large piece of cheesecloth on each end to serve
later as a handle. Lay the fish in the pan. Set the pan on your
range and pour over the fish sufficient **water** to cover it completely. Use a teakettle; then you won't have to lift the heavy
pan from the sink to the range. Keep track of the number of
filled teakettles you've used.

For each gallon of water (most teakettles hold 16 cups,
which is a gallon), add **½ cup lemon juice** or **½ cup vine-**
gar; 2 tablespoons salt; 1 cup light sweet white wine or **pale**

sherry; **4 sprigs parsley; 2 bay leaves; 4 peppercorns.** This is known as a "court bouillon." Let the water boil up over the fish, then quickly reduce the heat so it will simmer slowly. It will be done in about 10 minutes to each pound (2½ hours for a 15-pound fish), but keep watch over it, testing it with the prongs of a fork. Stop the cooking as soon as the fish flakes.

Lift the salmon carefully with the two ends of the cheesecloth. You can hold onto these with tongs on each side, if the cheesecloth is too hot for you. Set the fish down carefully on the edge of a counter or work table and slit the cheesecloth. Remove the cheesecloth from the topside of the fish, and, at this time, remove the skin and dark part of the flesh of the fish. Now turn the fish gently over the edge of the counter to a waiting platter of the proper size. You'll obviously need someone there to hold the platter. Careful is the mood here; the platter should be close by, poised. Now remove the rest of the skin and the rest of the dark flesh.

(You will notice, perhaps, that I have spoken about removing the head and the tail. Purists like to serve a fish with these parts intact. I'm not one of these. The eyes make me very nervous, as perhaps I deserve to be, under the circumstances.)

Keep the salmon in a warm spot while you prepare the following dill sauce. You can moisten the fish occasionally with a little hot court bouillon to keep it from drying out while it's waiting.

For the Dill Sauce: In the top of a double boiler, melt ¾ **cup (1½ sticks) butter.** Stir in ¾ **cup flour,** stirring around until smooth. Add gradually, **2 cups court bouillon** (the liquid in which you poached the salmon), strained, and **1 quart light cream.** Stir the sauce until thick and smooth. Season with **2 teaspoons salt,** ½ **teaspoon freshly ground pepper,** ¼ **cup chopped fresh dill** or **2 tablespoons dill weed.** Just before serving, add a little of the sauce to **6 beaten egg yolks,** stir it around with a fork, then return the egg yolk mixture to the sauce. Reheat the sauce, but don't let it boil. Pass with the salmon, which by this time you have ensconced in a circle of **parsley** and **cucumbers**.

The dill sauce can be done over direct heat, if you'll keep your eye on it every minute.

If you would like to serve the salmon chilled—a bit simpler, I suppose, at such a time—do not remove it from the court bouillon immediately after it is cooked. Let it remain, still in its cheesecloth coat, right in the bouillon, covered, for an hour. Then uncover it and let it come to room temperature. At this time remove the cloth and the skin as directed above and chill in the refrigerator for 24 hours, lightly covered with saran or aluminum foil.

For cold salmon, the following sauce is just right.

For Cucumber Sauce: Pare, chop, and drain **4 crisp fresh cucumbers**. Beat until stiff **2 cups heavy cream**, seasoned with **1 teaspoon sugar**, **½ teaspoon salt**, **⅛ teaspoon freshly ground pepper**. Add **½ cup white vinegar** and the cucumbers. Pile lightly in a bowl, pass with the salmon.

INGREDIENTS: 1 whole salmon, about 15 pounds; water to cover; parsley; cucumbers.

For the court bouillon: for each gallon water, ½ cup lemon juice or vinegar; 2 tablespoons salt; 1 cup light sweet white wine or pale sherry; 4 sprigs parsley; 2 bay leaves; 4 peppercorns.

For the dill sauce: ¾ cup butter; ¾ cup flour; 2 cups court bouillon (see above); 1 quart light cream; 2 teaspoons salt; ½ teaspoon pepper; ¼ cup chopped fresh dill or 2 tablespoons dill weed; 6 egg yolks.

For the cucumber sauce: 4 cucumbers; 2 cups heavy cream; 1 teaspoon sugar; ½ teaspoon salt; ⅛ teaspoon freshly ground pepper; ½ cup white vinegar.

FINE-NOODLE BAKE

Prepare **3 pounds fine noodles** as directed on the box. Lots of water, **1 teaspoon salt** for each pound, and a minimum of boiling time—about 2 minutes after the water comes back to a boil. Drain them thoroughly, rinse with cold water, and, unless you are ready for them fairly soon, refrigerate them. They can be cooked the day before or even two days before the important day.

This amount of noodles should fill two large casseroles, unless you have a really outsized one. Butter liberally your baking dish with about ¼ **pound** (1 stick) **butter.** Arrange the noodles in the casseroles and season them thoroughly with **salt** and freshly ground **pepper.** Mix together lightly **1 pint heavy cream,** whipped; and **1 pint commercial sour cream; 8 egg yolks; ¼ cup chopped parsley.** Fold this mixture into the noodles in the two casseroles. Sauté **3 cups soft bread crumbs** in ¼ **pound** (1 stick) **butter** until they are lightly browned. Sprinkle them around on top of the noodles. Bake until bubbly and brown in 375°F. oven—about 30 to 40 minutes. The casseroles can be prepared several hours ahead of time; the browning can be a last half-hour job.

INGREDIENTS: 3 pounds fine noodles; water; salt; ½ pound butter; pepper; 1 pint heavy cream; 1 pint commercial sour cream; 8 egg yolks; ¼ cup chopped parsley; 3 cups soft bread crumbs.

GRATED ZUCCHINI

A 10-minute job, once you've grated the zucchini. Grate **12 small zucchini squash,** washed and unpeeled, on a coarse grater so that you have thin strips. Set aside, covered with saran, in refrigerator until ready for the final preparation.

Heat a large black iron frying pan, toss in ¼ **pound** (1 stick) **butter,** let it sizzle and, over high heat, quickly wilt the zucchini. Keep it moving in the butter, turning it again and again, and, in a very few minutes you will find that it is starting to lose its starch. Don't let it soften completely; it should retain some crispness. Season with **1 teaspoon salt,** ¼ **teaspoon freshly ground pepper,** ½ **teaspoon sugar,** ½ **teaspoon marjoram.** Taste and, if you think you need more salt, or pepper, or anything, add it. You're the judge, there. Serve as soon as possible.

INGREDIENTS: 12 small zucchini; ¼ pound butter; 1 teaspoon salt; ¼ teaspoon pepper; ½ teaspoon sugar; ½ teaspoon marjoram.

SAUTEED FRUIT COMPOTE

A lovely tidbit, an extra. Peel 12 ripe bananas (ripe, not bursting—they need some body to hold themselves together) and cut them into ½-inch rounds. Melt ¼ pound butter and ¼ pound margarine in a heavy 12-inch skillet, add the bananas, 1 large (1 pound, 4 ounces) can pineapple chunks, drained, and sprinkle fruit with ½ cup light brown sugar. Heat slowly, turning with a pancake turner so that the fruit will sauté evenly. After 5 minutes, add 1 large can Bing cherries, drained. Continue to heat and turn for 2 minutes. Pour over the whole ½ cup light sweet red wine; heat 2 minutes longer. Serve in fruit dishes, hot from the pot, or pass to those who wish it.

INGREDIENTS: 12 ripe bananas; ¼ pound butter; ¼ pound margarine; 1 large can pineapple chunks; ½ cup light brown sugar; 1 large can Bing cherries; ½ cup light sweet red wine.

GREEK SALAD

You will want an enormous bowl of this, or two moderate-sized bowls. This recipe is for enough to fill your largest bowl, enough for all 25 guests at one mixing.

Wash, dry thoroughly, and break into small pieces 4 heads romaine lettuce, 4 heads iceberg lettuce, and 2 heads bibb or Boston lettuce. In a separate bowl, place 6 stalks hearts of celery, cut in diagonal slices; 6 unpeeled garden-fresh cucumbers (peel them if they're "boughten"), cut into small pieces (omit cucumbers if you're serving the salmon cold with the cucumber sauce); 6 scallions, trimmed and sliced thin; 8 ripe tomatoes, cut into small chunks; 1 green pepper, the seeds and spines removed, and the pepper chopped into small chunks; 2 dozen Greek black olives (these are packed in olive oil and are obtainable from your delicatessen); **4 small herrings,** cut up (also obtainable at most delicatessens; you can use 1 small jar herring tidbits if you can't get the herrings); **4 or 5 stalks of fennel,** also called finocchio, if you can come by it in your neighborhood; **1 tablespoon oregano; 1 cup cut-up cheese,** preferably provolone, though any similar soft cheese will do.

Refrigerate the greens, wrapped in a wet towel or pillow-case, and, separately, refrigerate the other ingredients of the salad, in their own bowl, covered with saran.

When ready to serve, combine the greens and the body of the salad in your bowl. Toss them together well. Then pour over the whole **2 cups pure olive oil, ⅔ cup wine vinegar.** Toss the salad with the dressing. Then, and only then, taste for **salt** and **pepper.** You'll need it but it will vary with the salt in the herring, so add it to your taste here.

INGREDIENTS: 4 heads romaine lettuce; 4 heads iceberg lettuce; 2 heads bibb lettuce or Boston lettuce; 6 stalks hearts of celery; 6 unpeeled garden-fresh cucumbers; 6 scallions; 8 ripe tomatoes; 1 green pepper; 2 dozen Greek black olives; 4 small herrings (or 1 small jar herring tidbits in wine); 4 or 5 stalks fennel; 1 tablespoon oregano; 1 cup cut-up provolone or other soft cheese; 2 cups olive oil; ⅔ cup wine vinegar; salt; pepper.

PUMPERNICKL WATERCRESS ROLLS

Slice fresh, soft **pumpernickl** very thin, or buy thin-sliced bread. Spread each slice liberally with softened **butter.** Place a sprig of **watercress** on one side of each slice and, starting there, roll the bread around the watercress. If the bread seems about to break, stop and help it along with a damp cloth. When the rolls are complete, fasten with toothpicks. Set them in a roasting pan on a slightly dampened cloth; arrange them close together and cover with another damp cloth. Refrigerate until needed. You can serve them as is, or slice them into rounds.

INGREDIENTS: 4 loaves fresh pumpernickl bread; 1 pound butter; 2 bunches watercress.

CREME AU CARAMEL

Sometimes called *crème reversée*, this is the classic caramel custard to be found in most French restaurants. Most of these custards, however, tend to be watery, thin, and occasionally actually tasteless. The recipe given here, on the contrary, will give you a beautiful, rich custard; fun to make; a triumph to serve. It will keep in the refrigerator, perfectly, for at least three days, so that, without a qualm, you can have it ready and waiting a day or two before the wedding.

You will have enough here for 24 custard cups or 4 1-quart molds. Bring **2 quarts rich milk** (or half milk and half light cream if your dairy doesn't provide milk with high butterfat content) to the scalding point, with **4 cups granulated sugar.** Don't let it boil. Set it aside a few moments to cool, then add it slowly to the well-beaten **yolks of 2 dozen eggs,** stirring all the time. Remember not to add the eggs to the hot milk, but the hot milk to the eggs. Add **2 teaspoons vanilla** and **1 cup light sherry.** Set the mixture aside for a few minutes. (Please note: You will not use the whites of these eggs, so freeze them in units of four, labeled, in glass jars. They can be called upon for mousses and white cakes; see strawberry mousse in my *Blueberry Hill Cookbook* and leftovers section of this chapter.)

Now make the caramel. This is more fun than you can imagine. Rather miraculous, actually, if you've never done it or seen it done. You start, in this case, with **3 cups granulated sugar** in a heavy saucepan. Set the pan over moderate heat, stirring it without a moment's pause. It will lump first, then melt, then darken to the color of caramels. Well, it *is* caramel, so why not? Have ready 24 custard cups or 4 1-quart Pyrex baking dishes or molds, and, working quickly, pour the caramel, about 1 tablespoon each time, into the cups, one at a time. Move the cups around and around until the lower half and as much of the sides of the cups as possible are coated with the caramel. The caramel sets almost as soon as it hits the cup, and will become hard, so you have to work fast.

The trick here is to keep the pan of caramel warm while you're working with the individual cups. If you will do one cup, keeping the pan of caramel warm while you're reaching for another, you can prevent the caramel from hardening before you've had a chance to get at it.

I strongly suggest, in fact urge, if you've never done this before, that you cut the recipe in four, and do just six cups with the first batch (¾ cup sugar). When you've done these successfully, do another batch, and so on.

The larger casseroles, surely, will go well for you; just four to do, a breeze.

Set the custard cups in cake pans or flat casseroles, set them in a 325°F. oven, and pour hot water around them to come at least one-third of the way up their sides. Then, and only then, add the custard, pouring it directly over the caramel. By adding the water and the custard after the cups are safely settled in the oven, you lessen the chance of spilling either of them.

Bake 30 to 40 minutes. Test the custard with a silver knife. When it comes out clean, the custard is done.

You can serve these warm or chill them. In this case, for this many people, chilled is the better way. But try them, some more relaxed time, when they're still warm. Velvet. When you're ready to serve them, it's fun to turn them out in little sauce dishes; the larger one should be turned out on a deep round platter. Set the sauce dish or platter tightly against the top of the custard dish or casserole and quickly turn them both over, keeping them tight against each other. The custard will fall down in perfect shape, and, *mirabile dictu,* the caramel which was hard as a rock before it went into the oven, is now a delicious, runny sauce.

This is, without reservation, my most favorite dessert. That's all I will say about it or for it.

P.S. If the custard doesn't come right out when you invert

it, turn the cups back upright and run a sharp knife dipped in boiling water around the edge. This time you'll have no trouble.

INGREDIENTS: 2 quarts rich milk; 4 cups granulated sugar; yolks of 24 eggs; 2 teaspoons vanilla; 1 cup light sherry; 3 cups granulated sugar for caramel.

NOTE: In the event you have trouble dividing, the following are the ingredients you will want for six of these custards; a family-size recipe.

INGREDIENTS FOR 6 CUSTARDS: 2 cups rich milk; 1 cup granulated sugar; yolks of 6 eggs; ½ teaspoon vanilla; ¼ cup sherry; ¾ cup granulated sugar for caramel.

TAKE-HOME CANADIAN WEDDING CAKES

These little cakes are in addition to the traditional wedding cake, which I shall assume you will have had baked and decorated by a professional baker. In the event you wish to bake your own, the recipe for this cake, multiplied by four, will give you enough batter for a cake to serve 100. Baked in regulation muffin pans, the recipe here will give you 36 small cakes; better still, if you will bake them in the very small tea muffin pans, you will have about 100. These are moist and fine keepers.

Cream thoroughly with your electric beater **1 cup best-quality lard** and **2 cups granulated sugar**. When this mixture is smooth and ungranular, drop in **2 unbeaten eggs**. Dissolve **4 teaspoons baking soda** in **2½ cups applesauce**, canned or homemade, and add it. The cake is improved, of course, if the applesauce is your own, made of tart apples. Combine the eggs and applesauce with the creamed lard and sugar and, when it is thoroughly mixed, add, one after the other, **4 cups flour, 1 tablespoon cinnamon, ¾ teaspoon ground cloves, ¾ teaspoon salt, 2 teaspoons vanilla, 2 cups seedless raisins, 1 cup broken pecans.**

Grease 3 dozen regulation muffin-pan sections with a good

vegetable shortening; if you are using the tiny tea-muffin tins, fill as many as you have and bake the cakes in relays. You should have about 8 dozen of the smaller size. Bake the larger cakes at 325°F. about 30 minutes or until they test done. The smaller ones will be done in about 15 minutes.

For Lemon Icing: Use your electric beater and beat at low speed until all ingredients are well combined. You will want ¾ cup (1½ sticks) **soft butter** or **margarine** (margarine may be used here quite satisfactorily; it does not have the rich texture of the butter, of course), **6 cups sifted confectioners' sugar**, the **grated rind** (just the yellow, keep away from the white) of **1 large firm lemon**, and, immediately after grating it, the **juice of said lemon** and **⅛ teaspoon salt**. When the ingredients are combined, increase the speed of your beater to high and beat for about 3 minutes. If the icing is too thick to spread, sparingly add **cream**; you should need no more than 1 teaspoon, so go easy. As soon as the consistency is correct for spreading, ice the cakes. If you have too much icing, refrigerate or freeze it; defrosted, it's as good as new.

For Plain Confectioners' Icing: A simpler, more traditional icing for these cakes is the plain confectioners' icing. Beat, in your electric mixer or blender, **3 cups sifted confectioners' sugar** and **6 tablespoons heated light cream**. Beat for 2 minutes at high speed. Add **almond or lemon extract** to your taste.

Set the individual cakes in small foil cups, just to fit. Set these on squares of saran, catch the saran in a bunch about 2 inches above the cakes and tie the packages with white ribbon; the cakes can then be taken home without damage. Be sure the bow is tied well above the icing.

INGREDIENTS:

For the cake: 1 cup lard; 2 cups granulated sugar; 2 eggs; 4 teaspoons baking soda; 2½ cups applesauce; 4 cups flour; 1 tablespoon cinnamon; ¾ teaspoon ground cloves;

¾ teaspoon salt; 2 teaspoons vanilla; 2 cups seedless raisins; 1 cup broken pecans.

For lemon icing: ¾ cup butter or margarine; 6 cups sifted confectioners' sugar; grated rind and juice 1 large lemon; ⅛ teaspoon salt; 1 teaspoon light cream.

For plain confectioners' icing: 3 cups sifted confectioners' sugar; 6 tablespoons heated light cream; almond or lemon extract.

TIMETABLE: Let's face it. This is a wedding. You just won't have time to do much, if any, cooking on the day itself. I'm assuming this is your daughter's wedding. So you will do as much as you can up to the night before the wedding and then, on the day itself, you will have somebody competent to take over.

Well then. The melons, which must be prepared no more than 2 hours or so before your luncheon, will have to be taken care of by someone other than you. Nothing to it, anyway. Have your husband pour the champagne at the right time, and there you are.

The soup should be on hand and ready well ahead of time. If you're going to serve it hot, all it needs is heating. If you're going to serve it cold, all it needs is serving. The sour cream in a bowl. The hot potato for the cold soup. That's the soup.

The salmon. If you have in your kitchen what is known as a jewel, plan on the salmon hot with the dill sauce. If not, prepare it the day before and serve it cold, with the cucumber sauce. (Note: If you're going to serve the salmon cold, have the soup hot. If the salmon is to be served hot, reverse the order. Don't have both hot; don't have both cold. One or the other. I said this before, and I say it again.)

Back to the hot salmon. It will bear waiting, warm, for about an hour, if you keep it moist as directed; the sauce too, can be reheated, so it's not actually a frantic matter.

The sauce for the cold salmon can be put together quickly. Have the ingredients in a neat private area, all together, and this will be no problem to anyone.

The noodle casserole can be prepared the night before or the morning of the party. Ready for the oven. In any case, cook the noodles well ahead—a day, two days.

The zucchini—the biggest job here is the grating. This should be done in the morning. The cooking takes a few minutes; let it take a few minutes of someone else's time. Arrange that matter, type the recipe for the seasoning on a card, tack it on the kitchen wall, and, if you can manage to come out to the kitchen, have a taste before it's served.

Salad greens improve after a spell in a wet towel in a properly functioning refrigerator. So prepare them early, tuck them away, and forget them. The other ingredients can be placed in a large bowl several hours ahead of the luncheon and they, too, can be forgotten. Comforting thought. The combining of the salad is simplicity itself. No fancy dressing. The ingredients of the salad provide most of the seasoning. Oil and vinegar, salt and pepper, as directed.

A nice way to serve the Greek salad is to have the "insides" dumped out of their bowl onto the greens, which I have always called, in salads, the "outsides." Your husband then, or another obliging male (perhaps the best man?) can toss them together for you. Hand him the combined oil and vinegar, let him continue tossing, and have a couple of bystanders taste for seasoning. A pepper mill close at hand, a salt shaker, more oil, more vinegar, if needed. Salad taken care of.

The pumpernickl rolls could be prepared days ahead and frozen, if you wish to avoid this fussy job at a busy time. Defrosted (and be sure they are thoroughly and completely so), they are in fine shape. Keep them well wrapped while they're in the freezer. If you don't have a freezer, make them the day before and refrigerate as directed. Again, get them back to room temperature—not cold—before serving.

The *crème au caramel* should be prepared the day before. All they need, then, is a careful turning out. These don't freeze well.

The cakes, of course, should be made days ahead of time

and kept, wrapped in saran in a good bread box or the re-frigerator. Don't ice them if you're going to keep them very long unless you plan to freeze them; then the icing will be done. The icing can be done the day before the luncheon. To return to the freezing, if you have this in mind, you can bake them when the engagement is announced; they'll wait for the wedding.

LEFTOVERS

The melon should have been cut to come out just even. If, however, you've miscalculated and have a melon left over, use it for the following recipe.

Lobster-Cucumber-Melon Salad

Cut your melon in half, scoop out the seeds, cut the melon into crosswise sections and, from the ends, scoop out about 1 cup of tiny melon balls or chop the melon into small squares. Remove the rind from the rings, or semi- or hemi-circles, whatever you have.

Combine 1 cup cooked lobster (a handy time to use the cup of lobster meat left from an earlier summer meal and frozen for this moment) or 1 cup crab flakes (preferably fresh, but canned crab, properly trimmed of its bones, will do) with 1 cup diced freshly picked cucumber, unpeeled, if fresh from the garden, and the cup of melon spoken of above.

Combine ¼ cup mayonnaise with ¼ cup commercial sour cream, 1 teaspoon lemon or lime juice, 1 tablespoon sugar, salt and pepper to taste, and lightly toss the lobster or crab mixture in this. Place the cantaloupe or other melon rings on a bed of leaf lettuce, fill with the lobster salad, top with capers. Garnish with fresh lemon or lime wedges. Serves 4.

INGREDIENTS: 1 cup melon balls; 1 cup cooked lobster or 1 cup crab flakes; 1 cup diced cucumber; ¼ cup mayonnaise; ¼ cup commercial sour cream; 1 teaspoon lemon or lime juice; 1 tablespoon sugar; salt; pepper; lemon or lime wedges.

Another fine thought re said melons: melt ½ cup currant jelly, cool it, fold it into 1 cup commercial sour cream. Serve it over unsweetened melon balls. Add a few blueberries.

The beet soup? Easy. If you've served it hot the first time, serve it cold the next time. Follow the directions as given in the menu. Other way around, if it is the other way.

The salmon! Ah, the salmon! The following recipe is so beautiful, encompassing as it does the leftover salmon, that I was torn between giving it to you as the main wedding luncheon dish and keeping it for a leftover. It will, for a fact, provide a perfect main course for another party luncheon, so don't underestimate it.

Salmon Gelée

Save all the bouillon and, the next day, add to it the **bones, head, backbone,** whatever **trimmings** you have **of the salmon,** and continue cooking the broth. Simmer it slowly for at least an hour until you have about 1 quart liquid. Strain and discard the bones and trimmings (unless you have a cat, licking his chops). If the bouillon is strong, you'll have a natural aspic which will jell without the addition of any more gelatine. You can test this by setting a small amount of it in the freezer for a few minutes. If it jells (before it freezes) you're in business. If it doesn't, soak **1 envelope unflavored gelatine** in **½ cup cold water.** Dissolve it after 5 minutes by setting it in hot water and, when it is dissolved, add it to the court bouillon. You shouldn't need the gelatine, however, not if you've done as I told you. Set the strained bouillon, with or without the added gelatine, in the refrigerator and keep an eagle eye on it.

On a fancy platter, lay out large pieces of the leftover salmon, trying to arrive at a shape something like a fish. If this is impossible, forget the realism and arrange the fish in a circle. You should have about **4 cups of leftover salmon.** As soon as the bouillon starts to jell—it should be the consistency of a rather runny madrilene—stir into half of it (1 pint) **1 cup mayonnaise** and **1 cup commercial sour cream,**

¼ cup chopped chives, 2 tablespoons dill weed, and 2 tablespoons chopped parsley. Fresh dill is better than dill weed, if you have some; 1 flower of fresh dill will do. Return this mixture to the refrigerator and, when it is firm enough to stay put, spread it over the cold salmon. You will not need all of it, but it's better to be safe than sorry, and, whatever you don't use would be an acceptable dressing for a salad of hearts of lettuce (a leftover from a leftover!). If you have been able to shape the salmon to resemble a fish, decorate the top of it with slivers of **green peppers, pimientos, stuffed olives,** and **hard-cooked egg slices.** The rest of the court bouillon, the other pint, should have jelled by this time. Chop it very, very fine and add to it ¼ **teaspoon garlic powder.** Arrange it in little piles around the fish and slide into the middle of each pile 1 **teaspoon of black or red caviar.**

You'll be hiring out to the Ritz next.

INGREDIENTS: Court bouillon; bones, head, backbone, trimmings of salmon; 1 envelope unflavored gelatine and ½ cup cold water, if necessary; 4 cups leftover salmon; 1 cup mayonnaise; 1 cup commercial sour cream; ¼ cup chopped chives; 2 tablespoons dill weed; 2 tablespoons chopped parsley; green peppers; stuffed olives; hard-cooked egg slices; ¼ teaspoon garlic powder; 1 teaspoon black or red caviar.

A quick go-over for the rest of the menu. The grated zucchini will do well (1) in a tossed salad, (2) combined with grated cooked carrots, well buttered, (3) combined with sliced, steamed summer squash, the yellow and the green a sunny contrast. The fruit compote can be served under or over vanilla ice cream as sort of a banana split. The Greek salad is hopeless. Don't try to keep it or use it again. The pumpernickl rolls should be refrozen and can come forth with the salmon *gelée.* The *crème reversée* is simply divine on top of leftover sponge or pound cake, topped with whipped cream. The take-home Canadian wedding cakes should have been taken home. If you have a few around, they're worth your whipping up a batch of hard sauce for. If they grow stale,

finally, steam them in your Bungalow Cooker and serve as a
hot pudding with a lemon sauce.

I haven't forgotten all those egg whites either. Use 6 of
them to make the following recipe.

Strawberry Soufflé

Mash with a fork **2 cups thawed frozen strawberries** (unless
you can find fresh ones, in which case, sugar them well and
mash them; reserve ½ cup of the strawberries). Beat stiffly
6 of your egg whites and add, bit by bit, **¾ cup superfine
sugar.** I truly mean bit by bit; if you throw the sugar in all
at once, the egg white will turn into marshmallow fluff. Use
it with peanut butter for a sandwich for your youngest.

Fold the strawberries into the egg whites, pour the whole
thing into a casserole, bake in a 375°F. oven in a pan of hot
water for 30 minutes. Serve at once with the reserved strawberries.

INGREDIENTS: 2 cups frozen strawberries or fresh strawberries;
6 egg whites; ¾ cup superfine sugar.

The recipe in August Family Menu for a white cake will take
care of many of the other whites. Meringues, too, call for
them. In any case, pack them away in little labeled jars in
your freezer—4 egg whites to a jar—and you'll have them
when you need them.

AUGUST

FAMILY MENU
Wa'n't It Hot Today, Though?

SUMMER SOUP ON THE ROCKS

LONDON BROIL

SKEWERED ONIONS

TOMATO, ASPARAGUS, AND MUSHROOM TART

HUSK-ROASTED CORN ON THE COB

AN AVOCADO IN THE HAND

ICED SALAD BOWL, DUNK SAUCE

GRILLED GARLIC ROLLS

A PERFECT WHITE CAKE WITH COFFEE OR PEACH CREAM

 Hot days, cool nights. That's the way we know August in Vermont. I remember, in New York, it was hot days, *hot* nights, and for this respite, I am grateful. Appetites don't have problems in Vermont, summer or winter.

This is an outdoor family supper. You can make a picnic of it, in a wooded glen, should it be too hot in your own back yard. Everything will pack in a picnic basket. All the cooking can be done on a grill or a hickory fire. The tomato and asparagus tart can be baked in the morning, wrapped in foil to be carried to the picnic, and warmed in same foil on the back of the grill.

215

A fun meal for a family of 6. Multiply for a company meal.

SUMMER SOUP ON THE ROCKS

Homemade chicken broth is best here. See page 13 for the making of it some cool, rainy day. Canned will do, in a pinch. To **1 quart rich chicken broth** add **1 tablespoon soy sauce, 1 teaspoon dill weed** or **1 large head of fresh dill,** chopped fine. Bring to boil, add **1 teaspoon sugar,** then chill, strain, and pack in a quart jar. Serve in old-fashioned glasses over **3 ice cubes** for each glass. A **twist of lemon** on top.

INGREDIENTS: 1 quart chicken broth; 1 tablespoon soy sauce; 1 teaspoon dill weed or 1 large head fresh dill; 1 teaspoon sugar; ice cubes; lemon twists.

LONDON BROIL

Start this in the cool of the morn. Marinate a **2½- to 3-pound flank steak** (the markets are now calling this London broil, but it's still flank steak) for at least 4 or 5 hours in **½ cup pure olive oil; 2 tablespoons red wine vinegar; juice of ½ lemon; 1 clove garlic,** peeled, split, and crushed in a mortar and pestle or a garlic press; **1 tablespoon light sweet red wine; 2 teaspoons salt; ¼ teaspoon freshly ground black pepper.** Mix the marinade thoroughly first, then lay the steak out in a large baking dish, large enough to hold it without crowding, pour the marinade over it, turn it over two or three times and, as we say in Vermont, "leave it lay." Turn it rather frequently, if you happen to be in the vicinity. It should be turned at least once every hour, anyway. When ready to broil it, drain it thoroughly first. If you're taking it along with you to another picnic spot than your own back yard, carry it, marinade and all, in a tightly sealed plastic bag. Drain it when you're ready to broil it, on the spot.

The coals on your grill should be glowing red when you start the London broil, so that the searing will take place quickly; this will seal in the juices. If you have a grill that can be controlled, raise the steak now, so that it will cook more slowly. If you haven't, simply remove the London broil for a few minutes, let the coals simmer down a bit, and continue broiling the meat. If you are doing this at home in an oven broiler, just reduce the temperature, after the searing, from high to moderate. Broil the meat for 5 minutes on each side. Test for rareness. It should be rare and ready for you, if you're that sort. If you like it better done, turn and broil 2 minutes more on each side. It will be medium, probably. If you want it well done, you'll have to look in another cookbook.

Set the London broil on a hot platter or a board; dress with ¼ cup (½ stick) **butter,** browned lightly first in a saucepan; slice the meat diagonally and serve with a toasted garlic roll and the skewered onions.

INGREDIENTS: 2½- to 3-pound flank steak (London broil); ½ cup olive oil; 2 tablespoons red wine vinegar; juice of ½ lemon; 1 clove garlic; 1 tablespoon light sweet red wine; 2 teaspoons salt; ¼ teaspoon pepper; ¼ cup butter.

SKEWERED ONIONS

This is really part of the London broil recipe. I've separated it, in deference to any of you who don't care as we do for onions. When you are marinating the meat, tuck in around it, moistening well with the marinade, **4 or 5 little white onions** for each person. Peel them first, of course. In this case, you'd want about 2 dozen, wouldn't you? Turn the onions in the marinade whenever you turn the meat. Drain them just before broiling and thread them on 6 small skewers. If you have bamboo sticks, they'll do fine. The onions need about 15 or 20 minutes grilling, so start them before the meat. Turn occasionally, baste with the marinade when they seem dry. At the last 5 minutes, sprinkle them with sugar, **1 teaspoon** over all (not 1 teaspoon each), and continue grilling. Serve with the meat.

If you decide against this, add an onion to the marinade for the sake of the London broil.

INGREDIENTS: Marinade from London broil; 2 dozen small white onions; 1 teaspoon sugar.

TOMATO, ASPARAGUS, AND MUSHROOM TART

If you don't have piecrust in your refrigerator or freezer, you'll have to prepare a 10-inch pie shell. Follow directions on page 287. If you have a freezer, as a matter of fact, it's a wise move to double the recipe which follows, make two tarts, freeze one, and next time you want one, you have it made—in more ways than one.

Sauté 6 slices lean bacon until they are not quite cooked through. Drain on paper towel and crumble into small bits. Arrange, in the bottom of the 10-inch pie shell we've been talking about (unbaked this time), thin slices of Swiss Gruyère or imported Swiss cheese, enough to cover every inch of pastry. The quantity will depend on how thinly it is sliced, but usually one package is about right for one pie shell —6 or 8 ounces. On top of the cheese, place the bacon bits.

Slice 2 firm tomatoes in thin slices. Poke out the seeds. Lay them on top of the cheese and the bacon. Set this much of the tart in the refrigerator while you prepare the rest of it.

Peel and chop coarsely 1 small onion. Wash and remove scales from the stalks of 1 pound fresh asparagus spears. Slice them diagonally into slices about ½ inch thick. Wipe dry, trim off the bottom of the stems, and slice vertically ½ pound fresh mushrooms.

Melt ¼ cup (½ stick) butter in a heavy skillet, large enough to hold the mushrooms and the asparagus. When the butter is melted, add the chopped onion, simmer it slowly until it is golden, not brown, and then add the mushrooms. Sauté them 3 minutes, then add the asparagus and continue sautéing over medium heat for another 5 minutes. Sprinkle over these vegetables 1 teaspoon flour, stir them around so that the flour is well combined with the butter, remove the saucepan from the range, and add, all at once, **4 large eggs,** well beaten; **½ teaspoon salt;** and **2 cups light cream.** Stir around well, scraping the juices from the bottom of the skillet, and turn it into the pie shell over the cheese and tomatoes. Scrape all the juices out of the pan.

Cover the edges of the crust with a 2-inch strip of aluminum foil, tucking it over and under the crust. This will prevent the crust from browning before the pie is done.

Bake at 375°F. (moderate) for about 40 minutes. Stop the baking when the custard is just set; don't overbake it. When a sharp knife will go in and come out clean, the tart is done. Serve hot, either directly from oven, or carry to picnic in a thermal basket.

NOTE: There are various substitutions possible in this recipe which, as you must have recognized, is a variation of a Quiche Lorraine. You can use any smoked meat such as ham or dried beef instead of the bacon. These would require no cooking; just add them as is. In the absence of fresh asparagus, frozen asparagus cuts will substitute. If they are very icy, wash them quickly under cold water before adding them to the mushrooms and onions or the ice will dilute and alter the flavor of the custard. Canned broiled-in-butter mushrooms can be used, but there's no substitute, really, for the flavor of a fresh mushroom—so look for the real thing, here, if you can.

INGREDIENTS: 6 slices lean bacon; 6 or 8 oz. Swiss Gruyère or Swiss cheese; 2 firm tomatoes; 1 small onion; 1 pound fresh asparagus; ½ pound fresh mushrooms; ¼ cup butter; 1 teaspoon flour; 4 large eggs; ½ teaspoon salt; 2 cups light cream.

HUSK-ROASTED CORN ON THE COB

A simple matter. Pick the corn or have it picked as close to suppertime as possible. If you have access to a road stand, fine; if you grow it yourself, better; if you have to buy it at a market where it arrives 24 hours after it's picked, forget this recipe. No more than 6 hours old is my rule for corn; preferably no more than 10 minutes.

Just before supper, or just before leaving for your picnic, strip the husks away from **12 freshly picked ears of corn**— golden bantam, country gentleman, or a variety my friend, the corn man, calls "Wonderful." I *think* he calls it "Wonderful." That's what it is, anyway. Don't remove the husks completely. You can throw away the tough outer layer, but keep a thick coating of them. By pulling them away from the ears, you are able to remove all the silk. Be sure you've got it all, fussy job though it is. Now smear the kernels thickly with **butter;** use a goodly amount, about 1 tablespoon for each ear. Return the husks to their natural place, tie them together with a string.

Arrived at the picnic, dip the corn quickly in cold water, in again, out again, then roast along with the onions, turning every so often, until the outer husks are dry and brown. This will take about 15 or 20 minutes, probably. Look into one and see if the kernels are done; they will be hot and tender and buttery, if they're ready. The time depends on the heat of your coals, of course.

> NOTE: If you want to boil the corn, do it in no more than 2 inches of liquid, half of which should be milk. The milk makes it possible to keep the corn for a while without water-logging it. Bring the liquid back to a boil after adding the corn (for this arrangement, you strip the husks from the corn), and in 3 minutes the corn should be just right for serving.

INGREDIENTS: 12 freshly picked ears of corn; ¾ cup butter.

AN AVOCADO IN THE HAND

The best thing about a picnic is the variety of foods that lend themselves to casual eating; foods which one usually associates with very lush, formal meals. Avocados, for instance. Take **3 ripe avocados** along. Slice them in half; give the pits to a child (never saw a child who didn't want an avocado pit to plant); squeeze the **juice of 1 orange** over them. Sprinkle with **salt**. Serve in the shell. A spoon or fork should be available. **Lemon juice** can substitute for orange, if you wish.

INGREDIENTS: 3 avocados; juice of 1 orange or 1 lemon; salt.

ICED SALAD BOWL, DUNK SAUCE

Chill for 3 or 4 hours all the ingredients which follow. Get them to the picnic in this state and, when ready to serve, set them out, casually arranged, in a large bowl of crushed ice. Your imagination can come into play here—nothing to stop you from changing this list. However, a lovely combination is achieved, both flavor and colorwise, by arranging with forethought to contrasts the following: **cherry tomatoes; large ripe olives; pineapple sticks**, drained; **scallions; large chunks green peppers; cucumber sticks; radishes** (stems left on, bottoms sliced off); **fennel** (you've heard me speak of this before; a delicious celery-anise-like flavor).

With this, the fol'owing salad-dressing dunk sauce: Mix together **1 cup mayonnaise, ¼ cup evaporated milk, 1 tablespoon prepared mustard, several dashes Worcestershire sauce, ¼ teaspoon garlic powder, 1 teaspoon horseradish** or **chutney** (the last two are optional; use one or the other, not both). Pile into serving dish, bury dish in crushed ice in center of platter of vegetables.

INGREDIENTS: Cherry tomatoes; large ripe olives; pineapple sticks; scallions; green peppers; cucumber sticks; radishes; fennel.
For the dressing: 1 cup mayonnaise; ¼ cup evaporated milk; 1 tablespoon prepared mustard; several dashes Worcestershire; ¼ teaspoon garlic powder; 1 teaspoon horseradish (optional) or chutney (optional).

GRILLED GARLIC ROLLS

A plain hard roll is best for these, with lots of soft center. Stay away from rolls that are all crust. The frozen club rolls available in supermarkets do well. Better still, if you have a fine bakery in your neighborhood, patronize it.

Cut **12 hard rolls** in half, lengthwise; spread each half with **1 tablespoon soft butter,** sprinkle with ⅛ to ¼ teaspoon **garlic powder** for each roll, depending on your attitude toward garlic. (If you wish, you can prepare **garlic butter** as in the recipe for July Tomatoes on page 175.)

Put the rolls back together as they were; toss them into a plastic bag or a brown paper bag, and carry them to the picnic that way. While the London broil is being sliced, set a large heavy iron frying pan on the now-vacated grill. Get the pan hot, then quickly heat 6 half rolls, butter side down, in the pan. As soon as they are lightly browned, serve, one-half roll per person, with the London broil. Repeat with the rolls as needed.

INGREDIENTS: 12 hard rolls; ¾ cup soft butter; 1 tablespoon garlic powder.

A PERFECT WHITE CAKE
WITH COFFEE OR PEACH CREAM

For years, faced with a plethora of egg whites in my freezer (see page 163 for freezing egg whites), I searched for a really wonderful white cake. Finally, through the largesse of a good friend, this cake came my way. It is now, unquestionably, the cake my children are fondest of; a perfect cupcake cake too. It freezes so well that I never bake just one recipe of it. I double it, which gives me, according to my whim, something like a good-sized layer cake, a loaf cake, and a dozen or more cupcakes; or all cupcakes; or some of one and some of the other. However, this recipe, as it is given here, will give you one three-layer cake or two loaf cakes, made in bread pans. You'll doubtless have one cake left over, but that won't be a worry, as you shall see when you come to the leftovers section of this menu.

Sift together **2¼ cups cake flour, 1 tablespoon baking powder,** and **½ teaspoon salt.** Cream together in your electric beater (turn the guide to "Cream," which is a fast speed) **½ cup margarine or butter** (either is fine here) with **1⅓ cups sugar.** When the batter is completely ungranular and very light, add **1 teaspoon vanilla.** Now add a little of the dry ingredients to the creamed mixture, then add part of **1 cup milk;** then add a bit more of the dry ingredients, a bit more milk, until you've added all the flour and all the milk. Beat well after each addition.

Beat **4 egg whites** until they are stiff, but not dry; stand in peaks, you know, glistening. If they are beaten too long, they become dry and fluffy and you'll never fold them into anything. Fold the egg whites into the batter. Be sure all the white has disappeared. Folding is a delicate job; do it carefully. If you beat things you're supposed to fold, you might as well not have whipped the egg whites in the first place. Under, around, over, that's folding.

Grease with a good vegetable shortening the bottoms of two bread pans (9 x 5 x 3 inches), then sprinkle them with a little flour. If you prefer, do the same with three 9-inch layer cake pans. Bake in a 350°F. preheated oven 30 to 40 minutes for the loaf cakes, 20 minutes for the layer cakes. Test before you take them from the oven; don't open the door of the oven before at least 30 minutes have passed for the loaves, 15 for the layers. If the cake springs back when you press it with your fingers, it's done. If a skewer goes in and comes forth dry and clean, the cake's done. Either test works.

If you're going to use the loaf pans, which I strongly recommend, you don't need to remove the cakes from them. Serve them right from the pan. For the layer cake, or should you wish to decorate the loaf cakes, let them cool on wire racks and, after about 10 minutes, turn them out and let them rest on the racks.

A simply marvelous (and marvelously simple) frosting for

this or any other plain white cake requires **1 pint heavy cream**, whipped quite stiff. Add **1 tablespoon sugar, 1 teaspoon vanilla,** and then, slowly, with a fork, blend in about **1 teaspoon instant coffee,** tasting all the while. When it suits you, fold in the stiffly beaten **white of 1 egg** (another egg white heard from!). This egg white will keep the whipped cream from collapsing. Spread over the cake and refrigerate at least an hour.

Don't care for coffee? Do the same with the heavy cream but, instead of the coffee, stir in **2 crushed ripe peaches, 1 tablespoon light brown sugar,** and the stiffly beaten egg white, as above. In fact, strawberries, blueberries, any fruit complements this cake singularly well.

INGREDIENTS:

> *For the cake:* 2¼ cups cake flour; 1 tablespoon baking powder; ½ teaspoon salt; ½ cup margarine or butter; 1⅓ cups sugar; 1 teaspoon vanilla; 1 cup milk; 4 egg whites.
>
> *For the frosting:* 1 pint heavy cream; 1 tablespoon sugar; 1 teaspoon vanilla; 1 teaspoon instant coffee; white of 1 egg. Or, instead of coffee, 2 ripe peaches and 1 tablespoon light brown sugar.

TIMETABLE: A timetable here is, really, superfluous. You're going on a picnic or eating in the back yard on a hot summer evening. Prepare the summer soup in the morning or, if you want to freeze it, on any cool day. Chill or defrost, respectively. The London broil is marinated in the morning, as are the onions; the tart is baked in the morning or well ahead of time, to be frozen until today. Reheat it just before leaving and keep it warm. The salad ingredients, with the dunk sauce—all a morning job. The corn a quick preparation task done either at the picnic grounds or just before leaving the house. Avocados? Bring them along, as is, with a knife to cut them and a utensil to perform the spooning out. The garlic rolls, prepared at home, are ready for grilling. The cake can be baked in the morning, or the day before or the week before; a frozen cake, defrosted, is as good as fresh. The coffee or peach cream should be prepared late in the afternoon, kept in a covered plastic container, in a bed of ice. You can use the ice later for the summer soup on the rocks.

When you arrive at the picnic, it's a matter of unpacking things, mostly, getting the grill going, and grilling, first, the onions, the corn, and then the London broil. Last of all, when the grill has room for them, do the garlic rolls. If everybody takes a hand, as they should, and do, for this sort of meal, you'll be fine. This is a very deluxe picnic, don't you think? Better invite somebody.

LEFTOVERS

The soup is delicious hot, so, if you have enough left to serve again, heat it. Slice into it whatever avocado pear you have about. If you haven't enough soup to use as a soup, you'll find this a perfect stock for a chow mein or, in fact, any Chinese meal.

Better still, let's use it with the leftover London broil. In fact, let's use whatever we can from this meal, in one dish:

Leftover Sukiyaki

Slice whatever meat you have left very thin. Get a large (10-inch) iron frying pan very hot, add enough **peanut oil** to cover the bottom of the pan, just (not swimming). Let the oil become wavy, add **1 fresh onion,** cut up in large sections, and let it slowly wilt and turn golden. This will require turning down the heat a bit, probably. If there are no onions left from the **skewered onions,** make this **4 fresh onions;** otherwise, add whatever onions you have left from the picnic, let them heat with the others for a minute, then push all the onions to one section of the pan. Now add the sliced **leftover London broil** (you should have about 10 or 12 thin slices); let it brown quickly, turning up the heat, and shift the pan so that it is the meat, not the onions, which are getting the intensity of the heat. Move the meat over near the onions in a section of their own. Now add 2 cups mushrooms, wiped dry, sliced through vertically, trimmed, and allow the mushrooms to sauté in their own section for 2 minutes. Now add whatever **leftover scallions** you have from the salad bowl with ½ **cup leftover summer soup,** 2 tablespoons soy sauce, 2 teaspoons sugar. Let the scallions stew 1 minute, so they are just wilted, and move them over near the meat.

You now have about three-fourths of the pan occupied. In the final section of the pan, place **2 or 3 cups spinach,** washed. Let this wilt quickly. Turn each section of food over in its own section; don't mix them together. If the sukiyaki seems dry, add a little more of the soup. Taste. Add more soy sauce or more sugar, according to your taste. As soon as everything is wilted, this can be served. There should be crispness to the vegetables, so don't cook to the stew state. Serve the plates, one at a time, using tongs, so that each person receives a portion from each section of food in the frying pan. Arrange the foods on the plates in wedges, so that they are not mixed; they will be an arresting sight. Top with **sliced radish rounds.** This will serve 6.

INGREDIENTS: Peanut oil; 1 fresh onion and onions left over from skewered onions or 4 fresh onions; leftover London broil; 2 cups mushrooms; leftover scallions; ½ cup leftover summer soup; 2 tablespoons soy sauce; 2 teaspoons sugar; 2 or 3 cups spinach; radishes.

The London broil, sliced cold, will make memorable sandwiches on dark bread with butter and sweet onions. Sautéed quickly and served with a fine Bearnaise sauce, it will make a meal of distinction. (You'll find a good recipe for a Bearnaise in many cookbooks, including the *Blueberry Hill Cookbook.*)

One of the best ways to use odds and ends of beef, such as the leftover London broil (or steak or roast beef or pot roast) is to combine it with eggs, either as an omelette, preferably Chinese style, seasoned with soy sauce and laced with green onions—or in this very lovely French way. In France it's called *oeufs à la tartare,* I am told, but I just call it "lovely eggs with beef."

Oeufs à la Tartare or Lovely Eggs with Beef

Use what you have left of the beef, cut it up into tiny bits (don't grind it) and I shall assume you have about 2 cups of the London broil. You can do this with as little as 1 cup, however. For 2 cups of the beef, you will want about 2 teaspoons very soft butter. Work the meat into the butter along with ½ teaspoon salt, a few grinds of fresh black pepper, and spread it evenly over the bottom of an earthenware baking dish or casserole for shirred eggs. You'll want a flat one; a Pyrex plate will do; shouldn't be larger than 6 inches. Break over the top of the meat 6 large fresh eggs, carefully. Don't break the yolks. Carefully smooth over the eggs ½ cup commercial sour cream. Sprinkle the top of the cream with lots of freshly ground black pepper. Place in moderate (375°F.) oven and bake 10 to 15 minutes. The eggs will have set and the top of the cream will be lightly browned. Serves 6 or 3, depending on whether you are one- or two-egg people. Some folks like catsup with this.

INGREDIENTS: 2 cups leftover London broil; 2 teaspoons butter; ½ teaspoon salt; pepper; 6 eggs; ½ cup commercial sour cream.

The tart, if much of it is left, ought to be frozen. Then, defrosted by heating from the frozen state to very hot, it is like new.

As for the remains of the salad bowl, just combine the olives (pit them first, if they're not already pitted), the pineapple sticks, now cubed, one or two chopped scallion tops, the green peppers (also cut up small), the cucumbers (ditto) and the radishes, with ½ cup mayonnaise, 1 tablespoon Durkee's dressing, and 1 teaspoon heavy cream. Add a few green grapes. Serve on a bed of lettuce. A delicious salad, particularly with cold meat or sliced sautéed London broil.

There are so many recipes using leftover corn, I just couldn't begin to mention all those I really like. Cut off the kernels with a sharp knife, catching whatever liquid comes with them; then make (1) a corn pudding, (2) corn fritters, (3) creamed corn.

Corn pudding I've told you about before. See the *Blueberry Hill Cookbook* for that one. A lovely corn fritter goes so:

Corn Fritters

Beat **yolks of 2 eggs** with electric beater until they are very thick and lemon in shade. Add, all at once, **1 cup rich milk, ½ teaspoon salt, ⅛ teaspoon freshly ground black pepper, ¼ cup flour, ¾ teaspoon baking powder, 1½ cups freshly cut corn** (off the cob). When it's well mixed, fold in, carefully, the beaten whites of the aforesaid 2 eggs. Beat the whites to a peak, you know, no more. The fritters can be fried in sizzling butter in a heavy pan, turned once, and served with hot syrup and bacon. You can also drop them from a tablespoon into a deep kettle of peanut oil, hot enough to light a match.

INGREDIENTS: 2 eggs; 1 cup rich milk; ½ teaspoon salt; ⅛ teaspoon pepper; ¼ cup flour; ¾ teaspoon baking powder; 1½ cups corn (cut from cob).

Velvet Corn

An unusual method of creaming corn requires **3 cups corn** cut from cobs. Add to these in a heavy saucepan, **2 small packages** (3 ounces each) **cream cheese, 2 tablespoons butter, ¼ cup milk,** and **½ teaspoon sugar.** Heat slowly until the cheese has melted into the rest. If it is too thick, add a little more milk. This is enough for 4 or 5.

INGREDIENTS: 3 cups corn (cut from cob); 2 small packages cream cheese; 2 tablespoons butter; ¼ cup milk; ½ teaspoon sugar.

If you have any garlic rolls left, cut them into ½ inch cubes, heat them in a slow oven, and use as croutons. Nice with left-over soup, or for a Caesar salad. They're great, too, heated with some Parmesan cheese, just until the cheese browns, and floated on a bowl of onion soup. A recipe for that soup is on page 266.

The cake can be kept indefinitely in the freezer and should be used as a base for ice-cream desserts or any dessert that calls for a dish lined with cake, such as a ladyfinger or sponge cake. It is perfect for such a dessert as this maple-coffee trifle.

Maple-Coffee Trifle

In the top of a double boiler, over direct heat, scald **1 cup milk** (get it hot, but not boiling; that's what scalding means) and stir it slowly into **3 egg yolks**, well beaten; **½ cup pure maple syrup**; and **¼ teaspoon salt**. As soon as this is combined, set it over the lower section of the double boiler which should have in it hot, not boiling, water, and cook, stirring, until you have a custard which will coat the spoon. It will be thick and smooth; takes 10 minutes or thereabouts in a double boiler. Try it, if you'd like, over direct heat, *low*. It'll cook much faster but so will it burn, too, if you're not careful. I prefer the direct method (in many other concerns, too), but I warn you, you must keep stirring and watching if you choose to make your custard this way. Remove from heat, as soon as it coats the spoon, and cool to room temperature.

Cut enough **leftover cake** to fill the bottom and sides of a 1-quart casserole. Combine **½ cup strong cold coffee** and **1½ tablespoons pure maple syrup** (rum can be substituted for the maple syrup) and pour this over the cake. Let it stand 10 minutes. Now pour over the cake the cooled custard. Chill at least 2 hours in the refrigerator, or 10 minutes in the freezer. Whip **½ cup heavy cream**. Add either **1 teaspoon sugar** and **½ teaspoon vanilla** or **1 tablespoon maple syrup**

to the whipped cream. Not both. One or the other. Sprinkle
with chopped **Brazil nuts** or **pecans**.

INGREDIENTS: 1 cup milk; 3 egg yolks; ½ cup and 1½ tablespoons maple syrup; ¼ teaspoon salt; leftover cake; ½
cup strong coffee; ½ cup heavy cream; 1 teaspoon sugar
and ½ teaspoon vanilla, or 1 tablespoon maple syrup;
Brazil nuts or pecans.

SEPTEMBER

PARTY MENU
September Song

COLD TOMATO CREAM
BROILED LAMB SQUARES
CHINESE FISH, DEVASTATING
LOBSTER CANTONESE
KIKUI FUJII'S CHINESE SPARERIBS
CAPER-FRIED RICE
PRESERVED KUMQUATS
PEARS SABAYON
BUTTERMILK-PINEAPPLE ICE

The tastes in a properly prepared Chinese meal are deliberately contrasted; the vegetables are crisp; the seafood or meat is tender. There is the sweet; there is the sour; the oils used are digestible. Eye appeal is always taken into consideration. In fact, it has long seemed to me that Chinese cooking is the most civilized in the world.

Serve this meal buffet style, so your guests can choose from the lavish array of foods. Arrange to keep the food hot while it's being served; I'll suggest ways. A supper party for 12.

COLD TOMATO CREAM

A cooling and delicious appetizer. Use your cocktail shaker for this one. Combine **9 cups tomato juice; 1 medium onion**, grated; **1 teaspoon sugar; 3 cups light cream.** Taste for **salt** and **pepper**; the amount of this will depend on the brand of tomato juice. Chill and at serving time shake with shaved ice, a cocktail shakerful at a time, and serve it right away.

INGREDIENTS: 9 cups tomato juice; 1 medium onion; 1 teaspoon sugar; 3 cups light cream; salt; pepper.

BROILED LAMB SQUARES

Half of a medium-size spring **leg of lamb** should be sufficient here. Cut the meat from the bone in squares, using a sharp knife (or ask your butcher to do this for you), 1 to 1½ inches on all sides, or as close to squares as you can manage it. Then cut the squares into very thin slices, about ¼ inch thick.

Mix together in a bowl a marinade of **2 cloves garlic,** crushed; **½ cup soy sauce; 2 tablespoons sugar; 1 tablespoon sherry;** and **½ teaspoon dry mustard.** Add the lamb squares, turn them over a few times so that the marinade has contacted every slice, and allow the meat to marinate (*sit* is a more vivid term) in this liquid for 2 hours, turning the pieces each half hour to be sure they are moist. When ready to serve these, lift the slices from the marinade with a slotted spoon and broil very quickly, turning when one side is brown. If you have a charcoal grill or even a small hibachi, your guests might broil their own, using bamboo sticks. The charcoal should be very hot so the meat will cook almost immediately. I prefer mine crisp, in fact, charred on the outside but still pink, hardly done at all, on the inside. If you do not plan to use a grill, place quite a few of the squares on a tray and broil quickly in a 500°F. oven, very close to the broiler unit. Turn once, brown the second side, and serve right away.

Toothpicks will work effectively here for service. Hot **Chinese mustard,** which is dry mustard, thinned down to a runny paste with cold water, may be placed in a little dish alongside, with similar dishes of **horseradish** and **soy sauce.**

INGREDIENTS: ½ medium-size spring leg of lamb (about 4 pounds); 2 cloves garlic; ½ cup soy sauce; 2 tablespoons sugar; 1 tablespoon sherry; ½ teaspoon dry mustard; side dishes of Chinese mustard (dry mustard), horseradish, soy sauce.

CHINESE FISH, DEVASTATING

This is one of the oriental dishes which can be, indeed should be, cooked before your guests' eyes. The preparation of the components of this dish can be taken care of in the morning; the actual cooking of the fish itself takes only a short while.

You will need **3 pounds of halibut** or **swordfish.** Have it cut from the center of the fish, which is the meatiest, at least 1 inch thick. If the fish is frozen when you buy it, defrost it only partially. You'll find it much easier to trim the bone away, which you are to do now, remove the skin, and slice the pieces of the fish downward, so that you will have small slices about ¼ inch thick each. If you have fresh fish, freeze it slightly, sufficiently to do the same; soft, fresh fish is difficult to slice neatly. When you have sliced all the fish, arrange it on a platter, neatly, the slices overlapping. Cover the platter tightly with saran and refrigerate the prepared fish fillets until you're ready to cook the entire dish.

While you are trimming and preparing the fish pieces, make a "court bouillon." To do this, boil together for 10 minutes **2 quarts water; 1 quart light sherry; 2 medium onions,** peeled and quartered; **¼ cup chopped parsley; 1 bay leaf;** and **1 teaspoon salt.** After the first 10 minutes of boiling, as you trim the fish, toss the bones and skin into this bouillon and, once all the fish trimmings are in, let the broth simmer for half an hour. Strain and measure the liquid. You'll need at least a quart. Refrigerate it until it is needed for the final preparation. The fish that is left on the bones is delicious. Pick it off the bones and refrigerate it, covered. It will make a fine leftover.

About an hour before you expect to serve this, prepare the other ingredients as follows: (1) **12 water chestnuts,** thinly sliced, set on a plate, symmetrically (these come in cans); (2) **4 cups thinly sliced fresh mushrooms** neatly arranged on another plate. You should trim the bottom of the stems of the mushrooms and, when they are sliced, drizzle some **lemon juice** over them to keep them from turning brown; (3) **1 cup chopped green onions** (or the tops of grown-out old onions) on another plate; (4) **1 cup chopped walnuts** on another plate; (5) **4 dozen edible podded peas** (snow peas), if available, on another plate. I've spoken of these before; they can be purchased in a Chinese grocery store if you happen to live in a city which has such; if you live in the country, you can grow them—easy as growing regular peas— just remember to harvest them before the peas develop in the pods; it's the pods which are eaten here. Snow peas can be frozen and will be useful and delicious right through the year. The last possibility for obtaining these, if you have no Chinese vegetable store in your city and cannot grow your own, is to see if the frozen-food section of your market can get them frozen commercially for you; this is possible in some sections of the country. In the absence of all three possibilities, **2 cups cooked peas** will do.

After you have arranged the aforesaid ingredients, cover them with saran and set them aside. Refrigerate all except the walnuts.

Prepare the batter for frying the fish, a simple task, accomplished by beating together with an electric or hand mixer, or even a wire whisk, **2 eggs, 2 tablespoons of the court bouillon, ½ cup sifted flour,** and **1 teaspoon soy sauce.** It will be very thick. When ready to serve, heat a 10-inch iron frying pan very hot; then add **peanut oil,** enough to cover the bottom of the pan, about ¼ inch deep, no more. When the peanut oil is hot and wavy, dip the little pieces of fish in the batter and fry them quickly in the oil. It will take about a minute for each piece; remove the fish as it is fried, setting it to one side on a piece of heavy brown paper. When all the fish is fried, arrange it on a deep platter and keep it warm while you make the sauce. Drain all excess oil from the pan.

Prepare the thickening in a small bowl before you start the sauce. First dissolve 2 tablespoons cornstarch in ¼ cup cold water, then stir in 1 teaspoon salt, 2 twists of the pepper mill, ⅛ teaspoon garlic powder, 2 teaspoons soy sauce, and 2 teaspoons sugar.

Retrieve all ingredients (i.e., the water chestnuts, mushrooms, onions, pea pods, and broth) from the refrigerator. Set the bowl of seasoned thickening close at hand; also the walnuts; and proceed, preferably with your guests gathered round.

Using the skillet, add to it the water chestnuts, the mushrooms, and the quart of broth. If you haven't a quart, add sherry to make it up. Simmer 2 minutes. Add cornstarch mixture. Stir it into the vegetables, add the snow peas if you have them, bring to a boil, and simmer 2 minutes. Add the thickening—and isn't it nice to have it all mixed and ready? Stir it into the vegetables, add the snow peas if you have them, bring to a boil, and simmer 2 more minutes, or just long enough to thicken the sauce somewhat. These short cooking times are important. These foods need no more time than this.

Pour some of the sauce over the fish fillets, sprinkle the top with the chopped green onions and the walnuts. Pass the extra sauce in a separate bowl.

Depending very much on your guests and your party set-up, the final cooking, both of the fish and the sauce, can be done with an electric skillet in the living room or dining room.

INGREDIENTS:

For the court bouillon: 2 quarts water; 1 quart light sherry; 2 medium onions; ¼ cup chopped parsley; 1 bay leaf; 1 teaspoon salt.

For the batter: 2 eggs; 2 tablespoons court bouillon; ½ cup sifted flour; 1 teaspoon soy sauce.

For the rest: 3 pounds halibut or swordfish; 12 water chestnuts; 4 cups thinly sliced fresh mushrooms; lemon juice; 1 cup chopped green onions; 1 cup chopped walnuts; 4 dozen edible podded peas (snow peas) or 2 cups cooked peas; peanut oil to fry; 2 tablespoons cornstarch; ¼ cup cold water; 1 teaspoon salt; pepper; ⅛ teaspoon garlic powder; 2 teaspoons soy sauce; 2 teaspoons sugar.

LOBSTER CANTONESE

The quantities given here would not be enough for 12 people if this were the only entree on the menu; the recipe actually produces 6 generous helpings. However, with so much to eat besides, **6 chicken lobsters** (1 to 1½ pounds each) will be more than enough. Have the lobsters split in half while still definitely alive, and ask the fish man to cut off the legs and claws for you. When you get the lobsters home, wash the shells thoroughly, crack the claws with a nutcracker so there won't be any trouble later about removing the meat. Set the lobsters on a welled wooden platter and, using a cleaver or poultry shears (both invaluable utensils in my kitchen), cut the lobster still in the shells into 2-inch lengths. The lobster liquid will accumulate in the well of the platter. Save it in a cup or a bowl. Place all the lobster, still in its shells, in a good-sized bowl. If there are any bits of shell around, get them out of there. Cover the bowl with saran. Refrigerate.

Again, as in the case of the fish recipe just preceding, prepare your thickening. Use a fork to beat lightly together in a small bowl, **1 tablespoon cornstarch, 1 teaspoon sugar, 2 tablespoons soy sauce, the lobster liquid** that you caught in its little bowl some time back and **cold water** to make ¾ cup. Cover the bowl with saran and refrigerate the thickening.

Have **2 pounds lean pork** ground with a medium blade. Heat thoroughly a large (12-inch) black iron frying pan, or a *wok* which is the authentic Chinese pan with a rounded bottom, and, when a drop of peanut oil will sizzle on contact with the pan, add **peanut oil** to cover the bottom to a depth of about ¼ inch. You should not use more than ½ cup oil in all. When the fat is hot and wavy, add the pork. At the same time, throw in **1 cup chopped scallions,** peeled and trimmed, tops, bottoms, everything, and **1 teaspoon salt** and lavishly grind your **pepper** mill over it all, seeing to it that the pork is well seasoned with the pepper.

When the pork is cooked through, a matter of mere minutes, add the **lobster pieces,** yes, shells and all, and sauté these with the pork for *1 minute* and 1 minute only. Add slowly, **3 cups chicken broth** (homemade, if you have some in your freezer, or a good quality canned broth). Bring the whole affair to a boil, then lower heat to a simmer and continue to cook for 5 minutes, turning the lobster pieces occasionally. Now add the thickening you have prepared and simmer for 2 minutes—just long enough to thicken the sauce slightly. A Chinese dish must be just barely thickened, not more than that. Beat **6 large eggs** thoroughly with a fork and, at the last moment, pour them over the lobster. Allow the simmering to continue 1 or 2 minutes, just long enough to start to cook the egg. Stir it around once, taste for seasoning— in this case meaning soy sauce or sugar—and serve, either directly from the frying pan or *wok,* or from a large chafing dish. Keep it hot while it's being served.

INGREDIENTS: 6 chicken lobsters (1 to 1½ pounds each); 1 tablespoon cornstarch; 1 teaspoon sugar; 2 tablespoons soy sauce; lobster liquid and cold water to make ¾ cup; 2 pounds lean pork; ½ cup peanut oil; 1 cup chopped scallions; 1 teaspoon salt; pepper; 3 cups chicken stock (homemade or canned); 6 large eggs.

KIKUI FUJII'S CHINESE SPARERIBS

This is a recipe sent to me by a lovely Japanese-American lady, with whom I had a sprightly correspondence about matters gustatory some years back. Her name is pronounced Kikwee Fujee, a rather pleasant combination of sounds. She seemed, though Japanese, to prefer Chinese cooking and one day she appeared at Blueberry Hill with a large shopping bag filled with authentic vegetables and groceries from New York's Chinatown. She had been shopping there the night before and, on the spur of the moment, she had urged her husband to take a "rittle lide" (a matter of 260 miles!) to present these good foods to the "rittle rady from Blueberry Hill." Her letters were long and rambling, the recipes colloquial (as are mine) and all really excellent.

Here, verbatim, is just one of her recipes: Kikui Fujii's Chinese Spareribs. My comments within the recipe are in brackets. "**4 pounds lean, young spareribs.** Keep whole. Trim off all excess fat possible. Grate 2 good-sized bits of **garlic** (2 cloves, if large) in 2-quart pan. Add **1 cup soy sauce** (half Japanese, half Chinese—richer flavor, Chinese), ⅔ **cup sugar, 2 teaspoons salt,** 2 shakes of freshly ground **pepper.** Bring to boil carefully. Stir. Sugar may burn. Smells good! Remove from heat.

"Place spareribs with curved side down on cookie sheets. Marinate (I don't use all), turn, about 2 hours. [She means, marinate 2 hours, turn every so often. I brush the marinade on the spots hard to reach, using a pastry brush.] In hot weather, refrigerate.

"Put in oven, 500°F., about 5 minutes, then to 350°F. and bake. Turn often, baste. Add more soy. I baste every 10 minutes. It burns, so add water judiciously (small amount, not to dilute flavor). At end, reduce heat to 300°F. About 1 hour in all. It's a rich brown. Smells wonderful! Tastes better.

"Then cut each rib off. Serve over rice with rich juices. **Scallions** on top, garnished, or **Chinese parsley.** It's so good!"

She's right. It's so good.

INGREDIENTS: 4 pounds lean, young spareribs; 2 good-sized bits (2 cloves) garlic; 1 cup soy sauce (half Japanese, half Chinese); ⅔ cup sugar; 2 teaspoons salt; 2 shakes of freshly ground pepper; scallions or Chinese parsley.

NOTE: I have used exactly this recipe for a Chinese barbecued pork tenderloin recipe. You would have, then, a perfect slab of pork, barbecued on the edges, moist and beautifully cooked inside. Serve this sliced thin on the diagonal, a bit of hot mustard on the side.

Not enough of us know about pork tenderloins. These are the tender strips of pork meat under the full loin of pork. If you can buy a whole loin of pork—which is a most economical method of buying it—the butcher will be glad to trim off the tenderloin for you. One tenderloin will serve two people, usually. If you wish to wait until you have enough for a larger group, wrap each tenderloin in saran as you get it, freeze it, and keep it until you have three or four more, or as many as you would like. The loin, bought whole, will provide you with this tenderloin, a center roast, 8 or 9 thick chops, and the ends can be cut up for chow mein or used for a family supper. It's not easy to carve, but the end meat is as delicious as the center. Speaking of pork tenderloins, try them as in this recipe:

Roast Herbed Pork Tenderloin

Marinate four pork tenderloins for a few hours at room temperature in a combination of 1 cup light sweet white wine, 1 bay leaf, 2 small peeled onions, cut up, 3 or 4 peppercorns, ¼ teaspoon salt, and ½ teaspoon rosemary. Heat a roasting pan in a very hot (475°F.) oven, add 2 tablespoons butter, let the butter sizzle, then drain and add the tenderloins. Turn them a few times so they're well covered with the butter and roast 10 or 15 minutes, until the meat begins to brown. Then add about a half cup of the marinade, including the onion, continue to roast, turning every 10 minutes. Cut into one of the tenderloins with a sharp knife after half an hour, and if there is any pink showing, continue roasting 10 more minutes or until the meat is definitely cooked through. More marinade can be added if the pan gets too dry. At the end, you should have just a little of the concentrated gravy. If the meat is done and the gravy is too thin, reduce it by cooking it over direct heat until it is thick. Add **2 tablespoons butter**, let it melt, add **1 tablespoon chopped parsley.** Slice the meat diagonally and serve with a little of the gravy. The leftover meat is gorgeous, cold.

INGREDIENTS: 4 pork tenderloins; 1 cup light sweet white wine; 1 bay leaf; 2 small onions; 3 or 4 peppercorns; ¼ teaspoon salt; ½ teaspoon rosemary; 4 tablespoons butter; 1 tablespoon chopped parsley.

CAPER-FRIED RICE

One cup of uncooked rice will afford you three cups of it, cooked. A handy bit of knowledge. For this meal, you will want to start with **4 cups uncooked rice.** I suggest that you use Uncle Ben's, cook it as it tells you to on the box, set it aside to cool, fluff it up, and refrigerate it overnight before using it for this recipe. Rice should always be bone dry before you try to fry it, that's another good rule to remember.

Heat a large (12-inch) black iron frying pan very hot. Add **peanut oil** just to cover the bottom of the pan, not any more than that, and let the oil get hot, too. It will wave. Add the 12 cups cooked rice and stir it around over low heat until the rice is thoroughly warmed. Push the rice to one side of the pan and, in the space left vacant, melt **1 tablespoon butter,** let it sizzle, and sauté in it **2 small onions,** peeled and chopped. If you will move the pan over so that the heat reaches the onion section, mostly, they will sauté quickly, and the rice will not be affected. You can move the rice occasionally, to keep it out of trouble. As soon as the onions are golden, combine the whole thing. This much can be done ahead. When you're ready to serve the rice, add ½ cup chopped parsley, ¼ cup soy sauce, and 4 eggs, well beaten. Stir this around and around until the eggs are lightly cooked. Add, last of all, ¼ cup capers, including the liquid that comes with them, and ½ cup shredded lettuce. Stir once more, and serve.

INGREDIENTS: 4 cups uncooked rice (12 cups cooked); peanut oil; 1 tablespoon butter; 2 small onions; ½ cup chopped parsley; ¼ cup soy sauce; 4 eggs; ¼ cup capers with liquid; ½ cup shredded lettuce.

PRESERVED KUMQUATS

We ran a little restaurant for a few winters in Florida and were able to buy kumquats at some of the orange groves. We would go into the grove of kumquat bushes and pick our own. I'm sure you know that these are tiny, elliptical oranges. We preserved them this way. Very easy and worth the effort, in any case. Cover 1 quart kumquats with water to cover, about 1 quart. Bring them to a boil, drain, cover again, bring to boil again, drain—well, do it three times in all. The last time, the third water covering, do not drain but boil until the kumquats are tender, about 10 or 15 minutes. Poke at them with a sharp fork to see. While they're boiling, prepare what is called a "simple syrup," in this case made of ¾ cup water and 2 cups sugar. Boil the sugar and water together for 5 minutes, then add the cooked and drained kumquats and simmer for 5 minutes longer in the syrup. That's all there is to it. Let the kumquats cool in their syrup and store in screw-top jars in the refrigerator. You'll have a great many out of a quart, and when you consider that they cost close to a dollar for a small jar in a fancy grocery store, they're a bargain if you can find the fruit where you live.

In the absence of fresh kumquats, buy them, preserved, in a jar. They contribute the right contrast of tastes to a Chinese dinner. Bittersweet, almost cleansing.

INGREDIENTS: 1 quart kumquats; water; 2 cups sugar.

PEARS SABAYON

For those who must have a glamorous dessert, here is one, indeed. Peel **12 fresh pears,** halve them lengthwise, core them, sprinkle them with **¼ cup light brown sugar,** and bake them at 375°F. in a shallow Pyrex dish with **1 cup fresh orange juice,** basting every few minutes, just until they are tender. This will take between 20 and 25 minutes. Don't discard the orange rind. Sliver it, eliminating all the white possible, and bring to a boil in cold water. Boil 2 minutes, drain. Add the orange peel to the sauce just as you remove the pears from the oven. Allow the pears to cool, then chill them in the refrigerator, covered with their own juice, until needed.

The sabayon sauce can be fixed several hours before you plan to serve the pears, or, if you have time, can be cooked close to dinner hour and served warm over the chilled pears. Beat together **12 egg yolks, 3 cups confectioners' sugar, ⅜ teaspoon salt,** and **1½ cups light sherry.** Cook in top of a double boiler over hot, not boiling, water, for 8 to 10 minutes, stirring constantly. As soon as it *starts* to thicken—don't wait for it to thicken completely—remove and cool. It will complete its thickening process away from the heat. Just before serving, whip **1 pint heavy cream** to hold a peak and fold it into the sauce. Pass from a bowl, to be spooned to the diner's whim, over the chilled, drained pears. Save the orange-pear sauce, whatever isn't used. What a leftover that will make!

INGREDIENTS:

For the pears: 12 fresh pears; ¼ cup light brown sugar; 1 cup fresh orange juice.

For the sauce: 12 egg yolks; 3 cups confectioners' sugar; ⅜ teaspoon salt; 1½ cups light sherry; 1 pint heavy cream.

BUTTERMILK-PINEAPPLE ICE

An alternate dessert, for those who prefer a light, cool morsel after such a meal (and count me one). Mix well **1** quart buttermilk, 2 cups superfine sugar, and 4 cups crushed pineapple, juice and all. Freeze until mushy in freezer trays; remove, and beat with wooden spoon very thoroughly, return to freezer trays or pile in serving dish, and freeze.

INGREDIENTS: 1 quart buttermilk; 2 cups superfine sugar; 4 cups crushed pineapple.

TIMETABLE: The day before, cook the rice, bake the pears, and fix the buttermilk ice. Almost every other part of this meal can be done during the day of your party, morning or afternoon. The last-minute cooking is to be done at the time of service. You won't be able to do everything yourself, so I'm hoping you will have a friend who will take over some of the chores. If you haven't, I've given you alternatives as I go along.

The following chores can be taken care of in the morning or afternoon, as noted:

1. *Cold tomato cream.* Combine. Chill.
2. *Broiled lamb squares.* Prepare marinade in morning. Marinate squares in afternoon.
3. *Chinese fish, devastating.* Prepare fish fillets in early afternoon. Arrange on plate, covered with saran, refrigerate. Make court bouillon with trimmings, strain it. An hour before serving, prepare all other ingredients for this dish; arrange them on plates; prepare batter; prepare thickening.
4. *Lobster Cantonese.* Prepare lobster in afternoon, when you've finished working on fish; prepare thickening. Chop scallions. Have pork, peanut oil, chicken stock ready.
5. *Kikui Fujii's spareribs.* Three hours before dinner, prepare marinade, cut ribs into serving pieces and marinate. (The same procedure goes for pork tenderloins, if you have decided to serve these instead of the ribs.) Two hours later, roast ribs as directed. You will need to be nearby, but, since this is 1 hour before dinner, you probably won't find it hard to be in the vicinity of the kitchen.

6. *Caper-fried rice.* Get all ingredients ready for this, including the frying pan. Mix the parsley and soy sauce with the eggs, ready for the final preparation.

7. *Pears sabayon.* Make sauce, except for the addition of the whipped cream. Have cream whipped and ready to stir into the sauce. The pears, you remember, were prepared yesterday and are ready in the refrigerator.

Ready to serve? Shake tomato cream in cocktail shaker with shaved ice. Remove ribs from oven, keep them in a warm spot, turn the oven up to 500°F. and quickly broil the lamb squares. If you have a hibachi, no need to take the ribs out of the oven, and you can let your guests spear the lamb squares themselves and cook them as they like them over the hibachi.

While your guests are enjoying the lamb squares, you, or your representative, should be frying the fish for the Chinese fish. If you have an electric frying pan, you can do this in sight of the guests; if not, do it or have it done in the kitchen. Arrange the fish on the platter. Now, if you can manage it, let your guests observe you put this dish together, quickly. You have all the ingredients arranged, beautifully, around you; let everyone watch while you add (1) the water chestnuts, the mushrooms, the broth; then, after 2 minutes, add (2) the thickening, which is ready, and the snow peas or the cooked peas. Simmer 2 minutes. That's all there is to it. Have someone serve the guests with little pieces of fish from the platter (chopsticks, if handled correctly, are the dainty method of service here), spoon over it the sauce, sprinkle the top with the chopped onions and walnuts.

While you're taking care of the Chinese fish, devastating, have a compatriot do the lobster (or vice-versa; you do the lobster while he or she does the fish). If you are planning to do all the cooking yourself, you should have the lobster done before you start on the fish. It's better, however, to have both come to a state of completion at one and the same time. Doing the lobster is even easier than the fish. It requires (1) cooking the ground pork with the scallions for about 3 minutes, (2) adding the lobster, shells and all, sautéing for 1 minute, (3) adding the chicken stock and simmering for 5 minutes,

(4) adding the thickening, already combined, simmering 2 minutes, and, finally, (5) stirring in the eggs. Everything ready to go in, what could be easier. Serve from frying pan.

The ribs are ready and waiting.

The rice you will find you will have been able to put together while either the fish or the lobster is being prepared. Heat your frying pan, add the rice, brown the onion (you may, if you prefer, sauté the onions separately some time earlier, and simply scrape them, onions and juices, into the pan of rice at this time), then add the egg mixture. As soon as the eggs are set, add the capers and lettuce, which have been standing by, waiting their turn.

The pears sabayon will require, at serving time, spooning into a beautiful cut-glass serving platter or bowl; the sauce, folded now into the whipped cream, in a fancy bowl nearby. The buttermilk ice is ready.

A complicated dinner? Not at all. Keep calm about the whole thing, have everything ready just as I've instructed, and you'll be fine. If you're completely on your own, fix the fish and the lobster a little ahead of the arrival of your guests and keep them hot in chafing dishes or on hot trays.

LEFTOVERS

Freeze what's left of the tomato cream. It's a delicate and delightful frozen appetizer; or pile it, frozen, on a bed of tender salad greens, serve with a sour cream dressing, sliced radish rounds on top.

Any cooked lamb squares that are left should be frozen and used in your next chow mein. Uncooked, they will keep for a week in the refrigerator to be charcoal-broiled at your convenience; frozen, they will be a comfort the next time you have unexpected cocktail guests. Don't even need defrosting; they'll defrost over the charcoal flames.

Leftover cooked lamb squares make delicious sandwiches; an onion, sweet, a natural with them. Uncooked, try them broiled on skewers alternating them with mushrooms, green peppers, pineapple squares, and onion sections.

The sautéed slices of fish, kept without sauce, make a

terrific late-night snack between slices of pumpernickl bread, moistened with mayonnaise or tartare sauce and lots of pepper. Or try them in the following soufflé.

Halibut or Swordfish Soufflé

Stir 1 cup of the fish, flaked, with or without the **fried batter,** into 1 cup of cream sauce; season it with **parsley** and a bit of **sherry.** Remove it from the heat. Add 2 **egg yolks** and fold in the beaten **whites of the same 2 eggs.** Bake in a buttered baking dish for 20 to 30 minutes or until set. Serve this right away. Soufflés are temperamental. (Note: To prepare a cream sauce for a soufflé, which perhaps is thicker than other sauces, melt 3 **tablespoons margarine,** stir in 3 **tablespoons flour,** make a smooth paste, and slowly add 1 **cup milk.** Cook until thickened. Season with ¼ **teaspoon salt,** a few grinds of your **pepper** mill.)

INGREDIENTS: 1 cup leftover fish; leftover fried batter (optional); 1 cup cream sauce; parsley; sherry; 2 eggs.
 For the cream sauce: 3 tablespoons margarine; 3 tablespoons flour; 1 cup milk; ¼ teaspoon salt; pepper.

Cucumber-Fish Salad

Another good use for leftover fish is this salad, prepared by marinating 2 **cups cooked fish** in ¼ **teaspoon salt, pepper, 1 teaspoon wine vinegar, 1 tablespoon pure olive oil,** a sprinkling of **garlic powder.** Two or three hours will do. Add 2 **cut-up small cucumbers,** freshly plucked; stir around, drain, and taste for seasoning, adding salt, pepper, and other seasonings if needed. Serve with 1 **cup whipped, salted cream** or **commerical sour cream;** grated **onion;** freshly ground **pepper;** grated **cucumber** or **dill weed.** Taste it as you go.

INGREDIENTS: 2 cups leftover fish; ¼ teaspoon salt; pepper; 1 teaspoon wine vinegar; 1 tablespoon olive oil; garlic powder; 2 small cucumbers; 1 cup whipped cream or commercial sour cream; onion; cucumber or dill weed.

The sauce for the Chinese fish, devastating, can be frozen and used for another meal. It's marvelous over fried shrimp, boiled lobster, crabmeat. The same holds true for the lobster Cantonese; it should be frozen as it is, reheated over boiling water, served. It will be nearly as good as new. You can doctor it up by adding some crisp fresh bean sprouts, drained, and a few new snow peas, if you have any. If you have little lobster and lots of sauce left, heat that and serve it over Chinese noodles with sliced cold pork, or over an egg foo yong. See my recipe for this in the *Blueberry Hill Cookbook*.

The Chinese spareribs are a natural for a midnight snack. They can be piled on top of any remaining rice in a casserole, greased with peanut oil. Tuck in some cut-up kumquats. If there's any marinade left, drizzle that around on top; cover with aluminum foil and heat just until it is steaming hot. Serve these with Chinese mustard.

If you have prepared (instead of, or in addition to, the ribs) the pork tenderloin, you should use it, sliced thin, for the most exquisite sandwich you've ever eaten, between slices of homemade white bread, a sweet onion sliced over it— much or little, as your taste in onions goes—the bread moistened lightly with mayonnaise. In fact, the pork tenderloin should be used as it is; its flavor is so perfect, it would be a shame to mask it with sauces and such.

Should you, nevertheless, prefer a hot dish made of it, lay the tenderloin in overlapping thin slices in a flat casserole, cover with foil and heat just to steaming hot. Meantime, prepare a thin sauce by stirring a teaspoon of soy sauce, a teaspoon cornstarch, ½ teaspoon sugar, and ¼ teaspoon garlic powder into perhaps a cup of cold chicken broth or consommé, and, as soon as the cornstarch is dissolved, bringing this to a boil. Taste for seasoning and serve sparingly over the pork tenderloin slices. Rice is fine with this, or vermicelli; the sauce can be varied by adding cubes of canned pineapple or little slivers of carrots and green peppers, parboiled a few minutes before adding.

The rice reheats fine in a frying pan; a little more peanut oil to get it started. It can, as well, be frozen; defrost preferably at room temperature; if you're in a hurry, defrost and heat in your Bungalow Cooker, the steamer without any holes in the bottom. This, since it's also called a Rice Steamer by its manufacturers, is obviously a natural for rice. Fluffs it right back up.

The kumquats are part of a lovely salad. Slit them and fill them with softened cream cheese. You'll know how to go on from there.

The orange-pear sauce, with whatever slivers of orange rind there are left in it, should definitely be saved and used another day. Make some thin crêpes (see page 195; the recipe for Blueberry dessert pancakes has a good crêpe recipe), roll them, heat the sauce, add a little cognac, heat it hot (or flambé it, if you have a touch of the dramatic), and pour it over the little pancake rolls.

The sauce sabayon, piled into a sherbet glass, chilled to help it hold its shape, makes a beautiful dessert on its own. Top it with shaved unsweetened chocolate, or—what else? —kumquats.

I haven't forgotten that you have a great many egg whites to use up. Use them for mousses, strawberry, apricot, or other fruits; they can be used for the very excellent white cake I give elsewhere in this book (page 222), or, in fact, any other white cake. A really terrific cake which calls for just the whites, and not the yolks, is what is known as a whipped cream cake. This is a classic recipe, not my own, but given to me by so many people and used by me for so many years, particularly to use up extra egg whites, that I think you ought to have it, if you thus far haven't. It goes like this:

Whipped Cream Cake

Sift together 2 cups cake flour, 1⅓ cups sugar, and 2¾ teaspoons baking powder. Whip until stiff 1 cup (½ pint) heavy cream. Combine the cream with 3 egg whites, beaten to hold a glistening peak. Add a pinch of salt. Fold into the cream-egg white mixture, ½ cup water, 1 teaspoon pure vanilla, and ½ teaspoon lemon extract.

Now carefully fold the flour mixture into the cream mixture, a little at a time, until it is all combined and there is no sign of any of the dry ingredients in the batter. Bake in two lightly greased and floured 9-inch layer cake pans, or in a regulation bread pan, at 350°F. It will need about 25 minutes in the cake pans, and perhaps 35 or 40 minutes in the bread pan. Test with a skewer to see if it's done; the skewer will be as dry when it comes out of the cake as it was when it went in.

Cool 5 to 10 minutes on rack before removing cake from pan.

NOTE: This recipe will also make several dozen cupcakes.

INGREDIENTS: 2 cups cake flour; 1⅓ cups sugar; 2¾ teaspoons baking powder; 1 cup heavy cream; 3 egg whites; salt; ½ cup water; 1 teaspoon vanilla; ½ teaspoon lemon extract.

Always Soft Chocolate Frosting

A fine frosting for the cake above is this chocolate frosting.

This is a delicious bitter chocolate frosting. Place in a saucepan 3 tablespoons cornstarch, ¼ pound unsweetened chocolate, 2 tablespoons butter, 1 cup sugar. Pour over all 1 cup boiling milk. Cook very slowly for 15 minutes, stirring every 2 or 3 minutes. At the end of 15 minutes, beat hard for 1 minute. Cool for 5 minutes. Add 2 teaspoons vanilla and a speck of salt. Makes enough for 1 cake or 12 cupcakes.

INGREDIENTS: 3 tablespoons cornstarch; ¼ pound unsweetened chocolate; 2 tablespoons butter; 1 cup sugar; 1 cup milk; 2 teaspoons vanilla; salt.

SEPTEMBER

FAMILY MENU
Love Those Potatoes!

HOT CLAM BROTH, CHEESE WAFERS
CHARCOAL-BROILED CALVES' LIVER
OLD-FASHIONED CREAMED POTATOES
BROCCOLI WITH PEANUTS
TOMATO FRITTERS
CUCUMBERS AND RED ONIONS IN SOUR CREAM
POTATO ROLLS WITH SUN-COOKED STRAWBERRIES
SCANDINAVIAN SPICE CAKE

It is a rather well-known fact that at Blueberry Hill, given an opportunity, I will serve any sort of starch other than a potato. I'm a fancier of rice, tame or wild, kasha, barley, noodles. Sometimes a considerable length of time goes by without my serving a potato in any form.

There is, however, one potato recipe which contradicts the whole thing, as far as I am concerned, and this one is as old as the hills. It is the truly old-fashioned creamed potato recipe which you will find in the menu that follows. There is no resemblance between these potatoes and any other potato you may ever have eaten—certainly no connection between them and the ordinary creamed potato. I won't talk about this any more, but I will urge you, but urge you, to try them!

The rest of the menu is a perfect autumn supper for the family. A friend, invited in, will count himself fortunate. Service for 6, a proper family size.

HOT CLAM BROTH, CHEESE WAFERS

The clam broth comes in a bottle. Heat it. If you have had steamed clams at any time through the summer and have saved the broth in your freezer, serve it now. I assume you will have strained it to remove the sand and shells before you froze it. Just hot is right.

The cheese wafers are so easy to bake, you'll never want to buy them again. Cream together well with your electric mixer, at very high speed, **½ pound grated sharp cheddar cheese, ½ cup (1 stick) soft butter, ½ teaspoon salt,** and, if you'd like, a **dash of cayenne pepper.** When thoroughly combined and smooth, add, gradually, **1½ cups flour,** sifted, continuing this process until you can form the mixture into a roll about 1 inch in diameter. Near the end, when it gets too thick for the beater blades, let your floured fingers take over the job. Wrap the roll in saran and refrigerate it for 2 hours; if you're impatient, set it in your freezer for 10 minutes. Same result.

Slice into thin wafers with a sharp knife and bake in a 350°F. oven for 8 to 10 minutes, or until lightly browned. These are delicious hot or cold. You may keep the roll, unbaked, in your refrigerator, slicing and baking the wafers as you need them; they'll be at their best, that way. You can, as well, freeze them either before or after baking. You will have about 8 dozen wafers, none too many.

INGREDIENTS: ½ pound sharp cheddar cheese; ½ cup butter; ½ teaspoon salt; cayenne pepper; 1½ cups sifted flour.

CHARCOAL-BROILED CALVES' LIVER

The flavor of calves' liver grilled over charcoal is, truly, unsurpassed. You can do this in your oven under the broiler, of course, but it will not be so special. We use a grill that can go into the fireplace when it's too cool outdoors for cooking and eating.

Have 3 pounds calves' liver cut into steaks, 2 inches thick. Brush each side with soy sauce, sprinkle with freshly ground black pepper. Grill over medium coals, brushing with melted butter, five or six times. You'll use about 3 or 4 tablespoons. The steaks will need 12 to 15 minutes to be rather on the rare side, still quite pink inside, but so much of this timing depends on the heat of your coals that you'd be wise to cut into the steaks as they go along to see how they're going. At the last moment, place the steaks very close to the coals to crisp and brown on the outside.

INGREDIENTS: 3 pounds calves' liver; soy sauce; pepper; 3 or 4 tablespoons butter.

P.S. If you've done these in your oven, you might like to add a bit of wine to the drippings in the bottom of the pan, let it cook up and add it to the liver before serving. Taste it first; you might like a bit of seasoning such as salt, pepper, or garlic powder.

OLD-FASHIONED CREAMED POTATOES

The star of the menu! Please note that no flour is necessary. The potatoes themselves produce the necessary thickening.

You must not use baking potatoes or new potatoes. Peel and cut into ¼-inch-thick lengthwise slices, 8 medium-sized old potatoes. Cut the slices into matchstick slim slivers, 2 inches long by ¼ inch wide. Keep the potatoes in cold water as they are peeled and sliced, until you have them all ready.

Use a heavy black iron frying pan, about 9 or 10 inches in diameter, and place in it a full pint of light cream. Drain the potatoes thoroughly, add them to the cream with 2 teaspoons salt, a liberal sprinkling of freshly ground pepper. The amount of pepper is up to you. Lots of pepper seems right for this dish. Also you will want 1 tablespoon butter.

Bring to a boil, then immediately reduce heat to a simmer and allow the potatoes to cook slowly until the cream is the consistency of heavy cream. This should happen in about 20 or 30 minutes. If the potatoes were cut slim enough, they ought to be done just about this time. If they aren't, add a little more cream. If you've run out of cream, add milk with another lump of butter. You should stir the potatoes from time to time. As soon as the potatoes are cooked through, yet not mushy, this delectable dish is ready, each potato firm and on its own. Don't overcook these. At the end, sprinkle 1 tablespoon chopped parsley over the potatoes. Taste for salt; you might need as much as another teaspoon; you might not. Taste and see.

INGREDIENTS: 8 medium-sized old potatoes; 1 pint light cream; 2 teaspoons salt; pepper; 1 tablespoon butter; 1 tablespoon chopped parsley.

BROCCOLI WITH PEANUTS

The peanuts are a fillip for the young; a delightful taste, in any event. Wash and trim the tough ends of 2 bunches fresh broccoli. Cut them lengthwise into serving-size pieces. Add 1 teaspoon salt and steam, quickly, to a state of tenderness. If you haven't a steamer, improvise one with a colander over hot water. It must be covered tightly. Broccoli, as is true with all other green vegetables, must not be overcooked, nor lose its color. A fork should go easily into the toughest part of the stem and, once this point is reached, you must definitely stop the steaming process. In fact, if you have to keep the vegetable a little while before you can serve it, you should remove the hot water from beneath it long enough to reduce the temperature of both the top and the bottom. Then you can return the top and keep it warm over its rightful bottom. This is, to me, one of the great advantages of steaming over pressure cooking; a steamer can be opened for checking purposes without endangering the life and health of the cook. Something very final about a pressure cooker, I think. The food is in there and by golly it's going to stay in there. You have no control at all.

Melt ¼ cup (½ stick) **butter,** watching it sizzle up, then lightly brown. At this point add **2 tablespoons chopped peanuts.** Let the butter with the peanuts sizzle up again, then immediately pour it over the broccoli, which by this time, should be arranged neatly on a heavy platter that can withstand the heat of the sizzling butter. Taste for **salt** and **pepper.** Add them if needed.

> NOTE: I have been serving all green vegetables—broccoli, asparagus, green beans, even peas—from platters rather than casseroles. It makes it possible to distribute the butter and seasonings all at one time and evenly, not to speak of the beauty of symmetrically arranged green vegetables. With deeper dishes, you must do the seasoning in layers, much more time-consuming, and then, in tossing and turning the vegetables, you are inevitably a bit rough, resulting in visual chaos.

INGREDIENTS: 2 bunches fresh broccoli; 1 teaspoon salt; ¼ cup butter; 2 tablespoons chopped peanuts; salt; pepper.

TOMATO FRITTERS

Drop **6 firm, medium-large red tomatoes** into a pot of rapidly boiling water, one at a time. Each tomato should be left in the water for 1 minute, then removed with a long-pronged fork. The skins will slide off. Slice them into thick slices; let them sit on a plate to drain out the excess liquid and seeds. You may poke out the seeds with a knife, if you wish. Season the tomatoes with **salt,** freshly grated **pepper,** and a **pinch of sweet basil** for each slice.

Beat together **1 beaten egg, ½ cup milk, 1 tablespoon melted butter, ¾ cup flour, 1 teaspoon baking powder, ¼ teaspoon salt.** The batter should be smooth and thick; if it isn't, add a little more flour; if it's too thick, add a little more milk. You're after the texture of a pancake batter.

Get a large frying pan very hot, add to it **2 tablespoons butter** and **2 tablespoons peanut oil.** When the fat is hot, dip the tomato slices, each in its turn, in the batter, drop them carefully in the sizzling fat, and sauté over moderate heat until each side is nicely browned. Add additional fat, if you need it, as you go along. As the fritters are done, remove them to a paper towel to drain for a minute, then to a warm platter. Serve next to the creamed potatoes. They are natural companions.

INGREDIENTS: 6 firm, medium-large red tomatoes; salt; pepper; basil.

For the batter: 1 egg; ½ cup milk; 1 tablespoon butter; ¾ cup flour; 1 teaspoon baking powder; ¼ teaspoon salt.

To fry: butter and peanut oil.

NOTE: For an alternate tomato dish, should you wish to avoid frying these, season your slices as noted above, sprinkle over them a few bread crumbs, dot them with butter, and brown them under the broiler. If you're doing the calves' liver in the oven, these to-matoes can go right along under the broiler with them. Just before serving and after the tomatoes have softened a bit, sprinkle them with a little brown sugar, dot them with a little more butter, and return them to the broiler until the sugar is bubbly and crisp.

CUCUMBERS AND RED ONIONS
IN SOUR CREAM

Soak **6 medium garden cucumbers,** thinly sliced, unpeeled (or peeled cucumbers, if not garden fresh) and **1 sweet red onion,** sliced into thin rings, in **iced salted water** for several hours. Drain, just before serving, and arrange on a platter, the red and the green alternating. The soaking process can cover the entire day, if it's more convenient for you to fix these in the morning. Cover with ½ **cup commercial sour** cream, mixed with 1 tablespoon sugar, 1 teaspoon white vinegar, ¼ teaspoon celery seed.

INGREDIENTS: 6 medium garden cucumbers; 1 sweet red onion; ice water; salt.

For the dressing: ½ cup commercial sour cream; 1 tablespoon sugar; 1 teaspoon white vinegar; ¼ teaspoon celery seed.

POTATO ROLLS

These rolls should be made at a time when you have **1 cup mashed potatoes** left over from another meal. You can do these rolls at any time that's convenient, freeze them, and defrost them today in a heavy brown paper bag. You'll want a corrugated grocery carton on hand for the rising.

Add **2 cakes yeast** or **2 packages active dry yeast** (check the date for freshness) to ½ **cup lukewarm water.** The yeast will dissolve within 5 minutes. During that time bring to the scalding point—which is below the boiling point but means very, very hot—**1 cup rich milk.** Add to this ¾ **cup** (1½ sticks) **margarine.** If you're a purist, make it **butter.** Stir around with ½ **cup granulated sugar, 2 teaspoons salt,** and watch everything dissolve in the heat of the milk. As soon as you can find no loose specks of sugar or salt, add **1 cup mashed potatoes.** Combine until well mixed. If the potatoes are cold when you start, go ahead with the next step. If they're hot (you'd need 2 or 3 freshly cooked potatoes, to make the 1 cup of mashed potatoes you want), wait for everything to cool to room temperature. Then, and only then, stir the yeast mixture and add it, along with **3 cups sifted flour,** to the potato mixture. Beat **2 large eggs** well, and mix them in. You should be able to do this all with a heavy wooden spoon. Now start adding more **flour.** You will probably need an additional **2 to 2½ cups sifted flour.** As you add the flour now, the dough will be dry enough to transfer it to a floured bread board.

Knead the dough with floured hands; kneading, in the

remote possibility that this is a term foreign to you, means lifting up the dough, folding it over, and pressing it down with the heel of your hand. Repeat this, adding flour as you do so, until you have used most or all of the 2 or 2½ cups. The dough at this point should be very smooth, elastic in fact, and will blister when pulled apart. It will not stick to the board, either, when this point has been reached, not even when there isn't much flour on the board.

Grease a large bowl with any fresh vegetable shortening; turn the dough in the bowl several times so that it, too, is well greased, and cover the bowl with a damp dish towel. Set the bowl in a corrugated grocery carton with a cover, cover it, and let the dough rise in a rather warm spot out of drafts. In an hour, or when the dough is double in height, cut it down with several slashes of a dull knife. It will deflate, quickly.

Now form 3 dozen rolls. Small balls of dough make very acceptable rolls. (If you want cloverleaf rolls, three small balls dropped into a greased muffin pan, with one small ball on top, takes care of that.) Place your rolls on a greased cookie sheet, put the sheets back in cartons that will hold them, and let them rise again for about half an hour, covered. Brush the tops of the rolls with **melted butter** and bake for 15 minutes in a rather hot oven, about 400°F. Check them after 10 minutes; they might be done before you think they should be. Might take 20 minutes. Depends on their size and the accuracy of your oven. Makes, as I said above, 3 dozen rolls. Get them off their pans while they're hot.

INGREDIENTS: 2 cakes yeast or 2 packages active dry yeast; ½ cup lukewarm water; 1 cup rich milk; ¾ cup margarine or butter; ½ cup granulated sugar; 2 teaspoons salt; 1 cup mashed potatoes; 5½ cups flour; 2 large eggs; 2 tablespoons butter.

SUN-COOKED STRAWBERRIES

This recipe is given here, in the month of September, because we have at this time the perfect meal for this lush preserve. Obviously the strawberries must be cooked when they are ripe, which is more apt to be in June than in September. I suppose in California you have strawberries all year round, don't you, so this is a moot question. Once you've eaten strawberries cooked in the sun, you are spoiled for all other strawberry jams. It is even possible to do this in a city apartment if you have a sunny window on which you can set a shelf to hold the berries.

Weigh **strawberries**. Take an **equal amount of sugar**. This is an amount equal in weight, not in bulk. Hull the berries, and run cold water over them to remove any sand left after the hulling. Place the berries in a bowl with the sugar and let them stand at room temperature overnight. In the morning, lift the berries from the bowl with a slotted spoon and place them on a deep platter, large enough to hold them all without piling them one on top of another. Be careful not to mash them. There will be considerable syrup left in the bowl. Place this in a saucepan and heat it to the boiling point, stirring to dissolve the sugar if there is any still granular. Pour the syrup now over the berries and place the berries in the sun out of doors with a sheet of glass covering the platter. The glass should rest no more than ¼ inch above the berries. Turn the berries carefully twice a day. If it is sunny most of the day, the berries might be thick enough to place in jelly glasses by night. If not, place the platter in the sun another day. It might take as much as 3 days. Bring them in at night, keep them in a cool spot, and set them out again the next sunny day. If it rains, keep them cool until the sun comes out again and resume. When the juice around the strawberries is thick, scrape the berries with the juice into hot sterilized jars and seal them with paraffin. Keep in cool, dark place.

INGREDIENTS: Strawberries; equal weight of sugar.

SCANDINAVIAN SPICE CAKE

A marvelously light cake, perfect for freezing. Grease the bottom and sides of an 8 x 8 x 2-inch baking pan. Vegetable shortening is best for this. Sift together **1½ cups sifted flour, ¼ teaspoon salt, ½ teaspoon ginger,** and **½ teaspoon ground cloves.** (Note: One day, preparing this cake, I found myself out of ground cloves; instead, I ground some whole cloves, naturally not as finely as they are ground commercially. The cake was wonderfully flavored. I now grind the cloves by hand most times.)

Cream together at high speed in your electric mixer **¼ pound** (1 stick) **margarine** or **butter, ¾ teaspoon baking soda,** and **1 cup firmly packed dark brown sugar.** When this mixture is very smooth and ungranular, add **1 egg,** unbeaten. Beat this in thoroughly, until the mixture is thoroughly combined.

Now beat in the sifted dry ingredients, alternately with **½ cup commercial sour cream,** beating each time only until smooth. Don't overbeat at this point.

Bake in the prepared pan in a 350°F. oven for 30 or 40 minutes. Turn the cake out on a wire rack or serve directly from the pan. Serve warm with **½ pint heavy cream, whipped.** A very nice, less rich, way of decorating the cake, if you are not serving it warm, is to cool it thoroughly, place a paper lace doily on top of it, hold the doily down with toothpicks, and sprinkle **confectioners' sugar** over the cake. When you remove the doily, the design will be clearly marked and very attractive.

INGREDIENTS: 1½ cups sifted flour; ¼ teaspoon salt; ½ teaspoon ginger; ½ teaspoon ground cloves; ¼ pound margarine or butter; ¾ teaspoon baking soda; 1 cup firmly packed dark brown sugar; 1 egg; ½ cup commercial sour cream; ½ pint heavy cream, or confectioners' sugar.

TIMETABLE: Such an easy meal to put together. If you have a freezer, you might well have already on hand the clam broth, the cheese wafers, the potato rolls, and the spice cake. The strawberries will have been sun-baked in their own good season.

In the absence of a freezer, here's how this quite simple meal would go together. The cheese wafers, by all means, should be prepared at your leisure, to the stage of the roll of dough, wrapped in saran. This might be done in the morning, or two or three days beforehand. At your leisure, as I said.

The spice cake can be baked in the morning, if you're nervous about leaving cakes to the last minute. A good idea. Cooled, covered with saran, served in the evening, it's almost like new. When you feel confident of your culinary control, however, I advise you to bake this while dinner is in process so that it comes out of the oven hot and fresh, at its most perfect state. If you have frozen it, reheating it restores it to this benign frame of being.

Also in the morning, cut up the cucumbers and the onions and place them in their bowl of ice water. Also prepare the dressing for them, a 2-minute job, and place it in the refrigerator in a covered bowl.

About two hours before dinner, prepare the dough for the rolls. It should take about 10 or 15 minutes only before the dough can be set in its carton to rise for the first time. Now peel and cut up the potatoes as directed, and leave them in cold water until you're ready for them. Also wash and prepare the broccoli—it's a good idea to soak this vegetable for a while in cold water too, although, should you not have allowed as much time as I have here, you will find that a thorough washing and inspection will be satisfactory. Make it thorough.

Place the broccoli in the top of your steamer; break up the peanuts and set them near the broccoli for their last-minute addition; butter in pan for sizzling later.

One hour before dinner, take care of shaping the rolls and setting them to rise again. Peel the tomatoes, slice them, and set them on a plate to drain. Measure out the dry and the liquid ingredients for the batter, if you're making fritters.

Don't combine the batter yet. If you're broiling the tomatoes, they can be seasoned and prepared for broiling at this
time and arranged on the broiler tray; no batter is needed
here, as you know. Season the liver and, if you're doing it
in the oven, arrange it next to the tomatoes. If you're char-
coal-broiling the liver (and I hope you are), this would be
the right time to get the grill in shape, coals arranged, ready
to be lit.

One-half hour before dinner, start the potatoes. Light the
grill. Place clam broth in saucepan to be heated. Slice cheese
wafers, heat the oven for them (350°F.). Drain the cucumbers and onions. If you're going to bake the cake at the
last minute, put it together now; it'll take no more than 15
minutes, surely less. When you've done it a few times, I'll
wager 10 minutes will do it. Don't forget to look at those
potatoes every so often.

Time for the last items. Dress the cucumbers with the
sour cream mixture. Place them on the table. Bake the cheese
wafers; heat the broth. It's fine to serve the broth with the
wafers wherever you all happen to be, unless you have a
strong sentiment about the whole family sitting down at the
beginning of each meal. My experience has been that there's
something warming and friendly about serving the first
course informally in your living room or den—that is, since
the children have grown up sufficiently to respect rugs and
wearing apparel.

While the family is having the broth, bake the rolls. You'll
have to turn up the oven right after baking the wafers, from
350°F. to 400°F.; give it about 5 minutes to reach the
higher temperature, then bake the rolls. While the rolls are
baking, broil the calves' liver—your husband's job if it's
to be done on the grill—and, while this is going on, you
steam the broccoli, a mere matter of starting the heat under
it. If it's fritters you're serving with the liver, combine the
batter, heat the butter and peanut oil for them, and, dipping
the tomatoes into the batter as you go, start sautéing them.

The rolls are ready. Take them out, hot, hot, and serve
them to your now seated family with lots of butter and

the strawberries. Your husband should now produce the calves' liver; the broccoli, meanwhile, can be arranged on its platter. It will take about as long to brown the butter and add the peanuts as it does for you to get the broccoli in its proper juxtaposition. I combine both operations so, just as it is needed, you will have the butter and peanuts ready. Set this on the serving table with the creamed potatoes in their own pan between the broccoli and the liver. The tomato fritters, which should be ready by this time, can now be placed on their platter next to the broccoli. If you find yourself confused at the thought of watching the tomatoes and turning them when needed, while still getting the rest of the meal on the table, rearrange your schedule to get the tomatoes fried and ready before you set up the serving table. They keep, but they're nicer, much nicer, if you do them at the last moment. Then, as you know, you can broil the tomatoes as directed, omitting the fussier frying procedure entirely.

Written down, this seems like a lot of things to do at once, but it isn't. You can see, I'm sure, the advantage of some sort of rolling serving table, on which you can set the foods directly from the oven to the range—saves so many steps and, more important, confusion.

As soon as you have taken the rolls from the oven, reduce the heat again to 350°F., wait a few minutes, and place the Scandinavian spice cake in the oven. Set your timer and, unless your family eats at a phenomenal speed, you will find that they will be just ready for their dessert when the timer will ring for you to come after the cake. Unsurpassed it will be, hot, with whipped cream passed at the table. As I said before, if you prefer to bake it in the morning, it will be a most satisfactory, quite delicious cake cooled and trimmed via the lace-doily method.

LEFTOVERS

Leftover clam broth combines with tomato juice for a fine, cold appetizer. It can also be added to a can of minced clams with lots of butter; a clove of garlic, minced; and parsley;

to be cooked down for a fine clam sauce for spaghetti. The cheese wafers go on as they are; strips of the dough can be cut, rolled between the palms of your hands and baked with sesame seeds on top, for a good cheese stick accompaniment for cocktails.

Leftover calves' liver makes another meal if you will cut it in squares, string it on skewers with sautéed large mushrooms, squares of partially cooked bacon, pineapple chunks, these alternated the length of your skewer, and quickly grilled over charcoal; the bacon should keep it well moistened. You don't need to cook these; just get them hot. An excellent brunch kabob.

Another way. Cut up the liver, again in squares, salt them, pepper them, dust with a bit of flour, and sauté very quickly in butter. A chafing dish is nice for this. When the liver is hot, add ½ cup guava jelly (and do you know what a delicious flavor guava jelly has?), heat long enough to melt the jelly—about 5 minutes—and serve.

The potatoes, piled into a buttered baking dish, topped with grated sharp cheddar, will need a little milk or cream to keep them moist while they're heating in a moderate oven. When they start bubbling, slide them under the broiler to brown. Au gratin potatoes. You can tuck some strips of the leftover liver in among them, or any other cold meat. Ham is particularly good. In absence of any meat, some of those little cocktail frankfurters, resting on top and heated right along with the potatoes, are quite delicious. Might omit the cheese then. Might not. Imagination and whim—these make cooking a delight.

Make a salad with the leftover broccoli. I can think of a bed of romaine lettuce, the leftover broccoli, a hard-cooked egg (either sliced, chopped, or pressed through a sieve), sweet onion rings, grapefruit sections. Dress the whole with a sharp Italian dressing or with one of my favorite, simplest dressings: 2 tablespoons sugar, 2 tablespoons white vinegar, and 1 cup light sweet cream.

Another quick casserole: a buttered baking dish, a layer of leftover cooked broccoli, a layer of leftover creamed potatoes thinned down a bit with cream, a topping of leftover broiled tomatoes, a dusting of Parmesan cheese. Bake it hot. A moment under the broiler finishes it nicely.

The leftover cucumbers in their sour cream sauce can be dropped into hot borscht, last minute, of course. These will be good for this purpose for about 24 hours.

The potato rolls freeze, reheat beautifully, freeze again. Break them open, roughly, butter them lavishly, toast under broiler, serve hot with jam for tea, or with hot pastrami or corned beef and mustard for a Sunday night supper. The right place for a pickle is sliced right into the middle of this sandwich. These potato rolls make a quite delicious bread pudding too.

I can think of two lovely bread puddings. Here they are.

Orange Bread Pudding

A simple matter of soaking **1½ cups torn-up leftover bread** or, in this case, **potato rolls**, in **3 cups rich milk**. When the bread has taken up most of the milk, add **2 beaten egg yolks**, **½ cup sugar**, and the **grated rind of a California orange**, no white, as I've said before. Combine well, and bake in a Pyrex dish set in a shallow tray of water, in a 375°F. oven for 45 minutes to 1 hour, or until a knife, inserted in the custard, comes out clean. Beat the **2 egg whites** (left over from the egg yolks used in the custard) until they will hold a moist, glistening peak. Gradually add the **juice of the orange** (same orange), folding it in carefully, and, still beating, slowly, slowly add **¼ cup superfine sugar**. Heed the admonition here for deliberation, as nothing will break down a meringue more quickly than hastily added sugar. When the sugar is completely beaten in, pile the meringue haphazardly over the top of the pudding and brown quickly in the oven, just long enough to make this a thing of beauty. Serves 6 or 8.

INGREDIENTS: 1½ cups torn-up leftover bread or potato rolls; 3 cups milk; 2 eggs; ½ cup sugar; 1 California orange; ¼ cup superfine sugar.

Coffee Bread-and-Butter Pudding

To do this, combine in a saucepan 1 cup very strong coffee, 1 cup light cream, and 2 cups of milk. Bring it to the scalding point, which is short of boiling. Spread 6 potato rolls (which you have sliced into thin slices) with butter, just enough to cover each cut surface. About 3 tablespoons would be right. Leave crusts right there. Cut the bread into cubes, now, and add to the coffee mixture. Beat 2 eggs slightly, add ½ cup sugar, ½ teaspoon salt; mix well and add to the bread mixture with 1 teaspoon vanilla. You may or may not add ½ cup white raisins, depending on how much you like raisins. Pour the whole into a 1½-quart casserole, sprinkle with ¼ teaspoon nutmeg, set the casserole in a shallow dish of warm water and bake at 325°F. for about 1 hour; you test with a knife as for the other pudding, and keep it baking until the knife comes clean—might be another 15 minutes. Serve warm or cold with plain or whipped cream. This will serve 8.

INGREDIENTS: 1 cup very strong coffee; 1 cup light cream; 2 cups milk; 6 leftover potato rolls; 3 tablespoons butter; 2 eggs; ½ cup sugar; ½ teaspoon salt; 1 teaspoon vanilla; ½ cup white raisins; ¼ teaspoon nutmeg.

Try a few of the sun-cooked strawberries in your tea. This is an old-country trick. Fill some tart shells with them, top with whipped cream. But mostly, save this jam and use it for your special friends in its pristine form.

The Scandinavian spice cake will serve its normal life span without deterioration. Freeze it if you want it to continue to taste oven-fresh. Otherwise remember it sliced plain with fruit, under ice cream, sliced and covered with a lemon custard sauce. Finally, should it stale at last (hard to conceive but it could happen), slice it thin, toast it, butter it, and serve it for tea with—what else?—sun-cooked strawberries.

OCTOBER

An Autumn Evening

FRENCH ONION SOUP
VEAL AND EGGPLANT CAPRI
SYRIAN PILAF
CAPERED CARROTS
SLICED TOMATOES, ITALIENNE
SHELTER ISLAND BREAD
DATE SHERBET OR GUAVA SHELLS WITH CREAM CHEESE

A lovely dinner for a few fast friends on an autumn evening. Have a look at the purple hills, the sunset. Take a walk across the fields. Light the fire. Try to resist the aroma of fresh-baked bread filling the house: the perfect mood, the perfect meal. For 8.

FRENCH ONION SOUP

A true Parisian onion soup. Use a heavy pot, a large one, about 3- or 4-quart capacity. Get it hot, the pot, first. Then, when a bit of fat will sizzle on contact, place in the pot ¼ cup (½ stick) **butter** or, preferred here if you have it or can get it, **rendered chicken fat.** (You "render" chicken fat by placing all the fat you can get off a nice old hen in a heavy saucepan. Add a cut-up onion and simmer it until all the fat

266

is "rendered" forth. Another term for this, particularly used with pork fat, is "tried out." Same thing. When the chicken skin, which clings to some of the fat, and the onions are crisp, you will have a clear, true chicken fat. Strain the fat into a jar. Set a silver spoon in the jar; then it won't crack from the contact with the hot fat. Refrigerate the fat until you need it. It will keep for an indefinite period of time. The cracklings that are left can be seasoned with a bit of salt and pepper and nibbled with a cocktail or a glass of tomato juice.)

When the fat is hot, add **4 cups thinly sliced onions** (you'll need about 8 medium onions to achieve this). Over low heat, stirring occasionally with a wooden spoon, brown the onions thoroughly. This will take about 15 minutes. You want them dark brown, but not burned. Watch them. You can't hurry this process, so don't try. Now add **2 quarts chicken broth.** (Homemade is best; see page 13, but you can use a good quality canned broth if you have to. *Don't* use bouillon cubes.) Add **2 thick slices dry French bread** (a firm bread is needed here—French or Italian is best). Simmer, covered, 30 minutes. The bread will disappear. Season with **salt** and **pepper** to taste. I can't possibly tell you how much because I don't know how well seasoned the broth was when you started. So taste first. Add a little salt and/or pepper. Taste again, and again, until it's right.

You can set the soup aside now, uncovered, for a few hours. If you prepare it the day before, refrigerate it as soon as it is cool. On a warm day (and some October days are that), chill it quickly in a bowl of ice cubes. Chicken broth sours easily. Get it into the refrigerator as soon as possible, do.

When ready to serve the onion soup, fill earthenware soup bowls with the hot soup (reheated just to boiling), place a **toasted slice of French bread** on each bowl so it floats on the soup. Sprinkle with **1 teaspoon grated Parmesan cheese** for each bowl. Brown the cheese quickly under the broiler, setting the bowls on a tray to do this expeditiously. If you have your broiler preheated when you start the browning, it's a matter of minutes. Set the bowls on under-liners on the table. Call your guests. Soup's on!

INGREDIENTS: ¼ cup butter or chicken fat; 4 cups thinly sliced onions (8 medium onions); 2 quarts chicken broth; 1 loaf day-old French bread; salt; pepper; 8 teaspoons Parmesan cheese.

VEAL AND EGGPLANT CAPRI

This is a very favorite veal dish in the Masterton menage, though I must admit the children carefully set the eggplant to one side. John and I adore it, however, eggplant and all, as do our guests.

Wash, dry, and slice **1 firm large eggplant** into 8 thin slices, unpeeled. Don't use the eggplant if it looks tired; the skin will be tough. The slices should be about ¼ inch to ½ inch, no more, in thickness. Sprinkle each slice with **salt, pepper,** and a very light sprinkling of **garlic powder.** A good estimate of the amount you would need would be about ¼ teaspoon salt, a few twists of the pepper mill, and ⅛ teaspoon garlic powder for each slice. Sprinkle each slice then with ½ **teaspoon flour,** each side. Set them, overlapping, on a tray.

Ask your butcher to slice, paper thin, **3 pounds of veal** from the leg, as for scallopini. These slices should be from the very center of the leg, such as are used for cutlets. If you want to be very extravagant, ask for a loin of veal and have the little tenderloins trimmed off and sliced for you. These are more symmetrical, and very beautiful. But the leg is fine. After the butcher has sliced them, ask him to pound them with a cleaver. My butcher likes to chill the veal in his freezer for a little while; says it cuts more easily when it's cold. Don't be afraid to ask for this service in your supermarket; the butchers there in the big back rooms are glad to oblige. Lends a bit of variety to their day.

Season the veal just as you did the eggplant, with salt, pepper, garlic powder, and flour. The veal can sit on a wooden tray until you're ready for the preparation. This dish is so easily and quickly prepared that it can be done right before your guests, using an electric skillet, if you wish. Me, I let my guests come into my kitchen and talk to me while I fix it in an old-fashioned iron frying pan on my gas range. It takes about 10 minutes, in all, to prepare this for a party of 8.

Heat a black iron frying pan, 10 inches in diameter, very hot. Then drop in a large lump of **butter,** enough, when melted, to fully cover the bottom of the pan, about 2 tablespoons. As you need it, keep adding more butter, never letting the pan get dry. You will probably use 6 or 8 tablespoons before you're through. As soon as the butter is melted and sizzling, drop the eggplant slices in, one at a time. The eggplant will brown very quickly—don't let it burn; turn down the heat if you have to, or add more butter—and, as soon as it is tender to the fork, turn it with a pancake turner, brown on the under side, and remove to a heated platter, set in a warm, turned-off oven. Arrange the eggplant neatly on the platter, now. To the same pan add, again, enough butter to fully cover the bottom of the pan, let it sizzle up, and, piece by piece, add the veal. Fill the whole pan with the veal, let it brown quickly, turn and let the underside brown. Don't use high heat under the veal, as veal toughens easily. Moderate heat will do the job. As soon as the veal is lightly browned on both sides (about a minute on each side does it), remove it to the platter with the eggplant, arranging slices right on the eggplant. Add the rest of the veal to the pan, in one or more stages, and, with the last slices of veal, as soon as they are brown, add **1 cup Marsala wine** or **cocktail sherry** and **1 lemon,** sliced very thin. Let the wine boil up over the veal; remove the veal to the platter and continue boiling the wine until it is reduced by one-half. Stir all the brown juices around into the sauce.

Pour the sauce over the veal and the eggplant. Serve from the platter or, if you prefer, carefully return the eggplant-veal servings to the frying pan, spoon the sauce over it, and serve from that.

INGREDIENTS: 1 firm large eggplant; salt; pepper; garlic
powder; flour; 3 pounds veal cutlet or from loin; ¼
pound butter; 1 cup Marsala or cocktail sherry; 1 lemon.

SYRIAN PILAF

One time I was doing a radio broadcast, promoting my first
cookbook. It was at a restaurant and I was being interviewed
by a disc jockey. It was two o'clock in the morning, a rather
odd time and way to promote a cookbook, it would appear.
However, in the audience, and vocally so, was a nice man
from Joliet, Illinois, who asked me, in a lull in the interview,
if I could make, or had a recipe for something he called
"pfaff." "That's the name of a sewing machine," I said, laughing. "No, no," he argued, "pfaff! pfaff! My wife makes it!
It's rice!" "Oh," I said, "so do I!" And here is my favorite
recipe for it, I believe quite authentic. Wish I had the name
of that man!

Heat a heavy 8-inch frying pan. When it is hot, melt in it
2 tablespoons butter or margarine and let it sizzle. Add 1
clove garlic, minced (this is optional, depending on your
own affinity for garlic) and 1 cup uncooked dry long-grain
rice. Stir the rice around until it is a golden brown. This
takes about 5 minutes. Be sure to stay by it, stirring all the
time until the rice is the proper tint, because it will burn
before your very eyes if you aren't careful. It puffs a little
at first, looks white and cooked and then browns. Now start
adding chicken broth, about ¼ cup at a time. The chicken
broth should be, preferably, homemade, but canned will do.
Very soon the rice will absorb the broth, and, at this point,
add another ¼ cup. Continue doing this, just throwing in
a little broth whenever the rice appears dry. You can do
this while you're occupied with other things, of course. It
takes about 30 minutes and, in all, you should use 2 or 3
cups of the broth. The amount of broth varies with the
rice, so have at least a quart of the broth on hand. Be sure

the broth is all absorbed when you consider the rice done. At this point, add a few **pignolia nuts** and ¼ **cup currants** or **raisins** simmered in enough **white wine** to cover for just 10 minutes. This plumps them up. If there's any wine left when you want to add them, add the wine, too, and let the rice boil just long enough to absorb the wine. Add **1 table-spoon melted butter**, season with **salt** to taste (depends on how salty the broth was), and toss with a fork. This will produce enough rice for 8. If you want some for leftovers, add half again as much of all ingredients. You'll have enough for 12—which means 8, and leftovers.

INGREDIENTS: 3 tablespoons butter or margarine; 1 clove garlic; 1 cup dry long-grain rice; 1 quart chicken broth; pignolia nuts; ¼ cup currants or raisins; ½ cup white wine; salt to taste.

CAPERED CARROTS

A natural with the veal and the pilaf. Wash and scrape **16 large carrots.** Cut them in thin slices, lengthwise, about 3 inches long. The thinner you slice them, the sooner they will be done; in the summer, should you wish to prepare this, when tiny carrots are available, do them whole. Lay the sliced carrots in a casserole with a lid, and sprinkle them with **1½ tablespoons light brown sugar, 1 teaspoon salt,** and **⅛ teaspoon pepper.** Dot with **2 tablespoons butter.** Add **water** just to cover the bottom of the dish, about ¼ inch deep, and cover the dish tightly. Bake in a 350°F. oven for 1 hour or until the carrots are tender. When they are tender, and just before serving, add **1 tablespoon undrained capers** (using whatever juice comes with them in the spooning). Keep warm, covered, or reheat just before serving. I urge you to try these.

INGREDIENTS: 16 large carrots; 1½ tablespoons light brown sugar; 1 teaspoon salt; ⅛ teaspoon pepper; 2 tablespoons butter; water; 1 tablespoon undrained capers.

SLICED TOMATOES, ITALIENNE

This is a lovely way to treat a tomato. Peel, by dropping into boiling water, removing almost at once, **4 large, ripe tomatoes.** The peel splits and is easily removed. Arrange the tomatoes in overlapping slices on a large, oval platter, preferably white. These look nice on a white plate.

Prepare the following dressing: Mash **1 clove garlic** in a wooden bowl with a wooden spoon. Add **1 tablespoon wine vinegar, ½ teaspoon salt,** and grind some fresh black **pepper** over the whole bowl. Suit yourself on the amount of this; you know how much pepper is enough, I'm sure. Mix until the salt is thoroughly dissolved, then add **3 tablespoons pure imported olive oil** and mix well. Pour two thirds of this over the tomatoes.

Now, again over the tomatoes, scatter small pieces of onion, using **½ sweet Bermuda onion** in all. Also scatter on **¼ cup chopped fresh parsley.** Pour the rest of the dressing over the onions and parsley. Let the tomatoes sit in the dressing for about 15 minutes before serving. Beautiful they are; delicious they taste.

INGREDIENTS: 4 large ripe tomatoes; 1 clove garlic; 1 tablespoon wine vinegar; ½ teaspoon salt; pepper; 3 tablespoons olive oil; ½ Bermuda onion; ¼ cup chopped parsley.

SHELTER ISLAND BREAD

Bread is another thing. Homemade, particularly! Think what this will do for your ego. I'll get right down to business here. Do as I say, now!

Mix **2 cakes of yeast** or **2 packages active dry yeast** with **½ cup sugar.** This will be a dry mixture. Let it stand, covered, in a warm spot for 15 minutes. What do you think! It will have liquefied! Magic. While the yeast is sitting around, mix together in a quart milk bottle or carton ⅓ **quart water and ⅔ quart milk**. Put this in a large pan on top of your range—a small dishpan will do (you are going to add a lot of flour so you should have a large enough utensil—nothing more frustrating than running out of bowl-room). Add to the liquid **2 tablespoons butter** and **2 tablespoons salt** and heat this until it's hot to the touch—say, like dishwater. The butter will melt, of course. Remove it from the stove. Beat thoroughly **3 eggs** and add them to the liquid. Clean the beater by beating it in the liquid. Now add the yeast mix. Easy so far, isn't it?

Get yourself a **5-pound sack of good unbleached flour**. Sift about a cup at a time into the liquid, mixing with a large, wooden spoon. If you have a willing husband at hand, it's a help. *You* add the flour, let *him* stir; not vice versa. Anyway, keep adding the flour, one cup at a time, until the dough is dry and stringy and you can't stir very easily any more. Then start mixing with your hands, no other way to do it, still adding the flour. The satisfaction of this you'll never know until you try it. When it comes free of the pan and is in a ball shape, you are ready to start kneading in flour. With the dough still in the big pan, start kneading (Do you know what kneading is? It's pressing down with your fists and pulling up from beneath.), adding flour all the time, until the dough is easily handled without being sticky. You must keep your hands floured, obviously, all through this process. You won't have to knead very long, either, before this stage is reached. You will have used, by this time, most of the 5-pound sack.

Turn the dough out on a flour-dusted table top or large bread board. Divide the dough into three parts, cutting through it with a floured knife to do this, and, keeping the table top well dusted, continue kneading each loaf until the dough is of satin quality. It will appear to have blisters on it. Probably 30 or 40 times each loaf will do it. Don't bother to wash the table top.

Grease 3 standard-sized bread pans or, if you prefer smaller loaves, 6 half-sized bread pans with any good vegetable shortening. Don't use butter to grease pans for baking—tends to burn. Don't look for trouble, after all. Place the dough in the pans and put them in a corrugated box with a good tight closure. Put the box in a closed-up place, like an oven, or a closet or, if your closets are like mine—full of everything—set it in a corner of your sofa with a pillow on top. The point is, you want to keep it out of drafts. Let it stay there about 3 hours. The loaves should be double in size. Turn them back on the dusted table top and knead each loaf 50 times. Call that husband if you're too tired.

Put each loaf back in its pan, stretching it to fill the entire bottom of the pan. The bread will rise more evenly if you do. Put the pans back into their box as before and let the dough rise again, about an hour. The loaves should be double in size again. Don't worry if they rise more than this. This bread can't spoil—it's wonderful, any way you do it.

Bake 50 minutes for the standard sized breads (check after 30 minutes, if you're using the smaller loaves) in a preheated 325°F. oven. You can even start this bread in a cold oven; if you do, start it at 375°F.; after 10 minutes, turn the temperature down to 325°F. and continue baking for 40 minutes.

When you take your loaves from the oven, rub them with **butter** while they're still hot—it adds to their attractiveness. If you like your bread soft, tie it in a plastic bag as soon as it's cool, one bag for each bread. If you like it crusty, let it sit in the air an hour or so before you do this. You can freeze this bread perfectly, or, if you haven't a freezer, it will keep in a plastic bag for about a week. In the summer, keep it in the refrigerator. French toast, made of this bread, is unsurpassed. Also, it's marvelous for toasting. The recipe as given makes, as I said, 3 large loaves or 6 small ones. It's easy to cut in two, if you wish. Why you would wish, I don't know.

INGREDIENTS: 2 cakes yeast or 2 packages active dry yeast; ½ cup sugar; ⅓ quart water; ⅔ quart milk; 2 tablespoons butter; 2 tablespoons salt; 5 pounds unbleached flour; butter (optional).

DATE SHERBET

This dessert won first prize at a food show I attended as a judge. It's not really a sherbet but it's served in sherbet glasses, so let it be sherbet.

Bring to a boil in a saucepan **3 cups water** and **3 cups dark brown sugar**. Add to this syrup **3 tablespoons cornstarch** dissolved in **½ cup water**, stirring constantly. Cook until the mixture thickens. Remove from heat and add **¾ cup dates** and **¾ cup walnuts**, diced and chopped respectively. Pour into 8 sherbet glasses and cool. Serve with **whipped cream;** ½ pint heavy cream will do, sweetened with **1 teaspoon sugar** and **½ teaspoon vanilla.**

INGREDIENTS: 3½ cups water; 3 cups dark brown sugar; 3 tablespoons cornstarch; ¾ cup dates; ¾ cup walnuts; ½ pint heavy cream; 1 teaspoon sugar; ½ teaspoon vanilla.

GUAVA SHELLS WITH CREAM CHEESE

A very sophisticated dessert which consists simply of the **guava shells** which come in cans, filled with **cream cheese,** softened with **heavy cream.** Serve these with salted crackers.

INGREDIENTS: Guava shells; cream cheese; heavy cream.

TIMETABLE: The bread can be baked, in fact *should* be baked, any time except the day of your party. This is a project of magnitude for many cooks and shouldn't be confused with party preparations. However, if you have a freezer, this or any other bread will benefit, if anything, from freezing. Bring it forth about 2 hours before you plan to use it and let it thaw, unwrapped, at room temperature. About 15 minutes before serving, set it, in a brown paper bag, in a 350°F. oven, making sure it's very hot before you cut it. It can be thawed in the oven the same way, but this is risky. Sometimes the center takes longer than it should to defrost. It should be cut in thick slices, on a bread board, at the table.

If you haven't a freezer, refrigerate the bread and reheat it in the same manner.

Also to be prepared ahead, and, if you'd like, frozen in cartons, is the onion soup. This fares well by this treatment. If you have no freezer, the soup can be prepared the day before or two or three days before and left in the refrigerator. In any case, it's really better after it has sat around a day or two, which is a truism applying to all soups and stews.

So you have, already prepared, the bread and the soup. The morning of your dinner party, prepare the date sherbet, a whiz to do, taking less time than it takes to tell of it, almost. The dressing for the tomatoes can be stirred up, as well, in the morning; the cream cheese can be softened with heavy cream and left in a pretty glass bowl, covered with saran until needed. Take it out of the refrigerator when you start to serve, so it will soften again and be easy to spread.

Early in the afternoon, prepare the carrots with the seasonings, arranging them in their casserole and setting them aside, covered. At about 5:00 o'clock, place the carrots in the oven and forget them for about an hour and a half. Prepare the pilaf as directed, and, while that is cooking, a process which necessitates your staying at the range anyway, prepare the veal for cooking, seasoning it and trimming it into neat slices. This should take you through about 6:00.

Reheat the onion soup; remove the pilaf from the heat, if it is done, which it should be, and place it in a warm spot on the back of the stove. Go get dressed.

The rest of the preparation is quick and shouldn't take more than 15 minutes.

Assuming you want to serve at 7:00, heat the casseroles for the soup and, at the same time, place the bread in the oven to warm. Slice the eggplant, season it, and leave it, with the veal, near the frying pan you're planning to use. Slice the tomatoes, pour the dressing over them, and set them on the table to soak in the flavors of the dressing and, of course, to be passed when the guests are assembled. The carrots will be done—should have been at about 6:30—and should be ready to be served. They will stay very hot and steaming in the casserole so long as you don't remove the lid.

A lovely way to serve the soup is on little trays in the living room. The toasted bread and the hot broth with the rich, brown onions are sufficient unto themselves. No need for any other bread or crackers at this point. If you're against this method of serving soup, as soon as you have browned the Parmesan cheese call your guests into the dining room, where the soup will await them.

If your guests have had the soup in the living room, however, it's easy to ask them into the kitchen to watch you prepare the veal and eggplant. If they're in the dining room, and you don't want to leave them, use that electric skillet. If neither of these devices works, just prepare the veal while they're having their soup. The point is, don't fix the veal and then let it sit. It's so much better right out of the frying pan. When the veal is nearly done, quickly reheat the pilaf, if it seems to have cooled off—this over direct heat, tossing with a fork. The veal, the pilaf, and the carrots, then, can be served by the host—an exquisite plateful, and, at the same time, the hot, hot bread, steam rising slowly as it is cut, can be sliced into thick, crusty slices, perfect for finishing up the last bit of gravy on the plate, as well.

The date sherbet is ready when you are; so are the guava shells. Give your guests their choice of these; urge them to try the guava, even if it's new to them. The coffee steaming, the talk good. A satisfactory dinner party, to say the least.

LEFTOVERS

There's nothing better than leftover onion soup. It goes on and on like Tennyson's brook. It would be sacrilege to add a thing to it; though, given a too small amount to make a meal of its own, I can't think of a thing wrong with adding all the leftover pilaf and every one of the leftover capered carrots to it. This would make almost a stew, of course, and, if you want a soup, a can of chicken broth would take care of that problem. As to the veal and eggplant, believe it or not, there is no better sandwich in the world than a cold veal sandwich.

The gravy congeals somewhat, and, on a thick slice of Shelter Island bread, heavily buttered, it has a flavor of its own. If there's a lot of eggplant around, mash it up, sauté an onion in it, stir in whatever tomatoes you have left from the tomatoes Italienne (draining them, first), season the whole thing with salt, pepper, and garlic powder to taste and add a pinch of sugar. Arrange this in a small open casserole, dot the top with grated Parmesan cheese, and bake in a 450°F. oven until the cheese is brown.

The date sherbet is delicious for several days and, if you don't want to serve it as a dessert a second time, omit the whipped cream and serve it with a slice of baked ham. If you have some whipped cream left, fold it into a tablespoon of creamed horseradish and serve this as a dressing for the, now, date-nut salad, setting the whole affair on a bed of shredded Chinese cabbage or romaine lettuce.

The Shelter Island bread, itself, as suggested with the recipe, is marvelous toasted; it's a rather coarse bread, as many homemade breads are, and makes a terrific bread pudding. (See my recipes for bread pudding on pages 264 and 265.) And don't neglect the crusts, should you come upon some. Sprinkle them with sugar and cinnamon, after first spreading them thickly with butter, and brown them lightly under the broiler. Best cinnamon toast you've ever had.

The veal itself can be ground, mixed with its own gravy, and rolled into thin biscuit dough like a jelly roll and baked until the dough is baked through and brown. Slice thinly and serve hot as an hors d'oeuvre.

OCTOBER

HOT MULLED SHERRIED CIDER
ROAST PORK WITH SAUERKRAUT
NEW POTATOES, MILLIGAN
HOT UNCOOKED TOMATOES
BROCCOLI PECAN
GLAZED STRAWBERRY APPLES
CRANBERRY BREAD
MAMA'S LEMON PIE

Call it supper. Call it dinner. If you're like us, you'll love eating it in the kitchen.

It's a family dinner, simple, still thoughtful. And if friends drop in, you've nothing to be ashamed of. A meal planned for 4, with provision for leftovers.

HOT MULLED SHERRIED CIDER

Pour **1 quart apple cider** into a saucepan. In a square of cheesecloth, tie together the following: **½ teaspoon whole cloves, ½ teaspoon whole allspice, 2 sticks cinnamon** (do not try to use powdered cinnamon; you'll ruin the whole thing!)

and, with ½ cup light brown sugar, packed down to measure correctly, drop the little bag into the cider. Bring the cider to a boil, turn the heat down to simmer, and forget about it for 10 or 15 minutes. Won't matter if it goes for 20, actually. Lift out the cheesecloth bag. Toss it away. Add ¼ cup good, preferably pale-dry sherry. (Note: A good rule to follow on sherry or any cooking wine is that, if it's good enough to drink, it's good enough to cook with.)

That's all there is to that! Hot mulled sherried cider. Keep it hot. Serve it hot. Ought to go for 4 people with seconds. (A very delicious variation of this is to do the same with cranberry juice. Same recipe all the way around.)

INGREDIENTS: 1 quart apple cider; ½ teaspoon whole cloves; ½ teaspoon whole allspice; 2 sticks cinnamon; ½ cup light brown sugar; ¼ cup sherry.

ROAST PORK WITH SAUERKRAUT

For this marvelous dish, you should use either fresh sauerkraut which often can be purchased right out of the crock in delicatessen stores in large cities, or, exactly as good, the plastic-packaged sauerkraut available now in most supermarkets. This is usually labelled "New Kraut." Did you know, by the way, that sauerkraut contains only 25 calories in an average serving? Good for you, too.

A very good roast for this dish is what is called a "picnic." This is the shoulder of the pork. The meat is very flavorful and you can get nice large cuts for your first meal for four. There is loads of meat left over to be used for sandwiches and, as I will show you later, for a marvelous leftover dish using the remaining sauerkraut as well as the leftover potatoes you will have around. The picnic roast has a tough skin on it when you buy it. Don't worry about this; you'll remove it later.

Set a 5- to 6-pound fresh picnic roast (or half a fresh ham, or 7 or 8 pork chops left together—matters little, except in timing) on a rack in a shallow roasting pan. Sprinkle it liberally with salt and **pepper**. Stick **5 or 6 slivers of garlic** in the fat, or sprinkle with **garlic powder** (not garlic salt). Slice **a medium onion** and set slices in slashes you can make in the fatty part of the roast which, by the way, should be top-side. Insert a meat thermometer (a *must* in all roasting, and you'd better get a metal one. The glass ones have a way of breaking right in the middle of the roast). The thermometer should be placed in the meaty part of the roast, making sure the point of it touches neither bone nor fat. The tip of the thermometer is the part that does the registering; this should be right in the middle of the meat.

You'll need about 3 hours at 300°F. to roast a 6-pound roast—that's 30 minutes to a pound—so set the roast in a preheated oven 3 hours before dinner time. Let it roast quietly for an hour, then remove it from the oven and, with kitchen shears, snip through the tough skin, which is now quite loose because of the heat of the oven. You'll see that the shears will cut right through this skin and you can then pull it off. Now sprinkle the newly exposed fat with some more salt and pepper and garlic powder, add a few more onion slices, and return the roast to the oven.

Continue the roasting for another hour. Remove the pork from the oven again. Lift it from the pan, setting it on a tray nearby. Remove the rack. (You can wash it now—won't need it again). Pour off all but about 3 tablespoons pork drippings. Drain **2 pounds sauerkraut** (this is the large bag) and add it to the drippings. Cut, right into the pan, **1 large tart apple**, unpeeled (though cored), and **1 onion**, peeled, cutting them both into smallish cubes, and, finally, **1 small clove of garlic**, peeled and minced very, very fine. Stir the whole thing around with two forks until the sauerkraut is well lubricated with the drippings. Spread it around evenly in the pan; then set the roast on top of the kraut and return the pan to the oven. Continue roasting for about another hour, still at 300°F. At 15-minute intervals thereafter, stir all the sauerkraut around again, lifting the roast a bit each time so the sauerkraut under *it* gets stirred into the rest, too.

Now, as soon as you have added the sauerkraut, start

watching your roast thermometer. The pork is done when it reads 185°F., and this is one meat you want *done!* Might take an hour, might not. The thermometer knows. When it says done, believe it. This should be served from a large, deep, old-fashioned platter, the pork nestling in the sauerkraut.

> NOTE: If you should want to make this for 2 people, roast 6 chops left as one. Don't need to worry about removing skin here. Otherwise, follow directions above, cutting all quantities in half. It will take less time depending on the size of the chops. Check with the thermometer. Add the sauerkraut after the first half hour. If there are 8 of you, I advise using half a fresh ham— very meaty, little waste. This being the case, you'd want to multiply all ingredients by two; and it will take 4 or 5 hours in all.

INGREDIENTS: 5- to 6-pound fresh picnic roast or half of a fresh ham or 7 or 8 pork chops; salt; pepper; 5 or 6 slivers garlic (or garlic powder); 2 medium onions; 2 pounds sauerkraut; 1 large tart apple; 1 clove garlic

NEW POTATOES, MILLIGAN

In Vermont in October the potatoes are being dug. In goes the pitchfork, out come the potatoes, 20 or 30 of them on a vine. For this recipe you'll need new potatoes and butter, that's all! The smaller the potatoes, the better. You'll want 6 or 8 tiny ones for each person; 4 if they're not so small. You'll want some for leftovers too.

Melt **4 tablespoons** (½ stick) **butter** in a small pan, so it's fairly deep. Drop washed, unpeeled **new potatoes** (as many as you need) into the butter, a few at a time. Shake the pan until the potatoes are shiny all over. Lift them out with a slotted spoon, set them in a square of heavy-duty aluminum foil. Make a package, tightly sealed, of about a dozen tiny potatoes or half a dozen larger potatoes in each. Don't stack the potatoes in any package. One layer does it.

Set your packages in a 300°F. oven (along with the pork roast) and bake. They take as long as they take, you know; the little ones should be done in 1 hour; larger ones have been known to take as long as 1½ hours. You can tell when they're ready by squeezing them a bit—you don't need pot-holders for foil, it stays cool. If they respond to a squeeze, they're done. You can open a package and test to be sure, if you wish. However, they keep for a long time in the foil so why not put them in the oven about the same time as you're taking the skin off the pork roast, unless you're doing the small roast. They might be done a little early, but you'll be content. You want them ready when you are, that's the point. They don't need any seasoning—for me, that is. You might want salt and pepper, but try them without it, first.

INGREDIENTS: 4 tablespoons butter; 2 to 3 dozen new potatoes.

HOT UNCOOKED TOMATOES

These are best with the ripe local tomatoes still in the market or bought at farm stands. When they start selling tomatoes to you in those little cellophane packages, you can put this recipe away until next year.

Skin **1 firm ripe red tomato** for each person. You do this by dropping them, one at a time, into rapidly boiling water, letting them sit there less than a minute, removing with a long-tined fork. The skin slips off. If there's a blossom in the tomato, leave it. It looks pretty and does no harm. Let the tomatoes sit on a plate until dinner time.

A few minutes before serving, heat **butter** in a small heavy kettle so that it comes up about ½ inch—about a quarter pound will do. Sprinkle the tomatoes with **salt, pepper, sweet basil**—lightly does it—set them carefully in the pan. Just when you're ready for them, turn the heat up high, and, stirring them constantly but carefully, keep them moving in the butter until they're hot through. They shouldn't cook. Just be hot. Five minutes should do the job. If you have a heavy saucepan with a tight lid, you can leave them in it over a moderate heat, and they will be evenly heated through without attention. Remove carefully to a platter. Serve whole, basting with butter at the moment of serving and sprinkling again with a bit of sweet basil.

INGREDIENTS: Firm red tomatoes, 1 for each person; ¼ pound butter; salt; pepper; sweet basil.

BROCCOLI PECAN

A simple, quite elegant vegetable. Steam **2 bunches fresh broccoli** or **3 boxes frozen broccoli** until just tender—not less than tender, not more. All who know me realize how I feel about my steamer—it does things to vegetables that God intended. If you haven't a steamer, boil the broccoli in an infinitesimal amount of salted water. The sauce couldn't be more elementary. Brown **½ cup** (1 stick) **butter** (don't burn it, brown it! a nice difference). Just before you plan to serve, add to this butter, reheated at this moment, **¼ cup chopped pecan meats** (or **walnuts,** or, perfection itself, **pistachio nuts**) plus **1 teaspoon tarragon vinegar.** Let it boil up, not over, and pour it over the broccoli. If you're a great one for sauces, you can make twice as much as this, and indulge your fancy.

INGREDIENTS: 2 bunches fresh or 3 boxes frozen broccoli; ¼ pound butter; ¼ cup chopped pecans, walnuts, or pistachio nuts; 1 teaspoon tarragon vinegar.

GLAZED STRAWBERRY APPLES

Peel **3 large hard apples,** such as Cortlands or Jonathans. Core them and slice them into 3 or 4 rings each, about ½ inch thick. Bring to a boil **1½ cups granulated sugar, 2 cups water, ½ cup strawberry jam,** and **6 or 7 red cinnamon candies.** Let this simmer together at least 10 minutes, until it looks a little thick. Then drop the apple rings into the sauce, 3 or 4 at a time. They should simmer, not boil hard, until a fork will go into them easily. This should take about 5 to 10 minutes. Remove them with tongs and place them, over-lapping, on a white platter. Continue until you've done them all. They will look pink and, immediately on hitting the platter, transparent. Watch the syrup; if it gets too thick, it will become candy and you'll be in trouble. If it seems to be thickening too much, add some more sugar and water in the same proportions as at first. When all the apples are cooked, you can pour the extra syrup over them; it will jell some-what and will remind you of an apple orchard on a May day.

INGREDIENTS: 3 large hard apples (Cortlands or Jonathans); 1½ cups granulated sugar; 2 cups water; ½ cup straw-berry jam; 6 or 7 cinnamon candies.

CRANBERRY BREAD

Quick breads such as this are just that—quick. There are the dry ingredients. There are the wet ingredients. Bring them together, mix them quickly, bake. No fooling around if you want a bread that is light, tender, delicious. And, endear-ing quality, simple.

A 1-pound bag or box of cranberries will make 2 standard-sized cranberry breads. However, I like to use very small bread pans; mine measure about 3 x 6½ inches on the bottom and are 2 inches deep. They're available in hardware stores. They produce four nice little loaves, each one about right for 4 people (though I've seen one hungry man consume a whole bread in five minutes flat) which means that the uneaten loaves can be kept, intact, each in its own little pan—frozen or refrigerated—to be reheated when wanted. Good as new. Better, maybe.

Before you do anything else, cut into halves 1 pound fresh cranberries, using a sharp knife and a wooden board. Then start the bread. Set your oven at 350°F.

Sift together 4 cups flour, 2 cups sugar, 1 tablespoon bak-ing powder, 1 teaspoon baking soda, 2 teaspoons salt. There you have it. The dry ingredients.

In another bowl combine ¼ cup (½ stick) melted margarine or butter (doesn't matter which, here), 1½ cups orange juice (either fresh or frozen), the grated rind of 1 lemon (and you must watch while you're grating it so that you do not grate any of the white, bitter part), and 2 well-beaten eggs. These are, of course, the wet ingredients.

Now do as I say. Quickly pour the wet ingredients over the dry ingredients. Mix with a large spoon *just to dampen*. No longer! Sprinkle 1 tablespoon flour over the cranberries (1 pound of cranberries is also 4 cups). Toss the cranberries in the flour a second, this to keep them from sinking to the bottom of the batter. Then fold them into the batter, just enough to see that they are thoroughly distributed.

Grease your pans very heavily with a vegetable shortening like Crisco or Fluffo or such, throw in a teaspoon of flour, toss it around until the flour is a thin coating on the bottom of the pans. Discard excess flour, if any. Divide the batter into the four little pans or the two big ones. The batter is thick and heavy and will need a little help. See that the sides are built up a little higher than the middle—makes a more level bread at the end. Place in oven. The little loaves get done in about 30 minutes; the larger ones take about 40. They are done when a skewer goes in and comes out dry; not before. If you have just one oven and it is busy at 300°F. with the roast and potatoes, you should prepare this bread in the morning. You can reheat it right in its pan when you want it; just be sure it's hot, steamy when you cut it, and you're on the right track. If you have made this bread any time in the past and it has been frozen, just set the loaves, uncovered, in their frozen state in your 300°F. oven for at least 30 minutes. They'll be hot enough then and like new. I always slice the breads and let my guests serve themselves right out of the bread pans. Two small pancake turners are just right for clasping and lifting each slice out in its turn. This is an easy recipe to cut in two, if you must.

INGREDIENTS: 1 pound fresh cranberries; 4 cups flour; 2 cups sugar; 1 tablespoon baking powder; 1 teaspoon baking soda; 2 teaspoons salt; ¼ cup margarine or butter; 1½

cups orange juice; grated rind 1 lemon; 2 eggs; 1 tablespoon flour.

MAMA'S LEMON PIE

I won't get started on the attributes of this lemon pie. A very
beautiful, very romantic pie. Uses 6 eggs. Don't begrudge
one!

You can bake the pie shell in the morning. Fix the filling
in the late afternoon, and, when you take your roast out of
the oven, all you need is 15 minutes at 350°F. (a little higher
than it was before) to finish it off.

First, bake Elsie's pie shell. This is my old piecrust recipe
and, though I am avoiding repetition, in this cookbook, of
recipes which are in my earlier cookbook, in this case I will
repeat one recipe. The reason for this is that it is still the
best piecrust recipe I know. This recipe makes two 10-inch
shells. Bake them both. Freeze one. As I have said before,
think of tomorrow. If you haven't a freezer, simply roll up the
unused piecrust in a ball, wrap it securely in either saran or
aluminum foil, and refrigerate. It will keep perfectly for at
least two weeks.

Mix, with a fork, **3 cups flour,** sifted with **½ teaspoon salt,
2½ teaspoons sugar, ⅛ teaspoon baking soda.** With a pastry
blender or two knives, cut in **1 cup** (½ package) **fine quality
lard** (no other shortening will do) until you have little pieces
the size of peas. I'm sure you know what "cut in" means,
but, if you don't, it probably sounds like Greek. It means to
cut through the flour and shortening again and again until
they are combined. A pastry blender does this job.

In a separate small bowl, beat **1 egg, 2 tablespoons lemon
or orange juice** (the orange juice is a new twist to the old
recipe; try it!), and **2 tablespoons cold water.** Add this mixture of liquids, a bit at a time, to the flour mix. Stir it
around, first with a fork, then with your floured fingers, then
press it lightly together with floured hands. Lightly. *Voila!*
Piecrust! It rolls out as nicely as you please, thin as you'd

like. About ¼ inch is the right thickness. Be sure the rolling pin is kept floured and the surface under the pastry is kept floured and you won't have any trouble with sticking.

This quantity crust will also fill three 9-inch piepans, if you prefer that size to the 10-inch. An easy way to transfer the crust to the piepan is to roll it up on a floured rolling pin, being sure there's some flour on the crust so it won't stick to itself, move the rolling pin over to the piepan, then unroll it. It will settle right in place. Flute the edges by pinching them symmetrically, make a few cuts on the bottom of the shell to keep it from puffing, tuck a 2-inch strip of aluminum foil around the edges of the crust, over and under (this will keep them from getting too brown but will permit them to take on a light golden color), and bake the shell or shells in a 425°F. oven for about 10 minutes. Set aside to cool. This part of the pie can be made in the morning, or, if you have a freezer, any time at all. The shell won't need to be defrosted before filling.

Next comes the filling. Do this fairly late in the day, in fact, just before you have a clear oven to finish the pie. Separate **6 large fresh eggs.** Set **1 egg white** aside for later. In the top section of a double boiler, using a hand or electric egg-beater beat the 6 egg yolks until light and lemon colored. Add **½ cup sugar,** beating again until ungranular, and add **the juice of 2 lemons,** grating the **rind of 1 lemon** into the mixture first. Add **2 tablespoons cold water.** Set the pan over the bottom section of the boiler, with rapidly boiling water underneath. It'll take 10 or 15 minutes to get thick while you stir constantly. I personally think that's too long to stir anything constantly, so I do this directly over the heat, stirring like crazy, and it gets thick in 3 or 4, never more than 5, minutes. Doesn't burn, either. Don't wait to remove it from the heat until it's very thick. Do it as soon as you see the texture taking on the thickness. It will continue thickening after you remove it. Let cool, stirring once or twice, away from the range, while you beat 5 egg whites (remember, you kept one aside) with **½ cup sugar.** You should have the egg whites nearly stiff before you add the sugar, which you do gradually. It should stand up in peaks. Mustn't be dry. Fold the whites into the yellow mixture carefully, folding until there are no specks of white to be seen. Fill your baked shell. It will be chock full.

Now beat the remaining egg white with ¼ **teaspoon salt** and **1 tablespoon sugar,** just as you did before. Drop it in tablespoons around the edge of the pie. It will make a pretty ring. Bake in a 350°F. oven until the meringue is lightly browned, about 15 minutes. Serve it warm. It's heavenly. Serve it, next day, cold. Couldn't be better.

INGREDIENTS:

For the pie shell: (makes two 10-inch shells) 3 cups flour; ½ teaspoon salt; 2½ teaspoons sugar; ⅛ teaspoon baking soda; 1 cup lard; 1 egg; 2 tablespoons lemon or orange juice; 2 tablespoons cold water.

For the filling: 6 large eggs; ½ cup sugar; juice of 2 lemons; rind of 1 lemon; 2 tablespoons cold water; ½ cup and 1 tablespoon sugar for meringue; ¼ teaspoon salt.

TIMETABLE: Early in the day or, if you prefer, in the early afternoon, you can prepare the cider. Bring it to a boil, then leave it over very, very low heat or in a warm spot on the back of your stove until you're ready for it. Bring it back to a boil then and serve it. The tomatoes can be peeled, ready for heating at the last moment.

If you have just one oven, as most of us have, you'd best prepare your pie shells in the morning or early afternoon, since you'll need a 425°F. oven for this. As I mentioned in the recipe, you'd be wise to roll out the two pie shells, and either bake them both, in which case you'll have another pie shell ready for another pie, or bake the one you're using tonight and freeze the other which can then be used for a Quiche Lorraine or an apple pie—any pie that requires an unbaked shell. Or you can roll the extra dough in foil and refrigerate it for another day. After you've baked your shell, let it cool, and refrigerate it until you're ready to fill it. Keeps it light.

As soon as you've finished the pie shell, you should turn the oven down to 350°F., and, while it's cooling down, prepare your cranberry breads. Bake these now and set them aside, in their pans, on the top of the range. They should be reheated for about 10 minutes when you're ready for them.

By 4:00 o'clock in the afternoon your oven should be available for the roast which calls for slow roasting at 300°F. If you happen to have two ovens, you won't need to do any of this baking ahead of time but can prepare your breads and pie as late as 5:30 for a 7:00 dinner.

Roast in the oven at 4:00. Remove it to get the outer skin off at 5:00. Put the potatoes in at 5:00 when you return the roast to the oven. Add the sauerkraut at 6:00. Now make the pie filling; pile it into the pie shell, but don't put it in the oven yet. Now's the time to prepare the broccoli, combine the ingredients for the sauce as directed—all except the final steaming of the vegetable. Glaze the apples. Look at the roast thermometer. As soon as it hits 185°F., remove roast from oven and raise oven temperature to 350°F. Dab meringue topping on pies, set pies in oven; also the breads. Heat tomatoes as directed to just hot. Pass a mug of hot cider (doesn't have to be served in the dining room). Steam the broccoli and heat its sauce. We like to set the pork on a carving board and place the sauerkraut in a fairly deep large platter for serving—it's easier to spoon it up. Arrange the broccoli on a separate platter. The apples can be served from their platter or set around the roast. The potatoes should stay in their foil wrappers until served. The breads, as you know, go on the table in their own bread pans. The pie, which should be lightly browned by this time, should be cooling during dinner but does not need to be cold to be served.

LEFTOVERS

This particular meal, at our house, always is followed by a leftover dish we call by a long title, but that's what it is, and it is supreme.

Leftover Pork with Leftover Sauerkraut with
Leftover Potatoes Supreme

Sauté **1 small onion,** peeled and chopped not too fine, in **2 tablespoons butter** in a previously heated black iron frying pan, moderate size. When the onion is golden, not brown to speak of, add **4 cups leftover pork,** cut into bite-size pieces (you can do this with lamb or beef, as well) and **2 cups left-over potatoes Milligan,** peeled and cut up into similar sizes. Let sizzle around a little, stirring to combine until heated through and a little crisp. Then stir in **1 to 2 cups leftover sauerkraut,** or whatever amount you have, which is of course full of pork drippings and onions and apples of its own. Stir this around, then add **½ cup commercial sour cream.** Be sure the meat mixture is not boiling hot, or the sour cream icy cold when they're joined or they'll curdle. Room temperature is the rule, always, when adding sour cream to any cooked dish. Then add **½ teaspoon dill weed or dill seed** (both are obtainable in the spice shelves of markets) or, and this is best of all, **1 sprig of fresh dill,** chopped fine. (Note: Dill is a *great* thing to grow, should you have a garden. Like a weed it flourishes. Freeze it at frost time—chopped, a tablespoon to a small saran package.) Reheat just to boiling; do not boil—again it's sour cream you're dealing with, and this separates if boiled. Taste for salt, which you probably won't need. You might need pepper, but taste first. That's one of my cardinal rules in cooking; taste, taste, and taste again. Know what you're serving before you serve it. This dish can be served directly from its frying pan. A perfect supper or lunch dish.

As for the rest of this meal, leftovers should present no problem. The cider keeps indefinitely; should be refrigerated, of course, and heated when wanted. If you don't want to drink it again, use it to baste a ham—a perfect function for it. The tomatoes can be mashed up, heated, a bit of sugar added, and, at the last moment, some heavy cream. Stir the mixture around and you have an unusual and quite divine tomato side dish. Or you can cook them with a few sautéed onion bits and green pepper bits, add a spoonful of capers, and pour them over an omelette. Then, of course, added to some fried and crumbled chopped meat with a little tomato paste, a bit more basil and a little oregano, you have a quite acceptable spaghetti sauce. Any broccoli leftover may be heated and covered with a rarebit. There's a good one in the *Blueberry Hill Cookbook*.

Keep that cranberry bread you haven't used, even if it's sliced. Freeze it in the pan, covered with foil. Defrost it, uncovered, in a slow oven—the top becomes damp if you leave the foil on. Should you have frozen a bread that was sliced, you should slap a bit of foil on the cut edge to keep it soft while defrosting—not on the top, though. This bread is divine sliced thin and spread with softened cream cheese. Serve it at afternoon tea or with a fruit salad at lunch.

Mama's lemon pie? Just try it cold, that's all I will say. If you have some left after three days, my suggestion would be to chop it up a bit, place it in a baking dish, heat it, and serve it with lightly whipped cream, almost like a sauce— or with soft ice cream. But don't ever throw any of this out!

NOVEMBER

PARTY MENU
Nothing Less Than Wonderful!

CREAM OF CHESTNUT SOUP
A VERY PARTY TURKEY
HALF-WILD RICE
BRAISED WATERCRESS
BAKED PUMPKIN CASSEROLE
CRANBERRY CHUTNEY
TOSSED SALAD, BLUEBERRY HILL
SOUR CREAM CURRANT MUFFINS
FROSTED GRAPES, CHEESE TRAY

November, at Blueberry Hill, is a month special to itself. Thanksgiving on the way; murmurs of Christmas coming. The beauty of the hills is a purple beauty, soft, velvety, exposed. The children are indoors a bit more, down cellar more frequently with John, rubbing wax on skis. A walk through the woods is a hushed thing; the trees bare, tall, grace incarnate. A cathedral; the carpet of leaves crunching lightly underfoot, giving forth a peculiar freshness.

This is a very lovely November dinner; not necessarily for Thanksgiving, though it can be that. For 8.

CREAM OF CHESTNUT SOUP

The word for this soup is superb. Since it does require the shelling of a considerable number of chestnuts, it's a fine idea to get the children in, or your husband, even your neighbors, to help. If such help is not available, turn on a Mozart sonata while you're shelling the chestnuts, and *listen* to it.

Prepare **2 pounds chestnuts.** And this is the way to shell all chestnuts, for whatever recipe they are required. Slit each chestnut with a sharp knife—two slits each, crossed. Cover them with boiling water and boil them for 15 minutes. (For this recipe the chestnuts should not be completely tender yet. If you do want thoroughly cooked chestnuts, let them continue to boil for 30 minutes or until one of them, tested, is soft). Remove them *one at a time* (this is the trick here—they must stay in hot water, each one, until you're ready for it) and let cold water run on each chestnut in turn. The skins will come off very quickly and the membrane, as well. Set aside.

In a heavy 3- or 4-quart saucepan, sauté lightly **1 large sweet onion,** peeled and cut up, in ¼ **cup** (½ stick) **butter** or **margarine** until the onions are lightly browned. Now add to the sautéed onion the prepared chestnuts, **2 large carrots,** peeled and cut up small, and **1 quart rich chicken broth** or **turkey broth,** preferably homemade. Since you'll have the carcass of the turkey available, why not make it turkey broth? (See page 13 for chicken broth; same rules for turkey broth.) Simmer until the chestnuts are quite soft, about 15 more minutes, then pour the liquid through a colander. The chestnuts and onions and carrots, which have been held back in the colander, should now be pressed through it. A Foley food mill is ideal for this job if you have one, or you can buzz the mixture in a blender. In any case, it must be *sans* lumps. Return the chestnut mixture to the broth and bring it all back to a boil. Remove it from the heat, add **1½ cups heavy cream, 2 tablespoons sugar, ½ cup pale dry sherry.** Taste for **salt** and/or **pepper** and add if needed; the amount necessary will depend on the seasoning in the broth you have used. Serve without boiling again. If you cool it and reheat it, don't boil it.

INGREDIENTS: 2 pounds chestnuts; 1 large sweet onion; ¼ cup butter or margarine; 2 large carrots; 1 quart rich chicken or turkey broth; 1½ cups heavy cream; 2 tablespoons sugar; ½ cup pale dry sherry; salt; pepper.

A VERY PARTY TURKEY

For this you will use only the breasts, legs, and second joints of the turkey. I find it easy to disjoint the turkey with a sharp knife, but you may want to ask your butcher to separate the legs, including the second joints, and to trim out the breasts. The trimmings (bones and remainder of the carcass, the wings, the backs) will make a fine strong turkey broth as noted earlier to be used in the sauce and in the chestnut soup. There'll be lots of bits of turkey meat, too, which can be used in the leftover turkey dishes I shall tell you about in this and the family menu.

Here we are employing the small turkey broilers. With a sharp knife, remove the meat from the legs and second joints of 2 turkey broilers, each weighing about 5 or 6 pounds. (You can toss the bones into the broth, along with the skin and gristle and muscle, which you should cut away.) Discard the skin and grind the meat with 2 tablespoons chopped sweet onion and 2 tablespoons chopped parsley in a food grinder, using a fine blade. It grinds easily and quickly. In a separate bowl, combine 2 egg whites, ¾ cup heavy cream, 2 teaspoons salt, 2 or 3 twists of the pepper mill, and ¼ teaspoon ground sage (optional). Beat with a wire whisk until just combined, then add to the ground turkey mixture and mix thoroughly, this time with a fork. Set in the refrigerator for an hour to chill or, if you're in a hurry, place it in the freezer for 5 minutes. Now cut the turkey breasts in half and make a slit in the thickest part of each to create a pocket.

Season the inside of the pocket with **salt** and freshly ground **pepper** and stuff with the ground turkey mixture, which you have just prepared and chilled.

Butter the bottom of a shallow baking dish, good looking enough to go to the table later, using at least **1 tablespoon of butter.** Lavishly, is the intention. Sprinkle the turkey breasts with **salt** and freshly ground **pepper** and arrange them symmetrically in the dish. Sprinkle the breasts with **½ cup soft fresh bread crumbs,** torn from bread without crusts. Dribble over the top **¼ cup melted butter.** This much can be done in the early afternoon. Keep it refrigerated, covered with aluminum foil, until an hour before you want to serve it. (Note: If you wish to prepare this ahead, you can, at this point, freeze the prepared breasts. See comment on this in timetable.)

About an hour and a half before dinner, set in the oven at 375°F. the turkey breasts, still covered with the aluminum foil. After 45 minutes, remove the foil and continue to bake, browning the crumbs and basting with the juices in the pan if the breasts seem dry. As soon as the breasts are thoroughly done—in about 25 to 30 minutes—lift from pans, arrange on serving platter, and serve with the following sauce.

For the Sauce: (Prepare this at any time in the afternoon, to be reheated at serving time.) Melt ½ cup (1 stick) **butter or margarine** in a 1-quart saucepan. Slice **½ pound fresh mushrooms,** including most of the stems (slice them vertically, trimming off stem ends, first—wipe with damp cloth, if they are gritty) and sauté them in the butter just until they start to wilt. This will be in 3 or 4 minutes. Push the mushrooms to one side of the pan and, stirring constantly, add **2 tablespoons flour; ½ teaspoon salt;** dash of freshly ground **pepper; 1 cup milk** and **1 cup turkey broth** or **2 cups milk,** if you haven't prepared any turkey broth, adding liquid slowly. Stir until the mixture comes to a boil. Then add a small part of it to the **2 egg yolks** (left from the egg whites used in the stuffing) well beaten, and return it to the sauce.

Again I remind you not to dump the egg yolks into the hot sauce; they will lump. Do not boil after the egg is added. Now mix in the mushrooms from the side of the pan, and add ½ cup Marsala wine or a light white wine or a pale dry cocktail sherry. The Marsala is the best. Heat, but do not allow it to boil again. Set the sauce aside. It will not be a thick sauce. If you prefer a thicker one, increase the flour to 3 tablespoons. Reheat it, *without boiling*, when you want it.

To serve, slice the turkey breasts down through the stuffing, so that each portion will have a center of the stuffing. Pass the sauce, spooning it over each serving. This is a beautiful business, these stuffed breasts—very gala, very professional, and, despite the length of this recipe, very simple to execute.

INGREDIENTS: 2 turkey broilers, 5 to 6 pounds each; 2 tablespoons chopped sweet onion; 2 tablespoons chopped parsley; 2 egg whites; ¾ cup heavy cream; 2 teaspoons salt; pepper; ¼ teaspoon ground sage (optional); 5 tablespoons butter; ½ cup soft bread crumbs.

For the sauce: ½ cup butter or margarine; ½ pound fresh mushrooms; 2 tablespoons flour; ½ teaspoon salt; pepper; 1 cup milk and 1 cup turkey broth (or 2 cups milk); 2 egg yolks; ½ cup Marsala or light white wine or pale dry cocktail sherry.

HALF-WILD RICE

Just that. Half wild. Prepare 1 cup Uncle Ben's rice as directed on the box. This is simple and foolproof. Just be sure you have a heavy kettle with a tight lid. I guess by this time you know how important to fine cooking such a kettle is. Also prepare 1 cup wild rice as follows: Place it in a fine sieve. Wash it with cold water, letting it run on the rice for several minutes, lifting the rice meanwhile with your hands to let it really get cleaned thoroughly. Remove any apparently foreign particles. Bring 1 quart water to boil. Add 1 teaspoon salt. Stir rice into this, slowly. Then leave it alone for about 40 minutes, letting it bubble merrily away. You needn't touch it. As soon as the water has boiled away, the rice is done. You will have 3 cups of it. Do both this and the white rice in the morning or the day before. At the time of serving, place **1 tablespoon butter** in a heated chafing dish or electric skillet. Let the butter melt, then add the cooled rice, both kinds, tossed around a bit in the cooling, for lightness' sake, and heat very, very slowly. It keeps fine, covered, over the lowest possible heat. It will seem all wild.

INGREDIENTS: 1 cup Uncle Ben's rice; 1 cup wild rice; 1 quart water; 1 teaspoon salt; 1 tablespoon butter.

BRAISED WATERCRESS

In a 10-inch black iron frying pan or electric skillet, melt ¼ **cup** (½ stick) **butter.** Finely mince **2 cloves garlic** and simmer them in the butter for 2 minutes. Cut the stems of **6 bunches watercress** into tiny bits and add to the skillet. Simmer for 5 minutes. Break up the leaves of the watercress and add them to the skillet. Sprinkle with ½ **teaspoon salt** and ¼ **teaspoon sugar.** Cook, stirring once in a while, until the watercress leaves are thoroughly wilted, about 3 minutes. Serve immediately, if possible.

INGREDIENTS: ¼ cup butter; 2 cloves garlic; 6 bunches watercress; ½ teaspoon salt; ¼ teaspoon sugar.

BAKED PUMPKIN CASSEROLE

This recipe can be made with canned pumpkin, but it is infinitely better if you will prepare your own pumpkin pulp. This is true for pumpkin pies, as well, if not more so. To do this, cut a *small* (no larger than a honeydew melon) pumpkin (an important emphasis—large pumpkins tend to be watery) in half, dig out the seeds and pith, turn it face down on a tray and bake slowly, at about 325°F., for about an hour or until you can pierce it very easily right through the skin. Remove it from the oven, scoop out the pulp, and mash it. That's all there is to it. Measure it and proceed. A small pumpkin will usually yield more than you can use for two pies.

In a large bowl, stir together until quite thoroughly combined, the following: 3 cups pumpkin pulp, 3 tablespoons brown sugar, 2 tablespoons melted butter or margarine, ½ teaspoon mace, ½ teaspoon nutmeg, 1 teaspoon powdered ginger, 1 teaspoon ground cloves, ½ teaspoon cinnamon, 2 eggs, slightly beaten, and ½ cup pecans, broken.

Turn this mixture into a 1-quart, lightly greased, earthenware or Pyrex casserole. Put over low heat in a small saucepan ½ cup light brown sugar and ¼ cup maple syrup. Stir constantly until the sugar is dissolved, then bring the syrup to a boil. Remove it from the heat, but at once! Let it cool a little and, at this time, arrange **pecan halves** symmetrically around the edges of the casserole. Pour the syrup evenly over the top and bake 40 minutes at 375°F.

This is rich going; servings should not be large. You can double it if you are serving hearty eaters.

INGREDIENTS: 3 cups pumpkin pulp (homemade or canned); 3 tablespoons brown sugar; 2 tablespoons melted butter or margarine; ½ teaspoon mace; ½ teaspoon nutmeg; 1 teaspoon powdered ginger; 1 teaspoon ground cloves; ½ teaspoon cinnamon; 2 eggs; 1 cup pecans; ½ cup light brown sugar; ¼ cup maple syrup.

CRANBERRY CHUTNEY

One pound of cranberries will make a quart of this. Just combine in a saucepan 2 cups water and 2 cups granulated sugar. Bring this to a boil, and let it boil for 5 minutes. Then add, all at one time (don't you love recipes that tell you to add everything all at one time?) the following: 1 pound picked-over fresh cranberries (or frozen, if you have them in your freezer), ¼ cup cider vinegar, 1 cup seedless muscat raisins (though plain seedless or white raisins are fine), 2 tablespoons light brown sugar, ½ teaspoon ground ginger (optional, but a good touch), and ½ teaspoon salt. Simmer, stir-

ring occasionally until all the berries have popped and the
mixture is fairly thick, about 10 minutes. The chutney can
be served hot if you wish, when it will be somewhat liquid.
If you chill it in the refrigerator, it will jell nicely. Hot or
cold, it's beautiful to behold—and to consume!

INGREDIENTS: 2 cups water; 2 cups granulated sugar; 1 pound
    fresh or frozen cranberries; ¼ cup cider vinegar; 1 cup
    seedless muscat raisins; 2 tablespoons light brown sugar;
    ½ teaspoon ground ginger (optional); ½ teaspoon salt.

TOSSED SALAD, BLUEBERRY HILL

This will be an exception to my rule generally followed for
this book of not repeating, if possible, any recipe as it appears in my *Blueberry Hill Cookbook*. I have had so much
comment on, and requests for, my own tossed salad, which
I serve at the farm quite regularly, that I am going to repeat
it here for the readers of this new book. As a matter of fact,
I can't imagine giving you twenty-four menus without including this salad in at least one of them. I trust the owners
of my first cookbook will forgive this repetition. It's the
best tossed salad I know, and I think it's worth repeating
here.

First, prepare the greens, better known in my vernacular
as the "outsides." For eight people you should have the
equivalent of two medium heads of iceberg lettuce. This
should be made up of 1 medium head romaine and other
greens as available, which might be iceberg or Boston lettuce,
chicory, escarole, bibb lettuce, watercress, or spinach greens,
in any combination to suit your fancy and the availability of the
greens. Wash the greens thoroughly, drain, wrap in a damp
towel or plastic bag, and place them in the refrigerator to
chill. About an hour before you plan to serve the salad, tear
the greens into fairly large pieces. Rub a salad bowl (large
enough so that the salad will fill no more than two thirds of
it, which gives you room for tossing) with a cut clove of

garlic. Discard the garlic. The greens can be placed in the bowl as they are, unless they are still damp, in which case you should line the bowl with two or three thicknesses of paper towels. Remember to discard these before you start tossing the salad. Place three thicknesses of waxed paper on top of the greens.

On the waxed paper, set what we call the "insides." I suggest you do this to keep the tomatoes and other parts of the insides from soaking the greens in case you have to wait awhile before tossing the salad. On the waxed paper place **2 medium-sized ripe tomatoes,** cut into chunks; **1 small cucumber,** peeled if store-bought, unpeeled if garden fresh, and cut into similar-sized chunks; **1 small white or red sweet onion,** peeled and sliced into rings; **1 California navel orange,** peeled and the segments cut from between the membranes; **½ cup seedless white grapes; 4 or 5 crisp radishes,** sliced into thin rounds; **½ avocado pear,** peeled and cut into chunks the same size as the tomatoes and cucumbers; **2 tablespoons crumbled Roquefort or bleu cheese; 1 small can rolled anchovies, oil** and **capers** added. (Note: This salad can be made without the orange, grapes, or pear, which are all window dressing, delicious but not really necessary. The other ingredients, however, are an integral part and should not be eliminated. In the absence of a fresh orange, a can of mandarin oranges, drained, could be used.)

Cover the top of the whole salad, "insides" and "outsides" with waxed paper, and refrigerate until ready to toss. Then, when you are about to serve, remove the paper towels, all the waxed paper layers, and combine everything quickly with light, deft tosses with your salad spoon and fork.

For the Dressing: Pour over the salad **1 tablespoon pure olive oil.** Toss all the greens with the oil, which will keep them from wilting. They must be coated with olive oil *first;* then proceed with the rest of the dressing. Sprinkle the salad with **salt, pepper,** and **garlic powder.** Toss the salad. Taste it. If you think it needs more seasoning, now's the time.

Mine usually does. So I add salt, pepper, and garlic powder. Toss it and taste again. I find that the time to season the salad is before the oil and vinegar are added.

Using a large salad spoon, pour into the bowl of the spoon, **1 teaspoon Worcestershire sauce.** With the Worcestershire still in the spoon, fill the spoon just to the top (about 1½ tablespoons) with **wine vinegar,** the best quality you can find. Pour this over the salad. Pour into the same spoon so it overflows quite freely, about **3 tablespoons of the finest imported olive oil.** If you do this with salad oil, please don't tell anyone you got the recipe from me.

Now start tossing. You will have the flavor here, not only of the olive oil, but of the oil from the anchovies. The cheese, too, provides a most important seasoning. Toss the salad lightly and taste it again.

All I can tell you, really, is that if you don't taste the garlic sufficiently to suit you, you should add some more garlic powder (*not* garlic salt). You may want a bit more salt and pepper. If the salad seems not tart enough, add a little more wine vinegar. If it's too tart, you will perhaps want a little more olive oil.

Serve the salad from the large bowl, letting the guests dig for their own anchovies.

INGREDIENTS: 1 medium head romaine; other greens as available to amount equivalent of 2 heads of lettuce (iceberg, Boston, chicory, escarole, bibb, watercress, spinach greens); 1 clove garlic; 2 medium-sized ripe tomatoes; 1 small cucumber; 1 small white or red sweet onion; 1 California navel orange; ½ cup seedless white grapes; 4 or 5 crisp radishes; ½ avocado pear; 2 tablespoons crumbled Roquefort or bleu cheese; 1 small can rolled anchovies.

For the dressing: 4 tablespoons olive oil; salt; pepper; garlic powder; 1 teaspoon Worcestershire; 1½ tablespoons wine vinegar; additional oil and vinegar and seasonings to taste.

SOUR CREAM CURRANT MUFFINS

Once you've tried these muffins, with or without currants, (or with or without blueberries, for that matter!), they will become a standby in your household. They need to bake only 15 minutes. You can do them ahead, if you wish, freeze them, and reheat them in the same muffin pans in which they were baked. You can, as well, do them in the morning and reheat them at dinner hour. A much better idea, I think, is to mix the wet ingredients in one bowl, mix the dry ingredients in another, grease your muffin pans and then, 15 minutes before dinner, combine the wet and the dry, fill the muffin pans, pop them in the oven, and accept the plaudits of the crowd.

Cream, with your electric mixer at high speed, **6 tablespoons** (¾ stick) **margarine or butter, 1½ cups granulated sugar,** and ½ **teaspoon salt.** Beat for about 3 minutes until very smooth and creamy. Make a hole in the middle, add **4 eggs,** beat them in the well until they're thoroughly combined, yolks and whites, and a light lemon color. Now beat them into the creamed mixture and add **1¾ cups commercial sour cream.** Beat to combine the cream. These are the wet ingredients.

In another bowl, mix with a fork **2¾ cups flour, 1 teaspoon soda,** and ¼ **teaspoon grated nutmeg.** These are, obviously, the dry ingredients.

When you're ready to bake these, heat the oven to 425°F. and, quickly, mix the wet and the dry. Don't waste time over this. As soon as the dry ingredients are thoroughly moist, stop. Fold in ½ **cup currants,** lightly floured. If you adore currants, make it 1 cup. Fill 3 dozen greased muffin-pan sections half full. Sprinkle each muffin with ¼ **teaspoon granulated sugar** or, if you like cinnamon, you can use **cinnamon-sugar.** Bake for 15 minutes. Let cool for 2 minutes, then loosen them from their pans. Serve them hot!

INGREDIENTS: 6 tablespoons margarine or butter; 1½ cups granulated sugar; ½ teaspoon salt; 4 eggs; 1¾ cups commercial sour cream; 2¾ cups flour; 1 teaspoon soda; ¼ teaspoon grated nutmeg; 3 tablespoons granulated sugar or cinnamon-sugar for topping.

NOTE: To turn these into memorable blueberry muffins fold in 2 cups floured fresh or frozen dry blueberries instead of the currants. This will give you 6 extra muffins, so allow space for them.

FROSTED GRAPES, CHEESE TRAY

Wash 2 pounds large sweet white or blue grapes. Cut them into little bunches with kitchen shears, drain. You should have 2 small bunches for each person. Mix, in one bowl 1 cup cold water and ½ cup white corn syrup. In another bowl, place about 1 cup granulated sugar. Holding the grapes by the stem, dip each bunch in the bowl of syrup, turn it around and around until it is thoroughly moistened, then dip into the bowl of sugar. A good way is to let the bunch sink right into the sugar, still holding the stem. As you pull it up, shake it lightly to get rid of the excess sugar and lay the grapes on a brown paper bag or paper towel to dry thoroughly.

Another good way to frost grapes is to beat lightly 2 egg whites (there's a use for those egg whites you've had in the freezer), dip the grapes in them instead of in the corn syrup, then in the sugar, and let dry.

These are very decorative, quite professional looking, and, not at all incidentally, very excellent to eat.

Serve with a cheese tray. In this, let your imagination be your guide. A fine Brie, which is my idea of the perfect cheese with fruit—creamy, rather strong yet delicate; a well-ripened and soft Camembert; Bel Paese, a bland cheese and, for that reason, acceptable to many people; and, of course and always, Roquefort, or the domestic bleu or Gorgonzola—all three cheeses having similarities, one of which is not the

price since Roquefort costs three or four times the price of
bleu, often. They're all good in their way. My point is, you
should experiment with cheeses; get away from the rubbery
processed cheeses we are promoted into buying by the tele-
vision industry—and remember, there is no more sophisticated nor more satisfying dessert after a fine meal than a
juicy pear or peach or persimmon, beautifully ripe, and a
slab of your favorite cheese. All the cheeses named here
should be served at room temperature; crackers and butter on
the side for those who wish them.

INGREDIENTS: 2 pounds white or blue grapes; 1 cup cold
water; ½ cup white corn syrup; 1 cup granulated sugar
(or 2 egg whites instead of the water and corn syrup).
For the cheeses: Brie, Camembert; Bel Paese; Roquefort,
bleu, or Gorgonzola; or any combination of these.

TIMETABLE: There are many day-before jobs in this
menu. The soup, for instance. Prepare it the day before and
refrigerate it. It freezes well, too, so there is nothing to
prevent your preparing it a week or two in advance.

The turkey dish, for instance. The breasts can be prepared,
stuffed, arranged in the baking dish, covered tightly with
a foil and refrigerated, all the day before. As in the case of
the soup, they can be frozen in the stuffed state which allows
you to get them ready at your leisure. Freeze each breast
in the foil-covered baking dish or individually wrapped in
saran or aluminum foil. If you'd like, you can bake them for
10 minutes before freezing; this, particularly, if the turkey
was a frozen bird when you bought it. Par-baked, if you
will, and wrapped, ready for action when called upon. Defrost them in the oven, not at room temperature. You'll need
to add 30 minutes to the baking time given in the recipe if
you are using frozen breasts.

The cranberry chutney, for instance. Prepare it the day
before the party, or three days before the party, even as much
as a week before the party. It has a long and happy refrigerator
life.

The rice, both kinds. Cook them the day before. The

pumpkin, if you're going to do this yourself instead of buying canned pumpkin. Bake it the day before, scoop out the pulp, mash it, season it, pile it into its baking dish, omitting only the topping and the decorative pecans. Cover with saran, refrigerate. Again, since pumpkin is a notably fine freezer, you can do this far ahead of time and freeze it in its baking dish.

So much done, so far ahead. Now comes the morning of the party. What's to do? Prepare the salad greens, wash them, break them up, leave them to chill in a linen towel in the refrigerator. Prepare the sauce for the turkey, set it aside. Also mix up the wet ingredients and the dry ingredients for the muffins, each in its own bowl. Set them aside. Wash and prepare the watercress as directed, stems on one piece of waxed paper, broken tops on another.

Afternoon? Already? Sit down and frost the grapes. About 4:00 o'clock, take the pumpkin casserole from the refrigerator to get it to room temperature before setting it in the oven —a particularly good idea if the casserole it's in is Pyrex or earthenware. Take the cheeses from the refrigerator to get them to room temperature. Grease the muffin pans.

Set the turkey breasts in the oven an hour and a half before dinner is to be served, remembering to add time to your reckoning if they've been frozen. Forget them, except for removing foil after 45 minutes, until they're ready to serve, when you will have the sauce, hot, to be poured over it, except for removing the foil and basting as directed. The pumpkin casserole goes in with the poultry.

Prepare the "insides" of your salad. Keep them cold, arranged in the bowl with the "outsides" as directed. If you have just one oven, you'll have to get the turkey breasts out before you do the muffins, but since they take only 15 minutes, this can work out all right. Raise the temperature to 425°F., combine the wet and dry ingredients for the muffins, fill the greased pans and start them on their way. If you've made the muffins ahead of time and frozen them, defrost them in the oven with the turkey. Takes 15 minutes. Heat the soup. Now finish the rice, leaving it in its chafing dish or electric skillet. Braise the watercress as directed, a 10-minute job.

Set the cranberry chutney on the table. Pour the water. Call your guests. Serve the soup. A lovely old tureen is called for here. Your husband or a suitable substitute can take over while you toss the salad. Done at the table, it is a fascinating entertainment for your guests. Maybe you can teach your husband to dress and toss the salad, or give him this book and let *me* teach him. Fine, if you can. That will leave you free to get the muffins out of the oven, loosen them, dump them into a basket lined with a linen napkin, and pass them. Stay in the kitchen and braise the watercress.

Assuming you're doing this party without serving help, you should have a rolling table on which to arrange the turkey breasts, cut just at serving time, the sauce ladled over the turkey, as the plates are filled; next should be the chafing dish or casserole of half-wild rice; next, the braised watercress, just ready (if this seems too much of a much, do this chore last before calling the guests; keep the watercress warm over low heat); beside the watercress comes the pumpkin casserole, the top glistening; and there you have a beautiful dinner, by gum. Roll it in, roll it in! Be seated, madam!

LEFTOVERS

The leftover possibilities for this dinner are so immense that perhaps you ought to have another party to use up the leftovers.

The turkey breasts, sliced cold and served with some of the chutney and a hot muffin, make an ideal late supper. Or reheat the turkey breasts in their own sauce in a warm oven. When it is hot and bubbling, sprinkle with grated Parmesan or cheddar cheese and brown quickly under the broiler. The rice can accompany it, reheated in a Bungalow Cooker or in a colander over hot water, and becomes newly interesting by the mere addition of some of the salted pecans you didn't need to use for your pumpkin casserole.

However, the greatest use you can make of the leftovers of this very party turkey is to prepare of it a mousse.

Turkey Mousse

Here's the way, and it's a recipe of its own: Sprinkle 1 **envelope unflavored gelatine** over ½ **cup cold homemade turkey broth.** (You know how to make a lovely turkey broth, I'm sure; I've referred to it before.)

Place the gelatine in the broth over low heat and stir it around until the gelatine is completely dissolved, no grains visible. Remove it from the heat and add another **cup of broth** and **1 tablespoon onion juice** or the scrapings with a sharp knife of half an onion. Set the mixture in the freezer or in a bowl of ice cubes and chill it until it is starting to set. It will be the consistency of unbeaten egg whites. Now fold into it **1½ to 2 cups diced cooked turkey,** including whatever stuffing you have left from the main meal, **2 tablespoons chopped, peeled cucumber, 1 tablespoon chopped ripe olives, 1 tablespoon chopped parsley,** and **1 cup heavy cream, whipped.** If there is any sauce around, it won't do any harm either. Toss it in. When everything is homogenously combined, turn it into a 1-quart (or larger, if you've had more turkey than I've expected you to have) mold, well-greased. You should use an oil without flavoring of its own, some sort of vegetable or peanut oil, to grease this mold. Taste and adjust seasoning.

Chill to firm—a matter of several hours at least—and unmold on a serving platter at the proper time. If you have trouble getting it out, set the mold momentarily in and out of hot water. Garnish with watercress. It will serve 6 or 8, depending on whether it's ladies or gentlemen.

INGREDIENTS: 1 envelope unflavored gelatine; 1½ cups cold homemade turkey broth; 1 tablespoon onion juice; 1½ to 2 cups diced cooked turkey; 2 tablespoons chopped cucumber; 1 tablespoon chopped ripe olives; 1 tablespoon chopped parsley; 1 cup heavy cream.

Let's see, now. The half-wild rice can be folded into beaten eggs, seasoned with soy sauce, salt, pepper, and chives and fried in little cakes in peanut oil. Delicious with cold meats, such as the sliced cold turkey breasts.

Nothing you can do with leftover braised watercress except toss it in whatever turkey broth you have unused, add a bit of sugar and a bit of sherry, and present with pride. Soy sauce makes it Chinese.

The chutney will cause you no worry. Just eat it. Or, the quantity reaching a low point, fold it into fresh melon balls, serve it with sponge cake and whipped cream. Add some vermouth to it and serve it over vanilla ice cream. Make a sandwich of it with cream cheese on nut bread. Fill a jelly roll with it, spread with whipped cream. No problem there.

The muffins, if you have the same experience we have with them, will not be around to be concerned over. Everybody in my house eats five of these at a clip. However, freeze them if you have them, reheat them in muffin pans when you want them. Split them, spread with butter and maple sugar, and toast them. Try them with a cup of tea at bedtime. A very favorite muffin.

The cream-of-chestnut soup should simply *not* be tampered with. I've kept it for as long as a week in the refrigerator and found it none the worse at that time. It's so deluxe that my advice would be for you to freeze it for your next party, if you've enough left for such a possibility.

The pumpkin casserole can be reheated with marshmallows on top; let the marshmallows brown and delight the young. As for the odds and ends of cheese, spread them on crackers, broil quickly for snacks at bedtime. The frosted grapes go into fresh fruit cups, particularly refreshing with mandarin oranges.

NOVEMBER

FAMILY MENU
Let Us Give Thanks

CRANBERRY-STRAWBERRY JUICE
TWO TURKEYS, TWO STUFFINGS
BRUSSELS SPROUTS AND ONIONS, BROWN BUTTER
SWEET POTATOES WITH BROILED ORANGES
MUSHROOM AND ZUCCHINI SALAD
MELBA TOAST
CRUSTLESS CRANBERRY PIE OR DELUXE MINCE PIE

 I can remember our first Thanksgiving at Blueberry Hill, the winter of 1949. It snowed early that year. There was a 28-pound turkey to be fixed for 20 hungry people; and I, who had virtually never done such a thing before, somehow had to manage it. We had time, even then, for an hour-long walk through the woods, which was a fairyland that day.

Each year since, Thanksgiving has been an important family time for us. With three daughters now, and a variety of friends, it is a gala affair. Though classified for purposes of this book as a family dinner, we have, in reality, a party; a beautiful Thanksgiving dinner; a family party.

To serve 12.

CRANBERRY-STRAWBERRY JUICE

Just thaw (by that I mean thaw *just* to this point and not beyond) **1 10-ounce package frozen strawberries,** stir it into **1 quart cranberry juice,** and mix thoroughly. Serve. You'll have to provide spoons for the strawberries.

If the day is cold and you'd prefer a hot appetizer, follow the recipe in the October menu on page 279 for hot mulled sherried cider, substituting cranberry juice for the cider. Serve hot in demitasse cups. This is a particularly fine hot drink, so do try it.

INGREDIENTS: 1 (10-ounce) package frozen strawberries; 1 quart cranberry juice.

TWO TURKEYS, TWO STUFFINGS

Two turkeys, with two separate stuffings, take half as long to roast as one large one; and it's fun to have the different tastes of these two, very unusual, stuffings. If you're a traditionalist and want a standard sausage and/or chestnut stuffing, you will find my favorite one in the *Blueberry Hill Cookbook.*

Two turkeys, 8 to 10 pounds each, dressed weight, should do here. Be sure they're thoroughly thawed. The best way to do this is to leave the turkeys out at room temperature for at least 12 hours. If you're in a hurry, set them in a low, low oven for about an hour to start them, but don't leave them there longer than that, since they will dry while they thaw.

Rub the turkeys, inside and out, with **salt** and **pepper.** Stuff loosely (see recipes for stuffings immediately following). You know there are two places to be stuffed, the large cavity and the smaller one by the neck. The dressing will swell so don't pack it in. Close the openings with poultry pins; they come on cards with heavy-duty string and are a bargain. Follow the directions on the card.

Hold the wings close to the body of each bird with skewers or poultry pins, tie the legs together, and set the turkeys on a double sheet of heavy-duty aluminum foil. If you have a large enough roasting pan, the birds ought to go in side by side in one pan; otherwise, use two, judiciously chosen for size to fit next to each other in your oven. Dot the turkeys with **butter,** insert a roasting thermometer between the breast and the drumstick (I heard the other day that a good place to have the thermometer is right *in* the stuffing), and wrap the birds completely in the aluminum foil.

Roast in a 300°F. oven about 20 minutes to the pound. That means, in the case of the 8-pound birds, they should be done in 160 minutes, or less than 3 hours. After 2 hours, remove all the foil, letting the juices pour back into the pan under the turkeys, and continue the roasting, basting every 15 minutes with the juices. When the meat thermometer reaches about 185°F., the turkeys will be done, and by this time they should be beautifully browned.

At the last quarter-hour of browning the turkeys, set around them a small bunch of **white grapes** for each person, baste them with the brown juices, and continue with the roasting. The grapes will be just heated through, slightly cooked and delicious. Baste them on and off.

Remove the turkeys and the grapes to a platter, one platter for each turkey, and keep them in a warm place for at least 15 minutes before serving. They will be much easier to carve if they are allowed this short wait.

For the Gravy: Heat the roasting pan in which you roasted the turkeys over direct medium heat until the juices are bubbling. Stir them around with a wire whisk and wait for them to become brown, if they were not this shade when you started. Now rub in, still with the wire whisk, ¼ **cup flour.** Keep rubbing the flour into the juices until you have a light brown paste. Pick up all the juices you can scrape from the corners of the pan. Let the paste (or *roux*, if you wonder what a *roux* is) cook over moderate heat for a minute or two. Then gradually add to it, rubbing all the time, **2 cups turkey broth,** which you have, with foresight, made by boiling the giblets and neck in well salted and peppered water to cover. If you add the broth slowly and keep stirring all the while, you will not have any lumps. Lumps come from impatience and only that. Pour all your liquid in at once, you have lumps. Take it easy, no lumps.

You should now have a smooth, thick gravy. Thin it down, still stirring, with **milk**, with more turkey broth, or with part milk, part **wine**, part broth. Choose your combination, and, now that the gravy is thinning out, you can add the liquid with more dispatch. If you like the idea of a rum flavor to your gravy, use mostly milk with perhaps ¼ **cup light rum.** If you want a giblet gravy, cut up the giblets, discard the gristle, and add them to the gravy. Taste it at the end for seasoning. I can't give you quantities on **salt** and **pepper** here. So much depends on the flavor of the broth you have used. Pour the gravy into a heavy saucepan, scraping it out of the corners of the roasting pan with a rubber spatula. Reheat it when you want it. Wash the roasting pan and get it out of your way.

For the stuffings, the procedure is as follows:

Cranberry Stuffing: Cut ½ **pound fresh cranberries** in halves with a sharp knife. Mix lightly with ½ **cup sugar.** Melt ½ **cup** (1 stick) **butter,** add **2 quarts soft bread crumbs** (loosely torn from 2-day-old bread), and combine with the cranberries. Add **1 cup white raisins, 1 teaspoon salt, grated rind of ½ lemon,** and ½ **cup turkey broth** (made from the giblets), or **canned chicken broth.** Toss lightly and stuff loosely into the bird as directed.

Rum Chestnut Stuffing: This is a very rich, lovely stuffing. You can bake it separately in a buttered casserole for 1 hour as a beautiful side dish with any poultry. If you really love chestnuts, reverse the quantities given so that you will have 6 cups chestnuts and only 2 cups bread crumbs, instead of the 2 cups chestnuts and 6 cups bread crumbs as given here. This recipe will be more than you will need for an 8-pound turkey; it is, in fact, sufficient for a 12-pound turkey, but you should definitely prepare a side dish of it for your freezer.

Toss all together **2 cups cooked, peeled chestnuts** (see

page 294 for directions on this), broken into rather small pieces, ½ cup (1 stick) **melted butter, ½ cup heavy cream, ½ cup light rum** (or sherry, if you prefer that flavor), **2 teaspoons salt, ¼ teaspoon pepper.** Combine ½ **cup melted margarine** with **6 cups bread crumbs** (loosely torn from 2-day-old bread) and ¼ **cup chopped parsley.** Mix lightly with the chestnuts and stuff loosely into the bird. Fit excess into a buttered baking dish, cover with foil or saran, and freeze; or bake now for 1 hour in a 300°F. oven along with the turkey.

INGREDIENTS:

For the turkeys: 2 8- to 10-pound turkeys; salt; pepper; butter; 2 pounds seedless white grapes.

For the gravy: ¼ cup flour; 2 cups turkey broth; 2 cups milk (or part milk, part wine; or part milk, part rum; or all turkey broth); salt; pepper.

For the cranberry stuffing: ½ pound fresh cranberries; ½ cup sugar; ½ cup butter; 2 quarts soft bread crumbs; 1 cup white raisins; 1 teaspoon salt; rind of ½ lemon; ½ cup turkey broth or canned chicken broth.

For the rum chestnut stuffing: 2 cups chestnuts; ½ cup butter; ½ cup heavy cream; ½ cup light rum or sherry; 2 teaspoons salt; ¼ teaspoon pepper; ½ cup margarine; 6 cups bread crumbs; ¼ cup chopped parsley.

BRUSSELS SPROUTS AND ONIONS,
BROWN BUTTER

Trim the outer leaves and stem ends of **2 quarts fresh Brussels sprouts.** Wash them. If you can't get fresh sprouts, **4 boxes frozen sprouts** is the amount needed. Steam them in your Bungalow Cooker or in a colander over hot water, until just done. It's important not to overdo sprouts or any other variety of cabbage. Test them with your fork from time to time and stop cooking as soon as they are tender. They must still have their bright green color, or they're overdone. If that happens, throw them out. Ten minutes should be enough.

As for the frozen sprouts, they should be started at the frozen state, and once they are thawed they will need no more than a few minutes to be cooked. A minute or two before you feel the sprouts are ready, add to them **2 cans or jars of tiny white onions.** These are already cooked and need just to be heated. Save the liquid in which the onions were packed, and add it, the first chance you get, to soup or sauce. You might use it today in the turkey gravy—it will do nothing but good. It's also a superb liquid for the gravy of a chicken or turkey pie.

As soon as the onions are hot, transfer the vegetables to a deep platter. Heat ½ **cup** (1 stick) **butter,** let it sizzle, then lightly brown, and pour it, still sizzling, over the sprouts and onions. Season with ¾ **teaspoon salt,** ¼ **teaspoon fresh black pepper,** a **pinch of summer savory** or **marjoram** (optional). Serve.

INGREDIENTS: 2 quarts fresh Brussels sprouts (or 4 boxes frozen); 2 cans or jars of tiny white onions; ½ cup butter; ¾ teaspoon salt; ¼ teaspoon pepper; pinch of summer savory or marjoram (optional).

SWEET POTATOES WITH BROILED ORANGES

Wash thoroughly and cover with cold water **12 small sweet potatoes,** unpeeled. Bring them to a boil, then simmer until they are not quite done. Timing for this depends on the size of the potatoes. Anywhere from 15 to 30 minutes ought to do it. Remove from saucepan and cool them enough to peel them. Slice them rather thin, about ¼ inch, and arrange the potatoes in overlapping rows in a 2- or 3-quart casserole, buttered lavishly with at least **2 tablespoons butter.** Grate the **rind of 1 large orange** (California's best, navel type) keeping away from the white, which is bitter. Sprinkle each layer of potatoes with light brown sugar, some of the grated orange rind, and ground nutmeg. You should use all the rind, about **2 tablespoons light brown sugar,** and about ¼ **teaspoon nutmeg** for the whole thing. Dot with

butter, using in all 3 tablespoons. Pour **1 cup light cream** over all. Bake at 300°F. for an hour. If you have room in your oven with your turkeys, an upper or lower shelf perhaps, the potatoes will fit right in with them; the temperature is the same. The potatoes, however, can be baked just before the turkeys go in the oven; in this case, cover the top of the casserole with foil and reheat them for about 15 minutes at dinner hour.

NOTE: If you should use frozen sweet potatoes, which are thoroughly cooked and usually sweetened, omit the sugar and bake only until heated through. They're not as good, but would be acceptable.

For the Broiled Oranges: Serve the potato casserole surrounded by broiled oranges. This is a simple matter of slicing **2 California oranges** in ¼-inch slices. You might as well slice the orange whose rind went into the potatoes. Marinate the slices for 10 minutes in a flat platter containing ½ **cup Italian dressing** (bought dressing is fine here). Drain and broil under a hot broiler unit about 500°F. for 5 minutes or until the rind has taken on a crusty, brown tinge. Arrange these slices around the edge of the potato casserole. Serve hot.

INGREDIENTS: 12 small sweet potatoes; 5 tablespoons butter; rind of 1 large orange; 2 tablespoons light brown sugar; ¼ teaspoon ground nutmeg; 1 cup light cream.
For the broiled oranges: 2 California oranges; ½ cup Italian dressing.

MUSHROOM AND ZUCCHINI SALAD

Start this in the morning. Wash **3 small zucchini squashes,** trim off the stem ends, and slice into very thin (⅛-inch) unpeeled rounds. Heat an 8- or 9-inch black iron frying pan (the only kind we have in our own kitchen) until it's goodly hot. A drop of water will sizzle, if you're not sure when that is. Pour into the pan **1 to 2 tablespoons olive oil,** enough to cover the bottom of the pan. Rock the pan around until the oil looks wavy, which means it's hot enough to start cooking, and drop into it the sliced zucchini. Sauté at high heat for 1 minute, stirring the zucchini around lightly, then turn down the heat, cover the pan tightly, and steam the vegetable over low heat for about 5 minutes. You want it just tender, still crisp and crunchy, so don't get your mind on other matters. Wipe ½ **pound fresh mushrooms** with a damp cloth if they're gritty. If they're immaculate, leave them alone. Trim off the tough bottom of the stems, slice them down through the caps and stems. You can do this while the zucchini is steaming in the frying pan. Now turn the zucchini into a bowl with the mushrooms, scraping all the juices from the pan into the bowl.

Over the zucchini and mushrooms, pour **¼ cup pure olive oil, 2 teaspoons wine vinegar, ½ teaspoon salt**, and **2 teaspoons Durkee's or Shedd's dressing**. These dressings are available in most supermarkets, at least in the East, and have a very individual flavor. If you can't find either of them, substitute a little prepared mustard and a little evaporated milk. Stir this all around and cover the bowl with saran. Refrigerate it, preferably all day, but at least 2 hours.

The great thing about this is that you not only have your ingredients for your salad, except for the greens, but you have, already prepared, a most delicious salad dressing.

Just before serving, fill a salad bowl the proper size for 12 with a combination of **Boston and romaine lettuce**, washed, dried, and crisp. You will want about 3 or 4 heads in all. You may use other greens if you can't get these two, but there is a crisp yet tender quality to the Boston and romaine lettuces which contrast perfectly with the marinated vegetables. Whatever you use, be sure it's ice cold, thoroughly dry and *broken*, never cut, into bite-size pieces. Turn the contents of the bowl (the zucchini, the mushrooms, and all the dressing, scraped from the bowl with a rubber spatula) over onto the greens. Toss lightly with a salad fork and spoon. Serve.

INGREDIENTS: 3 small zucchini squashes; 1 to 2 tablespoons olive oil; ½ pound fresh mushrooms; ¼ cup olive oil; 2 teaspoons wine vinegar; ½ teaspoon salt; 2 teaspoons Durkee's or Shedd's dressing; salad greens, preferably romaine and Boston lettuce, about 3 or 4 heads.

MELBA TOAST

A good accompaniment to the salad, easy to do ahead of time, and very nice for the conscience. Cut the crusts off day-old thin-sliced white bread. One loaf goes a long way. Cut into triangular quarters, then cut again, so that you have eight small triangles from each slice of bread. Place them on cookie sheets and bake in a slow (275°F.) oven for half an hour or more, looking at them occasionally. They will dry out, then brown lightly. Get them out of the oven then; if you don't they will steadily deteriorate. They won't need turning; for some reason, the underside browns right along with the top. Leave them uncovered, in a bread basket. If you've done these the day before, keep them in a plastic bag until needed. If they lose their crispness, recrisp them on open trays in the oven, at low temperature.

INGREDIENTS: 1 loaf thin-sliced day-old white bread.

CRUSTLESS CRANBERRY PIE

The very best of the cranberry pies. Grease a 10-inch pie plate. Spread over the bottom of it 3 cups fresh cranberries. (Notice there is no bottom crust. In fact, notice that this is not a pie in the accepted sense.) Sprinkle the cranberries with ¾ cup sugar and ½ cup chopped pecans or walnuts. Stir the sugar into the cranberries, right in the pie plate. Smooth out.

For the crust, beat in your mixer bowl 2 eggs until they are lemon colored and light. Add, gradually and still beating, ¾ cup sugar, ¾ cup flour, ½ cup melted butter, and ¼

cup melted margarine. When thoroughly combined and smooth, spread over the cranberries; you'll need a spatula for this, most probably. Bake in a slow (325°F.) oven for 45 minutes or until the crust browns. Serve this hot or cold, with or without cream. If cold, the crust will have a delightful chewy quality. Either way, it's a most unusual taste.

INGREDIENTS: 3 cups fresh cranberries; ¾ cup sugar; ½ cup chopped pecans or walnuts; 2 eggs; ¾ cup sugar; ¾ cup flour; ½ cup butter; ¼ cup margarine.

DELUXE MINCE PIE

A very rich pie. Prepare pastry for a 2-crust 9-inch pie (see page 287). Line your pie plate with half of the crust, fitting it well into place. Whip **1 cup heavy cream.** Fold it into **1 jar** (28 ounces) **fine-quality brandied mincemeat.** I don't like to give brand names and very rarely do, but the Crosse and Blackwell mincemeat has always seemed to me much crisper and like unto mother's than other brands. Of course, if you have mother's, that's another story. Use it.

See that there is no trace of the cream unassociated with the mincemeat and spread the mixture over the pastry. Sprinkle over the mincemeat now **2 tablespoons light brown sugar,** packed to measure accurately, and **2 tablespoons cake flour,** mixed together. Cover with the top crust, making various slits in the crust. I like to cut a design here—someone's initials, perhaps. Brush the top with **egg white.** (If you have some in your freezer defrost just enough to provide sufficient liquid for this purpose. Return the rest of the jar of egg white to the freezer.) Sprinkle sparingly with **granulated sugar,** perhaps 1 teaspoon in all. Seal well, flute the edges by pressing down at even intervals to form a rhythmic design, and cover the outside edges of the crust with a 2-inch strip of aluminum foil. Press the foil lightly against the edge of the crust, atop and beneath. Bake 30 to 40 minutes at 425°F., or until the filling bubbles through the openings in the top crust and the crust itself is beautifully browned. A marvelous pie, served warm. If you want to have a 10-inch pie, increase all quantities by 25 percent.

INGREDIENTS: Pastry for 2-crust pie; 1 cup heavy cream; 1 (28 ounces) jar brandied mincemeat; 2 tablespoons light brown sugar; 2 tablespoons cake flour; white of 1 egg; 1 teaspoon granulated sugar.

TIMETABLE: The day before is the time for preparing all those chestnuts. Also both stuffings can be prepared and re-frigerated in separate containers, covered, of course. Boil the sweet potatoes, unpeeled, and refrigerate them. Do your Melba toast, as much as a week ahead, if you wish; freezing is all right for this. Bake your mince pie ahead of time and freeze it. If you'd like to bake it the day of your Thanksgiving dinner, do it before you put the turkey in the oven; it can stand around, warm, for a good part of the day without trouble. Heat it hot when you want it. If it's frozen, it will need defrosting in, not out of, the oven; I'll tell you about that when the time comes.

We like to have our Thanksgiving dinner about 4:00 o'clock in the afternoon. If you plan this way, too, you should get the zucchini and mushrooms marinating, the greens washed and chilled, as soon as you finish breakfast. Then prepare the turkeys, stuff them with their 2 already-prepared stuffings, and get them in the oven by about 12:30. Start the giblets cooking for the broth you will want later. Prepare the sweet potato casserole.

Two hours before dinner, prepare the brussels sprouts, leave them in the top of the steamer, the onions drained and waiting nearby; ditto the herbed butter. Take the straw-berries from the freezer, start them thawing.

At 2:45 set the sweet potatoes in the oven with the turkey.

At 3:00, put the cranberry pie together. Don't bake it now; this will be baked after the turkey comes from the oven. As soon as you've finished preparing the pie, about 3:15, add the grapes to the turkey. Fifteen minutes later, slice the oranges, marinate them, and by 3:30 the turkeys should be ready to come out of the oven. Check the reading on the thermometer and, if the turkeys aren't ready, hold everything until they are. Set the turkeys on their heated platters and prepare the gravy, using the giblet broth which has been simmering slowly.

At 3:45, about 15 minutes before you're planning to serve dinner, combine the salad. Combine the strawberries with the cranberry juice. Take out the sweet potato casserole from the oven. Turn up the oven temperature to broil the oranges. Steam the sprouts and add the onions; heat the herbed butter.

At 4:00, serve the appetizers; life will be simpler if you do this in the living room, but it really doesn't matter. Soon the family can be sitting down, enjoying the salad and the Melba toast, and you can have set out the two turkeys, with two deep dishes for the stuffings as they are scooped out of the birds, the gravy in its deep, hot bowl, the sprouts and onions, the sweet potatoes with the just-broiled oranges. As soon as the oranges come out of the oven, turn it back down to 325°F., slide in the cranberry pie and the frozen mince pie. They will be just right when you're ready for them; the cranberry pie baked, the mince pie thawed and heated.

LEFTOVERS

Make a gelatin mold of the leftover cranberry-strawberry juice, using either unflavored gelatine or perhaps apple-flavored prepared gelatin. Fill little tea-sized muffin pans with this, turn them out, and there you have nice, useful centerpieces for individual fruit salad. Save a little of the juice to stir into some commercial sour cream, add a bit of sugar, and serve as a dressing for your salad.

How many things can you think of to do with leftover turkey? I can think of 10 or 11 right off. Turkey chow mein? (There's a good recipe for chow mein in my *Blueberry Hill Cookbook*.) Turkey hash? Here's how to make a good one. Chop 2 or 3 cups cold turkey very fine. Make a very rich cream sauce—this means you should use light cream instead of milk—and add 2 teaspoons minced pimiento, ¼ teaspoon thyme, salt and pepper to taste. Fry little pieces of bread (or use the leftover Melba toast bits), arrange them in a shallow oven dish, and cover the bread with the turkey in its sauce. Sprinkle a little grated Parmesan cheese over it all, brown under the broiler for a flash, or long enough to brown it and make it bubble. Serve with a tart currant jelly, a chutney (a cranberry chutney such as you have in the November party menu would be fine) and more fried bread or Melba toast.

Turkey leftover casserole? Just that. Layers of turkey and stuffing and gravy, alternated to the top of the dish. Bake to hot and bubbly.

Turkey in white wine sauce? A dish to remember. Simple too. Sliced turkey in a pretty casserole. Sliced cooked mushrooms on top. A rich cream sauce, with about one-fourth the liquid white wine. Season well. Add a bit of parsley. A sprinkling of Parmesan. Under the broiler to brown.

Oh, I could go on and on. Turkey sandwiches, spread, each one, with a tablespoon of your best dressing? If it's sausage dressing, it's the best.

Turkey slices in lemon-butter dill (or chive) sauce? This is simply butter brought to a bubbling boil, the foam skimmed off—clarified, to be precise—and grated rind of lemon, a bit of salt, a dash of pepper, and a tablespoon or so of chopped dill or chives, as your whim dictates, added. Pour this sauce over sliced turkey, heated first, slowly, in a bit of broth.

Another party dish such as turkey Marsala? Sprinkle large pieces of turkey breast with salt and pepper, dip in heavy cream, dust in flour, and sauté lightly in butter. Add ½ cup Marsala for enough turkey to serve 4, cover tightly, simmer 5 minutes. Lift the breasts to a heated platter, add ¼ cup heavy cream to the juices in the frying pan, reheat, add the white grapes left from dinner and, if you want to be fancy, 1 package of defrosted artichoke hearts. Heat, stirring, until everything is very hot. Pour over the turkey breasts and serve, garnished with watercress. This is a lovely recipe to remember for pheasant breasts, too.

Another way for a party? Season breast pieces with salt and pepper, then sprinkle with flour—not much—just a sprinkling. Sauté in clarified butter (as just described) just long enough to brown lightly. Remember, this turkey has been cooked before; doesn't need to be cooked again. Now add 1 cup sliced fresh mushrooms, ¼ cup sherry, 1 tablespoon chopped chives, and 1 cup heavy cream. Heat, don't boil, and serve with rice or stuffing which you have sliced into neat slices, dipped in flour, and fried to brown.

At the end, there's the carcass, from which one derives the turkey broth I've been talking about now and again. Cover the carcass with cold water, add a carrot, an onion, a bay leaf, some salt and pepper. Simmer, simmer. Freeze what you don't use right away. Comes in handy.

And for those final bits and pieces, think you not to toss them to the cat. One can make of these turkey croquettes seasoned with lemon juice and Worcestershire sauce—look for my recipe for ham croquettes in that other book of mine. Can't go repeating. The turkey croquettes are done the same way. Or, if it's an elegant mood you're in, there's the turkey mousse given you on page 308 or a simpler one which is just a croquette mixture—a heavy, heavy white sauce, that's what that is—(as in croquette recipe just mentioned) with some soft bread soaked in cream, mixed with beaten egg yolks, then folded into stiffly beaten egg whites and baked in a greased, covered mold for 45 minutes, about, in a very slow oven. Until it's firm, anyway. Serve this hot or cold. I repeat, elegant.

With any of these leftover dishes, serve what you have of the stuffings. They can be reheated in the oven, piled loosely, topped with butter to brown, and moistened with gravy.

A marvelous sauce to have around for leftover turkey is to be used when you're grilling turkey breasts. Add to the skillet, when you've removed the meat, a glass of black currant jelly. Mash it up, add ¼ teaspoon Worcestershire, ⅛ teaspoon dry mustard, juice of ½ lemon, and 2 tablespoons butter. Bring it to a boil, stir smooth, and pour it over the meat. This is a great sauce to be served with shoulder lamb chops or veal chops, as well.

A turkey salad comes to mind.

Party Turkey Salad

Cut up **2 or 3 cups of turkey**, toss it in ¼ **cup Italian dressing**, and allow it to marinate for about 2 hours. Add ½ **cup cucumber**, peeled and chopped, and **1 cup grapes**, whatever sort you have about, and, in fact, a little **melon** would be nice if you happen to have half of one on your hands. Taste for seasoning, and add **salt** and **pepper** to your taste with a little **celery seed.** Pile the turkey mixture on a bed of crisp washed lettuce, such as Boston, and top with a dressing made of ⅓ **cup mayonnaise,** ⅓ **cup commercial sour cream,** and **1 teaspoon sugar.** Sprinkle with **pecans.**

INGREDIENTS: 2 or 3 cups leftover turkey; ¼ cup Italian dressing; ½ cup cucumber; 1 cup grapes; melon; salt; pepper; celery seed; ⅓ cup mayonnaise; ⅓ cup commercial sour cream; 1 teaspoon sugar; pecans.

Try puréeing the Brussels sprouts in your food mill. Add butter and heavy cream in equal amounts, just enough to make a creamy consistency. Let the onions join them in the same process. Taste for salt and heat. I like sugar here.

Whip the sweet potatoes that are left, adding to them a tablespoon of butter, a pinch of cinnamon, and a tablespoon of cream for each cup of potatoes. Whip with your electric beater, and, while you're whipping, add a tablespoon of rum or a tablespoon of sherry, again for each cup of potatoes. Pile the whip into a buttered casserole, dot with butter, and heat until very hot and the peaks in the potatoes are brown.

I hope you've eaten all the mushroom and zucchini salad. The zucchini would make a nice antipasto-type thing, but you'd have to get rid of the wilted lettuce. Don't think it would be worth it.

The two pies do well as they go along. Reheat the mince pie to very, very hot, serve with hard sauce, with vanilla ice cream, or with sharp cheese. The pie will freeze, as I told you, and a nice way to do this is to freeze it in slices, so that you need defrost only as many slices at a time as you plan to use. The cranberry pie is kept, in my house, in the refrigerator. It doesn't last long, and each time another bit of it is consumed, there is heard in the air a sigh of appreciation. At the end, if you're down to bits, chop it up, heat it in individual custard cups, topped with (what else?) custard. This would suit the very young and the very old, but, with only enough for two or three, that ought to be a satisfactory arrangement.

DECEMBER

PARTY MENU

A Winter Brunch

CAFE RHUM
CAVIAR RINGS, GRILLED BREAD
OYSTER BISQUE
SCRAMBLED EGGS IN SOUR CREAM
CHICKEN LIVER KABOBS
PRUNES IN SHERRY WITH BACON
LEMON CURD
CHRISTMAS CRANBERRIES
BRIOCHES
SOUR CREAM LOAFERS

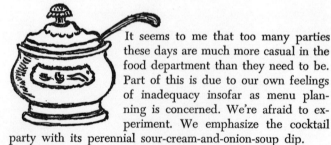 It seems to me that too many parties these days are much more casual in the food department than they need to be. Part of this is due to our own feelings of inadequacy insofar as menu planning is concerned. We're afraid to experiment. We emphasize the cocktail party with its perennial sour-cream-and-onion-soup dip.

Surely we can do better than that. The day of the gathering together of discerning friends to whom we may serve exquisite, precisely and perfectly prepared food is, hopefully, not gone.

This is a memorable brunch which belies such thinking. A

noon to two o'clock meal of a Sunday. Relaxed, casual, yes. But, starting with the delicious hot café rhum, every part of this meal is a conversation-starter. Your guests will think you're the greatest! Try it, won't you?

The amounts here will serve a gathering of approximately 20 people. There is no formal dessert, as you see. The same menu will do for a gala supper after theatre.

CAFE RHUM

Prepare, well ahead of time, **48 cups strong coffee.** Add to it, while still hot, **1 cup granulated sugar.** Cool. Add **3 cups heavy cream, 3 cups light rum.** Beat well, using rotary beater. Since 48 cups is the equivalent of about 2 gallons (measured in coffee cupfuls, not measuring cupfuls), you'll obviously want to do the beating in reasonable amounts. Just before serving, bring the mixture just to a boil. Serve very hot.

INGREDIENTS: 48 cups (coffee cups) strong coffee; 1 cup granulated sugar; 3 cups heavy cream; 3 cups light rum.

CAVIAR RINGS, GRILLED BREAD

Decide how many of these you wish to prepare; should you want one ring for each person, you'd need **40 eggs,** as each ring mold calls for 2. I don't think you'll want that many; with so many other things to eat, some of your guests will probably decide against the caviar. For this reason, I'm going to give you this recipe for 1 serving; you may multiply it as you wish. Thus, *for each serving,* butter an individual ring mold thoroughly. These are tiny things. Separate **2 eggs** carefully. Let the egg white go into the mold. Bake it in a slow (300°F.) oven and keep your eye on it; it will take from 10 to 20 minutes to set. You want it to be completely white and firm, but don't leave it in the oven longer than the period needed for it to reach this point. Chill and, just before serving, turn the ring out on a bed of parsley. In the case of this party, I'd suggest you use a silver tray, if you have one, and arrange your rings on that in a nice design. Fill each ring with **1 tablespoon caviar**, mixed with **¼ teaspoon grated onion**. (The sort of caviar here must be your own choice. Imported beluga would be gorgeous, but terribly expensive. Lumpfish or red salmon caviar makes a practical and delicious substitute.) While the egg whites are baking, simmer the egg yolks in **salted water**, kept on the quiet side, for 3 minutes or until they are cooked through. Refrigerate the yolks wrapped in saran, and, just before serving, press them through a fine sieve or ricer, pile them lightly in a bowl, and set it near the caviar rings. Lay **lemon wedges** here or there on the parsley bed. Grill small toast triangles as directed on page 43; arrange on a plate nearby. The guests can then help themselves at will.

INGREDIENTS (*for each serving*): 2 eggs; 1 tablespoon caviar; ¼ teaspoon grated onion; salted water; 1 lemon wedge; grilled bread.

OYSTER BISQUE

Here's your chance to use that beautiful tureen. Peel and cut into small cubes **2 small carrots**, **½ small onion**, **1 small celery stalk**, **2 stalks parsley**, and, if you can come by one without too much trouble, **1 leek**. Heat **¼ cup** (½ stick) **butter** in a heavy 3- or 4-quart saucepan and, when it is melted, add the vegetables, stirring them around slowly until they are shiny, about 3 or 4 minutes. This is called a *mirepoix* and is classic French procedure in the preparation of any bisque.

Drain **4 dozen oysters**, saving the liquor, and chop them very fine. They're resistant beasts, and I find the best method is to use kitchen shears, at least to start. Add them to the vegetables (the *mirepoix*) and stir them around for 3 minutes, over low heat. Add **2 cups light white wine** and continue simmering 3 more minutes. The authentic French bisque would now have you throw in the oyster shells (that is, if you've opened them yourself and scrubbed them) and simmer those a little while. Since I don't ever do it, I guess I'd better not advise you to; I just wanted you to know about it. The authentic bisque, too, requires that you now force everything—the chopped oysters, the vegetables, everything —through something known as a "purée machine," which would be a Foley food mill, I suppose. Do that if you prefer a very smooth soup. If you don't mind the little pieces in the soup, don't bother. I rather like a coarse soup, so I let well enough alone.

Soak 2 cups soft bread crumbs pulled from a sturdy bread, such as an Italian or French bread, in the oyster liquor. When they are thoroughly soaked through add this to the oysters and the vegetables, add 1 quart chicken broth or court bouillon (you might have some of this in your freezer as I have recommended on page 158), 1 quart light cream and 1 pint heavy cream. Heat, but do not boil. If the bisque is too thick, dilute with a little more light cream or wine. Taste for salt and pepper, which will vary with the sort of stock you have added. A nice touch at the end is 1 teaspoon Worcestershire, but this is quite optional.

This recipe will make enough small servings for most of your guests. If you were to serve this bisque as a main course at some future date, the recipe given here would serve 10 generously.

INGREDIENTS: 2 small carrots; ½ small onion; 1 small celery stalk; 2 stalks parsley; 1 leek; ¼ cup butter; 4 dozen oysters; 2 cups light white wine; 2 cups soft bread crumbs; 1 quart chicken broth or court bouillon; 1 quart light cream; 1 pint heavy cream; salt; pepper; Worcestershire sauce (optional).

SCRAMBLED EGGS IN SOUR CREAM

If eggs can be called divine, these are they. I suggest here that you do 8 eggs at a time, unless you know that more than this number will be used at once.

Have the water in the lower part of the double boiler hot,

not boiling. Melt ¼ cup butter in the top section; that's half a stick. In a bowl, beat together lightly with rotary beater 8 large eggs, ¼ cup commercial sour cream, ¾ teaspoon salt, ¼ teaspoon freshly ground pepper. If you object to the black specks in the eggs, use white pepper. When well combined, but not more than that, pour the egg mixture into the top of the double boiler with the butter. They will need little attention; just come back to them now and then and stir from the bottom as they begin to set and be sure to get them off the lower section as soon as they are completely set. They will be at their best if you don't let them cook longer than that. Serve them as they are ready.

INGREDIENTS: ¼ cup butter; 8 large eggs; ¼ cup commercial sour cream; ¾ teaspoon salt; ¼ teaspoon pepper.

CHICKEN LIVER KABOBS

These are do-it-yourself jobs. Again, this recipe will tell you how much you will need *for each serving*. Multiply as you wish. Sauté, for 2 minutes only, 3 healthy mushroom caps in 1 teaspoon butter, turning them around and around. Now string on skewers, in this order, 1 mushroom cap; 1 section (that means usually half) chicken liver, seasoned with salt and freshly ground pepper; 1 square Canadian bacon; 1 small firm chunk tomato, seasoned as are the livers. Repeat this, ending with another mushroom cap. This will give you two of everything except the mushroom. There'll be three of these caps. Let your guests broil these on a table hibachi, if you have one. Otherwise, you may broil them under the broiler unit of your range. Have nearby a small saucepan of melted butter; keep it melting on a candle flame while you are in need of it. The kabobs can be basted if needed.

INGREDIENTS (*for each serving*): 3 mushroom caps; 1 teaspoon butter; 1 section chicken liver; salt; pepper; 1 square Canadian bacon; 1 small firm chunk tomato; butter.

PRUNES IN SHERRY WITH BACON

Soak 1 pound large California prunes in 1 cup sherry overnight. Remove the pits, wrap each prune in half slices of lean bacon, secure each with a toothpick, and broil on a slotted tray under the broiler unit until the bacon is done and crisp. You'll need to watch these and turn them once or twice. Be sure that your tray has drainage so that the bacon fat will vanish as it appears.

INGREDIENTS: 1 pound large California prunes; 1 cup sherry; 1 pound lean bacon.

LEMON CURD

Lemon curd is a delightful pure lemon spread, well known in the British Isles and Scotland. Many of my British friends and guests have told me of it, and one of them gave me an assortment of recipes, which, after much experimenting, have resulted in this simple method. You will find that a jar of this curd, which is also called, in England by the rather unappetizing title "lemon cheese," will be the most popular item in your refrigerator. You will use it with toast at tea-time, with biscuits, scones; if you have a bit of piecrust around, you will want to use the curd for a tart filling. You'll need to be rather at leisure when you fix it. It keeps indefinitely in the refrigerator, although I cannot honestly say it's ever been allowed to in our house.

In the top of a double boiler, with the water beneath it simmering, not boiling, melt ¼ pound (1 stick) butter. Add to this 4 well-beaten eggs; the grated rind of 2 lemons; the juice of 4 lemons and enough additional bottled lemon juice to make up ⅔ cup; a few grains of salt; and 3 cups granulated sugar. Cook, stirring occasionally, until it is thick enough to spread. This will take about 45 minutes of cooking. Lower the heat when the thickening starts, so that the water in the bottom of the double boiler is truly not more

than a simmer. Transfer to a screw-top jar, and keep in refrigerator. Makes 3 or 4 jelly glasses full.

INGREDIENTS: ¼ pound butter; 4 eggs; grated rind of 2
    lemons; juice of 4 lemons and enough additional lemon
    juice to make ⅔ cup; salt; 3 cups granulated sugar.

CHRISTMAS CRANBERRIES

Boil for 3 minutes 2 cups sugar and ½ cup water. Toss in
3 whole cloves, 1 stick cinnamon, 4 cups cranberries, and
½ orange, finely chopped in food chopper, rind and pulp.
Cook over low heat until the cranberries start popping. Stir
occasionally. Remove from the range, add ¼ cup cognac,
and chill. You will have 3½ cups relish.

INGREDIENTS: 2 cups sugar; ½ cup water; 3 whole cloves; 1
    stick cinnamon; 4 cups cranberries; ½ orange; ¼ cup
    cognac.

BRIOCHES

This recipe was presented to me by two good friends, Bill
and Mildred Miller, who, as "The Millers," have run one of
the wittiest and most knowledgeable TV shows on food I
have ever come across. They've been entertaining audiences
in the Buffalo vicinity for many years (before TV, they
were on radio), and, along with lots of chatter, they manage to teach their lucky audiences how to cook really su-
perbly. This is their recipe for brioches; I've never found one
better. These brioches freeze well, so don't be discouraged
at the rather time-consuming procedure; the time can be
consumed on some other day than your party.

Dissolve in ½ cup warm water, 2 packages active dry
yeast, 2 tablespoons flour, and 1 teaspoon sugar. Allow to
rise in warm place until it is very light; won't take long.
Beat 8 eggs until they're lemon colored and light, then add
¼ cup sugar, 1 teaspoon salt, and blend well. Add, a little
at a time, beating well as you do, 4 cups sifted flour and ¾

cup (1½ sticks) **melted butter** or **margarine.** When all is combined, add another ½ **cup flour,** beat thoroughly. Add yeast mixture, beat again. Do as much of the beating as possible in your mixer. When it gets too stiff, use a wooden spoon. Allow the dough to rise in a warm place until doubled, which should take 1½ hours. Punch the dough down (which will thoroughly deflate it), cover with saran, and refrigerate it, still in its bowl, overnight.

You can either complete these the morning of your party or, as I suggested before, you can bake them ahead of time and freeze them. The dough will keep for several days, covered, in your refrigerator, if you prefer to bake them fresh for your brunch party. When ready to bake them, turn out the dough on a lightly floured board. Reserve one quarter of the dough. Roll the rest of it into cylinders 2½ inches in diameter. Cut these cylinders into pieces 1½ inches long. You'll get 12 from each cylinder. These will half-fill the traditional brioche molds that can be purchased from a French bakery supply house, or will do equally well in the large muffin pans. Make a cut through the center of each and shape small bits of dough from the reserved portion into the shape of a cone. Insert the small end of the cone into the cut. Allow the brioches to rest for about 20 minutes. Paint the tops with a mixture of 1 **egg yolk** and a little **water.** Bake at 450°F. for 15 minutes. Serve hot. Will make 24.

INGREDIENTS: ½ cup warm water; 2 packages active dry yeast; 2 tablespoons flour; 1 teaspoon sugar; 8 eggs; ¼ cup sugar; 1 teaspoon salt; 4½ cups sifted flour; ¾ cup butter or margarine; 1 egg yolk; water.

SOUR CREAM LOAFERS

The name "loafers" was coined by my youngest daughter, Laurey. My three girls love to help shape these flaky, croissant-like breakfast cakes, and one day, her head to one side, Laurey said: "Look, mommy," and she pointed to the attitude of the cakes, "they're loafing." Indeed, they were, all of them, in the most relaxed of attitudes. So this is what we call them. This is one of the recipes that I will *urge* you to try.

Sift **3½ cups flour** and **1 teaspoon salt.** Cut in **1 cup shortening** (make this half margarine, half butter, ¼ pound [1 stick] of each) with a pastry blender. When they are thoroughly combined, like cornmeal, dissolve **1 package active dry yeast** in **¼ cup warm water.** Stir the yeast into the flour mixture along with **¾ cup commercial sour cream; 1 whole egg** and **2 egg yolks,** well-beaten; and **1 teaspoon vanilla.** Don't try to do this with 2 eggs instead of 1 egg and 2 yolks. You really need the richness of the yolks; the loafers will not compare in flavor without it. Mix well, using your floured hands when it becomes difficult to use a spoon. You will have a smooth, silky dough. Cover it with a damp cloth, letting the cloth touch the dough all around. This will keep the dough soft; if you set the damp cloth over the top of the bowl, without touching the dough, you will have an unpleasant crust to cope with. Refrigerate the dough for at least 2 hours. If you're in a hurry, set it in the freezer for 10 minutes. You may now use the dough at any point (after the 2 hours) up to the following week. It keeps beautifully.

When ready to bake the loafers, cut the dough in half. Leave the section you're not working with in the refrigerator. Roll this half of the dough on a board sprinkled heavily with **flour** and with **sugar** or with **cinnamon-sugar,** if you like the flavor of the cinnamon. Roll the dough right on this flour and sugar into an oblong, 8 x 16 inches. Fold the ends toward the center, overlapping them. Sprinkle the top again with the sugar, keep the board floured and sugared, and roll out again to 8 x 16 inches. Fold the ends in again, sprinkle again, and roll out again. The third time you do it, continue rolling out the dough, so that you have it about ¼ inch thick. Cut the dough into strips 1 x 4 inches. Holding a dough strip by each end, twist it in opposite directions, stretching as you do it, so that you have a tightly twisted roll. Lay it out in a semicircle, in the shape of a horseshoe if you will, as if it were "loafing," and let it rest on an ungreased baking tray. Press the ends a bit to keep the twist where you left it. Repeat with the rest of the dough. Let the loafers rest for 15 minutes. Then bake at 375°F. for about 15 minutes or until delicately browned. Remove the loafers from the pan immediately and cool on a wire rack. You will have 4 to 5 dozen. Bake as many as you want at a time. For this party you may want to bake them and freeze them; that's all right, too. They defrost marvelously; don't even need to be heated, actually, to be good, though they're at their top form when they are hot.

INGREDIENTS: 3½ cups flour; 1 teaspoon salt; 1 cup shortening (half butter, half margarine); 1 package active dry yeast; ¼ cup warm water; ¾ cup commercial sour cream; 1 whole egg; 2 egg yolks; 1 teaspoon vanilla; flour and sugar or cinnamon-sugar for rolling.

TIMETABLE: Long before your brunch party, you can bake the brioches and the sour cream loafers. They can be frozen and reheated when you want them. If you're accustomed to baking, you can prepare the dough for the loafers a few days ahead of time, and, early in the morning of the party, roll them out and shape the crescents; then you can bake them at just the right moment. Don't worry about it, if you can't manage this, or if you have no help in the kitchen who can; the loafers really are terrific even after they've been frozen.

The lemon curd and the Christmas cranberries are both good keepers. Make them as much as a week or more before you want to serve them.

The day before your party, prepare the oyster bisque. Refrigerate it and reheat it when you're ready for it. Be sure that your tureen is heated too. That evening, set the prunes to soaking.

The morning of your party prepare the café rhum. If you can get hold of a large coffeemaker, fill that with the finished product, so that it can be served with a turn of the faucet. If not, heat it when you want it in a large soup pot, transfer it in small quantities to coffee servers; be sure it is steaming when your first guest arrives.

Next thing in the morning is the caviar rings. They're

easy; while you're baking them, boil the yolks and combine the caviar with the grated onion. Arrange the parsley on the tray, cut the lemon but keep it wrapped in saran until you want it. Refrigerate the rings and the grated yolks, which can be in their own bowl now. Grill your bread.

Now prepare the chicken liver kabobs, thread them on their skewers, cover them lightly, and refrigerate until you want them. Wrap the prunes in bacon, leave them on their tray, ready to be broiled. Combine the eggs with the sour cream and other ingredients for the scrambled eggs. Leave them in units of 8 eggs each in bowls. Give them a final flourish with a fork before cooking them.

Everything is ready. When your guests arrive, ply them with coffee. Before them on the tray is the caviar business —lovely looking. Wait until the guests have congregated before you heat the brioches and the loafers. They are at their best if they're served when they've reached their completely heated stage; if you keep them hot too long, they will grow crusty. Have the bisque ready to heat and start it going when you start to heat the breads; it will take about the same length of time.

Serve the bisque to those who want it; broil the bacon-wrapped prunes and scramble the eggs so that they will emerge more or less at the same time and be available for simultaneous consumption. Let the guests take care of their own chicken liver kabobs, or broil these after you've performed the bacon-prune bit. The grilled bread is available for those who want it; the brioches and the loafers are also ready, and on your table are two little dishes of the lemon curd and the Christmas cranberries. I'd advise you to have some black coffee for any guests who don't want the café rhum; you won't need much.

LEFTOVERS

The café rhum will keep in milk bottles in the refrigerator and will be quite delicious for several days. If you don't mind iced drinks in mid-winter, try it that way; add some instant coffee to compensate for the loss in strength from the ice. You can make a delicious dessert of this by stirring in some tapioca pudding to thicken it. Serve this in sherbet glasses with whipped cream.

If, perchance, you do have some of the caviar rings left, chop the whites, mix them with the yolks and the caviar that are left, bind with mayonnaise, sprinkle with chopped chives, and use it to spread the remaining grilled bread triangles for a delightful bite-size open sandwich to go with your leftover oyster bisque. Better still, chop any leftover chicken livers (if they weren't broiled in a kabob, simmer them for 2 or 3 minutes in salted water), and, mixed with the eggs and caviar, again with enough mayonnaise to bind them together, you have a nice paté. Serve it on a lettuce bed with a radish or two. You can use chicken fat instead of mayonnaise—a delicious taste.

The oyster bisque will freeze. Keep it for another party. If you happen to have any scrambled-egg components mixed up and not cooked, add to them whatever you have left, cooked or uncooked, of the chicken liver kabobs. You'll need to sauté the livers a minute or two first, but the rest can go in. If you have a likely amount of the livers and some tomatoes and bacon, etc., you will find that the eggs will probably serve just to hold them together. Melt some butter in a sizzling hot black iron frying pan, and, when the butter is hot, add the egg combination. While the bottom is browning lightly, lift the edges and let the liquid run down the sides and cook, too. When all the egg is just set, and still creamy on top, either fold together as you would an omelette, or turn and let the reverse side cook for just a minute. Slide onto a platter. This is a lunch in itself, and a delicious one.

The sherried prunes and bacon will make a nice side salad the next day, accompanying creamed cottage cheese on a bed of watercress. Make a dressing by combining ¼ cup of lemon juice with ½ cup superfine sugar and ¼ cup of the sherry left from marinating the prunes. If you've used a sweet sherry, cut down on the sugar.

The lemon curd, spread on the grilled bread and toasted

for a moment under the broiler, is a particularly delightful tea tidbit. Use it as suggested in the recipe, for everything that calls for lemon flavoring. Bake some cupcakes (that recipe for whipped cream cake on page 222 in the September party section is fine for these), drop a spoonful of lemon curd in each cupcake before baking, and see how you like them. Or if you have some leftover cupcakes around, slice them in half, spread with the curd, replace top. Fill some cookies with it. Fold it into vanilla ice cream, softened first, then refreeze.

The cranberries are a relish that will last as long as you let it. You'd better take out the cinnamon stick. Remember this, particularly, with curries.

DECEMBER

FAMILY MENU

New England Saturday Night Supper

MAMA'S VEGETABLE SOUP
BOSTON BAKED BEANS
GRILLED BUTTERMILK HAM STEAK
WITH HOT BUTTERMILK-MUSTARD SAUCE
HEARTS OF LETTUCE WITH CHEESE FLUFF DRESSING
PICKLED WATERMELON RIND
FRIED SALLY LUNN
SWEET-CHOCOLATE CAKE WITH WHIPPED CREAM
OR
OLD-FASHIONED ORANGE PIE

A blizzard in Vermont can be a frightening affair, if you're out in it; but there's no more satisfactory way to spend a Saturday night, given a roaring fire and a good New England supper eaten in the kitchen, than to be snug at home with the winds roaring and the snows gathering outside your door. The call then to supper, with all of us at home and together, is a signal for a family sufficient unto itself. And, if a friend is forced, or, indeed, is invited to stay the night, all the better. Good food, a tight house, a warmth of love. Supper is for 6.

339

MAMA'S VEGETABLE SOUP

My mama was a good, a consistently good, cook. Nothing fancy about Mama's cooking; in fact, sometimes we children thought it was pretty boring to have so many things the same. But if Mama found a recipe she liked, she stuck with it. Her spongecake, which is baked by so many readers of my earlier cookbook, was literally the only cake she liked to bake. She was right, too, I suppose; it's a perfect spongecake—why look further?

Mama felt that a vegetable soup should not be a beef-vegetable soup, or a chicken-vegetable soup. She made it without any meat or chicken stock at all and, through the long, slow cooking, it took on its own marvelous, robust flavor. This is it.

Start with **6 medium onions.** Cut them up and put them in a soup pot. Add **6 large carrots,** peeled and cut up. Add **1 small purple-top turnip; 1 leek** (if available); **6 or 7 full stalks of parsley; 1 cup celery tops,** including the leaves.

When all the vegetables are in the soup pot, add **2 quarts cold water.** Bring to a boil, add **2 teaspoons salt, ¼ teaspoon freshly ground pepper,** and reduce to a slow boil. Simmer for 1 hour. Mama now used whatever fresh green vegetables she could get in the market; this will depend on what part of the country you're in, but usually you can find some of these imported from California or Florida. She would add about **1 cup shelled fresh lima beans; 1 cup fresh green beans,** the ends trimmed and the beans cut or not, as you wish; **1 cup fresh wax beans;** and, after these had simmered for a half hour, she would add **1 cup fresh peas,** shelled measure. She would then continue to simmer the soup until the peas were tender, at least another 15 minutes. Mama never used tomatoes in this soup, if you will notice, nor green peppers, though there is no reason you shouldn't, if you'd like to. The soup should be rather thick, but, if it's *too* thick, you can thin it down with a little boiling water. Be sure the addition of the water is allowed to be assimilated before you call the soup done. This soup will take a variable amount of time in cooking; it doesn't hurt it to cook it longer than the 2 hours or so in this telling; all that will happen is that the vegetables will get softer. At the end, add **2 tablespoons butter,** let it melt, stir the soup around, taste for salt and pepper, adding seasoning if needed.

The second day it's better than the first. Why don't you cook it yesterday and serve it today? In the absence of fresh vegetables, you can use frozen, of course, but, unless you can get at least two of the green vegetables in the fresh form, I'd suggest you wait until they're available.

INGREDIENTS: 6 medium onions; 6 large carrots; 1 small purple-top turnip; 1 leek; 6 or 7 stalks parsley; 1 cup celery tops; 2 quarts cold water; salt; pepper; 1 cup shelled fresh lima beans; 1 cup fresh green beans; 1 cup fresh wax beans; 1 cup shelled fresh peas; 2 tablespoons butter.

BOSTON BAKED BEANS

This recipe was given to me by an English teacher, a man who used to love to spend Saturday afternoons baking beans. He was a New Englander, a witty fellow, and this is the way he wrote out the recipe. It's worth doing as he says, and, if you are one who has not tasted beans except from a can, this will truly be an experience for you. There is no similarity between these beans and the bought variety. I'll make a few comments at the end of the recipe.

"Don't attempt to bake beans if you have anywhere to go or anything else to do. You won't get baked beans. You will get boiled beans; and they are quite a different story. Bake them when the baby's sick, and you have to stay home all day. This is a 24-hour job.

"Use yellow-eyed or white beans. Take **2 generous cups of beans** and soak them overnight. In the morning put them on to boil until the skin curls when blown on (about 45 minutes to 1 hour).

"Put in the bottom of a bean crock a **6 x 8-inch piece of salt**

pork, cut in squares with the rind slashed every quarter inch; ¼ cup of sugar; and ½ cup of molasses. Add a large onion chopped fairly fine, and ½ teaspoon of dry mustard. The sugar and molasses can be increased or decreased according to whether you like beans sweet or less sweet. Use a crock. Bean crocks are both cheap and decorative, and compromising with aluminum or Pyrex simply means you are a person of mediocrity.

"Throw the beans on top of the mess already in the crock and add enough hot water to cover, but just to cover. See that there is an inch or two in the pot above the water to avoid boiling over. If this were to happen you would think you had a fertilizer plant. Cover tightly and put in an oven preheated to 350°F. Keep oven temperature even.

"Now this is the trick: during the baking the beans must be watched. When the water goes below the level of the beans, add enough, but just enough water, to re-cover— about a tablespoon or so. The water must be added every 15 minutes or so. That is why you can't go shopping on the day you are baking beans. Bake them for 8 to 9 hours. The beans, you see, must be boiled and in the oven by eight o'clock in the morning at least. A wonderful occupation for a rainy Saturday; the whole house will smell heavenly during the baking."

The amount of sugar and molasses given here does produce a very, very sweet bean. I would suggest that you cut this to 2 tablespoons sugar and ¼ cup molasses. Then, if you taste it near the end and you think you'd like more molasses, you are in control of the matter. Also, the direction about soaking the beans means with cold water to cover. The beans will swell up and there will be little water left, but add that, with the beans, when you start them baking. That's all.

INGREDIENTS: 2 generous cups yellow-eyed or white beans; 6 x 8-inch piece salt pork; ¼ cup sugar and ½ cup molasses (or 2 tablespoons sugar and ¼ cup molasses for less sweet beans); 1 large onion; ½ teaspoon dry mustard.

GRILLED BUTTERMILK HAM STEAK
WITH HOT BUTTERMILK-MUSTARD SAUCE

A quickie. Brush both sides of a 1½-inch-thick center slice of ready-to-eat ham with buttermilk. Use a pastry brush. Broil under very high heat, basting with buttermilk 4 or 5 times, turning as you do. It will glaze and will be very attractive. You won't want to spend more than 5 minutes for each side, if that; the ham is cooked already, you know—all you want to do is heat it.

For the Sauce: Beat 2 egg yolks until they are just blended; a fork does this quickly. Add ½ teaspoon dry mustard, 1 teaspoon flour, and ¼ teaspoon salt. Combine with fork or rotary beater until smooth. Heat 1 cup buttermilk and, when it is hot, add 2 tablespoons of it to the egg mixture. Combine and then dump the contents of the egg bowl into the saucepan with the buttermilk. Stir and heat until thickened. This will happen very quickly; eggs are that way, so don't think you have time to go away. Remove from heat immediately. Serve with the ham steak. You'll have a little over a cup of the sauce.

INGREDIENTS: 1½-inch-thick center slice ready-to-eat ham (about 2 pounds); ½ cup buttermilk.
For the sauce: 2 egg yolks; ½ teaspoon dry mustard; 1 teaspoon flour; ¼ teaspoon salt; 1 cup buttermilk.

HEARTS OF LETTUCE WITH CHEESE
FLUFF DRESSING

A few hours before serving, cut the core out of 1 large, firm head iceberg lettuce. Run ice-cold water into the cavity, let it rest there 5 minutes, then invert the head of lettuce and drain the water away, fully. Wrap the lettuce in a damp dish towel, refrigerate until serving time. Cut it into equal segments. One head of lettuce will make 6 very large sections; you may want less than that for each serving.

For the Dressing: A blender is a great help. Buzz until well mashed **4 ounces bleu cheese.** Add, blending quickly until smooth, **⅓ cup pure olive oil.** Stop the blender, add **½ teaspoon salt, ½ teaspoon grated lemon peel, 2 tablespoons lemon juice,** and **½ cup commercial sour cream.** Blend. Turn the dressing into a little serving bowl, refrigerate for 2 or 3 hours, then allow to return to room temperature for about an hour before serving. If there's any left, keep it in a covered jar in the refrigerator. It will last. Makes 1½ cups dressing.

At serving time, either place a large tablespoon of this dressing on each wedge of lettuce, or pass from the bowl.

INGREDIENTS: 1 large, firm head iceberg lettuce.
   For the dressing: 4 ounces bleu cheese; ⅓ cup olive oil;
      ½ teaspoon salt; ½ teaspoon grated lemon peel; 2
      tablespoons lemon juice; ½ cup commercial sour cream.

PICKLED WATERMELON RIND

Obviously, this is something you will have made during the watermelon season. Since you're eating it now, I've chosen this month to tell of it.

Peel and remove all green portions from the **rind of 1 large watermelon.** Cut into 1-inch cubes. It's all right to leave a little of the pink on, but too much of it will spoil the crispness of the pickle. Soak the cubes overnight in **1 quart cold water** with **¼ cup salt.** (If you do not have all the watermelon ready to pickle at one time, wrap the unpeeled and uncut rinds in saran or foil until you do have enough. The recipe, as well, can be divided in halves or fourths successfully.)

In the morning, drain the melon, cover with fresh **cold water,** bring to a boil, and simmer until the rind is nearly, but not quite, tender. This will be in about 20 minutes, usually, but it does vary by the size of the cubes and the variety of the melon. Be sure not to let the rind cook to a soft point. Drain again.

While the boiling is taking place, bring to a boil in another pan **4 cups granulated sugar, 2 cups cider vinegar, 4 teaspoons whole cloves, 8 sticks cinnamon,** and **¼ teaspoon mustard seed**. It's a good idea to tie the loose spices together in a little cheesecloth bag because you're going to want to remove them later. As soon as this comes to a boil, remove it from the heat and allow it to rest for 15 minutes. Now add the drained rind to the syrup and simmer until the rind is clear and transparent and thoroughly cooked, which will take approximately 15 minutes. Remove the bag of cloves and cinnamon and pack the pickle boiling hot with juice to cover into sterilized jars. Seal at once. There are now available nice jars with screw tops with the rubber rings right in the lids; they're fine for this. Small freezer jars are good, too. One pound of watermelon rind in the trimmed state will provide about three 6-ounce jars of the pickle. You probably would get about fifteen jars from a full watermelon.

INGREDIENTS: Rind of 1 large watermelon; water; ¼ cup salt; 4 cups granulated sugar; 2 cups cider vinegar; 4 teaspoons whole cloves; 8 sticks cinnamon; ¼ teaspoon mustard seed.

FRIED SALLY LUNN

The batter for these is the same as one would use for Sally Lunn muffins. Fried, they are a surprise, a delight, and lethally appetizing. Don't blame me if you eat six at a shot.

Sift into a bowl **1½ cups flour, 1 tablespoon baking powder, 1 tablespoon sugar,** and **½ teaspoon salt**. Separate **2 eggs**. Beat the yolks until they are thick and lemon colored. Add **¾ cup milk** to the yolks, mix well, and pour into the flour mixture. Add **½ cup (1 stick) melted butter** or **margarine** and mix thoroughly with your electric mixer. Beat **2 egg whites** until they will hold a peak, then fold them into the rest of the batter until no white is apparent.

If you want muffins of these, grease and flour 12 large muffin-pan sections, fill with the batter, dividing it evenly, and bake in a hot oven about 15 minutes until done.

However, try frying them just once, won't you? Get a black iron frying pan hot, add a **large lump of butter or 1 tablespoon sausage fat** or some of each, get the fat sizzling hot, and drop the batter in by teaspoonfuls. The little cakes will immediately rise, expand, and become sizable affairs, so don't try to do it by tablespoonfuls. Let them brown on moderate heat, adding fat as you think you need it—just don't let the pan get dry—and, in less than 2 minutes, they can be turned. It will take about 2 more minutes for the other side to brown and the insides to be completely baked. Test one by cutting it open before you serve it. You will get 3 or 4 dozen of the fried cakes and I doubt it will be enough for the six of you. These can be served for breakfast with butter and maple syrup, or with a rich preserve.

INGREDIENTS: 1½ cups flour; 1 tablespoon baking powder; 1 tablespoon sugar; ½ teaspoon salt; 2 eggs; ¾ cup milk; ½ cup butter or margarine; butter and/or sausage fat for frying.

SWEET-CHOCOLATE CAKE
WITH WHIPPED CREAM

Melt **1 package Baker's German's sweet chocolate in ½ cup boiling water.** Watch this as chocolate burns easily. Use a heavy saucepan. Remove it from the heat as soon as the chocolate has melted. Mix the chocolate and the water with a spoon and allow it to cool.

Cream **1 cup** (2 sticks) **butter or margarine** (perfectly acceptable here) with 2 cups granulated sugar at high speed with your electric mixer until the mixture is very light, very fluffy—in fact, creamed. Separate 4 eggs. Add, one at a time and beating well after each addition, the 4 egg yolks. Add the melted chocolate and **1 teaspoon vanilla.** Set this bowl aside.

Sift together ½ teaspoon salt, 1 teaspoon soda, 2½ cups sifted cake flour, and, alternating with 1 cup buttermilk, add to the chocolate mix. Take about three stages to do it; first the flour, then the buttermilk, and beat after each addition until smooth.

Now whip the 4 egg whites, and by this time you should know that they must stand in peaks, must glisten, must not be dry and fluffy.

Line three 9-inch layer cake pans with waxed paper. Easy. Just set one on top of a triple thickness of waxed paper, hold it down with one hand, draw around it with a pencil, cut all three at a time. They will fit. Divide the batter among these three pans and bake in preheated 350°F. oven for 35 to 40 minutes, or until a skewer goes in and out without becoming moist. Cool on cake racks.

For the Filling: Whip 1 pint heavy cream. When nearly stiff, add 1 teaspoon sugar and 1 teaspoon vanilla. Just combine.

You may fill the layers with the whipped cream, but, when I serve this cake, I like to take the layers from their pans when they're cool, stack them one on top of the other without any icing or filling and bring the cake to the table that way. Along with it I have a bowl of whipped cream. The cake is then cut, the wedges arranged on each dessert dish with a space between, and the cream is dropped on the cake in as sparing or lavish amounts as the person who is to eat it requires. Thus, if there is cake left, you do not have it covered with whipped cream, and it can be frozen and reused in other ways. Also, with three layers, it's fine to use just two of them for this cake, and freeze the other; then you have a good single layer available for another, completely different dessert. For two layers, ½ pint of cream, whipped, should be sufficient.

INGREDIENTS: 1 package Baker's German's sweet chocolate; ½ cup boiling water; 1 cup butter or margarine; 4 eggs; 1 teaspoon vanilla; ½ teaspoon salt; 1 teaspoon soda; 2½ cups sifted cake flour; 1 cup buttermilk.

For the filling: 1 pint heavy cream; 1 teaspoon sugar; 1 teaspoon vanilla.

OLD-FASHIONED ORANGE PIE

This is an alternate for those who would prefer a pie to a cake, after this dinner. And, if either is too much for some of you, don't forget the apple in the hand, spread with cheese, slice by slice. That's what I would choose.

You will want an **8-inch pie shell**, unbaked. Have you one in your freezer? Get it out. If you haven't, follow the recipe on page 287.

Cream together at high speed in your electric mixer **1 tablespoon butter** and **1½ cups granulated sugar**. When mixture is smooth and creamy, blend in, still beating, **¾ cup fresh orange juice, 2 tablespoons fresh lemon juice**, and **1 tablespoon grated orange rind**. (Obviously, you will grate the orange rind before you squeeze the orange.) Add **3 well-beaten eggs,** and continue to mix until well blended. Pour this filling into the unbaked pie shell, ready and waiting. Tuck a 2-inch strip of aluminum foil over and under the shell, to keep it from browning too much, and bake at 375°F. for 40 to 45 minutes, or until the custard is set. Cool. Peel **1 California navel orange,** removing all the white possible, and cut out neat segments with a sharp knife. Arrange these symmetrically around the edges of the pie. Whip **½ cup heavy cream**, add **½ teaspoon sugar** and **½ teaspoon orange extract**, and pile this in the center of the pie, inside the circle of orange slices.

INGREDIENTS: Unbaked 8-inch pie shell; 1 tablespoon butter; 1½ cups granulated sugar; ¾ cup fresh orange juice; 2 tablespoons fresh lemon juice; 1 tablespoon grated orange rind; 3 eggs; 1 California navel orange; ½ cup heavy cream; ½ teaspoon sugar; ½ teaspoon orange extract.

TIMETABLE: If you'll take my advice, you'll cook the soup the day before. That's yesterday. It'll mellow and you'll thank me for suggesting it. If this isn't possible, plan to do it early in the morning. Just remember to put your beans on to soak the night before you want to bake them.

Early morning, get at the bean job. Start them going. Prepare the dressing for your salad, wash the lettuce and get it at its chilling. Prepare your pie shell if you need one, and if you've decided on the pie rather than the cake. You may finish the pie, complete except for the whipped cream, and refrigerate it in the morning, or early in the afternoon. You'll have to interrupt the baking of the beans long enough to do the pie if you have just one oven.

Late in the afternoon, prepare the batter for the Sally Lunn. Cover the bowl with saran until you're ready to fry them. If you're going to bake the chocolate cake, prepare the batter now and get it in the three cake pans. Since this cake and the beans are done at the same temperature, you can bake the cake any time you'd like; the later the better; it's mouth-watering when it's still slightly warm at serving time.

Reheat the soup now and keep it steaming hot while you prepare the salads and set them on the table with the dressing. Now take the bean pot from the oven (beans will stay hot a long time in an old-fashioned bean pot); raise the oven temperature for the broiling of the ham steak. Baste the ham and broil it; while it's broiling, fry the Sally Lunn—a simultaneous operation. Keep the ham warm.

Call the family. Serve the soup and the Sally Lunn cakes. If your family is of the cooperative type, they might be willing to wait for you to broil the ham now; it'll be better than if it has been done earlier and kept warm. It's a quick task, but do whatever seems practical for your own family arrangements. When you go to the kitchen to get the ham, heat the sauce quickly. Serve the ham in thick chunks along with the beans. Fry some more of the Sally Lunn cakes, if you have any batter left.

The dessert, either the pie or the cake, is ready. Whip cream for either one, at the last. If I were eating this dinner, I'd have my dessert tomorrow!

LEFTOVERS

Add cut-up chunks of ham to the leftover soup. Break open the leftover Sally Lunn cakes, butter them, and toast them in your broiler. Serve with the soup for lunch.

Leftover Ham Cakes

A very good thing to do with leftover ham is to chop it up, measure it. If you have **2 cups of ham**, you will want **2 cups of bread soaked in milk**. Mix the ham and the soaked bread with **2 beaten eggs**, add **½ teaspoon powdered sage**, some **salt** if the ham needs it (taste it, that's how you'll know), and freshly ground **pepper**. Shape into little cakes, roll in flour and fry (sauté is the fancy word) in sizzling **sausage fat or butter**, as you would oysters; turn when the underside is brown. Serve with a **segment of lemon**.

INGREDIENTS: 2 cups leftover ham; 2 cups bread soaked in milk; 2 eggs; ½ teaspoon powdered sage; salt (if needed); pepper; sausage fat or butter for frying; lemon segments.

Ham croquettes are delicious affairs. There's a good recipe for one in my *Blueberry Hill Cookbook;* and don't forget about slicing leftover ham paper thin and frizzling it, by which I mean sautéing it in hot, hot butter, quickly so that it curls up and gets brown. This is right with scrambled eggs, or, creamed, as a filling for an omelette.

Sally Lunn Bread Pudding

The leftover Sally Lunn can be made into a nice bread pudding. If you have about **6 of the cakes** left, beat **3 egg yolks**, combine it with **1 cup of sugar**, beating until the granular look has left for all time, and add the Sally Lunn, toasted and cubed. Add **2½ cups scalded milk**, stir it all together, then fold in the **3 egg whites**, stiffly beaten, left from the 3 yolks, and bake in a 325°F. oven in a pan of water. Add some **raisins** before you bake it, if you like raisins. It should be set in something like an hour. Serve this hot with cream.

INGREDIENTS: 6 leftover Sally Lunn cakes; 3 eggs; 1 cup sugar; 2½ cups milk; raisins (optional).

If you're left with a very small amount of the vegetable soup, cook it down so that it's mostly all vegetables, very little soup (if the vegetables are really soft when you think you'd like to do this, strain them out and keep them to one side while you reduce the soup; add them later). Pour some heavy cream over them, taste for seasoning, and serve as a side dish with cold meat.

People make baked bean sandwiches. I don't, but that doesn't mean you shouldn't. I like to lay out the leftover baked beans in a flat casserole, arrange on top of them several neat rows of little cocktail frankfurters (the best of these are the little Kosher frankfurters which come in a plastic bag; they're frozen when you get them; bake them right from this state) and bake in a 375°f. oven until the beans are bubbly and the frankfurters are hot and sassy. If the beans are too dry for this treatment, stir into them enough boiling water to moisten them, and go on from there. A few cubes of pineapple can be tucked in and about.

As for the chocolate cake, the uses for this are infinite. Since whatever cake you have is free of icing or whipped cream, it can accompany just about any sort of fruit, fresh or stewed (my earliest memory of the true enjoyment of eating was an experience involving a tart, cold, red apple in one hand and a slab of chocolate cake in the other); slice it thin and top it with vanilla ice cream; go one step further and slice it thin and top it with vanilla ice cream and top that with hot fudge sauce. If you have much whipped cream left, slice the bits of cake you have left into thin slices, moisten them with a thick coffee syrup (2 parts sugar, 1 part strong coffee, boiled 10 minutes), spread with the whipped cream, and continue until all is used. Pour some rum over the top, let it soak together. Serve at dessert time.

The orange pie will survive in good state for about two days. You won't have trouble with it; you may be sure it will be eaten before then. It will freeze if you must; don't serve it to company, then.

DISHES FOR FREEZING

All the following dishes can be frozen. They should be reheated by the method followed in the original cooking, unless otherwise indicated in the recipe.

INDEX

To readers of this cookbook, and users of this index: It has been impossible to index all the leftovers ideas in this book, mostly because the preponderance of them have no names. Thus, except for those which are complete recipes in themselves, these are grouped under the heading of "leftovers" for each month concerned. An index of dishes for freezing precedes this index.

always soft chocolate frosting, 249

appetizers:
  artichokes, sour cream radish dip, 156
  café rhum, 327
  caviar mousse, 137
  cheese wafers, 251
  cider, hot mulled sherried, 279
  cider ice-cream float, 10
  clams and oysters, half shell, 54
  cranberry-strawberry juice, 311
  eggnog, 10
  fennel and black olives, 127
  lamb squares, broiled, 232
  melon and prosciutto, 67
  melon balls in white wine, 89
  melon champagne cup, 198
  mushrooms à la Greque, 16
  pineapple cubes dipped in grenadine, 101
  piroshkis, 108
  smoked salmon, pumpernickl, 28

appetizers (cont.)
  tomato cream, cold, 23
  tomato punch, hot, 28
apple-nut thing, 36
apple pie with cheese crust, 60
apples, glazed strawberry, 284
applesauce, golden, 81
apricot filling for cake, 21
apricot loaf, 144
April family leftovers, 106
April party leftovers, 98–99
artichoke hearts in wine, 142
artichokes, sour cream radish dip, 156
asparagus:
  or fiddleheads with buttered crumbs, 129
  and mushroom tart, tomato, 218
  with whipped cream, 114
August family leftovers, 225–230
August party leftovers, 211–214
avocado:
  in the hand, 220
  slices, clear mushroom broth with, 42

359